Tigers without Teeth

State and Society in East Asia
Series Editor: Elizabeth J. Perry

Tigers without Teeth

The Pursuit of Justice in Contemporary China

Scott Wilson

ROWMAN & LITTLEFIELD
Lanham • Boulder • New York • London

Published by Rowman & Littlefield
A wholly owned subsidiary of The Rowman & Littlefield Publishing Group, Inc.
4501 Forbes Boulevard, Suite 200, Lanham, Maryland 20706
www.rowman.com

Unit A, Whitacre Mews, 26-34 Stannary Street, London SE11 4AB, United Kingdom

British Library Cataloguing in Publication Information Available

Library of Congress Cataloging-in-Publication Data
Wilson, Scott, 1964– author.
Tigers without teeth : the pursuit of justice in contemporary China / Scott Wilson.
pages cm. — (State and society in East Asia)
Includes bibliographical references and index.
ISBN 978-1-4422-3616-5 (cloth : alk. paper) — ISBN 978-1-4422-3617-2 (electronic)
1. Civil rights—China. 2. Justice—China. 3. Civil society—China. I. Title.
KNQ502.4.W55 2015
344.5103'21969792—dc23
2014046132

∞ ™ The paper used in this publication meets the minimum requirements of American National Standard for Information Sciences Permanence of Paper for Printed Library Materials, ANSI/NISO Z39.48-1992.

Printed in the United States of America

Contents

Preface

Tigers without Teeth owes a great debt to many people. The research for this book was completed over the course of three trips to China in 2007–2008, 2010, and 2012. The School of Social Development and Public Policy at Fudan University hosted my initial research trip, covering a full academic year. I am deeply indebted to Professors Qu Tiepeng, Fang Lizhu, and Peng Xizhe at Fudan for helping to launch the research project. Without their assistance, I could not have undertaken research on civil society organizations and legal development, which was considered a particularly sensitive topic in the period just before the Beijing Olympic Games.

The research project was underwritten by a John B. Stephenson Fellowship from the Appalachian College Association and research grants from The University of the South. The Stephenson Fellowship afforded me the opportunity to conduct over sixty interviews with civil society organizations, attorneys, legal aid recipients, and international organizations in Shanghai, Beijing, Wuhan, Nanjing, and Kunming. Subsequent research trips in 2010 and 2012, supported by The University of the South, allowed me to continue with more than thirty focused interviews with civil society organizations, attorneys, state officials, and international groups on the rapidly developing fields of AIDS and environmental laws. Those interviews produced key insights on the political calculations behind which legal complaints make it into the courts and which ones do not. Thanks to the Appalachian College Association and the university grants committee at The University of the South for their generous support.

Many of the arguments presented in this book were first presented at conferences or published in journal articles. Vivienne Shue, Rachel Stern, Yu Haiqing, Wu Fengshi, Lu Yiyi, Kenneth Foster, Joan Kaufman and Rob Efird read conference papers and journal manuscripts and provided encouragement for the production of the work. Marc Blecher, Woody Register, and Charles Brockett read portions of the manuscript and offered their advice on how to craft the argument. Special thanks to Elizabeth Perry, the editor of the series in which this book appears, and Susan McEachern, editor at Rowman & Littlefield, for their interest in the book manuscript. Their advice and editorial skills improved the manuscript and led to its rapid publication. Anonymous reviewers also offered invaluable advice on ways to clarify and strengthen the book's argument. While many hands helped with the production of the book, responsibility for any errors is solely mine. My friends and especially my family in Sewanee provided support and much needed distractions over the course of researching and writing this book. My wife, Sherri Bergman, and my two daughters, Marisa and Kyra, spent a year with me in China while I conducted the first round of interviews in various Chinese cities. Without their love, support, and patience, I would not have finished the book.

I offer my deep thanks (and respect) for the many persons who agreed to be interviewed by me while in China. I was awed and humbled by the work that my interviewees have done and continue to do to halt the spread of HIV/ AIDS, fight polluters, reverse the stigmatization of people living with HIV/ AIDS, and advocate for disadvantaged citizens' rights, even filing lawsuits against corporations or state agents. Over the last six years, I have picked up Chinese and U.S. newspapers and seen many of my interviewees quoted in articles; sadly, some news reports described the detention or harassment of some of the persons whom I interviewed. Of course, the interviewees were cognizant of the political pressures that they faced because many had experienced political threats in the past. The fact that so many interviewees did not shirk in the face of state opposition to their activities left an indelible impression on me. In the book's pages, the interviewees remain anonymous in order to protect their well-being.

List of Acronyms

ABA	American Bar Association
AIDS	acquired immune deficiency syndrome
ART	antiretroviral (drug) treatment
CCM	country coordinating mechanism
CCP	Chinese Communist Party
CDC	Center for Disease Control
CHAI	Clinton Health Access Initiative
CLAPV	Center of Legal Aid for Pollution Victims
EIA	environmental impact assessment
EPB	environmental protection bureau
GONGO	government-organized nongovernmental organization
HIV	human immunodeficiency virus
INGO	international nongovernmental organization
MDG	millennium development goal
MEP	ministry of environmental protection
MOH	ministry of health
MSM	men who have sex with men

List of Acronyms

NEPA	National Environmental Protection Agency
NGO	nongovernmental organization
NRDC	Natural Resources Defense Council
OGIR	Open Government Information Regulations
PLWHA	people living with HIV/AIDS
SEPA	State Environmental Protection Agency
UNAIDS	UN Theme Group on AIDS
WHO	World Health Organization
WWF	World Wildlife Fund

List of Tables

Chapter One

Introduction: "Tigers without Teeth?"

A lawyer whom I interviewed in 2010 recounted his frustration with Chinese laws related to HIV/AIDS. During our meeting, he read aloud Article 3 of Regulations on AIDS Prevention and Treatment, which is as follows: "No work unit or individual shall discriminate against HIV/AIDS carriers. HIV/AIDS carriers and their relatives shall enjoy protection of their rights to marry, work, receive medical treatment, and receive an education."[1] The attorney paused then declared, "We think that it is great that the antidiscrimination clause is in the law. It is beautifully written, but we would like to have something that clarifies that persons assume responsibility for discrimination. We have an expression: 'If a tiger has no teeth, then no one fears it; if a tiger has a mouthful of teeth, then everyone will fear it.' Our law here is a case of a tiger without teeth. If you break the law, it can't bite you."[2] The lawyer's comments strike to the heart of many claimants' concerns: Chinese laws have the appearance of securing people rights, but a yawning chasm often exists between such legal expressions and actual protection of rights and interests. In order to defend their rights, Chinese citizens must rely not just upon laws but also extralegal pressure from civil society backers, the media, and protesters.

This book analyzes the efforts of two categories of disadvantaged citizens—environmental pollution victims and HIV/AIDS carriers—to pursue justice in China's legal system despite such toothless tigers. While much of the discussion takes up cases of civil litigation in China's courts, this is far more than a book about litigation. Many of the complaints analyzed in later chapters emerge out of protest and move through institutional channels, including the courts, with the help of civil society organizations. Most complaints never develop into full-blown cases in the courts because either the courts refuse to hear the cases or the cases are settled before hearings take place or verdicts are rendered. While all legal systems extend judges the right to refuse cases based on the merits of a complaint, Chinese courts refuse to hear complaints due to (inappropriate) political pressure from state or party officials not to try certain types of cases. For this reason, I examine some complaints that never make their way into the courts because of the courts' refusal to try them. Doing so reveals the politics of justice in China by analyzing not just court decisions rendered but decisions avoided.[3] The focus on the politics of justice, rather than the development of the judiciary as an institution, widens the scope of analysis to draw connections among contentious action, civil society, and litigation.

Tigers without Teeth argues that China's civil society and rights-based litigation have grown symbiotically, contributing to China's progress toward rule of law. For disadvantaged individuals pursuing justice in China's courts, financial backing and legal services provided by civil society organizations are crucial, a pattern that replicates the civil rights movement in the United States.[4] The story of pollution victims' and HIV/AIDS carriers' pursuit of justice is intertwined with the uneven rise of Chinese civil society. The rapidly growing number of domestic and international nongovernmental organizations (NGOs) in China provides resources to plaintiffs to maintain a steady supply of court cases and pressure on the courts to improve the quality of verdicts and rule of law.[5] To understand the politics of justice and development of rule of law in China, one must not merely look at court decisions but a broad scope of activity that includes protests, organization of civil society groups, and the writing of new laws and revision of existing laws in response to societal conflict and pressure.

DILEMMAS OF RULE OF LAW AND CIVIL SOCIETY IN NONDEMOCRATIC REGIMES

The pursuit of justice by individuals and even groups in China illuminates a series of grand questions: What roles do civil society and legal institutions play in China? Why has China's regime given space to civil society organizations and permitted rights-based litigation, both of which have the capacity to undermine the regime's authority? In a country where the leadership is bent on maintaining stability, how do officials balance the need to allow citizens to register complaints and the desire to prevent society from challenging the hegemony of the Chinese Communist Party? For the Chinese regime, which has held the reins of control for so long and over so many matters, how do the courts and civil society relate to regime legitimacy, when the litigants and organizations may expose problems generated by past and present policies? Finally, why does China's state respond more favorably to some social causes that have emerged in civil society than others? These questions point to a series of challenges and dilemmas facing China's regime as it tries to maintain legitimacy and stability in the face of growing social conflict.

Since Alexis de Tocqueville wrote *Democracy in America*, most analysts of civil society assume that robust associational life serves as a countervailing force against the state, strengthening existing democracies and perhaps serving as a harbinger of liberalizing or democratizing trends in authoritarian states.[6] The "velvet revolution" in Eastern and Central Europe in 1989 and the "jasmine revolution" or "Arab spring" beginning in 2010 in the Middle East and North Africa exemplify the way in which civil society mobilization can lead to challenges to nondemocratic regimes. Permitting the development of civil society, then, theoretically imperils aspects of Chinese Communist Party rule. China's regime has taken notice of both of these movements and stepped up surveillance and regulation of civil society to undercut the potential for such a movement,[7] but permitting limited development of civil society also potentially adds legitimacy to China's regime, at least in the short term.[8] International society and Chinese citizens call for increased participation in governance. From the regime's perspective, civil society organizations offer an opportunity to involve citizens in governance in a restricted and managed way, short of democratization.

Rights-based litigation also poses a dilemma for China's regime. Recent scholarship on the role of courts under authoritarianism as well as "cause lawyering" to advance rights or social change through the courts has highlighted the "judicialization of politics," in which conflicts related to governance are moved into the courts, a realm in which nonmajoritarian principles determine decisions.[9] From the vantage point of a nondemocratic regime, judicialization of politics has the benefit of channeling contentious politics off the streets and into the courts where institutionalized rules, established by the regimes themselves, govern. Settling societal and elite conflicts with reference to laws also lends the state legitimacy in the eyes of Chinese citizens and international society because it appears transparent and rules-based, as opposed to reliant on pure power and coercion. Two problems (or dilemmas) arise, however, for nondemocratic regimes who seek to use the courts to gain legitimacy. First, judges and courts are not passive actors but have their own interests, which they seek to advance. Court rulings that show independence from state or elite interests add legitimacy to the courts and rule of law in a country, so regimes that want to rely on the judicial system to add to state legitimacy set in motion a process in which courts often seek more professionalism, legitimacy, and power for themselves. Second, citizens in a nondemocratic state take seriously the regime's signals that it adheres to laws. Citizens then begin to demand adherence to laws and even revisions in the laws themselves, which may actually increase contentiousness, albeit transforming contentiousness into a mode that spans noninstitutionalized (protests) and institutionalized (litigation) forms.[10] The legal cases brought by citizens may also uncover information that tarnishes the regime's reputation.

The above dilemmas related to civil society formation and role of courts are extremely pertinent in post-Mao China, and they help to explain the regime's Janus-faced approach to rights-based litigants and civil society. As with Janus, the Roman god who oversaw beginnings and transitions, one face of China's state looks forward toward greater reliance upon laws and citizen participation to construct order while the second face of China's state looks to the past toward use of laws to rein in society and coercion to maintain stability. In the last two decades, Chinese civil society has grown in strength, and an increasing number of citizens have taken up legal means to pursue rights-based claims against the state.[11] While China's regime has sought to burnish its international and domestic credentials by increasing scope for civil society and judicialization of politics, the regime for the last decade has also focused on maintaining "stability" and constructing a "harmonious society." Providing economic growth and keeping destabilizing conflict in check are the underpinnings of China's path to "scientific development" and construction of "harmonious society,"[12] ideological constructs for the regime to legitimate itself, which sometimes require the state to ignore citizens' rights or use coercion to rein in conflict or threatening groups. Yet China's regime cannot dispense with rule of law and citizen participation because forces within and outside China's state call for them. To address these dilemmas, the party and state forces have sought to guide the process of civil society formation and rights-based litigation in the name of maintaining stability and harmony. To do so, China's regime has developed a set of agents who participate in civil society and defend citizens' interests in the courts in order to both lead and contain developments in those spheres. The dilemmas posed by partial opening to civil society organizations and rights-based litigation require a balancing act between social forces and activities, both inside the state and civil society, who can burnish or tarnish the regime's legitimacy.

CHALLENGES TO THE PURSUIT OF LEGAL JUSTICE

Drawing on laws that may not have teeth, average Chinese citizens face a herculean task of taking their cases to the courts to protect their interests and rights. Chinese laws that contain bold but general statements about crucial legal matters such as "freedom from discrimination" or the "right to information" may initially be difficult to apply because of their vague wording. Pitman Potter argues that such ambiguous wording allows local authorities greater leeway to interpret laws in ways that benefit local (state and business) interests.[13] The wording of Chinese laws, however, is not the only aspect of

China's legal system that can render laws "toothless." One problem that the above attorney identified is the lack of responsibility assigned to violators of Chinese rules and regulations. Even when responsibility for unlawful acts is assigned, the punishment system lacks teeth. Environmental lawyers complain that environmental protection bureau agents' fines are too negligible and court-awarded judgments too small to alter polluters' behavior.[14] A second problem of China's legal system is that the laws and regulations form a mosaic of inconsistent elements from different levels of government as well as distinct ministries and lawmaking bodies within the state. Some laws and regulations directly contradict one another, a problem that the central state is trying to remedy, while other laws and regulations draw distinctions between classes of people so that general legal principles cannot apply universally. For example, until May 2013, The Standards Used for Civil Servant Physical Examinations (Trial Implementation) allowed government units to discriminate against persons with HIV/AIDS or hepatitis (among other diseases) in hiring, while legal principles found in China's Constitution,[15] Labor Law, [16] Employment Promotion Law of the People's Republic of China on the Prevention and Treatment of Infectious Diseases,[17] and Regulations on AIDS Prevention and Treatment[18] called for nondiscrimination in employment (discussed further in chapter 5).[19] Third, when plaintiffs attempt to file complaints related to sensitive issues in the courts, judges may refuse to hear the cases. When courts refuse to hear complaints without written explanations, complainants have no recourse to appeal within the justice system. Fourth, China's regime has means to intervene in particularly sensitive cases—most rights-based litigation is deemed sensitive—either to keep cases from being heard or to affect the outcome of the case.[20] Selective intervention makes it more difficult for impact litigation cases to be tried and to render verdicts that advance social causes. Finally, China's legal system does not have a formal case law system in which courts follow the precedents set by earlier court decisions (*stare decisis*), which undermines the impact of a decision of one court on the legal system.[21] Within the judiciary, Chinese judges certainly read and likely follow other courts' verdicts, but they are not bound to replicate them. Judgments in new, sensitive case areas (including pollution and HIV/AIDS) may be, in fact, a clearer signal about the party-state's emerging opinion on a type of legal complaint than a determination of how abstract legal reasoning applies. These five points—weak punishment, a fragmented and contradictory legal corpus, refusal to try cases, selective intervention, and lack of binding precedents—form a significant gauntlet against plaintiffs winning complaints and undermine the impact of such court victories on development of rule of law.

Nevertheless, a growing number of Chinese citizens are turning to the courts to guard their rights and interests. During the period 1990–2011, the number of first trial civil cases by courts surged from 1.85 million to 6.61

million, which indicates both growing citizen legal consciousness and an increase in social conflict.[22] Many of the social conflicts resulting in the courts' caseload concern noncontroversial subjects, but *Tigers without Teeth* addresses sensitive (but not necessarily blacklisted) cases that pollution victims and HIV/AIDS carriers bring to the courts. Laws appear "toothless" to parties involved in controversial areas of litigation, but they can grow teeth when, pressured by activists and civil society organizations, legislators provide additional legal clarifications such as implementing instructions for laws or when courts render judgments that show how to apply abstract legal expressions. Given the odds against appearing in court and winning a judgment, the expected payoffs for litigation are not very good. Hence, many of the plaintiffs discussed in this book are animated to litigate out of a profound sense of having endured some injustice and a desire to right a wrong.

WHY STUDY ENVIRONMENTAL POLLUTION VICTIMS AND HIV/AIDS CARRIERS?

Tigers without Teeth focuses on China's responses to HIV/AIDS and environmental pollution because these are two looming global crises facing China. Though this book casts its analytical gaze on the activities of grassroots organizations, lawyers, and litigants in pursuit of justice, those microprocesses have important ramifications for the health of China's and even the world's environment and population. The fact that the United Nations' millennium development goals include targets to halt the spread of HIV/AIDS and to protect the environment indicates the global importance of these issues. Studies issued by the World Bank, the UN Theme Group on HIV/AIDS in China, and Chinese organizations, for example, are clarion calls on the magnitude of China's environmental and HIV/AIDS crises.[23] In recent years, several works have highlighted China's pollution problems and a few have chronicled China's HIV/AIDS problems, which have helped us to understand the causes that generated these problems.[24] What we lack is a thorough account of how civil society has responded by helping pollution and HIV/AIDS victims to defend themselves through advocacy and legal efforts in the midst of the crises.[25] This book seeks to fill that significant gap.

Estimates on the number of actual (as opposed to registered) cases of HIV/AIDS vary widely because the spread of HIV/AIDS in China has been difficult to document. Based on sample data collected throughout China, the government estimated that by 2011 approximately 780,000 persons were living with HIV/AIDS.[26] Some NGOs dispute that claim, however, arguing that the number is likely greater than 1 million HIV/AIDS carriers in China.[27] Statistically, the proportion of China's total population with HIV/AIDS is less than 0.1 percent, which, by international comparisons, is quite low.

Nevertheless, according to official reports, 28,000 Chinese AIDS carriers died in 2011, years after antiretroviral drug (ARV) treatment was widely available.[28] Heightened concern about China's HIV/AIDS epidemic is based on Chinese citizens' lack of general knowledge about the means of spreading (and preventing the spread of) HIV/AIDS, and the sharp increase of at-risk behavior, especially among China's youth. Michael Sidibe, the head of UN-AIDS, has (perhaps hyperbolically) warned that 50 million Chinese are at risk of contracting the disease.[29]

China's environmental devastation has been widely reported, and the statistics are frightening. In the 2010 "State of the Environment," issued by the ministry of environmental protection (MEP), the government reported that of China's two hundred main rivers, 16.4 percent were essentially useless even for industrial use. Of China's twenty-six major lakes and reservoirs, ten (38.5 percent) were graded as useless.[30] And those statistics on water quality marked an improvement from the previous years. The statistics on poor air quality in China due to industrial pollution also are staggering, but none are more so than estimates that ambient air pollution in China caused 1.2 million premature deaths in 2010.[31] Setting aside issues of degradation of land and sustainable agricultural production, China's public suffers from high rates of respiratory illnesses, waterborne diseases, and cancer. China's environmental problems imperil their citizens, the ozone, and the world's capacity to provide food for Chinese citizens.[32]

Both environmental pollution and HIV/AIDS necessitate forward-looking policies because perception of the problems lags behind their cumulative effects. Factories may emit toxic pollution in small amounts into the air, water, or soil that, initially, are scarcely noticed but accumulate and significantly affect crops and human health. From the point of initial exposure to HIV, the virus typically lies dormant in a person's body for eight to ten years before AIDS develops. If people are unaware of their contraction of HIV, they may have unprotected sex, donate blood, nurse their children, or share syringes when using intravenous drugs—all of which can unwittingly expose others to HIV/AIDS. As perception lags behind actual manifestations of pollution and HIV/AIDS problems, crises can brew and present daunting challenges to those seeking to contain and reverse them in the future. To borrow an analogy used by UNAIDS to describe China's HIV/AIDS crisis, such crises are like the "iceberg in the path of the Titanic"; only a small portion of the growing problem is evident above the surface of the water.[33]

To halt the spread of HIV/AIDS and environmental pollution, as well as to protect victims' rights, China needs better enforcement of its laws and regulations, which is why a study of legal action on these two issues is so important and timely. Although some of China's laws may appear to be toothless at first blush, we need to look more closely to see under what conditions the tigers can grow fangs to bite those people and organizations who infringe on HIV/AIDS carriers' and pollution victims' rights and to hold persons accountable for their responsibility for the growing crises. The stakes in these extraordinary legal confrontations couldn't be higher for the plaintiffs and activists who face life-threatening pollution and illness, for the officials and private actors who may face financial penalties or criminal charges for their violations of Chinese laws, and for the international community that must help China to rein in its pollution and stem the spread of the HIV/AIDS pandemic. International norms and formalized rules or legal expressions that have crystallized on environmental pollution and HIV/AIDS provide domestic actors with an important resource to mobilize and are more likely to result in concerted international pressure on China to address a particular subject of concern.[34] Chinese civil society organizations, attorneys, and litigants have been aided in their pursuit of justice by international actors who provide financial resources, technical knowledge, and political backing to China. Not only do funds flow through networks of domestic and international NGOs, but multilateral organizations such as the UN, through partnership programs, can legitimate groups and draw media attention to social causes.[35] Moreover, as China adopts (even in letter only, in some cases) laws that protect human rights in order to gain international approval, organizations and activists mobilize around laws to test the government's commitment to legal principles in court. Newly minted laws on the environment and HIV/AIDS combine with international financial resources to catalyze litigants in pollution and AIDS cases in this book.

While victims of HIV/AIDS and pollution may be primarily motivated by rights-based claims to justice and compensation, filing court cases serves a more important function, to protect the public interest. Increasing the penalties through tort claims (and potentially criminal charges) for polluting people's air and water or infecting people with HIV/AIDS raises the cost of hazardous behavior, and thereby discourages others from engaging in such behavior.[36] All Chinese are made better off when pollution abates and blood supplies are free of deadly and harmful diseases, and the world is made more secure by helping China to improve its human rights protections, stem the HIV/AIDS pandemic, and decrease its environmental pollution.

LINKING CIVIL SOCIETY DEVELOPMENT, LITIGATION, AND RULE OF LAW

In the fall of 2007, I set out to research the organizations and activists involved in China's struggle against pollution and HIV/AIDS. My work led me to interview over one hundred attorneys, legal aid recipients, government officials, activists, and representatives of grassroots organizations, multilateral organizations affiliated with the UN, and international nongovernmental organizations (INGOs). Those interviews provide detailed stories of Chinese citizens struggling to pursue justice by legal means to fill in the broad outline of Chinese legal development. The picture that emerges from the study reveals strong linkages between civil society development, rights-based litigation (or "cause lawyering"), and rule of law.[37]

To refer to "Chinese civil society" has only been possible in recent years and remains a point of controversy. During the Mao era (1949–1978), China lacked a civil society because the state did not allow private interests to aggregate and limited civil society organizations to those mass organizations directly attached to the Chinese Communist Party, such as the All-China Federation of Trade Unions and the All-China Youth Federation, which served as vehicles to transmit central policies and to recruit loyal party members as much as to articulate societal interests to the party-state. The state's strict control over social organizations thwarted the emergence of social movements and autonomous NGOs.[38] Beginning in the 1980s, China's incipient civil society was dominated by government-organized nongovernmental organizations (GONGOs), a term that strikes many as oxymoronic. Some have argued that Chinese civil society and GONGOs, in particular, bear the imprint of China's party-state, evincing a "top-down" or a "state corporatist" approach to civil society, instead of the bottom-up, autonomous associational model more typical of Western NGOs.[39] But over the course of the 1980s, new organizations began to emerge around China's budding capitalism, and scholars believed that China might be developing civil society.[40]

The momentum that Chinese civil society was just gaining in the 1980s culminated in the outpouring of calls for reform during the "Beijing Spring" demonstrations of 1989, often better known simply as the "June 4th" demonstrations for the day that the protesters were violently attacked. In the aftermath of the violent suppression of the June 4th 1989 protests, some authors charged that China had no civil society in opposition to the state and claimed that China lacked true NGOs.[41] After the post-1989 chill began to thaw, China incrementally reengaged with the international community, including attending United Nations–sponsored conferences on the environment and hosting the UN Conference on Women in 1995. Participation in the international conferences spurred authorities to become more open to, and even encourage the development of, NGOs. Recognizing the limits of their own capacity to address social problems, Chinese officials have created space for NGOs to fill gaps made by reforms.[42] Hence, the number of organizations grew as did their scope of action, leading scholars to argue against absolute state control over civil society.[43] Overall, the number of civil society organizations throughout China that are registered with the ministry of civil affairs and classified in the three official categories—social organizations (*shehui tuanti*), popular nonenterprise units (*minban feiqiye danwei*), and foundations (*jijinhui*)—has ballooned from just 4,446 in 1988 to 461,971 in 2011.[44]

Moreover, those figures do not account for a very large number of organizations that have not registered with the ministry of civil affairs. Although official figures of civil society organizations rarely categorize organizations by issue area, estimates suggest that civil society organizations, including official and unofficial groups, working on HIV/AIDS and the environment are two of the most robust sectors of Chinese civil society. Deng Guosheng, director of the NGO research center at Tsinghua University in Beijing, recently estimated that 3,500 officially registered environmental NGOs exist, and the number of unofficial NGOs is much higher.[45] The 2010 directory of civil society organizations and community-based organizations working on HIV/AIDS published by China AIDS Information Network lists over six hundred groups, some of which are not registered, but those numbers reflect only a partial catalog of the total number of organizations working on HIV/AIDS in China.[46] Commentators began to recognize that China's state permitted and even relied upon civil society groups, which led them to recalibrate their conceptual frames to describe the nature of state–civil society relations, blending authoritarian rule and civil society participation.[47]

Despite tight state controls over the registration and limitations on the activities of Chinese civil society organizations, they are not merely tools of the party-state. As Chinese civil society opened up, civil society organizations began to form networks with international organizations and foundations, which provided them with financial backing, increased their autonomy, and spurred them to develop new repertoires of action. Civil society proved flexible, resistant to suppression, and increasingly assertive. Some areas of civil society enjoyed greater scope for development than others; groups addressing HIV/AIDS and environmental pollution particularly benefited from the international attention and funding given to their causes. International groups came to China with goals ranging from raising the capacity of Chinese state and nonstate organizations by transferring technology and expertise to fostering civil society groups with the hope of empowering future agents of change to supporting confrontational groups that press for immediate, if incremental, steps to liberalize China. The growth and activities of the civil society organizations had a symbiotic relationship to less organized "contentious politics" and "rightful resistance" in Chinese society.[48] Even though civil society organizations were not always directly involved in activists' petitions and protests, they often provided advice and an organizational basis to activists.

By the time that I began research for this book, grassroots organizations' new repertoires of action also included legal means to press for rule of law and protection of rights. A handful of civil society organizations had begun to operate legal aid clinics, some focused on specific causes. The shift to litigation and other legal means to protect citizens' rights, the central focus of this book, is one of the most recent developments of civil society organizations and reflects a new element in their repertoire of actions that straddles contentious and institutionalized politics. The legal aid units attached to civil society organizations rely extensively on foreign funding, although some of it is "soft funding" in support of educational and training programs that spread legal consciousness rather than direct support for lawsuits.[49] Some of the legal aid stations attached to civil society organizations that I visited had elaborate networks of relations with foreign foundations and international NGOs that provided financial support and expertise on how to prepare cases in environmental and AIDS litigation. International funders, some with long-term political goals such as liberalization or democratization in China, were attracted to help domestic civil society organizations with legal aid. Even though Chinese civil society organizations may be reluctant to engage in confrontational practices such as protests, moving into the courts for litigation challenged China's state to live up to the claims written into its laws. By calling on the courts to enforce state laws, legal aid centers and plaintiffs both confront state officials in claiming rights and operate within institutions, in this case the legal system constructed by the state. Depending on the sensitivity of the types of cases pursued, the courts provide either a safe or potentially dangerous venue to claimants and organizations pursuing political goals. Litigation and other forms of legal contestation should be understood within the broad range of contentious action occurring in China.

Typically, litigation is not the first but nearly the last option for victims of pollution and AIDS. Many of the legal cases discussed in this book follow a pattern that entails their emergence out of social movements and citizens' efforts to petition authorities to address a grievance. Petitions turn to protests when grievances are denied or local officials ignore instructions from the petitioners' office to address a problem. The mobilization of grievances, backed by existing or emergent civil society organizations, attracts the attention of media and higher-ups in the party-state who, in turn, put pressure on local officials to resolve a case. In the most severe cases, complainants mobilize because they feel imperiled by growing evidence that toxic waste from local factories is destroying their crops and the health of people around them, or that they cannot gain access to medicine, insurance, or a job due to their HIV-positive status, which they may have contracted out of no fault of their own. Moving to the courts may not be the last effort, though, because plaintiffs may need to protest further or create media pressure to have their case heard and judgments enforced.

Civil society organizations provide more than financial resources and legal defense; social movements and civil society groups also raise legal consciousness among citizens and generate popular pressure on officials and the courts to act.[50] At various points in the transition from grievance to social protest to litigation, attorneys and civil society organizations enter the picture, disseminating information on laws and providing a legal frame to what initially arose out of anger or an informal sense of injustice. [51] Typically, an administrative solution is sought to quell the mobilization, but sometimes the cases enter the courts because they get out of the officials' control or the courts want to hear such a case. The latter possibility may be a rare occurrence, for as one attorney told me, "Generally speaking, the courts won't accept any case that they don't have to accept (*neng bu shouli, jiu bu shouli*)." [52] In other cases, savvy attorneys mobilize media attention or civil society groups in order to pressure courts to hear cases. [53]

Implicit in the above formulation is an assertion that political pressure influences the courts' decisions to hear cases and how to render judgments. "Judicial independence," which Tamir Moustafa and Michael McCann argue does not even exist in advanced democracies, is often viewed as an indicator of development of rule of law if not democratization. [54] Therefore, China watchers have paid close attention to the courts for indications of growing autonomy, but most observers have noted that state and especially party officials continue to exercise influence over China's courts. [55] Pressure from the party-state on China's courts takes at least three forms. First, central officials can make statements to the courts on general approaches to managing legal cases. For example, in 2011, Wang Shengjun, president of China's Supreme People's Court, called on the courts to emphasize mediation over litigation of cases, a nod to the courts' role in maintaining a "harmonious society." [56] A second form of institutionalized pressure on the courts occurs when an official, at the provincial or lower reaches of administration, calls on the courts not to hear a particular class of complaints such as all cases involving HIV/AIDS carriers, a ban that many activists assert existed in central Chinese provinces for much of the last fifteen years. [57] Finally, while China's constitution bans state interference in the courts, the Communist Party has a direct link to the courts in the form of the political and legal affairs committee (*zhengfa weiyuanhui*), which includes the party leader in charge of political-legal matters and representatives from the offices of civil affairs, state security, public security, justice, and the president of the court and procuratorate at each level of the bureaucracy. [58] The political and legal affairs committee provides guidance to courts on how to hear particularly sensitive cases. [59] The structural ties between the judiciary and state also undermine the courts' de facto autonomy. Local judges, who are appointed by the standing committee of the people's congress at the corresponding administrative level, are paid by the local state, a structure that encroaches on judges' autonomy and makes them susceptible to pressure from local officials.

While pressure from officials may set parameters on courts' behavior and plaintiffs' likelihood of success, citizen mobilization has emerged as a new source of political pressure on the courts to try cases. [60] The surge in protest in China has created greater pressure on Chinese officials to maintain stability, and the courts' role in such moderation and settlement of social conflict is a source of ongoing debate among Chinese officials. Later chapters show that media coverage of environmental disasters or denial of rights to HIV/ AIDS carriers preceded hearings and likely spurred the courts to accept such cases. While the courts are not purely passive actors in China because of growing professionalism and their modeling of international judicial behavior, they remain fundamentally linked to political forces from inside China's state and from civil society. Undulations in the courts' willingness to hear cases reflect the shifting balance of power between the varied interests in China's state and civil society.

UNDERSTANDING THE DIVERGENT STATE RESPONSES TO LOOMING CRISES

One of the chief findings of this book is that China's state has responded more favorably to the legal efforts of pollution victims than HIV/AIDS carriers. As chapters 5 and 6 show, both HIV/AIDS carriers and pollution victims encounter Chinese courts that deny them hearings. Nevertheless, in comparison to HIV/AIDS carriers, pollution victims have had more cases accepted by the courts and have a better track record of receiving favorable judgments. Indeed, many locales in China have developed their own environmental courts to hear important environmental cases. In contrast, China has developed policy measures to try to keep HIV/AIDS carriers out of the courts. It is impossible to give definitive proof that China's courts turn away more AIDS carriers than pollution victims who would like to file lawsuits because China's courts provide statistics neither for cases accepted nor for cases refused. However, circumstantial evidence—including the creation of environmental courts to enhance pollution victims' access to litigation, interviews with attorneys in both practice areas, online searches for court judgments, selective harassment of attorneys and civil society organizations working on AIDS issues, and published Chinese articles claiming that some provinces refuse to hear any cases on AIDS—all points in the direction of the judiciary's preference for hearing environmental cases over AIDS cases. China's divergent responses to civil society organizations and attorneys working on environmental pollution and HIV/AIDS, particularly the efforts to encourage and back legal claims by pollution victims and to discourage and deter legal claims by AIDS carriers, lay bare the varied interests within China's state structure and the bureaucratic pressure brought to bear on China's bench.

Why does the state respond more favorably to environmental protests and litigation than it does to HIV/AIDS carriers' protests and litigation? To understand Chinese officials' and courts' divergent responses to the two sets of claimants, one must abandon their notions of China as a single state with a unified set of interests.[61] Despite China's monolithic appearance as a one-party model, China's officialdom has vertical cleavages between ministries, provincial and regional distinctions, and horizontal rifts between central and local authorities. State responsiveness to complainants varies according to central-local positions in the administrative hierarchy, geographic area, and the type of cause.

By comparing environmental pollution and HIV/AIDS carriers' civil society organizations and legal efforts, *Tigers without Teeth* begins to identify explanations for variation in state responses to civil society mobilization and litigation as well as the connections between activism in the streets (in the fields, too) and in the courts. Studies focusing on a single sector of Chinese civil society such as the environment are limited because they cannot account for variation in state responsiveness, except among regions and between levels of the state. While regional and central-local state interests may diverge and, therefore, shape bureaucratic responses to a particular cause pertinent to some civil society actors, comparison of different segments of civil society and classes of litigants explains why some movements thrive more than others.

To preface the explanation offered here, I focus on the varying bureaucratic responses to social movements and litigants. *Tigers without Teeth* argues that the courts' divergent responses are shaped by the role of the two ministries directly involved in managing HIV/AIDS and environmental pollution, the ministry of health (MOH) and the MEP, respectively.[62] The MEP gains from pollution victims' activism and litigation by helping the ministry to monitor polluters who are under the control of rival ministries. Conversely, the MOH loses legitimacy when such activism and litigation by HIV/AIDS carriers casts light on the ministry's checkered past in terms of monitoring China's blood supply.[63] In a legal system still affected by government influence, the attitudes of the two ministries are pivotal in shaping the outcomes of cases in the courts. Both ministries seek to guard their interests and to advance them relative to other ministries, but they also must balance pursuit of their self-interest with a larger concern of maintaining stability and protecting the state from losing its position of ideological leadership. These twin goals color the actions of the two ministries and lead them to attempt to guide civil society and legal processes in a nondangerous direction.

The focus on bureaucratic interests offered here builds on political opportunity structure theory, which Timothy Hildebrandt argues explains the prospects for civil society organization.[64] From the perspective of pollution victims and HIV/AIDS carriers, elite divisions provide activists with potential patrons and protectors inside the state. Environmental pollution victims and activists have been able to take advantage of elite divisions to gain support for their efforts, which potentially benefit the MEP. Conversely, HIV/AIDS activists face a more unified set of state ministries that wish to keep AIDS-related cases out of the courts. The political opportunity structure approach and its focus on elite divisions has a great deal of explanatory power, but it does not help one to understand how state actors, even those allied with activists and litigants in civil society, try to protect the overall hegemony of the regime. To explain this balancing act by state officials, we need to draw from Gramscian theory on how states and elites attempt to interact with civil society to protect the regime's ascendance. In particular, Gramsci argued that intellectuals allied with the state help to construct consent to the state with ideology, but when ideological leadership wanes, the state can step in with coercion to uphold its hegemony.[65]

China's divergent responses to environmental pollution and HIV/AIDS are also potentially shaped by the varying ways that pollution and HIV/AIDS harm populations and how society views the two crises. It is difficult for anyone in a hazardous environment to hide from pollution and its effects because pollution does not respect property, village, township, county, provincial, or national borders. Factories in one locale that dump toxic waste into a river affect citizens' health downstream. In contrast, HIV/AIDS spreads widely but through limited forms of contact, so it deeply harms some subpopulations while not directly affecting others. The particular qualities of environmental pollution and HIV/AIDS in China have forged distinct societal attitudes toward victims of the two crises. Generally speaking, people exposed to environmental pollution are considered innocent victims whose lives were endangered by the polluters. HIV/AIDS carriers, in contrast, are stigmatized because of the modes of transmission of the virus. Some behavior that can transmit HIV/AIDS, such as intravenous drug use and unprotected sex with commercial sex workers or multiple partners violates social mores and laws in China. Even when people living with HIV/AIDS have not broken the law or engaged in at-risk behavior, the virus still has the capacity to stigmatize carriers of the virus.[66] The distinct characters of the two crises and societal perception of their victims place greater domestic pressure on China's state and courts to respond to pollution than to HIV/AIDS. Weighing against the impact of societal attitudes on China's state and courts are financial considerations of settling claims. Pollution victims not only seek compensation, but they also imperil, at least in the short term, China's economic growth model, which is the basis of the regime's legitimacy.[67] Environmental attorneys were quick to point out this issue as an impediment to their pursuit of litigation.[68] Given the widespread nature of environmental pollution and the more narrow effect of the HIV/AIDS epidemic, one might expect the courts to press for administrative solutions to the environment and judicial resolution of AIDS cases because the costs of addressing AIDS complaints are lower than tackling environmental pollution cases. Yet the reverse has occurred; the courts have been more willing to hear pollution victims' cases than HIV/AIDS carriers' complaints, which suggests that societal views do affect the courts' actions.

A LOOK AHEAD

The book's next six chapters are informally divided into two parts, followed by a conclusion. Chapters 2 through 4 address issues related to civil society in China. Chapter 2 provides an overview of China's civil society development, arguing that China's state actively contends for leadership of civil society in order to buttress its legitimacy. China's government has used regulations on the registration of civil society organizations to limit the types of groups that may officially operate and compete with GONGOs, as well as to drive wedges between grassroots civil society organizations and international funders. Despite these challenges, some grassroots organizations have proven surprisingly adept at sidestepping regulations and even collaborating with government officials.

Chapter 3 addresses the emergence of China's environmental and AIDS crises with special emphasis on how the institutional changes wrought in the 1980s rendered China prone to the two crises. China's environmental crisis has been several decades in development, as many authors have already noted.[69] Under Mao (1949–1976), China failed to develop appropriate regulations to monitor and regulate pollution, but the pollution problem intensified after 1978 when the reform era began. In the context of a weak regulatory system, China unleashed a set of policies that led to rapid industrialization, especially in the countryside where small enterprises operate. The numerous small factories dispersed throughout China's countryside provide enormous challenges to monitor, which have outstripped the capacity of the MEP with its meager resources and staff. Less well known is the story of the AIDS pandemic in China.[70] One of the reasons for the rapid spread of HIV/AIDS in China was reform of the state health-care system that privatized and decentralized many aspects of medical services. In the process of these reforms, regulation and monitoring capacity declined and a blood scandal broke out in central China, affecting upwards of 1 million persons according to some estimates.[71] In both the environmental pollution and AIDS crises, the liberalizing reforms after 1978 created a context in which polluting enterprises could operate with little fear of China's laws and blood collection agents could taint the blood supply with few repercussions.

Chapter 4 closely examines civil society organizations that work on environmental pollution and HIV/AIDS in China, their interaction with international actors (UN agencies, international foundations, and INGOs), and the challenges that organizations in the two sectors of civil society have faced. The chapter provides a detailed account of China's evolving approach to civil society organizations. Initially, state officials were afraid of civil society development but cognizant of the international expectations for civil society involvement in governance, so they granted NGOs very limited scope to operate. International funders and civil society groups tried to gain a foothold in China to expand the role for civil society organizations and, in some cases, to abet domestic civil society organizations that sought to liberalize Chinese politics. China's state has granted more scope for civil society in response to environmental and public health disasters.[72] In the last decade, China's state began to shift its civil society approach from control and suppression toward selective utilization of civil society organizations to carry out quasi-state functions. Civil society development reflects state attempts to balance several competing principles: subordinate organizations to the needs of state agents, maintain harmony in society, and garner international and domestic legitimacy with civil society and rule of law development.

The second section of the book, comprising chapters 5 through 7, highlights legal development related to environmental pollution and HIV/AIDS. Chapters 5 and 6 address legal cases and state responses to litigation on HIV/AIDS and environmental pollution, respectively. While both set of claimants have faced enormous challenges in pursuing their cases in the courts, a comparison of the cases in chapters 5 and 6 reveals the greater success of environmental pollution victims than HIV/AIDS carriers in litigation. Each chapter analyzes key legal cases that exemplify litigants' efforts to use somewhat loosely defined laws to protect their rights and interests. In the area of HIV/AIDS, litigants have attempted to sue government agents for disclosure of private information (especially their HIV-positive status), hospitals for medical malpractice in their exposure to HIV/AIDS, and employers and hospitals for discrimination by denying access to employment and health care. In the area of environmental pollution litigation, I focus on plaintiffs who have sued factories for damages to crops and personal health. The chapters also consider why courts have refused to hear lawsuits, which particularly affects HIV/AIDS carriers' pursuit of litigation, and the role of media and civil society pressure in addressing legal claims.

Chapter 7 examines the politics behind the recent emergence of environmental public interest litigation and revisions to laws related to such cases. In that chapter, I argue that organizations attached to the party-state apparatus are vying with grassroots organizations for leadership over who gets to defend the "public interest," a concept that is fundamental to any communist regime. The chapter lays bare the tensions between state-backed and grassroots organizations contending for leadership and support in civil society and in representing public interests in environmental courts. It also demonstrates how state officials have varying interests in how to resolve struggles over public interest litigation. The unfolding of environmental public interest litigation exemplifies the regime's attempts to gain legitimacy by leading and constraining the development of such lawsuits.

Chapter 8, the conclusion, draws out broad comparisons of the pollution victims' and HIV/AIDS carriers' movements and official responses. To use the terminology of the lawyer cited at the outset of the introduction, I explore what factors help toothless legal tigers grow teeth. I contend that the following four factors are helping to give Chinese laws more "bite": (1) international funding and diffusion of norms; (2) mobilization by Chinese protesters and media; (3) litigation that pushes the boundaries of prevailing rights considerations; and (4) allies within the regime that support rights-based claims brought by activists. The chapter also reflects on obstacles to advancing rights protection, including China's decentralized and fragmented judiciary and bureaucracy, as well as the fractured and uneven development of Chinese civil society. Finally, the conclusion considers the compatibility of advancing rights protection under the regime's ideology of "harmonious society" and the goal of maintaining stability. The trajectory of legal cases, law writing, and revising of existing laws gives moderate hope for giving China's laws more teeth and for greater inclusion of citizens in governance over HIV/AIDS and environmental pollution, although progress is uneven and occurs in fits and starts.

Tigers without Teeth contributes to our understanding of Chinese civil society and the role of litigation and legal development in nondemocratic countries. The book advances three core arguments. First, I contend that Gramscian analysis of state and civil society helps to explain Chinese officials' attempts to lead and constrain civil society as a whole. Second, Chinese courts are more responsive to pollution victims than AIDS carriers due to the political pressure placed on them by the environmental protection and public health bureaucracies, which have distinct interests with regard to litigation. Finally, an underlying argument in the book is that social protest and civil society development are important contributing factors to the development of rights-based litigation. The overall picture that emerges from the book is one of the state balancing its commitments to regime stability with the use of control and coercion against its need to defuse societal conflict with greater citizen participation in the form of civil society participation and litigation.

NOTES

1. *Regulations on AIDS Prevention and Treatment*, issued by State Council 29 January 2006 (Document No. 457), put into effect 1 March 2006.
2. Interview 78.
3. China also lacks a court record of all cases heard, which makes systematic analysis of decisions in China's courts nearly impossible. Rachel E. Stern, *Environmental Litigation in China: A Study of Political Ambivalence* (Cambridge: Cambridge University Press, 2013);

Rachel E. Stern, "On the Frontlines: Making Decisions in Chinese Civil Environmental Lawsuits," *Law & Policy* 32, no. 1 (January 2010), 79–103, and Pierre Landry, "The Institutional Diffusion of Courts in China: Evidence from Survey Data," in *Rule by Law: The Politics of Courts in Authoritarian Regimes*, eds. Tom Ginsburg and Tamir Moustafa (Cambridge: Cambridge University Press, 2008), 207–34, represent excellent research that attempts to overcome the lack of a court record to engage in some quantitative analyses of court decisions and norm diffusion in the courts.

4. Charles R. Epp, *The Rights Revolution: Lawyers, Activists, and Supreme Courts in Comparative Perspective* (Chicago: University of Chicago Press, 1998); Cary Coglianese, "Social Movements, Law, and Society: The Institutionalization of the Environmental Movement," *University of Pennsylvania Law Review* 150, no. 1 (November 2001), 85–118; and Christopher Coleman, Laurence D. Nee, and Leonard S. Rubinowitz, "Social Movements and Social-Change Litigation: Synergy in the Montgomery Bus Protest," *Law and Social Inquiry* 30, no. 4 (Autumn 2005), 663–736.

5. Epp, *The Rights Revolution*, makes a similar point with regard to advancing social causes in the courts under democratic regimes; Tamir Moustafa, *The Struggle for Constitutional Power: Law, Politics, and Economic Development in Egypt* (Cambridge: Cambridge University Press, 2009), discusses the importance of such a steady flow of cases in nondemocratic countries.

6. Alexis de Tocqueville, *Democracy in America*, translated by George Lawrence and edited by J. P. Mayer (Garden City, NY: Anchor Books, 1969); Robert D. Putnam, *Bowling Alone: The Collapse and Revival of American Community* (Simon and Schuster, 2001); Bob Edwards and Michael W. Foley, "Civil Society and Social Capital: A Primer," in *Beyond Tocqueville: Civil Society and the Social Capital Debate in Contemporary Perspective*, eds. Bob Edwards, Michael W. Foley, and Mario Diani (Hanover, NH: Tufts University and University Press of New England, 2001), 1–14.

7. Jeanne Wilson, "Colour Revolutions: The View from Moscow and Beijing," *Journal of Communist Studies and Transition Politics* 25, nos. 2 and 3 (June 2009), 369–95; Titus C. Chen, "China's Reaction to the Color Revolutions: Adaptive Authoritarianism in Full Swing," *Asian Perspectives* 34, no. 2 (2010), 5–51.

8. Fengshi Wu, "Environmental GONGO Autonomy: Unintended Consequences of State Strategies in China," *Good Society* 12, no. 1 (2003), 36. Marcia A. Weigel and Jim Butterfield, "Civil Society in Reforming Communist Regimes: The Logic of Emergence," *Comparative Politics* 25, no. 1 (October 1992), 9, discusses the way that party-sponsored organizations initially added to regime legitimacy under communist rule, though such groups eroded regime legitimacy as they increased their autonomy.

9. Tamir Moustafa and Tom Ginsburg, "Introduction: The Functions of Courts in Authoritarian Politics," in *Rule by Law: The Politics of Courts in Authoritarian Regimes*, eds. Tom Ginsburg and Tamir Moustafa (Cambridge: Cambridge University Press, 2008), 2. Moustafa, *The Struggle for Constitutional Power*; Austin Sarat and Stuart Scheingold, "What Cause Lawyers Do *For*, and *To*, Social Movements," in *Cause Lawyers and Social Movements*, eds. Austin Sarat and Stuart Scheingold (Stanford, CA: Stanford University Press, 2006), 1–34; and Sandra R. Levitsky, "To Lead with Law: Reassessing the Influence of Legal Advocacy Organizations in Social Movements," in *Cause Lawyers and Social Movements*, eds. Austin Sarat and Stuart Scheingold (Stanford, CA: Stanford University Press, 2006), 145–63, also address judicialization of politics and cause lawyering.

10. Kevin J. O'Brien and Lianjiang Li, *Rightful Resistance in Rural China* (Cambridge: Cambridge University Press, 2006).

11. Neil J. Diamant, Stanley B. Lubman, and Kevin J. O'Brien, "Law and Society in the People's Republic of China," in *Engaging the Law in China: State, Society, and Possibilities of Justice*, eds. Neil J. Diamant, Stanley B. Lubman, and Kevin J. O'Brien (Stanford, CA: Stanford University Press, 2005), 3–27; Mary E. Gallagher, "'Use the Law as Your Weapon!' Institutional Change and Legal Mobilization in China," in *Engaging the Law in China: State, Society, and Possibilities for Justice*, eds. Neil J. Diamant, Stanley B. Lubman, and Kevin J. O'Brien (Stanford, CA: Stanford University Press, 2005), 54–83; O'Brien and Li, *Rightful*

Resistance in Rural China (Cambridge: Cambridge University Press, 2006); and Stern, *Environmental Litigation in China.*

12. Kin-Man Chan, "Harmonious Society," in *International Encyclopedia of Civil Society*, eds. Helmut K. Anheier and Stefan Toepler (Springer US, 2010), 121–25.

13. Pitman Potter, *The Chinese Legal System: Globalization and Local Legal Culture* (New York: Routledge, 2001).

14. Interviews 26, 31, and 53.

15. *Constitution of the People's Republic of China*, adopted 4 December 1982, last amended 14 March 2004.

16. *Labor Law of the People's Republic of China*, promulgated by the president on 5 July 1994.

17. *Law of the People's Republic of China on the Prevention and Treatment of Infectious Diseases*, passed by the Standing Committee of the National People's Congress on 21 February 1989, revised 28 August 2004.

18. *Regulations on AIDS Prevention and Treatment*, issued by State Council 29 January 2006 (Document No. 457), put into effect 1 March 2006.

19. Scott Wilson, "Settling for Discrimination: HIV/AIDS Carriers and the Resolution of Legal Claims," special edition on "Governing AIDS" in *International Journal of Asia Pacific Studies* 8, no. 1 (January 2012), 35–55.

20. Randall Peerenboom, *China Modernizes: Threat to the West or Model for the Rest?* (Oxford: Oxford University Press, 2007); Stern, *Environmental Litigation in China.* Intervention in court proceedings can occur through informal ties (*guanxi*) between actors inside and outside the courts. Pitman Potter, "*Guanxi* and the PRC Legal System: From Contradiction to Complementarity," in *Social Connections in China: Institutions, Culture, and the Changing Nature of Guanxi*, eds. Thomas Gold, Doug Guthrie, and David Wank (Cambridge: Cambridge University Press, 2002), 179–96; and Scott Wilson, "Law *Guanxi*: Multinational Corporations, State Actors, and Rule of Law in China," *Journal of Contemporary China* 17, no. 54 (February 2008), 25–51.

21. James A. Goldston, "Public Interest Litigation in Central and Eastern Europe: Roots, Prospects, and Challenges," *Human Rights Quarterly* 28, no. 2 (May 2006), 496.

22. National Bureau of Statistics, *China Statistical Yearbook, 2012* (Beijing: China Statistics Press, 2012), 939.

23. World Bank and State Environmental Protection Agency, P. R. China (SEPA), *Cost of Pollution in China: Economic Estimates of Physical Damage* (Washington: World Bank, 2007); UN Theme Group on HIV/AIDS in China, *HIV/AIDS: China's Titanic Peril* (New York: United Nations, June 2002).

24. World Bank and State Environmental Protection Agency, P. R. China, *Cost of Pollution*; Elizabeth Economy, *The River Runs Black: The Environmental Challenge to China's Future* (Ithaca and New York: Cornell University Press, 2004); Lester Brown, *Who Will Feed China? Wake-Up Call for a Small Planet* (New York: Norton, 1995); Guomei Xia, *HIV/AIDS in China* (Beijing: Foreign Languages Press, 2004); and Sandra Teresa Hyde, *Eating Spring Rice: The Cultural Politics of AIDS in Southeast China* (Berkeley: University of California Press, 2007).

25. Stern, *Environmental Litigation in China*, provides an excellent account of the process of environmental litigation in China, but far less has been written about the struggle of HIV/AIDS carriers to litigate their grievances. Exceptions include John Balzano and Jia Ping, "Coming Out of Denial: An Analysis of AIDS Law and Policy in China," *Loyola University Chicago International Law Review* 3 (Spring 2006), 187–212; Wilson, "Settling for Discrimination."

26. Ministry of Health, *2012 China AIDS Response Progress Report* (Beijing: Ministry of Health, 2012), accessed 20 August 2014, http://www.unaids.org/en/dataanalysis/knowyourresponse/countryprogressreports/2012countries/ce_CN_Narrative_Report%5B1%5D.pdf.

27. Evan Anderson and Sara Davis, *AIDS Blood Scandals: What China Can Learn from the World's Mistakes* (New York: Asia Catalyst, 2007), 15.

28. Xinhua, "28,000 Die of HIV/AIDS in China in 2011," *China Daily*, 21 January 2012, accessed 23 August 2014, http://www.chinadaily.com.cn/china/2012-01/21/content_14488896.htm.

29. Agence France Presse, "China AIDS Campaigner Detained: Activists," Agence France Presse, 21 August 2010, http://www.google.com/hostednews/afp/article/ALeqM5i0DSDtElSxTCWgRZEoL7aXXQBIUg.

30. Huanjing Baohubu 环境保护部, *Huanjing Baohubu Zhengfu Xinxi Gongkai Gongzuo 2011 Niandu Baogao* 环境保护部政府信息公开工作2010 年度报告 (2010 Report on the State of the Environment in China) (Beijing: Environmental Information Center, 2011).

31. Edward Wong, "Air Pollution Linked to 1.2 Million Premature Deaths in China," *New York Times*, 1 April 2010,http://www.nytimes.com/2013/04/02/world/asia/air-pollution-linked-to-1-2-million-deaths-in-china.html, citing a study in the *Lancet*.

32. Brown, *Who Will Feed China?*

33. UN Theme Group on HIV/AIDS in China, *HIV/AIDS: China's Titanic Peril* (New York: United Nations, June 2002).

34. Kathryn Sikkink, "Patterns of Dynamic Multilevel Governance and the Insider-Outsider Coalition," in *Transnational Protest and Global Activism,* eds. Donatella della Porta and Sidney Tarrow (Lanham, MD: Rowman & Littlefield, 2005), 151–73.

35. Kim D. Reiman, "A View from the Top: International Politics, Norms and the Worldwide Growth of NGOs," *International Studies Quarterly* 50 (2006), 45–67.

36. Siri Gloppen, "Litigation as a Strategy to Hold Governments Accountable for Implementing the Right to Health," *Health and Human Rights* 10, no. 2 (2008), 21–36; Alex Wang, "The Role of Law in Environmental Protection in China: Recent Developments," *Vermont Journal of Environmental Law* 8 (Spring 2007), 195–223.

37. "Cause lawyering" is a term used in a variety of ways and is difficult to define. One fairly comprehensive definition is as follows: "not-for-profit legal work with and/or on behalf of individuals or groups who cannot afford to hire a lawyer, the ultimate aim of which is to achieve a progressive social change." Stephen Meili, "Consumer Cause Lawyers in the United States: Lawyers for the Movement or a Movement unto Themselves" in *Cause Lawyers and Social Movements*, eds. Austin Sarat and Stuart Scheingold (Stanford, CA: Stanford University Press, 2006), 512 (note 2).

38. Throughout the book, I use "nongovernmental organizations" (NGOs) and civil society organizations interchangeably.

39. Jonathan Unger and Anita Chan, "China, Corporatism, and the East Asian Model," *Australian Journal of Chinese Affairs*, no. 33 (January 1995), 29–53; and David Da-hua Yang, "Civil Society as an Analytical Lens for Contemporary China," *China: An International Journal* 2, no. 1 (2004), 1–27.

40. Margaret M. Pearson, *China's New Business Elite: The Political Consequences of Economic Reform* (Berkeley: University of California Press, 1997).

41. Timothy Brook and B. Michael Frolic, "The Ambiguous Challenge of Civil Society," in *Civil Society in China*, eds. Timothy Brook and B. Michael Frolic (Armonk, NY: East Gate Books, 1997, 3–16); and Jude Howell, "Prospects for NGOs in China," *Development in Practice* 5, no. 1 (February 1995), 5–15.

42. Bjorn Alpermann, "State and Society in China's Environmental Politics," in *China's Environmental Crisis*, eds. Joel Jay Kassiola and Sujian Guo (Houndsmill, Basingstroke: Palgrave McMillan, 2010); Peter Ho, "Introduction: Embedded Activism and Political Change in a Semi-Authoritarian Context," in *China's Embedded Activism: Opportunities and Constraints of a Social Movement*, eds. Peter Ho and Richard Louis Edmonds (London and New York: Routledge, 2008), 1–19; Howell, "Prospects for NGOs"; Joan Kaufman, "The Role of NGOs in China's AIDS Crisis: Challenges and Possibilities," in *State and Society Responses to Social Welfare Needs in China: Serving the People*, eds. Jonathan Schwartz and Shawn Shieh (London and New York: Routledge, 2009), 156–73.

43. Tony Saich, "Negotiating the State: The Development of Social Organizations in China," *China Quarterly*, no. 161 (March 2000), 124–41; Judith Howell, "Seizing Spaces, Challenging Marginalization and Claiming Voice," in *Exploring Civil Society: Political and Cultu-*

ral Contexts, eds. Marlies Glasius, David Lewis, and Hakan Seckinelgin (Abingdon and New York: Routledge Press, 2004); and Kaufman, "Role of NGOs."

44. National Bureau of Statistics, *China Statistical Yearbook*, 2012, 866.

45. Quoted in Sha Liu, "Environmental NGOs Grow across China but Still Struggle for Support," *Global Times*12 (June 2012), accessed 14 March 2014, http://www.globaltimes.cn/content/714330.shtml.

46. China AIDS Information Network, *2010 China HIV/AIDS CSO/CBO Directory* (Beijing: China AIDS Information Network, 2010). An article in China's press stated that there are nearly one thousand NGOs working on AIDS in China. Kai Cao, "NGOs Participation Help China Fight AIDS," *Xinhua*, 30 November 2012, accessed 23 August 2014, http://news.xinhuanet.com/english/china/2012-11/30/c_132009780.htm.

47. Jessica C. Teets, "Let Many Civil Societies Bloom: The Rise of Consultative Authoritarianism in China," *China Quarterly*, no. 213 (March 2013), 19–38; Timothy Hildebrandt, *Social Organizations and the Authoritarian State in China* (Cambridge: Cambridge University Press, 2013); Anthony J. Spires, "Contingent Symbiosis and Civil Society in an Authoritarian State: Understanding the Survival of China's Grassroots NGOs," *American Journal of Sociology* 117, no. 1 (July 2011), 1–45; Saich, "Negotiating the State"; Baogang He, "The Making of a Nascent Civil Society," in *Civil Society in Asia*, eds. David C. Schak and Wayne Hudson (Farnham, Surrey: Ashgate, 2003), 114–39.

48. These terms come from O'Brien and Li, *Rightful Resistance*; and Sidney Tarrow, *Power in the Movement* (Cambridge: Cambridge University Press, 1998), among others.

49. Stern, *Environmental Litigation in China*, makes such a point with regard to soft funding for environmental litigation in China. In contrast, legal aid stations operated for HIV/AIDS carriers that I interviewed received funding from international NGOs and foundations in support of their litigation efforts.

50. Epp, *Rights Revolution*; Coglianese, "Social Movements, Law, and Society"; Coleman et al., "Social Movements and Social-Change Litigation."

51. Law and society scholars raise a similar point in other contexts. Coglianese, "Social Movements, Law, and Society"; Coleman et al., "Social Movements and Social-Change Litigation"; and Levitsky, "To Lead with Law."

52. Interview 87.

53. Xin He, "Judicial Innovation and Local Politics: Judicialization of Administrative Governance in East China," *China Journal*, no. 69 (January 2013), 20–42; and Benjamin L. Liebman, "China's Courts: Restricted Reform," *China Quarterly*, no. 191 (September 2007), 620–38.

54. Moustafa, *The Struggle for Constitutional Power*; and Michael W. McCann, "Interests, Ideas, and Institutions in Comparative Analysis of Judicial Power," *Political Research Quarterly* 62, no. 4 (December 2009), 834–39.

55. Randall Peerenboom, *China's Long March toward Rule of Law* (Cambridge: Cambridge University Press, 2003), argues that China's courts have very limited autonomy due to judges' poor training and the interference of party and state officials in courts' decisions. Pitman Potter, "The Chinese Legal System: Continuing Commitment to the Primacy of State Power," *China Quarterly*, no. 159 (September 1999), 673–83, suggests that legal reforms are subordinated to the state's interests. He, "Judicial Innovation," sees some scope for limited judicial autonomy and innovation.

56. Stanley Lubman, "Civil Litigation Being Quietly 'Harmonized,'" China Real Time Report, *Wall Street Journal* (31 May 2011),http://blogs.wsj.com/chinarealtime/2011/05/31/civil-litigation-being-quietly-harmonized/.

57. Interview 47; Interview 72; Bin Zhou and Luo Huiru 周斌 罗惠如, "*Shuxue Ganran Aizibing Qun Fa Anjian Lvshi Daili Tantao*" 输血感染艾滋病群发案件律师代理探讨 (An Analysis by Attorneys Representing a Group Who Contracted HIV/AIDS from Blood Donations), Asia Catalyst (no date), accessed 16 July 2014,www.asiacatalyst.org/Blood_transfusion_AIDS_cases.docwww.asiacatalyst.org/Blood_transfusion_AIDS_cases.doc.

58. Peerenboom, *China's Long March*, 302.

59. Peerenboom, *China Modernizes*; Stern, *Environmental Litigation in China*; and He, "Judicial Innovation and Local Politics."

60. Gallagher, "'Use the Law as Your Weapon!'" 54–83; He, "Judicial Innovation and Local Politics"; and Liebman, "China's Courts."

61. Timothy Hildebrandt, "Development and Division: The Effect of Transnational Linkages and Local Politics on LGBT Activism in China," *Journal of Contemporary China* 21, no. 77 (September 2012), 845–62; Diamant et al., "Law and Society," 3–27; Joel S. Migdal, "The State in Society: An Approach to Struggles for Domination," in *State Power and Social Forces*, eds. Joel S. Migdal, Atul Kohli, and Vivienne Shue (New York: Cambridge University Press, 1994), 5–34.

62. In March 2013, the ministry of health was dissolved and combined with the State Family Planning Commission to become a new agency titled National Health and Family Planning Commission. The interviews for this volume were all conducted before the change in organization, so the volume consistently refers to the ministry of health. At time of writing it is also unclear what effects, if any, the reorganization will have on new agency's capacity to address AIDS.

63. As is the case with the ministry of environmental protection, the ministry of health is embroiled in rivalries with other state agents. Litigation, however, does not advance the interests of the ministry of health because it (and its agents), rather than its rivals (and their agents), is likely to be named as a defendant in lawsuits.

64. Hildebrandt, "Development and Division"; and Scott Wilson, "Introduction: Chinese NGOs—International and Online Linkages," *Journal of Contemporary China* 21, no. 76 (July 2012), 551–67.

65. Antonio Gramsci, *Selections from the Prison Notebooks*, trans. and ed. by Q. Hoare and G. Smith (New York: International Publishers, 1971); and Kate Creehan, *Gramsci, Culture, and Anthropology* (Berkeley: University of California Press, 2002).

66. A survey has shown that in China, HIV/AIDS carriers who contracted the disease through contaminated blood products are subjected to less discrimination than those who contract the disease through unprotected sex or intravenous drug use. Yanhai Wan, Hu Ran, Guo Ran, and Linda Arnade, "Discrimination against People with HIV/AIDS in China," *Equal Rights Review* 4, 15–25.

67. Susan Shirk, *China: Fragile Superpower* (New York: Oxford University Press, 2008).

68. Interview 86.

69. Economy, *The River Runs Black*; Judith Shapiro, *Mao's War against Nature: Politics and the Environment in Revolutionary China* (Cambridge: Cambridge University Press, 2001); and Bryan Tilt, *The Struggle for Sustainability in Rural China: Environmental Values and Civil Society* (New York: Columbia University Press, 2010).

70. Exceptions include Anderson and Davis, *AIDS Blood Scandals*; Joan Kaufman, "Turning Points in China's AIDS Response," *China: An International Journal* 8, no. 1 (March 2010), 63–84; and Edmund Settle, *AIDS in China: An Annotated Chronology 1985-2003* (Monterey, CA: China AIDS Survey, 2003).

71. The estimate comes from activist physician Gao Yaojie, who discovered the outbreak of HIV due to the blood scandal. Cited in Anderson and Davis, *AIDS Blood Scandals*.

72. Saich, "Negotiating the State"; Kaufman, "Role of NGOs"; Katherine Morton, "Transnational Advocacy at the Grassroots: Benefits and Risks of International Cooperation," in *China's Embedded Activism: Opportunities and Constraints of a Social Movement*, eds. Peter Ho and Richard Louis Edmonds (London and New York: Routledge, 2008), 195–215; Timothy Hildebrandt and Jennifer Turner, "Greening Activism? Reassessing the Role of Environmental NGOs in China," in *State and Society Responses to Social Welfare Needs in China: Serving the People*, eds. Jonathan Schwartz and Shawn Shieh (London and New York: Routledge, 2009), 89–110; Joan Kaufman, "Global Women's Movement," *Journal of Contemporary China* (July 2012); Scott Wilson, "Seeking One's Day in Court: Chinese Regime Responsiveness to International Legal Norms on AIDS Carriers' and Pollution Victims' Rights," *Journal of Contemporary China* 21, no. 77 (September 2012), 863–80.

Chapter Two

State Management of Civil Society and the Judiciary

Over the last two decades in China, the number of civil society organizations and the amount of legal contestation has greatly increased.[1] The growth and consolidation of civil society and the rise of rights-based litigation pose a potential threat to the Chinese regime's legitimacy and stability. Although China's Communist Party has staved off challenges to its power that brought about political transitions in Eastern European and the Former Soviet states, it has granted increasing scope for social movements and use of courts to defend citizens' rights. China's central government has become more permissive of social movements and legal contestation—in some quarters, state officials actively encourage both—but the state's tolerance for agitation and litigation is limited. Under the rubric of "*weiwen*" (protecting stability), China's state reins in activities that might tarnish the Communist Party's legitimacy and imperil its rule. China's regime is motivated by two competing principles: providing enough freedom of expression and ability to organize that citizens feel that their rights are secured, while avoiding the creation of new points of organized authority that become alternatives to the regime's leadership. How has China's regime sought to balance these competing goals, and how has that balance affected the development of civil society and legal activity? Additionally, how has the entry of international civil society organizations and funders affected the balance of forces arrayed in Chinese civil society, as well as Chinese commitments to rule of law?

I use Gramscian theory to argue that the state has attempted to intervene in civil society and litigation to protect its hegemony. Despite greater leeway for civil society organizations and litigation, China's regime has also (1) created a set of rules and regulations on the activities of civil society organizations and attorneys to contain societal opposition, (2) intervened to thwart close ties between international funders and domestic grassroots activist organizations, (3) created state-backed organizations to vie with grassroots organizations and activist attorneys to protect the Communist Party's role of representing the public interest, and (4) utilized institutionalized ties to the courts to exercise ideological leadership over, and limit the autonomy of, the judiciary. Chinese officials' responses to grassroots organizations and rights-based contentiousness have sought to balance state-constructed order and modest amounts of citizen participation in governance. This chapter begins by briefly summarizing some of the contending approaches to civil society and litigation as arenas of contestation with the state. Next, the chapter presents the state's mechanism to manage and contain opposition in civil society and the courts as well as some of the opportunities for civil society organizations to oppose the state.

CONTENDING APPROACHES TO CHINESE CIVIL SOCIETY

Chinese civil society development has confounded standard theories of civil society because of the coexistence of active state-backed organizations and more autonomous and contentious organizations. The former hints at state control, while the latter suggests autonomous forces from civil society acting as in opposition to the state.[2] Typically scholars and journalists have analyzed Chinese civil society dynamics based on expectations from a liberal model of civil society development. As civil society grows, opposition to the state strengthens either as a counterweight to authoritarian rule or as a check on democratically elected leaders. Although most scholars have rejected the notion that China's civil society is going to culminate in the creation of a democratic state, progress toward democratization remains a (if not *the*) benchmark by which civil society development has been judged.[3]

Chinese civil society does not follow the clean lines of demarcation between societal forces and the state, as described by liberal theories. Rather, the dynamics of Chinese civil society comprise a shifting balance of forces between the regime and activists in civil society, state participation in civil society, and a mixture of regime motives that include citizen participation and regime stability. The goal of regime stability itself leads to a variety of state actions from occasional ham-handed suppression of social movements and activist attorneys to inclusion of civil society in policy implementation and enforcement of regulations in courts. Some observers of China's civil society have tried to make sense of the varying types of groups and patterns of state-society interaction by coining new qualifying terms such as "corporatist" or "top-down" civil society or to suggest that China lacks a true form of civil society.[4] More recently, in order to convey the blending of the open and closed nature of China's civil society and the legal system, authors have coined various terms such as Jessica Teets's "consultative authoritarianism," Yongshun Cai's "managed participation," Anthony Spires's "contingent symbiosis," Peter Ho and Richard Edmonds's "embedded activism," and Andrew Mertha's "fragmented authoritarianism."[5] Although many Chinese and international civil society organizations harbor liberal goals of rule of law, human rights, and democratization (or more broadly, citizen participation), liberal theories about civil society and democratization are not particularly useful for explaining developments in Chinese civil society.

I argue that Antonio Gramsci's theoretical framework helps to explain the contestation that is taking place in Chinese civil society and courts. In contrast to liberal theories that view civil society and the state as autonomous from each other, one of Gramsci's key findings is that the state and its allies actively participate in civil society and attempt to exercise ideological leadership over citizens in civil society. The state allies itself with intellectuals that represent classes and organizations in civil society to articulate the regime's ideology and develop consent to its rule.[6] Through their efforts to spread ideological tenets in civil society, state-backed organizations help to make the dominant ideology commonsensical to citizens, thereby constructing consensus. To the extent that citizens accept or at least follow the ideology of the state, in civil society, the ruling forces have constructed cultural hegemony. When ideological leadership begins to break down, the state can employ coercion to maintain its control over society.

Gramsci developed his theory of hegemony and civil society based on his study of capitalist societies, but the model applies with even greater force to nondemocratic mixed economies such as China. Many civil society organizations in China depend on state officials for support, protection, and financial backing. Indeed, some civil society organizations are directly linked to state or party organs, a relationship which simultaneously undermines their autonomy from the state and enhances their access to the state policy makers. Complicating the lines of ideological debate and material base of contention, international actors have entered China, and the ideas and resources that they provide can reduce civil society organizations' dependence on the state.[7] In theory, international organizations can challenge state authority with the ideas that they spread and funds that they distribute.[8] China's state has reacted to this troubling trend not by cutting off ties altogether but by regulating and participating in networks that link international foundations and organizations with domestic civil society organizations.

Following Gramscian theory, I argue that China's grassroots and state-backed organizations in civil society are engaged in struggles over ideological leadership that have profound ramifications for state authority. While the contestation in Chinese civil society primarily occurs among domestic actors, international actors including international organizations, foundations, and international nongovernmental organizations (INGOs) help to shape the balance of power and contours of conflict. In addition to funding, INGOs have helped to build the capacity of their Chinese counterparts through training and professionalization. External funders, including INGOs, foundations, and UN agencies, have provided Chinese civil society organizations and cause lawyers with crucial material resources to carry on some of their activities. Finally, transnational networks of activists in universities, civil society organizations, and law firms have diffused techniques and repertoires of action including litigation and protests to China. The goals of international actors are mixed. While some international actors simply want to contribute to relatively apolitical efforts such as protecting endangered species, improved public health, and disaster relief, others would like to push China's political development, including protection of human rights, rule of law, and promotion of democracy. The latter organizations work with Chinese civil society organizations and activists toward a common goal of political reform or use Chinese organizations to advance foreign political goals for China.

Such an approach extends Gramsci's theory of civil society, which focuses on domestic actors, to include international actors. China's domestic civil society dynamics involve complex alliances and maneuvering involving China's regime, state-allied organizations, grassroots organizations, and international groups. All of the above social forces have mixed motivations that lead them to form strategic partnerships to pursue one goal in ways that undermine pursuit of other goals. For example, international funders and organizations support grassroots organizations as a counterweight to state authority, while also developing close ties to state agents and state-sponsored organizations who have the capacity to implement social and technical programs. Grassroots organizations seek a relationship with the state in the form of recognition, collaboration, and funding, and (at least some groups) want to maintain a degree of autonomy in order to criticize policies. State agents also interact in complex ways with civil society, simultaneously disciplining civil society organizations, sponsoring civil society organizations, and collaborating with international and domestic groups. None of the actors is fully autonomous, but none are completely dependent on the other parties. Similarly, the three sets of actors mix contention and collaboration.

The entrance of international groups and funders has caused a split among Chinese officials with regard to the activities of INGOs and grassroots organizations in civil society. Officials recognize the value of international cooperation including the expertise and material resources that international groups can offer to address problems such as pollution and HIV/AIDS, but officials also are anxious about the interests that international actors bring to China. In particular, officials fear that INGOs and foreign foundations seek to fund activist grassroots groups to incite a "color revolution" along the lines of those that occurred in the Ukraine or a jasmine revolution, as took place in Libya and Egypt. Such concerns are heightened by growing political restlessness in China; since 1995, public disturbances (including protests) have proliferated, numbering over 87,000 incidents in 2005, after which time the Chinese government quit publicizing the trend. Concomitantly, the number of officially registered civil society organizations skyrocketed during the period 2007–2012, growing from 354,000 to 460,000,[9] which does not even account for unregistered organizations.

CIVIL SOCIETY AND THE JUDICIARY AS ARENAS OF CONTESTATION

Liberal and Gramscian theories agree that social movements and organizations that operate in civil society have the potential to challenge the hegemony of a regime. The capacity to contest state dominance or legitimacy in courts, however, is a source of considerable debate. The core issue is whether legal battles can challenge the state because the state writes the laws and court procedures, and judicial institutions are part of the state. In other words, courts must operate within parameters established by the state, so citizens can use courts to challenge individual state actors but not the state and its hegemony. Some theorists argue that social movements in civil society and litigation are complementary in the sense that legal victories can affect societal values and societal values are supportive of legal change.[10] Attorneys and plaintiffs press to institutionalize gains for underprivileged classes of citizens in the courts, which social movements attempt to advance through more direct forms of contention such as protests. Court victories can give wind to further protest, which, in turn, can propel further gains through litigation.[11] More generally, social movements aim to raise popular consciousness of, or change how society frames, an issue, giving rise to more legal contentiousness, even generating legal reform. In turn, legal reforms and litigation can affect public perception, "with action by courts and other legal institutions sometimes lending legitimacy to the claims advanced by social movements."[12] According to the above viewpoint, courts and civil society activities can work in tandem to have a cumulative effect on the protection of underprivileged persons' rights, albeit the notion of "rights" as conferred by a state is consistent with the persistence of state hegemony in the face of legal challenges.

Others contend, however, that litigation can essentially hijack a social movement's activism by taking contentious activity out of civil society and placing it in courts. According to Tomiko Brown-Nagin, "social movements and juridical law are fundamentally in tension."[13] He further argues, "social movements that define themselves through law in the courts risk undermining their insurgent role in the political process, thus losing their agenda-setting ability."[14] Court cases might harm the development of social movements in at least four ways: by (1) handing control over the process of advancing groups' interests to lawyers who are practiced in negotiating compromises rather than pursuing ideals; (2) shifting social movements' contentious, noncompliant behavior into a venue (the courts) that effectively narrows contestation to the application of existing laws and regulations; (3) channeling resources to expensive litigation that may achieve "symbolic" gains in the courts but drain them away from direct contention that can substantively improve a situation[15]; and (4) slowing the process of rights-based contention by shifting from the immediate and direct action of social movement activists to legal representatives arguing cases at the measured pace of litigation and appeal processes.[16] In moving to the courts, social movements may demobilize and lose their capacity to press for further changes of laws or shift popular consciousness of an issue.

In liberal democracies, the judiciary enjoys a high degree of autonomy, and civil society activists have gained the right to protest and press for changes to state policies or laws. Those rights are less secure in a nondemocratic context such as China, where the regime deeply compromises judicial autonomy and restricts activists' and cause lawyers' activities. In China, civil society organizations are critical in helping cause lawyers to work on behalf of disadvantaged groups. The cost of preparing and arguing lawsuits in China is high, and most of the disadvantaged citizens who seek to defend their rights lack resources. To offer pro bono work to disadvantaged citizens and activists, lawyers must draw compensation and support from civil society organizations. Despite China's extraordinary record of economic growth, civil society organizations and disadvantaged groups remain impoverished due to restrictions on domestic fund-raising, which has opened a door for international actors (UN organizations, INGOs, and foundations) to fund civil society organizations and rights-based attorneys and to influence the direction of legal pressure brought on China's courts and government.

Categories of Civil Society Organizations and Registration Rules

One of the primary means for China's regime to moderate the pace of development and demands of civil society organizations is through its registration procedures. China divides civil society organizations (*shehui zuzhi*)[17] into the following three types, each with its own set of regulations for registration: social organizations (*shehui tuanti*), private noncommercial institutions (*minban fei qiye danwei*), and foundations (*jijinhui*, which are not discussed in this book). The above three categories represent the official types of civil society organizations, but activists and international observers have long noted that Chinese regulations on the registration of civil society organizations are arduous, and the ministry of civil affairs, charged with implementing the procedures, is reluctant to register many organizations, especially those that emerge without ties to China's state.[18] Social organization and private noncommercial institution are the two registration types that most civil society organizations seek to secure from the ministry of civil affairs, with private noncommercial institution status being easier to obtain because the social organization category is dominated by government-organized nongovernmental organizations (GONGOs). Table 2.1 includes the number of officially registered organizations with the ministry of civil affairs, but alongside such official organizations are many more civil society groups that register as (nonprofit) enterprises with the ministry of commerce or that fail to register altogether. Wang Shaoguang and He Jianyu found that there are four times as many improperly registered or unregistered organizations as official civil society organizations registered with the ministry of civil affairs.[19] Table 2.2 offers a general overview of the attributes of the various kinds of Chinese civil society organizations discussed below.

Under the current registration procedures, which are due to change in the near future, to apply for registration as a social organization with the ministry of civil affairs, or a local department of civil affairs, at the county level or above, a group must find a sponsoring unit (*zhuguan danwei*). A sponsoring unit must be a department of the state council (the highest executive organ of China's state) or the local government or be authorized by the local government to serve as a sponsor in the social organization's professional area. For example, an AIDS group would require a sponsor in the public health domain.[20] The department of civil affairs and the sponsoring unit form a dual oversight system to monitor and potentially restrict social organizations' activities. Regulations require that applicants have fifty or more members and assets of 30,000 yuan to register at the local level (100,000 yuan to register at the national level),[21] and the registration rules are designed to limit the scope of activities and number of organizations allowed to register. For example, the procedures bar registration of social organizations in the same or a similar field of activity as an existing social organization that is registered in a locale.[22] Such a provision can be used to grant a virtual monopoly on social services or advocacy to a state-backed civil society organization. Finally, the registration procedures forbid civil society organizations that are not national organizations from opening an office in more than one locale, effectively splintering civil society and limiting the geographic scope of such organizations' operations.

The rules governing private noncommercial institutions closely follow those for social organizations described above; private noncommercial institutions must have sponsors and may not replicate the work of another organization in the same functional area in a locale.[23] An important difference in the two sets of regulations, however, relates to limitations on the geographical scope of operations. Social organizations can be national (*quanguoxing*) in scope and register branch offices in locales outside of the original social

Table 2.1.   Number of Officially Registered Chinese Civil Society Organizations by Year and Type

Year	Total Number of Institutions	Social Organizations	Private Nonenterprise Institutions Run by NGOs	Foundations
1988	4,446	4,446		
1990	10,855	10,855		
1995	150,583	180,583		
1996	184,821	184,821		
1997	181,318	181,318		
1998	165,600	165,600		
1999	142,665	136,764	5,901	
2000	153,322	130,668	22,654	
2001	210,939	128,805	82,134	
2002	244,509	133,297	111,212	
2003	266,612	141,167	124,491	954
2004	289,432	153,359	135,181	892
2005	319,762	171,150	147,637	975
2006	354,393	191,946	161,303	1,144
2007	386,916	211,661	173,915	1,340
2008	413,660	229,681	182,382	1,597
2009	431,069	238,747	190,479	1,843
2010	445,631	245,256	198,175	2,200
2011	461,971	254,969	204,388	2,614

Source: National Bureau of Statistics. *China Statistical Yearbook* (Beijing: China Statistics Press, various years).

organization's place of registration.[24] Private noncommercial institutions, on the other hand, are not permitted to open branches or offices beyond their home location.[25]

It is also worth noting that the regulations on civil society organizations in China have been silent about registering international groups, although revisions to national registration regulations are scheduled to fill that gap. For decades high-profile INGOs have operated in China, cooperated with state offices, run conferences with local partners, and provided training to grassroots organizations and even officials, all without having registered with civil affairs bureaus. Most international groups have been left in a precarious legal position without appropriate registration. If Chinese officials judge the inter-

Table 2.2. Attributes of Various Types of Chinese Civil Society Organizations

	Social Organization (*shehui tuanti*)	*Minban Feiqiye* (private nonenterprise institutions)	(Non-commercial) Enterprises	Nonregistered
Registration	With Civil Affairs	With Civil Affairs	With Commerce	None
Sponsoring Unit	State or state-authorized agent in same functional field	State or state-authorized agent in same functional field	None	None
Relations with State	Many GONGOs, collaboration with state and state programs	Some collaboration and cooperative programs with state	Some personalized relations with officials, some collaboration and subcontracting in service delivery	Some personalized relations with officials, some collaboration and subcontracting in service delivery
Sources of Funding	State, international, domestic fund-raising	State, international	International, commercial operations, state subcontracting	International, commercial operations, state subcontracting
Personnel	Typically, staffed with full-time personnel	Small number of full-time personnel, volunteer base	Few full- or part-time personnel, volunteer base	Very few full- or part-time personnel, volunteer base
Capacity	Direct ties to government facilitate programs and some policy influence	Capacity to deliver programs and exert policy influence dependent on level of resources and state ties	Programs dependent on level of funding, mostly local operations, influence public opinion rather than direct contact with policy makers	Volunteer-based programming, many focus on influencing public opinion through social media rather than direct contact with policy makers

national groups to have crossed some undisclosed red line for acceptable conduct in China, lack of formal registration permits the Chinese state to close down the groups' activities. Such an attenuated position has under-

mined international groups' capacity to support local civil society organizations and to pressure China's regime to reform. In 2010, Yunnan Province
adopted experimental registration reforms that formalized the registration
procedures for international organizations. While the ability to register as
international civil society organizations is desirable, the rules on registering
collaborative programs with domestic organizations in Yunnan were cumber-
some enough that some international groups decided to depart China, although the effect of the regulations is uneven across civil society groups. [26]

The required sponsoring organizations, which must be attached to an
authorized state or Communist Party agent and are derisively called "moth-
ers-in-law" (*popo*) by Chinese, have been a major impediment to civil society development and autonomy. Very few grassroots organizations, what
many would call "true NGOs," can find a sponsor and receive government
approval to register with the ministry of civil affairs. As a leader of an NGO
explained, party and state organs have little interest in serving as sponsors:
"If a government organization acts as our sponsor, and we do good work,
they don't get any credit. But if we do poorly, then they take the blame. Their
calculation is that sponsorship doesn't pay; it's a simple calculation." [27]
Under those circumstances, very few grassroots NGOs can identify willing
sponsoring organizations, leaving them to register as (nonprofit) enterprises
with the ministry of commerce (a gray area of the law) or not to register at all
(outside the law). Registering with the ministry of commerce does not require a sponsoring organization and, by all accounts, is a very simple process. NGOs that follow this registration path, however, must surrender taxes
to the government on their operating revenue, including all donations and
grants. For many grassroots NGOs operating on a shoestring, the demand for
taxes is a real financial burden. Moreover, U.S. foundations, at least initially,
could not grant funds to "enterprises" and could not fund tax obligations.
According to Deng Guosheng's estimates, by 2012 China had five thousand
large grassroots civil society organizations and another 1 million small grassroots groups. [28]

The rules on registration of the various civil society organizations both
constrain the range of activities of organizations and provide mechanisms for
the state to limit and shape the development of such organizations. The
process of finding a sponsoring organization acts as a fine-gauge screen on
would-be NGOs that have strong political advocacy goals. The application
process allows the state to indirectly limit civil society development through
its subsidiary organizations that act as sponsors for grassroots NGOs. Forthcoming reforms in the registration process, which follow experiments with
registration procedures discussed below, will remove the requirement to have
a sponsoring organization as part of the application process. Early indications
suggest that the reforms, however, will still allow state agents at civil affairs
bureaus to shape civil society organizations' goals through the application

screening process. Restrictions on domestic fund-raising favor state-backed organizations, leaving grassroots organizations with no ability to publicly fund-raise, except through "special accounts."[29] The regulations on social organizations and citizen nonenterprise units also call for them not to "endanger national unity" or "harm the national interest."[30] The regulations leave the terms of such a loyalty test vaguely defined, which provides the authorities latitude to rein in organizations that engage in contentious political activities. Authorities are particularly sensitive to these concerns because sponsoring organizations (*zhuguan danwei*) share responsibility for the actions of the civil society organizations.

The elaborate rules on registration of social organizations have placed a premium on political connections and given rise to a special category of civil society organizations called GONGOs. GONGOs, which have direct ties to state or party organizations, are much more readily permitted to register as NGOs. Many of the founding directors of GONGOs are retired officials who form a social organization that remains tied to their former state or party unit. The state finds ready partners in GONGOs in its efforts to lead and contend with grassroots organizations in civil society. For example, in the HIV/AIDS area, GONGOs tend to be quite cautious in their advocacy for HIV/AIDS carriers, and their programs gravitate toward narrowly conceived medical issues that serve the interests of policy makers. Grassroots AIDS groups, on the other hand, are more likely to be contentious and advocate for new or reformed policies to protect AIDS carriers' interests. For example, in chapter 4 I analyze several groups that the state has closed down or harassed due to the groups' advocacy work—all of them have been grassroots organizations, and most of them were not registered with the ministry of civil affairs. Carolyn Hsu, however, asserts that civil society groups with close ties to the government—some of which are GONGOs—can use those ties to press for changes in state policies, whereas grassroots organizations—many of them improperly registered—tend to avoid challenging the state.[31] While it is true that some grassroots organizations avoid contact with the state and do not try to influence policies, those organizations that are engaged in legal advocacy and legal aid use state laws to correct state practice, which challenges the state's legitimacy. As I show in chapters 5 through 7, autonomous civil society groups that provide legal aid services are more likely to take on state agents than legal aid providers that are backed by the state.

Obviously, GONGOs are closely tied to official bodies, but some GONGOs try to push the limits of government tolerance. A staff member in one Beijing-based GONGO explained the political difficulties that the organization faced in its operations:

> Government officials are relatively nervous about our development and our growth. But, we are able to avoid confrontation with the government. . . .

Developing in this way, though, has led grassroots organizations and INGOs
to criticize us. . . . I explain to them that we first have to subsist, then we can
talk about the development of civil society in China. Sometimes the pressure is
very strong, and it comes from two sides.[32]

Although GONGOs remain controversial among grassroots civil society organizations in China for their relations with state authorities, they also have the potential to expand the scope of acceptable civil society behavior or serve as conduits to the government for grassroots partners.

Despite the construction of the registration procedures as a means to limit civil society development, many state officials ignore the letter and the spirit of the regulations. Typically, local officials are fully cognizant of the existence and activities of organizations that register as enterprises with the ministry of commerce rather than as one of the official civil society organization types with the civil affairs bureaucracy. Although they are placed in a compromising situation—not actually being commercial enterprises and sometimes engaging in advocacy work—officials generally allow them to operate. The pattern of operating on the margins or outside of the law with the knowledge and tacit approval of local officials reveals the regime's reliance on civil society organizations as well as such organizations' tenuous existence. The state can harass and/or shut down improperly registered civil society organizations that step out of line. At the same time, the state needs civil society organizations to meet functional needs in social service provision and to enjoy international legitimacy, issues that are explored further in chapter 4 of this book. Grassroots organizations' inappropriate registration allows the state to use such groups to meet its social service goals and shut down organizations that challenge the regime's legitimacy.

Sources of Civil Society Organization Autonomy

China's regulations on civil society organizations are designed to limit the autonomy of organizations by "keeping a potential enemy close at hand," while also trying to make civil society dependent on the state both for legitimacy and funding. Despite the state's tendency to manage and rein in civil society organizations, many civil society organizations that I interviewed sought to register and, in some cases, collaborate with authorities. Carolyn Hsu suggests that, in fact, China's state and civil society are interdependent, providing mutual benefits to the other party.[33] Civil society organizations' survival strategies draw organizations closer to the state, or at least pockets of state authorities, but many groups also wish to have the autonomy to advocate for their causes to officials.[34] The rest of this section addresses some of the factors that enhance civil society organizations' autonomy in China.

International Linkages and Funding

Chinese civil society organizations have been propelled by contact and collaboration with international organizations and transnational social movement organizations. For example, in the AIDS field, the UN Millennium Development Goals and the creation of the Global Fund to Fight AIDS, Tuberculosis, and Malaria helped to generate global resources for groups working to fight HIV/AIDS and to protect the rights of those affected by HIV/AIDS. Since 2003, China has received approximately 834 million dollars from the Global Fund. International nongovernmental organizations such as Marie Stopes International and foundations including the Ford Foundation and the Open Society Institute have provided significant funding to Chinese organizations, some of them advocacy-based. In the area of environmental governance and rule of law development, the Ford Foundation, World Wildlife Fund, and Natural Resources Defense Council among others have provided significant financial support and training to Chinese civil society organizations.

International funders approach China with the following two goals: to address problems such as pollution and public health concerns and to advance grassroots civil society or otherwise liberalize China's regime. Some international groups see Chinese state organs and GONGOs as long-term partners with capacity to develop and implement effective programs. International groups also can improve governance structures through cooperation. Such an approach, however, leaves few resources for grassroots organizations. The uncertain registration status of foreign foundations and INGOs in China lead foreign organizations to self-limit their programs and ties to grassroots organizations to avoid open conflict with Chinese authorities. International funding gives Chinese civil society organizations—both GONGOs and grassroots groups—capacity to pursue programs that test the boundaries of state tolerance, including provision of legal aid to disadvantaged citizens such as pollution victims and AIDS carriers.[35] Some international organizations that work on environmental issues, in turn, are attempting to liberalize China's governance. A field director of one such organization described its approach: "We see ourselves very much as supporting local reformers—people within the courts, people within the bar, people within the NGO community—that have new ideas or that are looking for new ideas to solve problems in China. We see ourselves as partners with them, helping them to access information from the outside that will be helpful to them, playing very much a bridge function."[36] The Ford Foundation, which has substantial programs in China, perceives its role as helping to build an infrastructure for civil society development.[37] A staff member of an international organization explained to me the balancing act that his group faces: "How can we build capacity in civil society and channel funds without wasting funds, without undermining any kind of work that is being done by the government and others, and without shooting ourselves in the foot? Obviously, if the government suddenly gets scared and shuts down everyone, it is not beneficial to anyone—not the NGOs and certainly not the people with HIV. It's like walking a tight rope."[38] An environmental attorney, however, noted the limits of international nongovernmental organizations' willingness to support civil society organizations that press for change: "INGOs want to cooperate with the government and universities, unceasingly hold conferences to research and publish books, produce superficial papers, manage a few good-looking but not very useful programs. They offer very little support for grassroots NGOs, especially activist organizations that seek to protect rights."[39]

International funders' goals lead donors to provide resources to state-backed *and* grassroots organizations, which has generated some controversy around who receives the funds. According to a study by Deng Guosheng and the Tsinghua University NGO Research Center, in 2011, only 1.32 percent of all Chinese charitable donations went to grassroots organizations, an indication of the financial challenges that grassroots groups face.[40] In contrast, over 51 percent of charitable donations went to the state or GONGOs, and nearly 40 percent went to foundations, most of which are related to the state. To gain access to vital funds, cash-starved grassroots organizations must turn to foreign donors or the state. According to Anthony Spires, during the period 2002–2009, U.S. funders to China gave 42 percent of their grant funds to GONGOs or the government, while only 5.6 percent of funds went to grassroots organizations.[41] Another 44 percent of the international funds went to academic units, which are under the control of the state, but can also include legal aid stations for disadvantaged groups. While the donation levels to grassroots organizations may seem paltry, they supplied roughly 90 percent of the funding to leading grassroots organizations (such as Friends of Nature and the Global Village) from 1995 to 2000.[42] Many civil society organizations wish to expand their autonomy from the state, but they need resources to do so. Restricted funding leaves most grassroots groups with weak capacity in the form of few regular employees and few resources to operate programs. While international resources available to Chinese civil society groups may be limited, they are an important source of autonomy and advance advocacy efforts.

Distance from State or State Partnership?

One of the main dilemmas that civil society organizations face is whether to register and seek close ties to China's state or not register and retain more autonomy. For some Chinese grassroots organizations, being outside of the state's gaze helps them to pursue advocacy programs. Such groups seek distance from the dual monitoring structure of the civil society organization registration system and the state's capacity to rein in and harass advocacy groups. Groups that push the boundaries of acceptable advocacy or that publicize the regime's agency or complicity in the emergence of social problems, including environmental pollution and the spread of AIDS through a blood scandal, are not likely to be permitted to register with the ministry of civil affairs. Instead, grassroots advocates are likely to register as enterprises with the ministry of commerce and evade, as much as possible, state monitoring and control in order to pursue contentious activities. An NGO director in Shanghai described the registration dilemma to me as follows:

> If you register as an NGO, the government can influence your programs because after you register you have a [sponsoring] unit . . . that can control the implementation of your programs. For example, if you have some program or some opinion that the government functional unit thinks is not good or too sensitive or radical, then the government supervisory unit can just cancel your program.[43]

Conversely, not registering with the government or registering as a commercial enterprise can leave one prone to government harassment and being shut down.

Other organizations find autonomy in the form of ties to the state. Many organizations that seek to alter Chinese policies or to advocate for disadvantaged groups would like to register with the ministry of civil affairs and cooperate with state authorities. The advantages of close ties to the state include patronage and protection provided by state organs.[44] Although official registration designates a party or state organ to be responsible for a civil society organization's activities, the actual monitoring of such organizations can be lax. In a sense, registration gives the civil society organization the state's imprimatur, which authorizes the group to carry out programs. In some cases, the sponsoring organ supports a civil society organization in order to add leverage for changing policies or protecting the rights and interests of disadvantaged groups. Doing so strengthens the hand of sponsoring organizations in interbureaucratic political struggles. In this sense, civil society organizations and organs within the regime may ally with one another in order to advance common causes.[45] While state monitoring and sponsorship serve as means to shape and restrain civil society formation, state ties can also create openings for policy changes and advocacy.

Regulatory Changes and Control over Civil Society Organizations

In response to criticism about state impediments to the registration of civil society organizations, beginning in the late 2000s, China's central government allowed local governments to experiment with new registration guide-

lines. Now the central government is poised to adopt some of these regulations for the entire country. Some of the main experiments were undertaken
by cities such as Shenzhen, Beijing, Chengdu, and Shanghai, and by provinces including Yunnan and Guangdong.[46] The main goals of the reforms
have been either to "open up" the registration process so that civil society
organizations would not be required to have a sponsoring organization or to
"regularize" the process of registration of certain types of civil society organizations, especially international organizations. Activists hoped that such reforms presaged China's reduction of state management of civil society. Unfortunately, recent legal changes on registration and access to international
funds have proved to be new means of state management of civil society.

Guangdong Province in south China has been a leader in revising registration rules for civil society organizations. In July 2009, Shenzhen, a city in
Guangdong, reformed its regulations to allow social organizations to register
directly with the bureau of civil affairs without having to find a sponsoring
organization. Building on Shenzhen's experience, in May 2012, Guangdong
Province issued new registration rules for the entire province. Initially, people believed this step would facilitate many existing organizations, currently
registered as enterprises or not registered at all because they could not find a
sponsor, to come forward and properly register with authorities. In the first
two months of the new provincial regulations, Guangzhou registered eight-
een new social organizations.[47] According to a Chinese press report, seven
hundred more organizations were able to register in the first three years of
the new, liberalized procedures in Shenzhen.[48]

Yet interviews with four Guangzhou-based civil society organizations in
2012 revealed that the procedures for registration are far from open and still
subject to state bias in the approval process.[49] According to personnel in two
HIV/AIDS organizations, civil society organizations would have been required to deposit 300,000 yuan in order to register as a civil society organization; to register as an enterprise only requires a 30,000-yuan deposit.[50] One
of two interviewed environmental organizations in Guangzhou, whose leader
had government connections, was invited to register as a social organization
(*shehui tuanti*), the most difficult registration status to obtain, and was not
required to put down any deposit; the other organization has had an application pending for two years without action.[51] The organization that successfully registered focused on educational programs related to the environment, an
area that does not endanger, but serves, the state's interests. Neither of the
HIV/AIDS organizations in Guangzhou had adequate resources or political
connections to register under the new regulations. Gay Friends and Relatives
Group, an NGO in Guangzhou, was not permitted to register directly with
authorities because there was no law clearly stating that being gay was legal.
To no avail, the leader of the group told the bureaucrat at the department of
civil affairs, "Everything that is not stated as unlawful is legal: there also is

no law stating that heterosexuality is legal."[52] A staff member at a multilateral organization noted that early results from the new regulations indicated that the state is willing to register civil society organizations that have cooperated with state agencies, are small in size, and do not act as political advocates for their constituents and members.[53] These observations align with the finding that controversial labor organizations that challenged the leadership of the party-sponsored All-China Federation of Trade Unions were denied registration under the new rules.[54]

Officials in Yunnan Province have used reforms on civil society registration to press international organizations that collaborate with, and fund many projects by, local civil society organizations to register or leave.[55] The new regulations allow international organizations to register in China, an important breakthrough due to the previous lack of any regulations governing international groups, but the regulations have proved a means of control, too. The purpose of the revised regulations is, in the name of "regularization," to compel networks of many international and domestic civil society organizations that operate in Yunnan to operate more transparently and under the watchful eye of state authorities. As of 2012, partly in response to the changes in the government's approach to managing them, many of the international organizations that worked on HIV/AIDS in Yunnan chose to withdraw from Yunnan and, in some cases, China.[56] The withdrawal of such organizations suggests that the provincial authorities have sought to hamper their operation rather than merely regularize it.

Other regulatory changes demonstrate state attempts to weaken ties between domestic and international civil society organizations. In 2010, the State Administration of Foreign Exchange (SAFE) issued a circular that generally tightened the rules on civil society organizations' receipt of foreign funds.[57] State officials have systematically used the revised regulation on foreign funds to harass civil society organizations that are too assertive about the state's deficiencies. The effects of the SAFE regulations are difficult to discern because of other factors that have affected withdrawal of international funds from China. Beginning in 2008, several governments as well as international funding agents and nongovernmental organizations began to withdraw funding from China, and that pattern of withdrawal has persisted to present.[58] In 2012, G7 countries determined not to provide funds to other countries in G20 countries, and the Global Fund to Fight AIDS, Malaria, and Tuberculosis cut off aid to G20 countries (excepting South Africa), which includes China. The withdrawal of international funding from China is affected by frustrations with China's regulations and a growing sense that China as a rising power has obligations to provide its own resources and to contribute to other countries.[59] The SAFE regulations are not so arduous to ward off many international foundations and nongovernmental organizations, but they make it very difficult for foreign funders to support improperly registered groups. For example, Oxfam was unwilling to provide support for unofficial civil society groups in Yunnan after the SAFE regulations, and new Yunnan civil society registration procedures were implemented.[60] Some sectors of civil society that have large numbers of improperly registered organizations, such as that focusing on AIDS, are likely to be disproportionately affected by the SAFE regulations.

China's state also attempts to prevent opposition from autonomous grassroots organizations by using GONGOs and state agencies to engage INGOs and foreign foundations. GONGOs have soaked up much of the available international funds and loosened the financial ties between grassroots civil society organizations and international actors. Many international funders prefer to work with GONGOs because they have more personnel, expertise, and, therefore, greater capacity to develop robust programs. Drawing from data on the distribution of funds to China from some of the largest U.S. grant makers during the period 2002–2009, Anthony Spires shows that the ministry of health received a remarkable 12.48 percent of the funds distributed by U.S. grant makers.[61] The ministry of health and the Center for Disease Control (CDC), as well as GONGOs attached to them, redistribute some of the international funds to grassroots organizations, but the routing of funds renders grassroots civil society organizations dependent on state agents because grassroots organizations often must subcontract service delivery to state agents or GONGOs to receive funds. The CDC and GONGOs use international funds to reach out to intravenous drug users, prostitutes, and MSM (men who have sex with men), but the channeling of funds through the CDC and GONGOs allows state agents to choose grassroots organizations that comply with state regulations (and avoid controversial advocacy) as partners.[62] In fighting HIV/AIDS, naturally a significant portion of funds goes to medical units and the CDC, all run by China's state and monitored by the ministry of health, but one might expect more funds to go to advocacy organizations who try to protect the rights and interests of HIV/AIDS carriers. If international funds are a source of autonomy for grassroots organizations, then GONGOs and state receipt of international resources limit grassroots organizations' capacity to provide autonomous opposition.

UNAIDS and the Rift with China's State over the Global Fund

A conflagration between China's government and the Global Fund exemplifies the (limited) role that international funders can play in pressing for grassroots civil society development. One of the most important catalysts for the development of grassroots civil society organizations in the HIV/AIDS field in China has been the 2001 creation of the Global Fund to Fight AIDS, Tuberculosis, and Malaria (hereafter, the Global Fund). In China, UNAIDS and the country coordinating mechanism (CCM), who administer the Global

Fund, have created a mixture of incentives and sanctions to encourage China's government to improve its human rights record on HIV/AIDS, offer more scope for the operation of civil society, and improve the flow of information, including information about the spread of HIV/AIDS in China. UNAIDS has been explicit in its commitment to framing AIDS as a human rights issue, and the Global Fund has leveraged the 834 million dollars in grants approved for China to advance civil society development. At a few crucial junctures, the CCM and UNAIDS have judiciously used their funds as inducement to affect Chinese government policy in subtle ways.

The first instance of the Global Fund shaping China's response to HIV/AIDS came with its 2002 denial of China's application to the fund. The denial of China's application created a strong financial incentive to more openly discuss and address the blood crisis in China's central provinces.[63] In the second application, the Chinese reported 800,000 cases of HIV, a figure drawn from UNAIDS estimates and much larger than earlier Chinese figures.[64] The 2003 application sought funding to support the China CARES program and greatly scaled up China's response to the epidemic. In 2006, the second instance of UNAIDS affecting China's approach to HIV/AIDS came with Round 6 of the Global Fund's grants, which was designated to support civil society development. In Round 6 of funding, 254 unregistered civil society organizations received 1.07 million dollars, just over 4,200 dollars per organization. In order to receive these funds, the civil society organizations had to be awarded grants by the Chinese CDC, usually in exchange for helping the CDC to conduct some of its work.[65] Despite the efforts of the CCM and UNAIDS to promote grassroots organizations, little money actually has reached grassroots organizations.

In May 2011 and in response to complaints from grassroots organizations about lack of funding, the CCM and UNAIDS temporarily suspended all allocations to China from the Global Fund. China's grassroots civil society organizations have long accused the government of hording all of the Global Fund monies by giving it to GONGOs attached to the Chinese state. China requires the CCM to give its share of the Global Fund to China's CDC, which then disperses part of the funds to grassroots organizations. Grassroots organizations argue that the CDC does not offer adequate funding to them, while the CDC complains that the grassroots organizations lack capacity to undertake projects.[66] Even prior to suspension of the Global Fund grants to China, NGO leaders complained to me about the CDC's and government's approach to grassroots NGOs. One longtime leader of an NGO said,

> They often say, "NGOs lack capacity." "NGOs don't have bank accounts." "We can't give you funds." "Everything about NGOs, including personnel, is unstable." In my many conversations with the government I hear these claims, but this is the government's fault (*zeren*), not ours. We try hard to grow, but

the government does not want us to grow. We are at the stage of "under construction." The government continuously uses us and controls us. [67]

The Chinese government uses grassroots NGOs to perform certain difficult tasks that the government cannot undertake and to attract international funding to fight HIV/AIDS, but funding often goes through state middlemen. Even when it hands over funds to grassroots organizations, the CDC has been known to take 5 percent of the funds in the form of handling fees. [68]

The suspension of aid in 2011 took place in the context of Chinese government harassment of important leaders and organizations working on HIV/AIDS and activist attorneys. In 2010, Wan Yanhai, who had previously been detained and interrogated several times, fled the country after he and his organization, Aizhixing, had been subjected to repeated investigations. In 2011, several human rights lawyers such as Teng Biao, Li Fangping, and Li Xiongbing were "disappeared" by Chinese police, only to be released weeks later. Both Teng Biao and Li Fangping were associated with Yirenping, a legal center that took on a wide variety of human rights cases but specialized in public health and discrimination matters, and Li Xiongbing worked with Wan Yanhai's group, Aizhixing. The actions of the CCM and UNAIDS were an attempted shot off the bow of China's leadership and CDC regarding its approach to civil society, specifically their reluctance to support, and tendency to harass, grassroots advocacy organizations.

During the 2011–2012 period when UNAIDS' and the Global Fund's relations with China's government came into conflict, international society began to sour on China as a recipient of funding (rather than being a donor country) to fight HIV/AIDS and other programs. Many foundations began to withdraw funds, and in 2012, the Global Fund board determined that no Global Fund monies would be allocated to G20 countries, of which China is a member, unless they had severe epidemics. Hence, at the end of 2012, all Global Fund monies to China for HIV/AIDS were to be phased out. Despite civil society organizations' complaints about inadequate funding, the Global Fund supplied approximately 60 percent of the funds used by grassroots organizations working on HIV/AIDS. [69] The Chinese state has expressed disappointment about the Global Fund's withdrawal from China, but it has committed state resources to fill any funding gap created by the vacuum. One long-term staff member at a number of INGOs working on AIDS in China worried, though, "The structure of the Global Fund has enlisted the voice of NGOs. Their country-coordinating mechanism has positions for people with HIV and grassroots NGOs. If the government were to take over, would it do the same thing?" [70] With regard to the pending shift from international to state funding, another civil society organization staff member in Beijing predicted, "The state certainly won't give money to organizations that are not registered. If the government only selectively allows some kinds of organizations to register, then they will also limit funding for some kinds of organizations."[71] The implied threat to civil society was clear: the grassroots organizations would enjoy less autonomy and inclusion in programs, and access to funds would likely require passing an ideological litmus test.

CHINA'S JUDICIARY

The role of civil society in pressing for rights protection is important, but any discussion of the advancement of rights must also take account of China's judicial system and the politicization of justice. In countries with autonomous courts, citizens have the ability to receive fair trials and challenge state authorities, and judges enjoy the freedom to try cases and render verdicts that may compromise state interests. In nondemocratic systems, courts can be important checks on arbitrary state power and, therefore, a venue for challenging the state's ideological leadership and coercive power. Of course, challenging state authority in courts is confined to legal principles written by the state itself. In countries lacking judicial autonomy, state officials can also influence courts and judges. But authoritarian states also face a dilemma in their desire to grant courts some autonomy to gain legitimacy while preventing courts from becoming sites of organized opposition to the state. Tom Ginsburg and Tamir Moustafa's groundbreaking work on courts under authoritarianism, in which courts serve as a "double-edge sword," captures an important aspect of China's judiciary. According to their analysis, "Courts help regimes to maintain social control . . . and enhance legitimacy. However, courts also have the potential to open a space for activists to mobilize against the state. . . ."[72]

Over the last thirty years, China's judiciary has made significant progress in developing rule of law, judicial expertise, and (even) limited judicial independence. Beginning in 2008, the Supreme People's Court has published "guiding cases" in order to create greater uniformity among the judiciary's decisions (discussed below), and in 2013 Xi Jinping has called for greater judicial autonomy in his 2012 speech to the National People's Congress (NPC), both of which are suggestive of growing judicial power.[73] China's judiciary has sought to enhance its power and to become somewhat more assertive, but other institutions such as the NPC have resisted ceding power to the judiciary.[74] Progress in judicial autonomy, however, has only partially offset the political influence that party and state officials can bring to bear on courts to determine what cases to try and the types of verdicts to render. Moreover, observers inside and outside of China have raised serious doubts about whether Chinese legal reforms have stalled or even begun to backslide since 2006 in the name of preserving social stability.[75] While the later chapters in this volume address the courts' handling of two sensitive case areas,

HIV/AIDS victims' and environmental pollution victims' claims, here I analyze the mechanisms that party-state officials can use to influence the judiciary and limit civil society's access to the courts to challenge state power.
China's courts have become an object of political struggle between civil
society forces allied with, and in opposition to, the state. In order to understand the courts' relationship to other political institutions, I outline what
progress has been made in enhancing judicial autonomy.

Party and State Influence over the Courts

China's constitution is explicit that courts shall "exercise judicial power
independently and are not subject to interference by administrative organs,
public organizations or individuals."[76] The article, in referring to "administrative organs," clearly bars state organs from interfering in the decision-
making processes of the courts. As Rachel Stern has pointed out, however,
the constitution is silent on the role of the Chinese Communist Party (CCP)
and its influence on courts.[77] In fact, the party has a number of institutionalized mechanisms with which to exercise influence on the courts and their
judgments in specific cases. For example, within each court, the CCP has
established party groups and party cells.[78] Each court also has a president, a
position filled by a vote of the people's congress at the same administrative
level. The court president holds political, rather than legal, qualifications,
rendering the person "sensitive to the Party's position on important cases."[79]
    Despite China's constitutional commitment to keeping the judiciary
autonomous from state interference, relations among China's institutions
create structural conditions for state organs and officials at each level of the
administration to influence the courts. According to Article 128 of the Constitution, courts at each level are "responsible to the organs of state power
which created them."[80] State organs from the central government down to
townships give courts at the same level a budget, as well as appoint and
review judges, which creates a context in which state officials can pressure
the courts not to hear cases or to render verdicts with an eye to protecting the
local or national regime's interests. State officials can invoke a version of
"local protectionism" to shield the party, state organs, or local businesses
from lawsuits in the courts. Interviews with attorneys and activists highlighted such instances of state pressure on courts to render protectionist verdicts and, more often, to deny hearings to legal claimants that might prove
embarrassing.[81]
    China's legal system has another institution, the procuracy, that is typical
of communist states and which encroaches on judicial autonomy. At each
level of China's administration, an office of the procuracy exists, which is
under the control of the corresponding level of state organs and responsible
for overseeing the judicial system.[82] The procuracy's supervisory role over

the courts can come into conflict with its other roles in the justice system. For example, the procuracy can serve as a plaintiff in some cases, in environmental public interest lawsuits and administrative lawsuits. When the procuracy, a supervisory agent of the court, appears as a plaintiff in a case, the autonomy and impartiality of the courts can easily be compromised.

Moreover, China's governance system includes political-legal committees (*zhengfa weiyuanhui*) under the party committee at each level of administration. The political-legal committees draw their membership from "the president of the court and procuracy, and the heads of the various ministries or bureaus including public security, state security, justice, civil affairs, and supervision."[83] While under the authority of the party committees, the membership of the political-legal committees is drawn from state organs, blurring, if not erasing, the lines of judicial independence from state intervention.[84] The political-legal committees, which offer general guidance to the courts and advice on particular cases, expand the scope of courts' considerations beyond the law to include broad political and social implications such as maintaining stability.[85] Depending on the appointees to the committees at various administrative levels, the political-legal committee can give greater emphasis to security concerns rather than rule of law. For example, Zhou Yongkang, who was the head of the ministry of security, served as the leader of the central political-legal committee during the period 2007–2012, when many commentators observed a tightening of reins on the courts and cause lawyers.[86]

While the above political constraints on China's courts render the bench susceptible to direct intervention and guidance in particular cases, a broader method of influence is the ideological leadership that the party can exercise over the courts. Benjamin Liebman notes that, beginning in 2006 with a "socialist rule of law campaign," China's regime emphasized the courts' ideological concerns and loyalty to the party, as ensured by the central political-legal committee.[87] The same ideological campaign sought to turn China away from an emphasis on Western rule of law.[88] Establishing the political parameters of acceptable court cases and judgments encourages the bench's self-regulation (some might say "self-censorship") to avoid politically sensitive cases that will draw the attention and admonishment of party and state leaders.[89]

Sources of Judicial Autonomy

One of the most important determinants of autonomy and authority of the judicial system is the quality of the judges who sit on China's bench. As Randall Peerenboom argues, judges' "low level of technical competence is a more serious problem than limitations on judicial independence."[90] Until passage of the 1995 Judges Law, China routinely appointed demobilized and

retired military officers who received a brief course in Chinese law to the
bench. The Judges Law has raised the standards of qualification for the bench
by requiring judges to pass an examination and to meet educational qualifications and professional experience.[91] China's bench has become more compe-
tent and assertive since 1995, but these improvements have not produced
judicial activism and attempts to establish legal precedents in lower courts.[92]
The issue of technical competence and training is particularly germane to
new areas of the law such as those governing the environment and AIDS.
Rendering correct decisions on these emerging issues requires judges to be
knowledgeable of the law and, in many cases, science. Judges' lack of
knowledge of specialized areas of the law and appropriate science leads them
to render verdicts that do not strictly comply with laws but also take into
account societal and economic considerations, a pattern that Rachel Stern
calls "rough justice."[93] "Rough justice" places decisions in the hands of
judges, but it is guided by informal conceptions of justice rather than strictly
formal legal considerations.

The other main source of judicial autonomy is the Chinese regime's stated commitment to rule of law. While the party-state has wavered on its
commitment to judicial autonomy (especially since 2006) and pockets of the
regime are firmly opposed to rule of law, leaders' frequent public pronounce-
ments on developing a society ordered by rule of law, dating back to Deng
Xiaoping's return to power in 1978, have affected popular views of the
judiciary's appropriate role. Spurred on by international groups, citizens and
attorneys have come to rely on legal settlement of social conflicts. The regime's stated commitment to rule of law means it cannot act in a ham-handed
way toward the judiciary. China's bench can use its growing knowledge of
abstract legal principles, partly gained from legal training programs sponsored by Western law schools and legal organizations, and the regime's
stated commitment to rule of law to carve out more authority for itself. As
noted above, however, the party and state have various indirect means, such
as budgets and personnel reviews, to influence the courts' actions and limit
judicial autonomy, which undermine legal formalism.

Civil Society and Reining in Cause Lawyers

While party and state forces pressure courts to limit judicial activism and
restrict plaintiffs' access to the courts, for more than a decade civil society
groups have worked with cause lawyers to use the courts to advance legal
claims to protect and advance citizens' rights. Cause lawyers and activist
civil society organizations have participated in a "rights-claiming" (*weiquan*)
movement, which attempts to extend rights to new claimants or, more often,
to claim rights in practice that the state has already extended in legal statutes.
Cases filed by cause lawyers place the courts in a difficult position because

the cases draw on legitimate legal claims, but enforcement of those rights may violate the regime's interest in maintaining social harmony and pursuing economic development goals, or challenge regime authority and legitimacy by highlighting official wrongdoing. Civil society organizations, typically with funding from international groups, provide resources and pressure outside of the legal system to support cause lawyers.

Yet China's regime has begun to use its allies in civil society to influence the direction of Chinese legal contention, especially by reining in cause lawyers. One of the party's main civil society allies in this regard is the All-China Lawyers Association (ACLA), which was founded in 1986. The ACLA is responsible for overseeing the development of lawyers, which also entails a disciplinary function. Beginning around 2006 when some legal observers argue that China began to "abandon the law," the ACLA started to constrain cause lawyering and emphasize social stability.[94] In 2006 the ACLA issued a "Guiding Opinion on Lawyers Handling Collective Cases" that required firms to exercise oversight on lawyers who wished to pursue joint litigation suits, which the regime views as threatening to social stability. In particular, two partners in a law firm must approve its attorneys arguing a joint litigation suit, and the attorneys' actions are to be supervised on a daily basis.[95] This constituted a not-so-thinly-veiled threat to cause lawyers and had a somewhat chilling effect on joint litigation lawsuits.

Since 2006, state authorities—mainly the ministry of justice—have issued a series of laws and opinions that have politicized the actions of attorneys. For example, the 2007 Law of the People's Republic of China on Lawyers (hereafter, Lawyers Law), which defines the obligations and protections that lawyers have within China's judicial system, had several articles that compromised the autonomy of attorneys to represent their clients in court. For example, Article 3 calls on lawyers to observe "ethics and discipline of the legal profession" and submit to "state supervision."[96] Article 40 contains provisions calling on lawyers to refrain from "disturbing public order" or "endangering public security," and not to interfere with the "normal proceedings of the court."[97] While these articles may seem innocuous, their vague wording allows the state to fine or even disbar a lawyer who incites contention related to a case inside or outside the courtroom.[98] In 2008, the ministry of justice began a campaign aimed at lawyers to construct "Chinese-style socialist legal professionals," the goal of which was to induce ideological commitment to socialism and to maintain a harmonious society.[99] The ACLA was charged with spreading this campaign to attorneys.

In March 2012, the ministry of justice used the ACLA to develop requirements on new attorneys that amounted to a loyalty pledge. Among other typical commitments such as to uphold the constitution and to protect the rights of citizens, the ACLA required new attorneys to "uphold the leadership of the Chinese Communist Party and the socialist system." Elizabeth

Lynch argues that the issuing of regulations and opinions on lawyers is tantamount to "legalization of suppression," giving a false gloss of rule of law to detention or disbarment of lawyers in order to rein in cause lawyering. [100] While the ACLA, along with it local affiliates, has opposed legal statutes that impede attorneys' pursuit of their work, the Lawyers Law also enlists its support in helping the state to monitor the activities of attorneys according to the regulations and opinions issued by the regime.

The state backs its efforts at ideological leadership of civil society with selective use of force. Since 2006, China's state has sought to intimidate high-profile cause lawyers without engaging in widespread attacks or harassment of lawyers. The state has subjected well-known cause lawyers, including Xu Zhiyong, Chen Guancheng, Gao Zhisheng, Liu Wei, and Teng Biao among others, to detention, interrogation, torture, disbarment, and incarceration for their work. In some cases, lawyers crossed clear "red lines" such as defending Falungong practitioners or advocating democracy, but in most cases, lawyers simply called on China's state to observe its constitution and laws. Lawyers interviewed for this book expressed a lack of clarity about the boundaries of acceptable conduct in their profession. [101] Selective use of coercion by the state is designed to rein in the enthusiasm of cause lawyers in a pattern colorfully described in Chinese as "killing the chicken to scare the monkey." Coercion is meant to intimidate civil society and cause lawyers to hew more closely to the lines of acceptable ideology and conduct. China's state has paired such intimidation tactics with ideologically charged campaigns on model judges and socialist rule of law, which emphasize mediation and social stability considerations in dispute settlement. [102]

CONCLUSION: CHINA'S STATE IN THE TRENCHES

One of the important conclusions advanced here is that China's state is not simply resisting the development of civil society and the judicial system but is actively taking part in both arenas to create hegemony and to protect its interests through ideological leadership. The state does so in order to maintain consensus in society about its right to rule, which requires it to intervene in several ways. First, the state attempts to limit discussion of its negligence. As one attorney explained, "in nonpolitical settings we can say all kinds of things about the government, but if we are in a public space and we say things that are clearly critical of the government, then it is unacceptable." [103] Second, an important component of the consensus is the appearance of the state as rising above its ties to particular interests and representing societal interests as a whole. As Robert Fatton notes, according to Gramsci, rulers attempt to transform their interest into "the embodiment of the general interest." [104] As discussed in chapter 7, the state is attempting to lead and limit the public interest litigation through one of its GONGOs in civil society, the All-China Environmental Federation. The state, then, is attempting to maintain a monopoly over representing the interests of all of society. Third, the state has developed a number of regulations that fragment civil society, deter registration of advocacy groups, and limit linkages between civil society organizations and foreign organizations. Fourth, GONGOs work with the state to advance its policies in civil society and to guide civil society away from challenging the authority of the state. GONGOs receive international funding due to their capacity to implement policies, leaving grassroots organizations who adopt a critical advocacy function weak and marginalized in civil society. Finally, the construction of rules and passage of new laws give an air of legal rationality to the regulations that modulate the development of rights-based litigation and civil society.

Grassroots organizations and international groups offer an alternative approach to the state's limitations on citizen participation in governance of the environment and HIV/AIDS. International funders have contributed important material resources to advocacy-based organizations that seek to protect citizens' rights and develop new models of citizen participation. The withdrawal of international funding from the HIV/AIDS issue in China, however, reveals the tenuous nature of such linkages between international and domestic organizations. In their wake, China's state is poised with funding to replace international resources, but the political implications of that shift in funding sources are transparent to all involved; advocacy-based organizations are likely to be brought to heel.

Finally, Gramsci's characterization of hegemony as consent backed by coercion ably explains the Chinese state's approach to civil society. China's state has attempted to gain consent in civil society, but some grassroots organizations have challenged that consensus. The state has selectively used coercion against organizations and activists that threaten the hegemony of China's officialdom. When necessary, the state allows activists to target particular negligent officials or to suggest revisions to policies, but the regime's leadership is left intact. While China's regime has developed sophisticated means to establish its hegemonic leadership to limit challenges from civil society and the legal system, divisions within China's state and party undermine such efforts. Pockets of the regime ally themselves with civil society organizations and litigants who challenge policies and pockets of the regime. Indeed, to the extent that the state appears tolerant of moderate dissent and responds to social conflicts, it can add to its legitimacy. The key for the regime (and its survival) is striking a balance between citizen participation in the courts and civil society to address unpopular aspects of CCP rule without generating powerful points of authority in civil society and in the form of an autonomous legal system.

NOTES

1. Elements of this chapter were originally published in Scott Wilson, "China's State in the Trenches: A Gramscian Analysis of Civil Society and Rule of Law Development," *Protosociology* 29 (2012), 57–76. The author wishes to thank the publishers of the journal for permission to reprint those elements here.

2. Gordon White, "Prospects for Civil Society in China: A Case Study of Xiaoshan City," *Australian Journal of Chinese Affairs* 29 (1993), 64.

3. Jie Chen, "The NGO Community in China: Expanding Linkages with Transnational Civil Society and Their Democratic Implications," *China Perspectives*, no. 68 (November–December 2006), 2–15; David Da-hua Yang, "Civil Society as an Analytical Lens for Contemporary China," *China: An International Journal* 2, no. 1 (2004), 1–27; Zhenglai Deng and Yuejin Jing, "The Construction of the Chinese Civil Society," in *State and Civil Society: The Chinese Perspective*, ed. Zhenglai Deng (New Jersey: World Scientific, 2010), 25–46; X. L. Ding, "Institutional Amphibiousness and the Transition from Communism: The Case of China," *British Journal of Political Science* 24, no. 3 (July 1994), 293–318; Baogang He, "The Making of a Nascent Civil Society," in *Civil Society in Asia*, eds. David C. Schak and Wayne Hudson (Farnham, Surrey: Ashgate, 2003), 114–39.

4. Jonathan Unger and Anita Chan, "China, Corporatism, and the East Asian Model," *Australian Journal of Chinese Affairs*, no. 33 (January 1995), 29–53; Timothy Brook and B. Michael Frolic, "The Ambiguous Challenge of Civil Society," in *Civil Society in China*, eds. Timothy Brook and B. Michael Frolic (Armonk, NY: East Gate Books, 1997), 3–16; Jude Howell, "Prospects for NGOs in China," *Development in Practice* 5, no. 1 (February 1995), 5–15; B. Michael Frolic, "State-Led Civil Society," in *Civil Society in China*, eds. Timothy Brook and B. Michael Frolic (Armonk, NY: East Gate Books, 1997), 46–67; Jonathan Schwartz and Shawn Shieh, eds., *State and Society Responses to Social Welfare Needs in China: Serving the People* (London and New York: Routledge, 2009); Deng and Jing, "Construction of the Chinese Civil Society," 25–46; Jiang Ru and Leonardo Ortolano, "Corporatist Control over Environmental Non-Governmental Organizations," in *China's Embedded Activism: Opportunities and Constraints of a Social Movement*, eds. Peter Ho and Richard Louis Edmonds (London and New York: Routledge, 2008), 44–68; and Jennifer Y. J. Hsu and Reza Hasmath, "Local Corporatist State and NGO Relations in China," *Journal of Contemporary China* 23 (2014), 516–34.

5. Jessica C. Teets, "Let Many Civil Societies Bloom: The Rise of Consultative Authoritarianism in China," *China Quarterly*, no. 213 (March 2013), 19–38; Yongshun Cai, "Managed Participation in China," *Political Science Quarterly* 119, no. 3 (Fall 2004), 425–51; Anthony J. Spires, "Contingent Symbiosis and Civil Society in an Authoritarian State: Understanding the Survival of China's Grassroots NGOs," *American Journal of Sociology* 117, no. 1 (July 2011), 1–45; Peter Ho and Richard Louis Edmonds, eds., *China's Embedded Activism: Opportunities and Constraints of a Social Movement* (London and New York: Routledge, 2008); and Andrew Mertha, "'Fragmented Authoritarianism 2.0': Political Pluralization in the Chinese Policy Process," *China Quarterly* 200 (December 2009), 995–1012.

6. Kate Crehan, *Gramsci, Culture, and Anthropology* (Berkeley: University of California Press, 2003), 138; A. Gramsci, *Selections from the Prison Notebooks*, trans. and ed. by Q. Hoare and G. Smith (New York: International Publishers, 1971), 12.

7. Fengshi Wu, "Environmental GONGO Autonomy: Unintended Consequences of State Strategies in China," *Good Society* 12, no. 1 (2003), 41.

8. T. Carothers and M. Ottaway, "The Burgeoning World of Civil Society Aid," in *Funding Virtue*, eds. M. Ottaway and T. Carothers (Washington: Carnegie Endowment for International Peace, 2000), 3–17; S. Golub, "Democracy as Development: A Case for Civil Society Assistance in Asia," in *Funding Virtue*, 135–58; M. Seligson, "Exporting Democracy: Does It Work?" in *Is Democracy Exportable?* eds. Z. Barany and R. Moser (Cambridge: Cambridge University Press, 2009), 222–41.

9. Xinhua, "Number of NGOs in China Grows to Nearly 500,000," *China Daily*, 20 March 2012, accessed 24 August 2014, http://www.chinadaily.com.cn/china/2012-03/20/content_14875389.htm.

10. Cary Coglianese, "Social Movements, Law, and Society: The Institutionalization of the Environmental Movement," *University of Pennsylvania Law Review* 150, no. 1 (November 2001), 116.

11. Christopher Coleman, Laurence D. Nee, and Leonard S. Rubinowitz, "Social Movements and Social-Change Litigation: Synergy in the Montgomery Bus Protest," *Law and Social Inquiry* 30, no. 4 (Autumn 2005), 671–73; Charles R. Epp, *The Rights Revolution: Lawyers, Activists, and Supreme Courts in Comparative Perspective* (Chicago: University of Chicago Press, 1998).

12. Coglianese, "Social Movements, Law, and Society," 86.

13. Tomiko Brown-Nagin, "Elites, Social Movements, and the Law: The Case of Affirmative Action," *Columbia Law Review* 105, no. 5 (June 2005), 1442.

14. Brown-Nagin, "Elites, Social Movements, and the Law," 1443.

15. Gerard N. Rosenberg, *The Hollow Hope: Can Courts Bring About Social Change?* (Chicago: University of Chicago Press, 1991), 341.

16. Brown-Nagin, "Elites, Social Movements, and the Law," 1509 fn. 368.

17. Here, I use the term "civil society organization" as a translation for *shehui zuzhi*, which is normally translated as "social organization." I use civil society organization to avoid confusion with another term, *shehui tuanti*, which is also translated "social organization." *Shehui zuzhi* is, in fact, a broad term that applies to a number of types of organizations that form part of civil society, while *shehui tuanti* is a particular registration type granted to some organizations.

18. Zengke He, "Institutional Barriers to the Development of Civil Society in China," in *China's Opening Society*, eds. Zheng Yongnian and Joseph Fewsmith (London and New York: Routledge, 2008), 167. Yiyi Lu, "NGOs in China: Development Dynamics and Challenges," in *China's Opening Society: The Non-State Sector and Governance*, eds. Zheng Yongnian and Joseph Fewsmith (London and New York: Routledge, 2008), 92–93, argues that the ministry of civil affairs lacks the capacity to register NGOs.

19. Calculated from Shaoguang Wang and Jianyu He, "Training Ground for Democracy: Associational Life in China," in *State and Civil Society: The Chinese Perspective*, ed. Zhenglai Deng (New Jersey, London: World Scientific, 2010), 305, table 11.

20. *Regulations on the Registration and Management of Social Organizations*, promulgated on 25 October 1998, decree no. 250, articles 3 and 6.

21. *Regulations on the Registration and Management of Social Organizations*, article 10.

22. *Regulations on the Registration and Management of Social Organizations*, article 13.

23. *Provisional Regulations on the Registration and Management of Non-Governmental, Non-Commercial Enterprises*, issued on 25 October 1998, decree number 251, articles 5, 7, and 11, for analogous rules on sponsorship and registration applications potentially being denied on the grounds of an already existing organization in the same or similar field or activity.

24. *Regulations on the Registration and Management of Social Organizations*, article 19.

25. *Provisional Regulations on the Registration and Management*, article 12. Another important difference between the two sets of registration requirements is that private noncommercial institutions do not have high capital and membership requirements but must simply designate a legal representative and document funding sources. *Regulations on the Registration and Management of Social Organizations*, article 10.

26. Jessica C. Teets, "The Evolution of Civil Society in Yunnan: Contending Models of Civil Society Management in China," *Journal of Contemporary China* (2014).

27. Interview 35.

28. Guosheng Deng, "The Decline of Foreign Aid and the Dilemma of Chinese Grassroots NGOs," *Religions and Christianity in Today's China* III, no. 1 (2013), 30.

29. An example of such fund-raising through "special funds" is the China Dolls case, an organization that established a special account to raise funds for its work on osteogenesis imperfecta, a genetic bone disorder. Hui Wang, "Grassroots NGOs Use Special Accounts to Raise Funds," China Development Brief, 15 June 2011, accessed 29 July 2014, http://chinadevelopmentbrief.com/articles/grassroots-ngos-use-special-accounts-to-raise-funds/. I appreciate an anonymous reviewer pointing out this exemplary case.

30. *Provisional Regulations on the Registration and Management*, article 4; State Council, *Regulations on the Registration and Management of Social Organizations*, article 4.

31. Carolyn Hsu, "An Institutional Approach to Chinese NGOs: State Alliance versus State Avoidance Resource Strategies." *China Quarterly* (forthcoming).

32. Interview 33.

33. Carolyn Hsu, "Chinese NGOs and the State: Institutional Interdependence Rather Than Civil Society," unpublished paper presented at the annual meeting of the American Sociological Association Annual Meeting, Hilton San Francisco, San Francisco, 2009, CAOnline, accessed 2014 August 18, http://citation.allacademic.com/meta/p305261_index.html.

34. Timothy Hildebrandt, *Social Organizations and the Authoritarian State in China* (Cambridge: Cambridge University Press, 2013), 15, describes social organizations and the state in terms of "codependency." The term captures the way China's state sets limited opportunity structures for organizations, some of which desire autonomy.

35. Fengshi Wu, "Environmental GONGO Autonomy: Unintended Consequences of State Strategies in China," *Good Society* 12, no. 1 (2003), 35–45, argues that international grants enhance GONGOs' autonomy from the state.

36. Interview 48.

37. John Fitzgerald, "A Response," *YaleGlobal Online* (28 March 2012), accessed 24 August 2014, http://yaleglobal.yale.edu/content/us-foundations-boost-chinese-government-not-ngos.

38. Interview 32.

39. Interview 102.

40. Deng, "The Decline of Foreign Aid," 28, is the source for the statistics in this paragraph.

41. Anthony J. Spires, "US Foundations Boost Chinese Government, Not NGOs," *YaleGlobal Online* (28 March 2012), accessed 24 August 2014, http://yaleglobal.yale.edu/content/us-foundations-boost-chinese-government-not-ngos.

42. Deng, "The Decline of Foreign Aid," 29.

43. Interview 2.

44. Albert Chen, "The Limits of Official Tolerance: The Case of Aizhixing," *China Rights Forum*, no. 3 (2003), 51, http://www.hrichina.org/sites/default/files/PDFs/CRF.3.2003/Albert_Chen.pdf.

45. Timothy Hildebrandt, *Social Organizations and the Authoritarian State in China* (Cambridge: Cambridge University Press, 2013), 12.

46. Jessica C. Teets, "The Evolution of Civil Society in Yunnan," and Karla W. Simon, *Civil Society in China: The Legal Framework from Ancient Times to the 'New Reform Era'* (Oxford and New York: Oxford University Press, 2013), 260–83, discuss social organization registration reforms in various locales.

47. Hua Ma, "The Situation and Predicament of Guangdong's New Government-Issued Regulations on Registration of Social Organizations," *China Development Brief* blog post, 4 September 2013, accessed 24 August 2014, http://www.chinadevelopmentbrief.org.cn/qikanarticleview.php?id=1400.

48. Cited in International Center for Non-Profit Law, *NGO Law Monitor: China*, 6 June 2013, accessed 24 August 2014, http://www.icnl.org/research/monitor/china.html/.

49. Interviews 93, 94, 95, and 96.

50. Interviews 93 and 94.

51. Interview 95; Hua Ma 马骅, "*Guangdong Xin Zhengxia Shehui Zuzhi Zhuce de Xianzhuang yu Kunjing*" 广东新政下社会组织注册的现状与困境 (The Situation and Predicament of Guangdong's New Government-Issued Regulations on Registration of Social Organizations), *Zhongguo Fazhan Jianbao* 中国发展简报 (China Development Brief) blog post, 4 September 2013, accessed 17 September 2013, http://www.chinadevelopmentbrief.org.cn/qikanarticleview.php?id=1400.

52. Ma, "*Guangdong Xin Zhengxia Shehui Zuzhi Zhuce.*"

53. Interview 96.

54. International Center for Non-Profit Law, *NGO Law Monitor: China.*

55. International Center for Non-Profit Law, *NGO Law Monitor: China*; Teets, "The Evolution of Civil Society in Yunnan."

56. Interview 90; Teets, "The Evolution of Civil Society in Yunnan."

57. State Administration of Foreign Exchange, People's Republic of China, "Notice of the State Administration of Foreign Exchange on Issues Concerning the Administration of Foreign Exchange Donated to or by Domestic Institutions," issued 25 December 2009, effective 1 March 2010.

58. Guosheng Deng, "The Decline of Foreign Aid and the Dilemma of Chinese Grassroots NGOs," *Religions and Christianity in Today's China* III, no. 1 (2013), 29.

59. LaFraniere, Sharon, "AIDS Funds Frozen for China in Grant Dispute," *New York Times*, 20 May 2011, accessed 18 August 2014, http://www.nytimes.com/2011/05/21/world/asia/21china.html?_r=1&hp.

60. Teets, "Evolution of Civil Society," 18.

61. Calculated from Spires, "US Foundations."

62. Jennifer Y. J. Hsu and Reza Hasmath, "Local Corporatist State and NGO Relations in China," describes a process of "tacit sanctioning" in the registration approval process, and the same sanctioning occurs in government contracting.

63. Joan Kaufman, "Turning Points in China's AIDS Response," *China: An International Journal* 8, no. 1 (March 2010), 71.

64. Kaufman, "Turning Points."

65. Hui Li, Nana Taona Kuo, Hui Liu, Christine Korhonen, Ellenie Pound, Haoyan Guo, Liz Smith, Hui Xue, and Jiangping Sun, "From Spectators to Implementers: Civil Society Organizations Involved in AIDS Programmes in China," *International Journal of Epidemiology* 39 (2010), Supplement 2, ii67.

66. Qian Li, "Health Funding Freeze Shows NGO Dilemma," *Global Times,* 25 May 2011, http://china.globaltimes.cn/society/2011-05/658765.html; LaFraniere, "AIDS Funds Frozen."

67. Interview 67.

68. Interview 67.

69. Interview 97.

70. Interview 90.

71. Interview 99.

72. Tamir Moustafa and Tom Ginsburg, "Introduction: The Functions of Courts in Authoritarian Politics," in *Rule by Law: The Politics of Courts in Authoritarian Regimes*, eds. Tom Ginsburg and Tamir Moustafa (Cambridge: Cambridge University Press, 2008), 21. Tamir Moustafa, *The Struggle for Constitutional Power: Law, Politics, and Economic Development in Egypt* (Cambridge: Cambridge University Press, 2009), 32, makes the same point.

73. Jinping Xi 习近平, "*Xi Jinping: Guanyu 'Zhonggong Zhongyang Guanyu Quanmian Shenhua Gaige Ruogan Zhongda Wenti de Jueding' de Shuoming* 习近平：关于 '中共中央关于全面深化改革若干重大问题的决定' 的说明" (Xi Jinping: Explanation Related to 'The Central Committee Decision on Major Problems Related to All-around Deepening of Reforms'), *Xinhuawang* 新华网 (News Network), 2013 November 15, accessed 2014 July 18, http://news.xinhuanet.com/politics/2013-11/15/c_118164294.htm.

74. Bjorn Ahl, "Retaining Judicial Professionalism: The New Guiding Cases Mechanism of the Supreme People's Court," *China Quarterly*, no. 217 (March 2014), 127.

75. Elizabeth M. Lynch, "China's Rule of Law Mirage: The Regression of the Legal Profession Since the Adoption of the 2007 Lawyers Law," *George Washington International Law Review* 42 (2010), 538 and passim; Carl F. Minzner, "China's Turn against Law," *American Journal of Comparative Law* 59 (2011), 937 and passim; Benjamin L. Liebman, "China's Courts: Restricted Reform," *China Quarterly*, no. 191 (September 2007), 624.

76. *Constitution of the People's Republic of China*, adopted 4 December 1982, last amended 14 March 2004, article 127.

77. Rachel E. Stern, *Environmental Litigation in China: A Study of Political Ambivalence* (Cambridge: Cambridge University Press, 2013), 25.

78. Randall Peerenboom, *China's Long March toward Rule of Law* (Cambridge: Cambridge University Press, 2003), 284.

79. Peerenboom, *China's Long March*, 285.

80. *Constitution*, article 128.

81. Interviews 47, 56, and 78.

82. *Constitution*, articles 129–133.

83. Peerenboom, *China's Long March*, 302.

84. Lynch, "China's Rule of Law Mirage," 578, makes a similar point.

85. Peerenboom, *China's Long March*, 303.

86. Keith Zhai, "Communist Party Committees Are Meddling Less in Courtrooms: Judges," *South China Morning Post,* 12 December 2013, accessed 24 August 2014, http://www.scmp.com/news/china/article/1378830/party-committees-are-meddling-less-courtrooms-judges; Lynch, "China's Rule of Law Mirage," 535–85; and Minzner, "China's Turn against Law," 935–84.

87. Liebman, "China's Courts," 622–28.

88. Liebman, "China's Courts," 628.

89. Liebman, "China's Courts," 626.

90. Peerenboom, *China's Long March*, 289.

91. *Judges Law*, issued on 28 February 1995, put into effect 1 July 1995, article 9. (Chinese version available at http://news.sina.com.cn/c/290364.html.)

92. Interview 89.

93. Rachel E. Stern, "On the Frontlines: Making Decisions in Chinese Civil Environmental Lawsuits," *Law & Policy* 32, no. 1 (January 2010), 83.

94. Lynch, "China's Rule of Law Mirage," 544.

95. Zhonghua Quanguo Lvshi Xiehui 中华全国律师协会, "*Zhonghua Quanguo Lvshi Xiehui Guanyu Lvshi Banli Quntixing Anjian Zhidao Yijian* 中华全国律师协会关于律师办理群体性案件指导意见" (Guiding Opinion on Lawyers Handling Collective Cases), issued 20 March 2006, accessed 20 January 2010, http://www.chineselawyer.com.cn/pages/2006-5-15/s34852.html.

96. *Law of the People's Republic of China on Lawyers*, adopted on 28 October 2007, promulgated and put into effect on 1 June 2008, article 3.

97. *Lawyers Law*, article 40.

98. Lynch, "China's Rule of Law Mirage," 558–62.

99. Lynch, "China's Rule of Law Mirage," 576.

100. Lynch, "China's Rule of Law Mirage," 540 and 568.

101. Interviews 57 and 77.

102. Liebman, "China's Courts," 627–28; Minzner, "China's Turn against Law," 949–55.

103. Interview 77.

104. R. Fatton, "Gramsci and the Legitimization of the State: The Case of the Senegalese Passive Revolution," *Canadian Journal of Political Science* 19 (1986), 730.

Chapter Three

The Development of China's Environmental and HIV/AIDS Crises

The post-Mao leadership of China can certainly take pride in the country's astounding economic takeoff, but it has been accompanied by the emergence of troubling environmental and public health disasters. China's environmental crisis, which shows few signs of abating, is well documented by Chinese and international authors.[1] Less well known is the pattern of development of HIV/AIDS in China.[2] This chapter analyzes the emergence of China's environmental and AIDS crises and the causes of their emergence. The account pays special attention to how institutions—both rules governing the environment and HIV/AIDS and the state organs that monitor and address these crises—contributed to the development of China's environmental crisis and spread of HIV/AIDS. Such an approach advances our understanding of why state forces turned to civil society organizations for help in addressing these issues (the subject of chapter 4), as well as the causes for litigation brought by pollution and HIV/AIDS victims (analyzed in chapters 5 to 7). In the chapter, I devote greater space to the emergence and spread of the HIV/AIDS epidemic in China because it less well understood and documented than the environmental crisis.

China's environmental crisis and spread of HIV/AIDS are significantly different in many ways, including their severity. Yet the two crises share three important characteristics in their development: (1) both crises spread because the regulations governing these issues were underdeveloped and, therefore, ill-suited to check the spread of polluting activities or HIV/AIDS, (2) the state organs charged with overseeing the crises were underfunded and poorly prepared to manage the crises, and (3) economic and administrative reforms, which had the effect of giving incentives to local actors in the public health and economic fields while also limiting regulatory oversight, impeded control over pollution and the spread of HIV/AIDS.

INSTITUTIONS AND EPIDEMICS IN CHINA

Since 2003, China's central government deserves praise for its resolute attempts to tackle HIV/AIDS. Chinese authorities have slowed the spread of HIV/AIDS by some modes of transmission and taken steps to provide anti-retroviral drug treatment to infected persons, but the number of people living with HIV/AIDS continues to grow and the number of annual deaths due to AIDS accelerates. According to the 2012 Chinese ministry of health report on HIV/AIDS, "National prevalence remains low, but the epidemic is severe in some areas."[3] Since the country's first contact with the virus, China's institutional weaknesses and transition to a marketized health-care system have impeded the public health community's response to HIV/AIDS. Only when international pressure on China to improve its public health system grew in reaction to the 2003 SARS epidemic did authorities effectively respond to HIV/AIDS. Three main institutional factors affected the spread of HIV/AIDS in China: (1) marketization and globalization, (2) the regulatory approach to high-risk behaviors, especially the early criminalization of such behaviors, and (3) the weak capacity of the ministry of health, both in terms of resources and authority relative to other ministries and state agents.

Marketization and Globalization

The shift from a closed society and planned economy during the Mao era (1949–1978) to a globalized society and market-based economy during the current era has facilitated the spread of HIV/AIDS throughout China. The early outbreaks of HIV/AIDS in China occurred on the periphery of Chinese society in areas with high incidence of intravenous drug use and inhabited by large numbers of ethnic minorities. Although the CCP's leadership virtually eradicated drug abuse during the Mao era, since 1978 an increasing number of people, including the new middle class, are using intravenous drugs including heroin and cocaine. The number of officially registered drug users has grown from 70,000 in 1990[4] to over 2 million in 2013,[5] the majority of whom are heroin addicts. The trend in registered drug addicts, which understates actual drug use, emerged despite Chinese authorities' attempts to crack down on drug use and moralistic campaigns against "spiritual pollution" in the 1980s and 1990s.[6] The spread of HIV/AIDS, especially in the early periods of development of the epidemic, followed the lines of drug trafficking from the southwestern province of Yunnan eastward and northward.

Transnational communication networks have introduced and normalized new patterns of sexual behavior among youth and same-sex Chinese communities. The beginning of China's recent sexual revolution coincided with the first cases of HIV/AIDS in China. Since the 1980s, a growing number of high school and college students have engaged in premarital sex often without the protection of condoms. Sexual promiscuity has grown, not just in the younger generation, but also in older segments of society. Pan Suiming, a widely respected Chinese sociologist and researcher of Chinese sexual trends, found that Chinese sexual promiscuity is positively correlated with wealth. In a nationwide survey, Pan found that the top 5 percent of China's male income earners were 32 times more likely to visit a prostitute than the bottom 40 percent of male income earners.[7] In the same survey, male factory managers, owners, and bosses had, on average, 6.27 to 6.41 extramarital sexual partners, more than any other category surveyed.[8] As China's middle class has developed, it has engaged in greater levels of sexual activity and promiscuity.

In addition, HIV/AIDS spread throughout China as a consequence of the movement of people, which the economic reforms have facilitated. The number of internal migrants in China, known as the "floating population," ballooned to 221 million migrants by 2011.[9] Originally, Chinese citizens' movement was restricted due to a residency permit system that assigned rural people to live and work in the countryside and urban citizens to reside in a particular city. As China developed private markets for social services, housing, and labor allocation, a mass internal migration occurred, some of it between cities and a very large share from rural to urban areas. In China, migrants who tend to be in their early careers and most sexually active years have contributed to the spread of HIV/AIDS between urban and rural areas and between cities.[10] Some migrant women, in particular, have moved to wealthier coastal cities to become commercial sex workers. Chinese market reforms have catalyzed the spread of HIV/AIDS geographically and among all segments of Chinese society.

Legislation and Stigmatization

A key to AIDS prevention is creating a context in which potential HIV/AIDS carriers feel that they can come forth to be tested without threat of arrest or stigmatization, which points to the importance of regulations governing AIDS. Chinese laws and regulations neither caused the spread of HIV/AIDS (with the possible exception of the absence of protocols for collecting and testing blood from donors until 1998, which contributed to the spread of AIDS through the blood supply) nor engendered stigmatization of people living with HIV/AIDS; they did, however, indirectly contribute to both. China's regulatory approach to high-risk populations including intravenous drug users, sex workers, and men having sex with men (MSM) has (at least for the majority of the reform period in the case of MSM) criminalized and/or stigmatized their behavior. In the early years of AIDS in China, China's state response to HIV/AIDS mixed three approaches: attempts to keep it at bay by regulating foreign interactions, laws to criminalize high-risk behaviors, and morality campaigns to discourage high-risk behaviors.

Chinese citizens and some officials tended to look at the spread of HIV/AIDS in China as caused by loose moral behavior primarily confined to ethnic minorities; therefore, AIDS carriers were considered deserving of their consequences.[11] Alongside moralizing campaigns, authorities sought to fight the epidemic by "striking hard" against criminal drug use and commercial sex work. Initially, laws against prostitution and drug use were made more restrictive, and enforcement was stronger.[12] Until the late 1990s, China's approach to intravenous drug use mixed punishment and hortatory campaigns. Simple drug use is not considered a criminal offense under the Criminal Law, but drug users are subject to detention under the Law of the People's Republic of China on Penalties for Administration of Public Security.[13] Intravenous drug users are subject to ten days' detention and 2,000-yuan fines.[14] Police can subject intravenous drug users to forced random urine tests and HIV testing.[15] Some of the measures taken had harmful consequences for the fight against the epidemic by "promot[ing] concealment of risk activities,"[16] which made it more difficult for officials to contact and monitor intravenous drug users.

Until 1998, condoms were considered to be "sexual toys" and, therefore, were highly regulated. The 1998 "Education Principles for the Prevention of Spread of AIDS" clarified that condoms were an important tool in limiting the spread of STDs.[17] Nevertheless, not until December 1, 2007, did public security departments announce that they would no longer arrest women who possessed condoms on charges of prostitution.[18] Until that time, scattered reports showed that the police occasionally arrested women carrying condoms, presuming that only prostitutes carried condoms. Consequently, prostitutes and women interested in engaging in protected sex were discouraged from doing so.

In China, MSM relations were never formally outlawed, but same-sex relations were considered a psychiatric disorder until 2001. Those practicing same-sex relations were subject to criminal and psychiatric treatment.[19] Until 1997, China's Criminal Law vaguely defined "hooliganism," and the police used that legal basis to arrest and detain MSM.[20] In some cases "hooliganism" was used even after 1997 to harass MSM. Handbooks that guided psychiatric practice in China considered same-sex relations a disease.[21] If discovered to be a MSM, a man could be placed in detention under psychiatric supervision or in labor reform. The psychiatric view of same-sex relations had a chilling effect on the MSM community and contributed to societal bias against MSM. To hide their true sexual identity and to stave off parental pressure to carry on the family line, homosexuals often marry and have a child, raising the risk of HIV/AIDS spreading between heterosexual and MSM populations. The stigmatization of MSM and the threat of detention made it difficult for state officials to contact MSM and stem the spread of HIV/AIDS epidemic among the MSM community. International foundations affected China's stance on this issue: "Some foreign funders insisted that some of the funds be given to homosexual groups. Prior to removal of the psychological label of disorder placed on same-sex relations, homosexuals formed civil society groups, but they were not in the open. They were very active doing work on AIDS from the start because they feared the spread of AIDS in their community."[22]

Ministry of Health

Until recently, one of the contributing factors to the spread of HIV/AIDS in China has been the disarray of the ministry of health and the health-care delivery system.[23] The Maoist leadership made substantial improvements in the health-care system, especially extending basic health-care services into the countryside. In 1960, China had just 24,849 rural health clinics, but by 1978 the government greatly extended the reach of health-care provision with 55,018 rural clinics. Under Mao, China also developed separate health insurance programs for those in the urban areas and in the countryside.[24] While it is easy to overstate Mao's accomplishments in the provision of health care, it is certainly correct that the percentage of citizens with access to health care has declined during the reform (post-1978) era.

Since 1980, China's government has been seeking to reduce its role in providing welfare for its citizens in order to limit state outlays and to make consumers pay more realistic prices for previously subsidized goods and services. In the health-care field, China's state has greatly decentralized control over hospitals and doctors, inserting greater responsibility for managing their budgets. Individuals, at least the minority of citizens who can afford to, are asked to buy health insurance from private companies. These reforms have fundamentally altered the nature and range of coverage of Chinese health care. Although China's public health system has long displayed an urban and coastal bias in its provision, the reforms exacerbated the inequities. Before the health-care reforms, approximately 90 percent of China's population was covered by the state medical system, but a survey in 2004 found that approximately one-half of urban households and just fewer than 16 percent of rural households had medical insurance.[25] The government introduced a Cooperative Medical System in the countryside in 2003, but the coverage of the new system requires substantial patient payments and provides little help to rural citizens.[26] Moreover, the fundamental reform of health care left the system in disarray, unable to provide for many citizens due to rising costs and limited extension of services into the poorer, rural sections of China.

It is difficult to measure the weakness of the ministry of health in isolation from the capacity and use of the health-care system, because the ministry provides limited historical data on its personnel. Anecdotally, civil society groups and doctors who worked on AIDS issues noted that the ministry lost interbureaucratic battles with the department of propaganda and especially the ministry of public security. As a proxy for the health-care bureaucracy's capacity to deliver services, China's total expenditure on health care, encompassing central and local government and individual payments, increased from 11 billion yuan in 1978 to 1,754 billion yuan in 2009 (in current yuan). That large leap in expenditure, however, masks some very important trends that make the health-care system look less robust. First, the expenditure on health care as a percentage of GDP only inched up from 3.02 percent to 5.15 percent over the same period. China's inflation of prices during China's market transition, as well as an increase in medical expenses that accompany an aging population, explain why health-care expenditure has not grown very much as a share of the total economy. Second and more importantly, after 1978, China's health-care reforms reduced the role of the central government and increased the burden on individuals for health-care provision. In 1978, individual citizens contributed 20.4 percent of China's total health-care payments, but that figure rose to 59.96 percent in 2001 before dropping to 37.46 percent in 2009. The central government contributed 32.16 percent to the total health-care expenditures in 1978. The figure peaked at 38.69 percent in 1986 and fell to 15.69 percent in 2002 before slowly rising to 27.46 percent in 2009. The slow rise in government share of health-care expenditure began to increase again in 2003 after the SARS incident pointed out the shortcomings of China's health reform efforts.[27] Local governments picked up the remaining share of health-care costs. These trends in the sharing of the health-care cost burden are shown in figure 3.1. Finally, while health expenditure as a share of GDP has increased, use of the health system has actually decreased. The percentage of hospital beds occupied and the length of hospital stays has declined,[28] so while there is greater capacity on the supply side of health-care provision, citizens have inadequate resources on the demand side to utilize the health-care system. Moreover, the number of doctors and hospital beds per person in the countryside actually declined in the 1980s.[29] In other words, the growth in expenditure is more a function of rising costs than it is expansion of access and use.[30]

The twin reform goals of decentralization and individual responsibility affected the spread of AIDS in two ways. First, poor areas concentrated in the countryside and China's interior, where health-care provision was deficient, became the regions with the highest incidence rates of HIV/AIDS. China does not provide data with specific numbers of HIV/AIDS cases by

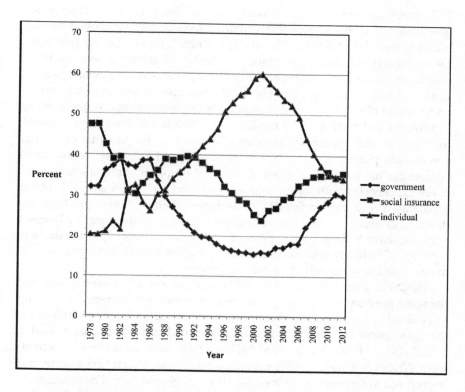

Figure 3.1.   Sources of Total Health Expenditure in China, in Percentages
Source: National Bureau of Statistics, China Statistical Yearbook (Beijing: China Statistics Press, various years

province, but they do publish maps indicating the number of such cases in each province in a given interval. In 2009, three provinces—Yunnan, Guizhou, and Sichuan—were estimated to have 80,000 to 120,000 cases of HIV/ AIDS (the most in China). Four provinces (Guangdong, Xinjiang, Henan, and Guizhou) were estimated to have 40,000 to 80,000 cases of HIV/AIDS. Excepting wealthy Guangdong, which has a very large share of the floating population that find work in foreign-invested enterprises, the other six provinces are among China's twelve poorest provinces. Second, the decentralization of expenditure made it more difficult to monitor and respond to national epidemics such as HIV/AIDS and SARS in two ways. As health-care providers were made responsible for their own finances, they shifted toward profitable enterprises and procedures. Unfortunately, monitoring of diseases yields no profit, so tracking infectious diseases fell by the wayside. Government expenditure on health promotion and disease prevention fell from 0.11 percent of GDP in 1978 to just 0.04 percent in 1993, and that was after AIDS had already begun to spread in China.[31] The public health reforms indirectly gave rise to mismanagement of China's blood supply (described below), which spread HIV/AIDS (and hepatitis) in China's poorer, central provinces. Decentralization reduced the ministry of health's capacity to monitor blood collection agents under its supervision at the grassroots level, while market-ization of health care gave local hospitals financial incentives to cut corners on testing of blood donors and plasma for infectious diseases. Without strong institutions and clear lines of regulation, protocols and laws were violated. The state's weak regulatory capacity is evinced by the fact that even after commercial plasma stations were ordered shut in 1995, some continued to operate for more than five years. Even local hospitals, particularly in rural counties, persisted with illegal commercial blood exchanges and without the capability to test plasma for HIV. The decentralizing reforms put local au-thorities in charge of appointing and paying most of the costs of hospital administration.[32] Hence, the number of health-care personnel did not decline, but lines of authority were decentralized so that the central ministry could not mandate and monitor policies at the local level.

The 2002–2003 outbreak of SARS brought on a wave of international and domestic pressure for China's government to improve its capacity to respond to epidemics, causing the government to substantially increase funding for the fight against HIV/AIDS.[33] In 2002, China had only ten doctors trained to treat AIDS, and only one hundred AIDS patients received antiretroviral treat-ment (ART).[34] China's public health system was clearly inadequate and unprepared to respond to the brewing HIV/AIDS epidemic. The propaganda department's controls over information about HIV/AIDS impeded average citizens from readily learning about how the disease spread and allowed prejudice and discrimination against HIV/AIDS carriers to persist. At the time, condom use was not even recommended to help stop the spread of HIV/AIDS.

As part of a new approach, in 2003, the state rolled out the China Com-prehensive AIDS Response (China CARES) program, greatly improving in-stitutional capacity to respond to HIV/AIDS. The five-year program estab-lished 127 program sites throughout China where there were concentrations of high-risk populations, including those with known outbreaks due to the blood scandal, intravenous drug use, and commercial sex work. At the sites, China tracked the epidemic with sentinel surveys and provided information on HIV prevention.[35] Prior to the program, 39 of the 127 program sites lacked screening laboratories for HIV/AIDS, which had prevented basic tracking and treatment of HIV/AIDS carriers.[36] The program's core compo-nents included the "Four Free, One Care" (*simian, yiguanhuai*) policy, which guaranteed, among other things, free ART for qualifying AIDS carriers. The program enrolled over 23,000 people in free ART. After a successful trial period, the China CARES program and the Four Free, One Care policy was expanded to all of China. By 2011, 76.1 percent of qualified adult AIDS carriers received ART.[37] These measures and the increased funding for HIV/AIDS and health care in general helped to put the ministry of health and the CDC on better footing and to scale up China's capacity to respond its HIV/AIDS epidemic. China also elevated the ministry of health to a cabinet ministry in 2008, which helped to raise its profile in China's administrative hierarchy. China's ministry of health remains overburdened and relatively weak, but its capacity to tackle the HIV/AIDS epidemic has been greatly improved. In March 2013, the ministry of health was dissolved and combined with the State Family Planning Commission to become a new agency titled National Health and Family Planning Commission. The interviews for this volume were all conducted before the change in organization, so the volume consistently refers to the ministry of health. At time of writing it is also unclear what effects, if any, the reorganization will have on the new agency's capacity to address AIDS.

The Spread of HIV/AIDS in China

In 2009, China had an estimated 740,000 HIV/AIDS carriers, a very large figure. In the context of China's vast population, however, only 0.057 percent of the population had HIV/AIDS, which is quite low, especially in comparison to prevalence rates in sub-Saharan African populations.[38] NGOs and scholars have contended that China has underreported the number of cases of HIV/AIDS (and deaths from AIDS) related to the politically damaging and massive blood scandal described below.[39] For example, Aizhixing, a prominent Chinese NGO, estimates that there are 1 million HIV/AIDS cases in China.[40] The following account chronicles the spread of China's HIV/AIDS epidemic by breaking up the history into four periods, while table 3.1 gives data on China's AIDS epidemic according to the emergence of new HIV cases broken down by category of transmission over time.

1985–1989

In 1985 and 1986, China recorded its first HIV cases, all of which involved contact with foreign persons or purchase of foreign blood products (for hemophiliacs).[41] The first HIV cases coincided with a political movement to root out bourgeois liberalization, associated with foreign investors and the (ill) effects of foreign culture in China. The movement, which targeted loosening sexual mores, prostitution, drug use, and political liberalism, colored Chinese attitudes toward HIV/AIDS.[42] A retired Chinese public health official explained, "With AIDS, people said it was an instance of capitalism or self-indulgent decadent lifestyle due to China's new opening to the world."[43] Such a viewpoint affected China's approach to HIV/AIDS in two ways. First, Chinese officials developed the mistaken impression that HIV was only a

Table 3.1.   Newly Reported Cases of HIV in Past Years by Mode of Transmission (percentage of total cases)

Year	Heterosexual	MSM	Intravenous Drug Use	Blood	Mother to Child	Unknown
1985–2005	11.3	0.3	44.2	29.6	1.1	13.5
2006	30.6	2.5	34.1	17	1.5	14.3
2007	38.9	3.4	29.2	9.5	1.5	17.5
2008	40.3	5.9	27.9	7.7	1.3	16.9
2009	47.1	8.6	25.8	5.5	1.4	11.6
2010	54.9	10.8	22.1	4.5	1.3	6.4
2011	62.6	13.7	16.9	3.3	1.2	2.2

Source: Ministry of Health. *2012 China AIDS Response Progress Report.* Beijing: Ministry of Health, 2012, 25. Last accessed 20 August 2014. http://www.unaids.org/en/dataanalysis/knowyourresponse/countryprogressreports/2012countries/ce_CN_Narrative_Report%5B1%5D.pdf

foreign virus to be kept at bay through quarantining measures. Second, officials saw high-risk behaviors as either criminal or morally deficient, both of which required state crackdowns.

Attempting to keep HIV/AIDS outside of China led to a host of regulations designed to secure China's borders. For example, Chinese immigration regulations for foreigners passed in 1986 barred people with HIV/AIDS from entering the country,[44] a regulation that stayed on China's books until 2010.[45] Chinese citizens who returned from abroad were required to submit to mandatory HIV/AIDS testing. Foreign blood products were banned from entering China.[46] In 1987, China's first national plan on HIV/AIDS focused attention on keeping the epidemic out of China rather than addressing internal prevention measures,[47] and Chinese regulations allowed authorities to incarcerate and quarantine anyone with such diseases. China also established monitoring stations in areas that were frequented by foreign tourists and businesspersons, for example in special economic zones.[48] During this initial time period, the number of reported HIV/AIDS cases remained quite low and were concentrated in Yunnan Province on China's southwestern border.

1989–Mid-1990s

In 1989, an outbreak of HIV/AIDS occurred in ethnic minority areas of Yunnan Province. The outbreak occurred near the "golden triangle" region of Myanmar (Burma), Vietnam, and Thailand, an area of ethnic migration across borders and with high levels of illicit drug use and prostitution. The number of reported HIV cases rapidly grew in China with the reemergence of drug trafficking. In 1994, 73 percent of the total reported HIV cases were intravenous drug users, but that figure had dropped from 88 percent in 1990.[49] Initially, nearly all of the new HIV cases were in Yunnan, and in 1990, 98 percent of Yunnan's HIV/AIDS cases came from the Dai ethnic group in which drug use is prevalent.[50] UNAIDS estimated that by 2000, 80 percent of intravenous drug users in Ruili County and 75 percent in Wenshan County, Yunnan Province, had contracted HIV/AIDS.[51] By 1994, China had a total of 1,774 documented cases of HIV/AIDS, and over 80 percent of the cases were in Yunnan.[52]

The monitoring methodology used by China at the time may also explain the preponderance of documented HIV/AIDS cases in Yunnan by underreporting the spread of HIV/AIDS to other provinces. Yunnan established a strong sentinel survey and monitoring system in 1991, prior to China's launching a national system in 1995.[53] So the documentation of Yunnan cases was likely more accurate (and made the epidemic there appear much worse) than for other provinces. In fact, later reports acknowledged that during the period 1989 to the mid-1990s HIV/AIDS spread from Yunnan to neighboring provinces through drug trafficking networks.[54] Finally, China's nascent sexual revolution provided a new, important path of transmission; during this period, sexual activity was beginning to overtake intravenous drug use as the most rapid cause of the spread of China's HIV epidemic.

Mid-1990s–2001

During the mid-1990s, the most important and distinguishing feature of the development of China's HIV/AIDS epidemic was the blood scandal that occurred in central provinces. The blood scandal is popularly associated with Henan Province, but it arose in five provinces in China's center. While other countries have had tainted blood plasma infect citizens with HIV, the incidents have been mostly isolated and brought a quick response from government agents.[55] In contrast, China's blood scandal demonstrates multiple layers of broken regulations and safety procedures on the handling of blood by private and government agents, as well as the breakdown of regulatory systems in the shift to hospitals operating on market principles. Local officials suppressed news of the blood scandal in China for years, resulting in a prolonged, widespread outbreak of HIV/AIDS among blood donors and patients receiving blood transfusions.

Poverty and a shift toward a market economy drove the blood scandal. In China's central provinces, impoverished farmers and migrant workers sought to supplement their meager income by selling their blood. In 1995, rural citizens in four provinces hit hardest by the blood scandal—Henan, Anhui,

Shanxi, and Hubei Provinces—earned an average of just 1,232 to 1,511 Chinese yuan (approximately 150 to 175 dollars) per year.[56] In deeply impoverished villages, average incomes were much lower. At the time, villagers earned roughly 5 dollars for each 32 ounces of blood that they sold;[57] selling blood could more than double the income of poor rural households. The blood collectors who came to be known as "blood heads" (*xietou*) were private actors who used reckless procedures. Officially, blood collection agents needed to be authorized by the government and to follow protocol on blood collection. In fact, few private blood agents did receive official authorization, though many likely operated with the tacit knowledge of local officials. Indeed, Wan Yanhai, whose organization, Aizhixing, helped to publicize the blood scandal in China, alleges that the Henan provincial health department had a policy of blood and plasma commerce, which it promoted throughout the province.[58] The privatization and insertion of profit motives into health-care provision eroded the state's capacity to directly monitor actors and even created incentives for hospitals to enter into the commercial blood market.

In the collection of blood, blood heads failed to test their donors for HIV/AIDS and other infectious diseases such as hepatitis. Syringes and tubing were reused to collect blood from multiple donors. Blood plasma was pooled and put through a process called centrifugation, which spins the blood and forms concentrated plasma. The concentrated plasma could be more inexpensively distributed to hospitals in other parts of the country than whole blood. Blood agents took the leftover portion of the red blood cells after the centrifugation process and injected it back into blood donors, so that the donors could avoid anemia and would be able to donate blood again more quickly than if they waited for the body to reproduce plasma.[59] For their part hospitals failed to test blood plasma for HIV/AIDS and other infections before using it for transfusions into patients. Some hospitals routinely collected blood from donors without checking for HIV/AIDS in order to give patients blood transfusions. The effect of this process was to spread AIDS among blood donors and those receiving blood transfusions.

Word of the blood scandal arrived in Beijing by 1995, but Henan officials attempted to suppress efforts to report the scandal. They were largely successful for five years. According to Wan Yanhai, doctors and journalists who first began to report on the outbreak of the blood scandal in Henan were all fired or pressured to suppress their findings.[60] After learning of a potential outbreak of HIV/AIDS in China's central provinces, public health officials went to investigate. A 1996 survey in Fuyang, Anhui (one of the affected provinces), revealed 12.5 percent of local blood donors had contracted HIV. Another study found an astonishing 65 percent HIV infection rate among residents in Wenlou Village, Henan, one of the "AIDS villages."[61]

In 1995, the central government issued an order to halt all commercial blood collection ventures.[62] A year later, the ministry of health responded to the emerging blood scandal by drafting the Law of the People's Republic of China on Blood Donation (hereafter Blood Donation Law),[63] which was passed in 1997 and promulgated in 1998, a full three years after the first public reporting of the scandal. Article 10 of the Blood Donation Law requires all collected blood to be tested for qualification, including absence of HIV/AIDS infection, while Article 8 bans operation of blood collection stations for commercial purposes.[64] Passage of the law provides clear evidence of the central government's early knowledge of the breaking epidemic due to the blood scandal. Between 1996 and the first years after the passage of the new law, attempts by the ministry of health and CDC to tighten safety controls over commercial blood donation practices, however, made little progress. A retired official who worked in the public health field at the time explained to me why the MOH and CDC failed in their efforts:

> Many locales had no experience testing blood for HIV, had no means to test blood, and didn't know what to do. So, although the regulations required them to test blood donors, many locales failed to comply. The stations were told to stop their work, but their economic interest in maintaining operations was great. They made a lot of money off of selling blood. . . . A lot of locations said the law was useless because they could not implement it.[65]

According to the former official, the new regulations on blood donation only started to be implemented in 1999 and 2000. Although commercial blood stations had been ordered closed as early 1995, in 2004, Chinese health officials admitted that up to 20 percent of China's blood supply still was provided by paid donors.[66] Nevertheless, the proportion of Chinese people with HIV/AIDS who contracted it from the blood supply has dropped significantly since 2006, an indication of government control measures gaining traction and, sadly, the dying off of many people who were infected by the blood supply.

In 2000, the first media reports, filed by international papers and China's *Southern Weekend*, discussed the blood scandal in China's central provinces. The story broke because of the bold work of Dr. Gao Yaojie, a doctor from Zhengzhou, Henan, who visited villages to investigate and treat the HIV/AIDS patients that began to develop in the 1990s. Her reports were first aired in a newsletter published by Aizhixing, an NGO run by Wan Yanhai, who left his position in the ministry of health over disagreements about its handling of HIV/AIDS and to establish Aizhixing. In 2001, deputy minister of the ministry of health Yin Dagui discussed the spread of HIV/AIDS through blood transfusions in China's central provinces.[67] Two weeks later, Yin was fired from his post.[68] In 2002, Chinese authorities arrested Wan Yanhai for revealing "state secrets" due to his publication of Gao Yaojie's work on the blood scandal. Clearly, officials at all levels of the government sought to suppress news of China's widespread blood crisis.

The government sought to hide the catastrophe outside of official circles until 2003, when the country coordinating mechanism (CCM) of the Global Fund to Fight AIDS, Tuberculosis, and Malaria indirectly forced the government's hand. In 2002, China had applied to the CCM for funding to fight HIV/AIDS, but their application focused on the problems of intravenous drug users in Yunnan, downplaying the blood crisis in central provinces.[69] The CCM, however, turned down the proposal due to the Chinese government's failure to acknowledge the blood crisis. When China reapplied to the Global Fund in 2003, the application was explicit about the blood scandal and the need for funds to provide ART to tens of thousands of AIDS victims affected by it.[70] An important figure in the AIDS public health field who worked with the CDC at that time argued that the blood scandal was a turning point in the influence of international groups on China's government: "When the issue of AIDS in Henan broke, no one in China was allowed to know about it. People didn't discuss it in China, and there was no media reporting. But in the international community, the WHO, UNAIDS, the UN, and other international bodies put a lot of pressure on the government to come out with the information, so they started to speak up about it."[71]

The number of HIV/AIDS cases that arose from China's blood scandal has long been a source of dispute and conjecture, and there are a number of reasons why estimating and documenting HIV/AIDS cases caused by the blood scandal has proved difficult. First, when China established its sentinel survey system in 1995, it tracked five categories of people: patients with sexually transmitted infections, prostitutes, drug users, truck drivers, and pregnant women.[72] The early sentinel surveys overlooked blood donors and MSM—two important categories of HIV carriers in China—by not tracking them. Second, most of the sentinel survey sites were in cities, but China's HIV outbreak was most severe in the countryside, especially in Yunnan and the central provinces affected by the blood scandal. China lacked adequately trained public health personnel to monitor, prevent, and treat HIV/AIDS in rural areas,[73] so surveys likely underreported cases in many of the emerging problem areas.[74]

The central government rarely makes public an official number of total HIV/AIDS cases caused by the blood scandal,[75] preferring instead to offer annual reports on the estimated number of existing and new cases and the modes of transmission. In its 2003 reapplication to the Global Fund, the ministry of health offered that there were 80,000 persons infected with HIV in China's central provinces due to the blood scandal,[76] while in 2006, the ministry of health and UNAIDS put the figure at 69,000.[77] Gao Yaojie, the doctor who first documented the blood scandal, has estimated the number of people infected by the blood scandal to be approximately 1 million.[78] A 2000 study of Shangqiu County, one of the worst hit by the scandal, found that 84 percent of the 100,000 residents had developed HIV/AIDS. According to Asia Catalyst, the study of Shangqiu County was commissioned by the government but then was suppressed when the results were reported to officials. [79]

In addition to the above problems with estimating HIV/AIDS cases in the countryside and among blood donors, the official figures tend to obscure two other factors. First, the estimations focus on those *living* with HIV/AIDS, so they do not take into account the *deaths* of HIV/AIDS carriers prior to and during the periods of sentinel surveys. Undetected for a long period of time and then covered up by local officials, many people died of AIDS contracted through the blood scandal that never made it into official estimates. Second, the official figures indicate a high number of documented deaths (7,700 in 2010)[80] and estimated deaths due to AIDS (20,000 to 30,000 per year for the years 2005–2009), but authorities do not break down the deaths by mode of contracting HIV/AIDS. [81] Such aggregated figures mask the severe toll that the blood scandal had in central provinces.

By the end of the period under study, China had an exponentially increasing number of newly reported HIV/AIDS cases each year. In 1995, the number of newly reported cases was 1,567, but in 2001, there were 8,219 new cases reported. [82] By the end of 2001, China had 30,736 cumulative reported cases of HIV/AIDS. The number of actual cases—sentinel survey methods were still quite rudimentary in China in 2001—was much higher due to the rapid spread of HIV/AIDS through the blood scandal and the political pressure to suppress information about the outbreak in central China.

2001–Present

Since 2001, HIV/AIDS in China has developed to more closely resemble the epidemic in other parts of the world. While the number of persons who contracted HIV/AIDS from blood donations and blood transfusions remains quite high, since 2005 few new such cases have emerged. According to official statistics, people living with HIV/AIDS contracted from the blood scandal comprised 29.6 percent of all of China's HIV cases during the period 1985–2005, while accounting for just 6.6 percent in 2011. [83] In recent years, the fastest-growing number of HIV/AIDS cases is due to unprotected sexual intercourse, and the MSM community has emerged as the fastest-growing category of HIV-infected persons. In 2011, of the estimated 48,000 new cases of HIV, the ministry of health calculates that 46.5 percent resulted from heterosexual transmission and 17.4 percent from same-sex transmission, [84] but the incidence rate among China's small MSM community is very high. In 2011, the ministry of health estimated the prevalence rate among the MSM community to be 6.3 percent. [85] Intravenous drug users remain a significant

share of the total HIV/AIDS carriers, and that group has the highest prevalence rate of all categories of HIV/AIDS carriers, estimated to be 6.4.[86]
Mother-to-child transmission, too, has infected children (in 2009, 1.4 percent
of the total number of HIV cases), so all age categories of society have been
infected.[87] In 2011, UNICEF estimated that 496,000 to 894,000 children had
been affected by HIV/AIDS, either by being infected with the virus or having
their parents infected with the virus.[88] By 2009, over 90 percent of all rural
counties and urban districts throughout the country have reported incidences
of HIV/AIDS.[89]

Since 2001, Chinese authorities essentially have brought the AIDS epidemic under control, but they have achieved mixed success reaching out to
high-risk communities with their educational programs. Among the high-risk
categories of people tested in sentinel surveys, MSM showed the lowest level
of knowledge about HIV/AIDS transmission.[90] In 2009, MSM were 12 percent less likely to have reported using a condom last time they had anal sex
(73.1 percent) than commercial sex workers reported the last time that they
had intercourse (85.1 percent).[91] Sex workers, despite the growing number of
HIV/AIDS carriers resulting from heterosexual transmission, have not constituted a particularly large portion of the HIV/AIDS-infected population.
The 2011 sentinel survey estimates indicate that the prevalence rate among
commercial sex workers is just 0.3 percent, far above the prevalence rate for
the entire population but much lower than the rates for MSM and intravenous
drug users.[92] The government's harm-reduction approach to commercial sex
workers seems to have gained traction, resulting in a relatively low incidence
rate of HIV/AIDS. Over the course of this period, China's HIV/AIDS epidemic has spread to typical high-risk groups, bringing China's epidemic
more in line with international patterns of HIV/AIDS.

INSTITUTIONAL ORIGINS OF CHINA'S
ENVIRONMENTAL CRISIS

Having reached the stage of being a national and even global crisis that
affects global warming and food security, China's environmental pollution is
a daily staple in today's newspapers. While the cumulative effects of China's
environmental pollution are well known outside of academic circles, the
institutional origins of China's environmental crisis have received less attention.[93] As with the above account of the causes of China's HIV/AIDS epidemic, China's environmental crisis emerged as a consequence of three institutional factors: (1) the meager set of regulations and laws that governed
environmental pollution at the outset of China's intensive industrialization,
(2) economic reforms that prioritized economic growth over environmental

stewardship, and (3) the low capacity of the ministry of environmental protection (MEP) to rein in polluters.

Environmental Regulations

Since 1978, China has legislated a robust set of environmental laws and regulations to govern pollution and protect the environment, but the development of environmental rules came quite late and after a pattern of lightly regulated industrialization had already taken shape. During the Mao era (1949–1978), the regime's environmental record was woefully poor. The state produced just one piece of broad environmental regulation, pursued political campaigns that sought to conquer rather than preserve the environment, and did not create an organ dedicated to overseeing environmental concerns until 1972.[94] Early industrialization arose in the absence of regulations, and the rapid proliferation of factories after 1978 commenced with inadequate pollution controls. In 1979, China produced its first significant piece of environmental legislation, the Environmental Protection Law of the People's Republic of China (hereafter, Environmental Protection Law).

Chinese environmental laws and regulations lack clarity and "teeth." Many basic laws provide a general framework or strategy for addressing an issue, requiring subnational state units to develop more detailed rules to put national laws into practice.[95] Chinese laws and regulations on environmental protection now cover all of the necessary areas of pollution, but their language is vague, filled with terms such as "should" rather than "must," and fails to clarify responsibilities for enforcement.

China's environmental regulatory field can appear a patchwork quilt of rules and regulations authored by state organs at different levels of government and competing bodies at the same level of administration. Some laws and regulations contradict one another, a problem that the central government is trying to rectify. While the highest laws are produced by the National People's Congress, ministries are also authorized to produce laws and regulations. The MEP shares overlapping jurisdictions with a number of ministries and agencies related to managing water, land, forests, and industry, which can lead to the production of inconsistent regulations on pollution levels and pollution abatement procedures. A factory may comply with one set of regulations but be out of compliance with another.[96] In addition, legislatures (and bureaus and departments) at the various levels of administration are authorized to produce laws and regulations that affect environmental protection. Subnational laws should not contradict national laws, but subnational state organs may produce regulations and laws on an issue prior to the passage of national legislation, leading to inconsistencies.

A final problem with Chinese environmental regulations is the weak fines and enforcement measures built into the regulations. Until the 2014 revision of the Environmental Protection Law, the fines that environmental officials can levy against polluters typically have been far less than the costs of adding pollution abatement technology, and sometimes returned in the form of tax breaks to the violators.[97] Consequently, polluters prefer to pay small fines rather than remedy their polluting ways. For years, environmental protection bureaus retained a portion of the fees that they levied against polluters to underwrite their budgets, giving them an incentive to fine polluters rather than rectify the production process. In the late 1990s, the government stripped authorities of the power to retain a part of the fines,[98] but some environmental units have persisted in such behavior.

Economic Institutions

An important contributing factor to China's extraordinary economic takeoff was a series of rural and fiscal reforms in the early and mid-1980s. The reforms decentralized control over financial resources into the hands of local officials to invest and spur economic growth, as well as loosened or relinquished state control over economic assets and markets to create strong incentives for individuals to undertake new or expanded lines of production. Loosened restrictions on private agricultural and sideline operations encouraged expansion of production without consideration of environmental consequences. Reforms spurred China's early economic growth, especially in the countryside, but the same reforms also established a set of institutional designs that put China on a collision course with environmental disaster. Two reforms, in particular—the fiscal and (related) cadre responsibility systems, and rural industrialization—played prominent roles in China's "pollute first, clean up later" growth model.

The cadre responsibility system, introduced in the early 1980s, linked officials' salaries to meeting or exceeding targets. The targets (or evaluative criteria) for cadres are divided into three types: "guidance," "hard," and "veto" targets.[99] Most of the economic targets are hard targets that determine if an official receives a full salary and, if targets are exceeded, bonuses. Failure to meet veto targets such as fulfilling the one-child policy or to maintain local order, results in punishment.[100] Until 2006, environmental requirements were deemed guidance targets, which had little effect on officials' salaries.[101] For many local officials, a simple calculus exists—more production, more pay—creating a personal incentive to expand industry.[102] Local officials who manage retained funds for public undertakings invest in "collective enterprises" to promote economic development and job growth and increase their salaries. Although the MEP has introduced new criteria that recognize the importance of sustainability, such as the "green GDP" model, into the cadre evaluation system, the basic incentive structure that has given rise to pollution-intensive growth persists. The cadre responsibility system has been the key institution to propelling economic growth, mollifying the population, and promoting CCP legitimacy.

In the early 1980s, the central authorities revised the revenue-sharing arrangements, which gave more revenue to local authorities in order to spur investment in collective and nonstate operations.[103] During the 1980s, the number of factories in China soared, many of them small- and medium-size enterprises located in China's vast countryside, often referred to as "township and village enterprises (TVEs)." In 1985, still the early stages of China's economic takeoff, 1.57 million township and village factories operated.[104] By 1998, the last year in which TVEs were counted as a distinct category of factories, their number had risen to over 20 million.[105] Of the total industrial output in China, the share of TVEs rose from a baseline in 1978 of 9 percent to 28 percent in 1996.[106] Typically, local authorities controlled such enterprises, which remained outside the planning of central state authorities. The takeoff of collective enterprises in the countryside was very steep until, in 1994, the central government revised the fiscal system to reassert a greater measure of central control over locally retained revenue. Local authorities, however, created mechanisms to get around the strictures. For example, local authorities amassed "extrabudgetary funds" that could not be transferred to other locales or monitored by central authorities.[107] The proliferation of small- and medium-size factories scattered throughout China's countryside has created challenges for monitoring and regulating pollution.

While I focus mainly on industrial pollution and resulting legal cases in this book, agriculture, mining, forestry, and other economic activities also have contributed to China's environmental crisis. Just as is the case with industrial growth described above, improved incentives to expand economic production came at the expense of sustainability and pollution controls. For example, incentives to farmers encouraged cultivation of land that was marginally productive and overgrazing of land, contributing to soil erosion and deforestation. These factors have contributed to a decline in China's soil quality, in the most acute cases, desertification. Similarly, mining firms have undertaken hazardous mining activities and unlawful disposal of waste (both chemicals and silt), damaging water supplies, biodiversity, and agricultural production, not to mention public health.

The Environmental Protection Bureaucracy

One of the challenges that China faces in tackling pollution and environmental regulation is the weakness of the MEP. Although in 2008 the MEP became a "super ministry" with full rank in the State Council, its current standing, which many still claim is weak, belies its humble origins. The MEP's precursors go back to 1974 when China's State Council established the office of the leading group of environmental protection in the State Council to oversee daily environmental affairs and planning.[108] In 1982, that office was folded into the new ministry of urban and rural construction and environmental protection. Two years later, the National Environmental Protection Agency (NEPA) was created within the ministry of urban and rural construction and environmental protection. In 1988, NEPA split from its previous ministry, establishing its independence, although it only had 120 employees at the central agency.[109] A decade later, the state raised the profile of NEPA to the State Environmental Protection Agency (SEPA) and made it a ministerial-level agency, though still below the level of top ministries. Finally, in 2008, SEPA was transformed into the ministry of environmental protection, giving the organization full ministerial credentials and putting it on more equal footing with rival ministries.

A clear signal of the MEP's monitoring challenge and relative weakness is the number of personnel in the ministry. In 1985, China's environmental protection bureaucracy at all levels of administration totaled just 22,921 personnel, and each was required to monitor, on average, nearly 15 million (2005 constant) dollars of GDP. While the total staff in the environmental protection bureaucracy expanded to 205,334 persons in 2012, each staff member was required to monitor, on average, over 22 million (2005 constant) dollars of GDP. The MEP began from a position of relative weakness, and in terms of the amount of economic activity that each member of the bureaucracy must monitor, the ministry's position has worsened.

One of the challenges that the MEP faces is lack of clarity of its authority both in terms of its power to author regulations and its jurisdiction over implementation of regulations. Other state organs such as the national development and reform commission (in charge of climate change, emissions, and management of energy efficiency) have competing interests over environmental policies, and the commission has often clashed with the MEP, arguing for weaker environmental regulations than the MEP desires.[110] The MEP also is pitted against the ministry of industry and information technology, which oversees industrial development, on the issues of environmental regulations and enforcement. In general, the MEP has suffered from inadequate authority in struggles with other ministries over environmental protection.[111]

The MEP is hamstrung in its enforcement efforts by the administrative organization of China's bureaucracy. First, environmental protection units are found at each level of state administration from the central down to township or district levels of administration, but the authority to enforce regulations, including levying fines, is overlapping among the various levels of environmental protection administration. As Chen Gang points out, a pollution issue in a municipal district could be handled by district, municipal, provincial, or even central environmental protection units, and in this system of unclear jurisdiction and authority, the first environmental unit that discovers the environmental problem generally handles it. [112]

Second and more important, the environmental protection bureaus are enmeshed in both a vertical environmental protection administrative hierarchy and horizontal ties to government bodies at the same administrative levels. Within the environmental protection bureaucracy, bureaus provide environmental plans and advice to lower environmental protection units. More important are the horizontal ties that environmental protection bureaus have to local government; environmental protection bureaus receive their budgets not from the environmental protection bureaucracy but from the government at their level of administration. For example, a township environmental protection department receives its budget from the township government. [113] Similarly, appointments of leaders in environmental protection bureaus at each administrative level are made by corresponding government units at the same level of administrative hierarchy and not by higher-level administrators in the environmental protection bureaucracy. Appointments to the environmental protection bureaus have been affected by political considerations or nepotism rather than professional qualification. [114] Even at the provincial level, governments appointed environmental protection bureau directors who lacked an environmental background in three-fourths of the cases. [115] Such political appointees as provincial environmental protection leaders set the tone for the entire environmental protection bureau staff and affected its capacity. [116]

The cadre responsibility system and administrative ties to environmental protection units combine to weaken local environmental protection units' autonomy from the local government and polluters. Local governments both invest in factories that pollute and provide the budgets (including the officials' meager salaries) to environmental offices that are charged with reining in polluters. Government officials are reluctant to appoint environmental protection leaders who might undermine their evaluations by prioritizing environmental protection over economic expansion. Consequently, environmental protection units at the lower reaches of administration are quite weak. [117] Administrative and budgetary linkages compromise the ability of environmental officials to enjoy autonomy in enforcing policies. The frequent outcome of China's administrative structure is local protectionism with limited central capacity to gain compliance with its policies. Even diligent local environmental protection agents may be swayed by local leaders' call for ignoring pollution regulations in order to spur job growth.

The MEP is generally regarded as understaffed and short-funded for the herculean task before it. In addition to the incentive structure that emphasizes economic growth at the expense of environmental protection, China's numerous small- and medium-size enterprises (especially in the countryside) require an extensive network of officials with appropriate resources. Simply, the environmental protection bureaucracy lacks the personnel, funding, and technology to systematically monitor rural industry.[118] Many environmental protection bureaus in the countryside do not even have monitoring equipment to test factories for compliance with pollution standards.[119]

The MEP has developed monitoring systems to implement national regulations on pollution. For major factories, the MEP uses continuous monitoring systems, and the factories are charged with reporting their emission levels to the MEP or its agents. One of the problems that the system faces, however, is factories tamper with the monitoring devices or even turn them off. To halt such obstructions, the MEP has developed teams that travel to factories to collect independent samples, which are then used to verify the reports from the continuous monitoring systems. Still, some factories have been caught turning on pollution filters or dialing down emissions when investigators arrive, only to turn up their prohibited emissions after the officials depart or when local citizens cannot observe.[120] The MEP can apply the monitoring system to large factories in cities, but it has much weaker regulatory capacity and practices for factories in the countryside. An official at an INGO in Beijing lamented, "The MEP is very clear—they just pick a few large factories to monitor. These key point factories are checked once a month. As for the other factories, secondary factories are checked just once a quarter. All other factories are checked once a year. In the countryside, small factories are not monitored at all."[121]

CHINA'S ENVIRONMENTAL DECLINE

The Communist era, especially the period of Mao Zedong's rule (1949–1978), often is blamed for the state's destructive approach to the environment, which set China on its current course for environmental destruction. While the Mao era significantly contributed to environmental degradation, both Mao's predecessors and successors bear a great deal of responsibility for the current state of China's environment. Indeed, as Robert Weller and Peter Bol suggest, the notion of the state maintaining harmony between society and nature has long held sway, but "this view did not result in the conscious establishment of environmentally sound practices."[122] For example, since the eighteenth century, Han Chinese have encroached upon the steppe in Mongolia and attempted to supplant Mongol land-use practices and introduce those followed by the Han majority in China. That shift led to overuse of the soil and the spread of desertification.[123] Similarly, during the late dynastic period (prior to 1911), massive deforestation occurred, which caused water and soil management issues such as flooding, salinization, and erosion.[124]

The Mao Era (1949–1978)

Maoist China perpetrated a number of environmental sins of commission and omission. First, Mao's attacks on intellectuals, especially during the Cultural Revolution (1966–1976) marginalized scientists and science in policy-making processes just as the world and China were becoming more aware of the importance of protecting the environment. Mao spread economic development policies through politically charged campaigns that suppressed rational, scientific criticism. [125] The Great Leap Forward (1958–1960) was the first and most devastating of these campaigns to inflict damage on China's environment in a rushed attempt to industrialize. During that period, China cleared forests, engaged in ill-conceived, large-scale rural industrialization, and gave short shrift to agricultural production, among other unwise policies, culminating in the loss of an estimated 18 to 42 million lives. The same disregard for science also spurred population growth, which Mao believed strengthened China's development potential but put stress on China's environment. [126]

Second, a recurring theme in Maoist propaganda and agricultural policy was to "take grain as the main link" and to open new land for agricultural production. Such exhortations and policies compelled Chinese farmers to clear forests and bring poor-quality land under agricultural production. During the Cultural Revolution, approximately 3 million acres of land deep in China's interior were reclaimed for agricultural use. [127] The cultivation of poor land and reduction of forests depleted the soil and exacerbated inherited problems of erosion and flooding; in some cases, the habitats of scarce animals were destroyed. [128]

A third problem caused by Maoist policies was the unregulated expansion of industry. In particular, the spread of industry to China's countryside, in pursuit of a political goal to close the socioeconomic gap between the rural and urban populations, caused a great deal of damage to China's farmlands. Beginning under Mao and continuing through the present, rural industry has had the following two harmful effects on agriculture: (1) industry encroaches upon farmland, causing a decline of agricultural production, and (2) industry emits pollution into the groundwater and air that harms crops, livestock, and farmers. While Mao's political motivations to expand industry especially in the countryside are understandable and maybe honorable, in retrospect, it is easy to identify how his industrial policies began a pattern of development that harmed China's environment and undermined its food production.

Finally, Maoist China committed a sin of omission; it failed to develop environmental regulations and regulatory agencies until the early 1970s. And, as described above, the first incarnations of environmental protection units lacked independence and sway over policies. The failure to develop policies to regulate economic organizations and their impact on the environment meant that leaders after Mao began their own economic development programs without effective regulations.

The Post-Mao Era (1978–Present)

During the course of the Deng era, central authorities have become increasingly concerned with environmental damage and control measures over pollution, but divisions among ministries and agencies undermine pollution abatement efforts. In general, China has greatly improved the quality of laws and regulations governing the environment since 1978, but enforcement lags behind. Despite improved environmental regulations, economic growth and development of new industries have outstripped pollution abatement efforts. So even as China has improved the efficiency of its use of resources and has begun to shift its energy production away from its heavy reliance on coal and other fossil fuels, China's rapid growth has caused a steady increase of pollutants to be emitted. During the post-Mao era, villagers witnessed accelerated development with the application of new chemical fertilizers and pesticides, expansion of industry, and mining of resources, all of which contributed to local environmental damage. [129]

1978–1991

Two of the early actions by the post-Mao regime were the revision of the Constitution in 1978 and passage of the Environmental Protection Law in 1979. Into the Constitution, the regime inserted the following provision: "The state protects and improves the living environment and the ecological environment, and prevents and remedies pollution and other public hazards." [130] The Environmental Protection Law (Trial Implementation) called on state administrative units to establish organs designated to protect and monitor the environment. [131]

Despite the development of more environmental regulations and laws, a host of environmental problems—all forms of pollution, deforestation, soil depletion, and desertification—were intensified by the dramatic growth of economic activity. During this period, poorly regulated rural industrialization emitted pollution into waterways, the soil, and the air. Decollectivization of agricultural production, while encouraging entrepreneurship, also put more pressure on the land when farmers brought poor soil under cultivation, applied chemical fertilizer, and cropped too intensively. Forests were cleared for wood fuel, lumber used in new home construction, and timber for furniture production. Rapidly improving living standards began to have devastating consequences for China's environment.

1992–2004

The beginning of this period is marked by China's participation in UN Conference on Environment and Development (UNCED) in Rio de Janeiro. The conference helped to diffuse vocabulary related to "sustainable development," which began to alter China's analysis of its economic model. China's participation in conferences and adoption of international discourse on the environment did not, however, have an immediate effect on environmental pollution. In 1994, the Huai River turned black from industrial pollution being dumped into the river and the streams that feed into it. Millions of pounds of fish died, people along the river who used its water became ill, and people were left without access to clean water for weeks.[132] Such incidents heightened societal and government concern about the impact of pollution on the environment. In 1996, the government targeted fifteen types of small-scale rural industries for forced closing because of the heavy toll of their pollution, which led to the shuttering of sixty thousand rural enterprises in January 1997.[133] Although this marked an important step in fighting pollution in China's countryside, rural industries have posed a persistent, serious problem for environmental protection agents.

Deforestation continued during this period with a "market-driven cut" in 1998 that depleted China's forests further.[134] That same year, China experienced significant flooding on the Yangzi River, which Chinese leaders partially attributed to deforestation in Sichuan Province, the western reaches of the river. In response, China ordered an immediate halt to timber harvests in western Sichuan Province.[135]

The state through the MEP planned to reduce emissions of pollution into the atmosphere and water, but prevention measures could not curb pollution in the face of rapid economic growth. During this period, China greatly improved on their environmental efficiency measured by the amount of energy used in producing a unit of gross domestic product, and in the amount of carbon dioxide and sulfur dioxide emitted in producing goods. Unfortunately, growth of production outpaced improvements in the production process, leading to more pollutants being emitted. For example, during the tenth five-year environmental plan of 2000–2005, China exceeded its targets for sulfur dioxide emissions by 42 percent and for COD (chemical oxygen demand) discharge into the water by 8 percent.[136]

2004–Present

In the period since 2004, Chinese authorities have taken several steps to improve environmental protection efforts, although it is instructive that the period also coincides with what some legal scholars call China's "turn away from the law."[137] In fact, the enhanced environmental protection efforts during this time period relied on some advances in environmental litigation, especially environmental public interest litigation described in chapter 7, and strengthened bureaucratic approaches to enforcement of environmental protection measures.

During this period, China's cadre evaluation system gave more weight to economic criteria than to environmental protection measures. In 2004, the SEPA (the precursor of the MEP) developed a "green GDP" model that attempted to measure the environmental impact of development on China's GDP and to include the green GDP metric in the cadre evaluation system. In the first two years of calculating the green GDP, the economic cost of environmental degradation worsened from 2004 to 2005, the opposite of the desired effect of instituting such calculations. According to Alex Wang, the government did not publicize the embarrassing information and abandoned the use of green GDP in 2006, but the idea of using environmental criteria as fundamental components in cadre evaluation had taken root. [138]

In 2005, the SEPA cracked down on lax enforcement of environmental impact assessment procedures. According to China's Environmental Impact Assessment Law, construction for every new economic organization or expansion of an existing one requires a study to be completed of the expected environmental impact, though the rules are often ignored or done in a negligent way. As part of an "environmental storm" campaign, the SEPA halted construction of thirty factories that had failed to undertake proper environmental impact assessments. [139] The halt was temporary, but the message from SEPA was that it was going to exercise its power to ensure better enforcement of the environmental impact assessment rules.

During the eleventh five-year plan (2006–2010), several environmental targets were made binding and allocated to the leading officials at various levels of the state administration (e.g., provincial governors and city mayors). Progress toward meeting environmental goals was measured by targets in three categories: (1) "project reductions," consisting of investments in environmental infrastructure, (2) "structural reductions," including closing down polluting factories, and (3) "management reductions," entailing improvements in monitoring and enforcement. [140] Wang argues that the recalibrated cadre evaluation system strengthened enforcement of pollution control measures and allowed the administrative bureaucracy to effectively respond to several incidents involving heavy metal pollution in 2009. [141] In 2012, the same environmental targeting was applied to the case of PM2.5, a finer-gauge measure of particulate matter in the air than China's previous standard, PM10. [142] While official data from China support the claim that the new evaluation system has improved environmental protection, the environmental protection bureaucracy still lacks adequate monitoring capacity (especially in the countryside) and local officials are prone to falsifying data. [143] The overarching goal of the green GDP and revamped cadre evaluation system appears to be avoidance of mass disturbances related to the environment, and the regime, in order to protect its legitimacy, is emphasizing bureaucratic measures over reliance on environmental litigation.[144]

At the same time, China's regime also developed specialized environmental courts and environmental public interest litigation as new judicial tools to address pollution problems, discussed in greater detail in chapters 6 and 7 of this book. So during this period, the Chinese state employed both bureaucratic and judicial means to reduce pollution without fully involving citizens directly in the practice of environmental governance. Rather, the regime sought to respond to the pollution with litigation led by state-related civil society groups (GONGOs) and bureaucratic management. As noted above, the SEPA was made into the MEP and given full ministerial standing, which nominally added to its strength in interministerial struggles.

The environmental protection bureaucracy has been a leader in responding to the state's new Regulations of the People's Republic of China on Open Government Information. Each unit of government is charged with providing public information on the daily state of the environment in its location, which creates pressure on officials to improve environmental protection. The issue of airborne particular matter, which reached dangerous levels in major cities such as Beijing at the end of 2011, is a good example of pressure brought by the new information regulations. The U.S. embassy in Beijing and consulates in other parts of the country began to report the pollution levels at PM2.5, particulate matter that exceeds 2.5 micrometers, which is in line with international measurement and reporting standards. According to the more refined measurements, air pollution and particulate matter were at hazardous levels in many locations. In January 2012, Chinese authorities adopted new measures for particulate matter at PM2.5. The adoption of new standards and continuous reporting by urban areas creates greater transparency about China's pollution problems and heightens citizens' consciousness of the issue. Information empowers citizens to demand that governments address pollution problems.

CONCLUSION: INSTITUTIONAL ORIGINS AND RESPONSES TO CRISES

The above narratives of the development of HIV/AIDS and environmental devastation in China underscore how both institutional changes and weaknesses propelled the spread of AIDS and pollution. The narratives also reveal some of the bureaucratic conflicts and responsibilities for the crises. In the case of HIV/AIDS, China's MOH and its CDCs have been responsible for reining in and responding to the epidemic. While the department of propaganda has some control over public service messaging related to AIDS and the ministry of public security tackles some of the behavior of high-risk populations such as intravenous drug addicts and sex workers, the MOH has been primarily responsible for handling the response to HIV. Due to the MOH's weakness and poor funding, it has limited capacity to address the spread of HIV/AIDS. Working with civil society and international organizations, it has enjoyed success in bringing the epidemic under control, although HIV is spreading more quickly through sexual activity, and many Chinese citizens continue to engage in unprotected sex.

In addressing environmental pollution, the MEP faces challenges on several fronts. First, the MEP is poorly funded, despite its elevated status and funding levels, which limit the ministry's capacity to carry out its work. Second, central and local authorities have conflicting interests, even within the environmental protection bureaucracy. The central environmental protection ministry cannot always bring local officials to heel on following emissions standards. Finally, the environmental protection bureaucracy struggles with other ministries and bureaucracies over the substance and implementation of environmental protection measures. The MEP's attempts to add teeth to environmental protection laws and regulations meet with stiff resistance from other state units, which leads the MEP to depend on civil society groups to help rein in polluters.

The public health and environmental crises have revealed the limited capacity of China's institutions to contain and remedy the problems. While China has significantly improved the laws and regulations in these areas, the environmental protection and public health bureaucracies have limited capacities to implement policies and regulations. To improve their capacity to implement policies, both ministries need civil society input (discussed in chapter 4). The two ministries' historical failures to implement policies and secure citizens' safety from pollution and contaminated blood have left state agents susceptible to protests and lawsuits (analyzed in chapters 5 to 7).

NOTES

1. Lester Brown, *Who Will Feed China? Wake-Up Call for a Small Planet* (New York: Norton, 1995); Elizabeth Economy, *The River Runs Black: The Environmental Challenge to China's Future* (Ithaca and New York: Cornell University Press, 2004); Jun Ma, *China's Water Crisis* (Pacific Century Press, 2004); Robert B. Marks, *China: Its Environment and History* (Lanham, MD: Rowman & Littlefield, 2011); Judith Shapiro, *Mao's War against Nature: Politics and the Environment in Revolutionary China* (Cambridge: Cambridge University Press, 2001); Judith Shapiro, *China's Environmental Challenges* (Cambridge, Polity Press, 2012); Vaclav Smil, *China's Environmental Crisis: An Inquiry into the Limits of National Development* (Armonk, NY: M. E. Sharpe, Inc., 1993); Rachel E. Stern, *Environmental Litigation in China: A Study of Political Ambivalence* (Cambridge: Cambridge University Press, 2013); Bryan Tilt, *The Struggle for Sustainability in Rural China: Environmental Values and Civil Society* (New York: Columbia University Press, 2010); and Lei Xie, *Environmental Activism in China* (Abingdon: Routledge, 2009).

2. Sandra Teresa Hyde, *Eating Spring Rice: The Cultural Politics of AIDS in Southeast China* (Berkeley: University of California Press, 2007); Edmund Settle, *AIDS in China: An*

Annotated Chronology 1985–2003 (Monterey, CA: China AIDS Survey, 2003); and Guomei Xia, *HIV/AIDS in China* (Beijing: Foreign Languages Press, 2004).

3. Ministry of Health, *2012 China AIDS Response Progress Report* (Beijing: Ministry of Health, 2012), 5, accessed 20 August 2014, http://www.unaids.org/en/dataanalysis/knowyourresponse/countryprogressreports/2012countries/ce_CN_Narrative_Report%5B1%5D.pdf.

4. Ingo Ilja Michels, Yu-xia Fang, Dong Zhao, Li-yan Zhao, and Lin Liu, "Comparison of Drug Abuse in Germany and China," *Acta Pharmacologica Sinica* 2007, no. 10 (October 2007), 1508.

5. Xinhua, "China's Registered Drug Users Top 2 Mln," *Xinhua*, 25 June 2013, accessed 24 August 2014, http://news.xinhuanet.com/english/china/2013-06/25/c_132485980.htm.

6. Zunyou Wu, Sheena G. Sullivan, Yu Wang, Mary Jane Rotheram, and Roger Detels, "Evolution of China's Response to HIV/AIDS," *Lancet* 369 (24 February 2007), 680.

7. Suiming Pan, Yingying Huang, and Dun Li, "Analyses of the 'Problem' of AIDS in China," originally published in *China Social Science*, no. 1 (2006).

8. Pan et al., "Analyses of the 'Problem' of AIDS in China."

9. Xinhua, "China's 'Floating Population' Exceeds 221 Million," *Xinhua*, 1 March 2011, accessed 20 August 2014, http://www.china.org.cn/china/2011-03/01/content_22025827.htm.

10. Pan et al., "Analyses of the 'Problem' of AIDS in China."

11. Norman Kutcher, "To Speak the Unspeakable: AIDS, Culture, and the Rule of Law in China," *Syracuse Journal of International Law and Commerce* 30, no. 271 (Summer 2003), 281–82.

12. Wu et al., "Evolution of China's Response," 680.

13. *Law of the People's Republic of China on Penalties for Administration of Public Security*, passed by the Standing Committee of the National People's Congress on 28 August 2005, put into effect 1 March 2006.

14. John Balzano and Ping Jia, "Coming Out of Denial: An Analysis of AIDS Law and Policy in China," *Loyola University Chicago International Law Review* 3 (Spring 2006), 204.

15. Yanhai Wan, Ran Hu, Ran Guo, and Linda Arnade, "Discrimination against People with HIV/AIDS in China," *Equal Rights Review* 4 (2009), 17.

16. Wu et al., "Evolution of China's Response," 680.

17. Ministry of Health et al., "Education Principles Related to the Spread of AIDS," issued on 8 January 1998 by the Ministry of Health, Central Party Propaganda Ministry, National Education Committee, Ministry of Public Security, Ministry of Justice, Ministry of Culture, Ministry of Cinematic Broadcasting, National Reproductive Planning Committee, and News Broadcasters.

18. Xinhua, "Condoms No Longer Proof of Prostitution," *Xinhua*, 1 December 2007, accessed 20 August 2014, http://www.chinadaily.com.cn/china/2007-12/01/content_6292045.htm.

19. Zunyou Wu, Sheena G. Sullivan, Yu Wang, Mary Jane Rotheram, and Roger Detels, "The Evolving Response to HIV/AIDS," in *Chinese Social Policy in a Time of Transition*, eds. Douglas Besharov and Karen Baehler (Oxford Scholarship Online, 2014), 279.

20. USAID and Health Policy Initiative, *Assessment of the HIV Legal Environment: Yunnan, China* (Kunming, China: RTI International, 2008), 10.

21. Joan Kaufman, "Turning Points in China's AIDS Response," *China: An International Journal* 8, no. 1 (March 2010), 69.

22. Interview 71.

23. Interview 32; Congressional-Executive Commission on China, Roundtable on HIV/AIDS, "China's HIV/AIDS Crisis: Implications for Human Rights, the Rule of Law and U.S.-China Relations," testimony by Bates Gill, 9 September 2002, 4.

24. Jin Ma, Mingshan Lu, and Hude Quan, "From a National, Centrally Planned Health System to a System Based on the Market: Lessons from China," *Health Affairs* 27, no. 4 (July/August 2008), 939.

25. Martin King Whyte and Zhongxin Sun, "The Impact of China's Market Reforms on the Health of Chinese Citizens: Examining Two Puzzles," *China: An International Journal* 8, no. 1 (March 2010), 2 and 14.

26. John Cai, "Turning Away from Dependence on the Economic System: Looking Forward and Back on the Reform of China's Health Care System," in *Economic Transitions with Chinese Characteristics*, eds. Arthur Sweetman and Jun Zhang (Montreal and Kingston: McGill-Queen's University Press, 2009), 136–37.

27. Karen Eggleston, "Health Care for 1.3 Billion: An Overview of China's Health System," Asia Health Policy Program working paper no. 28 (Stanford, CA: Stanford University, Walter H. Shorenstein Asia-Pacific Research Center, 2012), 10.

28. Ma, Lu, and Quan, "From a National, Centrally Planned Health System," 941.

29. Xingzhu Liu and Junle Wang, "An Introduction to China's Health Care System," *Journal of Public Health Policy* 12, no. 1 (Spring 1991), 110.

30. Ma, Lu, and Quan, "From a National, Centrally Planned Health System," 941.

31. Ma, Lu, and Quan, "From a National, Centrally Planned Health System," 944.

32. Mariam Claeson, Hong Wang, and Shanlian Hu, "A Critical Review of Public Health in China," unpublished paper, August 2004, accessed 19 August 2014, http://siteresources. worldbank.org/INTEAPREGTOPHEANUT/Resources/publichealth,09-13-04.pdf.

33. Jonathan Schwartz, "The Impact of Crises on Social Service Provision in China: The State and Society respond to SARS," in *State and Society Responses to Social Welfare Needs in China: Serving the People*, eds. Jonathan Schwartz and Shawn Shieh (London and New York: Routledge, 2009), 135–55.

34. Mengjie Han, Qingfeng Chen, Yang Hao, Yifei Hu, Dongmei Wang, Yan Gao, and Marc Bulterys, "Design and Implementation of a China Comprehensive AIDS Response Programme (China Cares), 2003-2008," *International Journal of Epidemiology* 39 (2010), ii48.

35. Han et al., "Design and Implementation," ii47.

36. Han et al., "Design and Implementation," ii49.

37. Ministry of Health, *2012 China AIDS Response Progress Report*, 42, accessed 20 August 2014, http://www.unaids.org/en/dataanalysis/knowyourresponse/countryprogressreports/2012countries/ce_CN_Narrative_Report%5B1%5D.pdf.

38. Ministry of Health, *China 2010 UNGASS Country Progress Report (2008-2009)* (Beijing: Ministry of Health, 2010), 21, accessed 20 August 2014, http://data.unaids.org/pub/Report/2010/china_2010_country_progress_report_en.pdf.

39. Evan Anderson and Sara Davis, *AIDS Blood Scandals: What China Can Learn from the World's Mistakes* (New York: Asia Catalyst, 2007), 15; and Wan et al., "Discrimination against People," 15.

40. Wan et al., "Discrimination against People," 16.

41. Elena S. H. Yu, Qiyi Xie, Konglai Zhang, Ping Lu, and Lillian L. Chan, "HIV Infection and AIDS in China, 1985 through 1994," *American Journal of Public Health* 86, no. 8 (August 1996), 1116; Simona Bignami-Van Assche, "Estimates and Projections of HIV/AIDS for Yunnan Province, China," *Population Review* 43, no. 2 (2004), 73.

42. Interview 51.

43. Interview 51.

44. *Rules for the Implementation of the Law of the People's Republic of China Governing the Administration of Entry and Exit for Foreigners*, approved 3 December 1986 by the State Council, promulgated 27 December 1986, article 7(4).

45. *Decision by the State Council Regarding Revision of "The Detailed Instructions on Procedures for Foreigners Entering and Exiting China,"* issued by the State Council on 19 April 2010, http://www.chinaaids.cn/n16/n1193/n4073/380299.html, revised article 7(4), removing AIDS as grounds for denial of entry into China. However, the revised article replaced "persons with AIDS" with "persons with serious psychological disorders, communicable tuberculosis, or infected with other diseases that can pose a serious threat to public health" (author's translation).

46. Ministry of Health and General Office of Customs of China, 1986, *Notice on Banning Importing Factor III and Other Blood Products*, issued 1986.

47. Balzano and Jia, "Coming Out of Denial," 196.

48. Vincent E. Gil, "Sinic Conundrum: A History of HIV/AIDS in the People's Republic of China," *Journal of Sex Research* 31, no. 3 (1994), 212.

49. Yu et al., "HIV Infection and AIDS in China," 1117.

50. Yu et al., "HIV Infection and AIDS in China," 1118.

51. UN Theme Group on HIV/AIDS in China, *HIV/AIDS: China's Titanic Peril* (New York: United Nations, June 2002), 15.

52. Yu et al., "HIV Infection and AIDS in China," 1117.

53. Bignami-Van Assche, "Estimates and Projections of HIV/AIDS," 73.

54. Wu et al., "Evolution of China's Response," 679.

55. Anderson and Davis, *AIDS Blood Scandals.*

56. National Bureau of Statistics, *China Statistical Yearbook, 1996* (Beijing: China Statistics Press, 1996).

57. Frank Langfitt, "China's Inaction Carries AIDS Toll," *Baltimore Sun*, 30 August 2001, accessed 24 August 2014, http://articles.baltimoresun.com/2001-08-30/news/0108300116_1_infected-henan-aids-education.

58. Human Rights Watch, "Locked Doors: The Human Rights of People Living with HIV/AIDS in China," *Human Rights Watch* 15, no. 7(C), 62.

59. Anderson and Davis, *AIDS Blood Scandals*, 15.

60. Yanhai Wan万延海, "*Mai Xue Chuanbo Aizibing he Guojia Jimi* 卖血传播艾滋病和国家机密" (The Transmission of AIDS through Blood Sales and National Secrets), Aizhi Action Project press release, 28 December 2002, accessed 15 August 2014, http://www.peacehall.com/news/gb/pubvp/2002/12/200212290253.shtml.

61. Neil Renwick, "The 'Nameless Fever': The HIV/AIDS Pandemic and China's Women," *Third World Quarterly* 23, no. 2 (April 2002), 380.

62. Anderson and Davis, *AIDS Blood Scandals*, 15.

63. *Law of the People's Republic on Blood Donation*, adopted on 29 December 1997 by the Standing Committee of the National People's Congress, promulgated as Order No. 93 by the president on 1 October 1998.

64. *Law of the People's Republic on Blood Donation*, adopted on 29 December 1997.

65. Interview 51; see also Anderson and Davis, *AIDS Blood Scandals.*

66. Anderson and Davis, *AIDS Blood Scandals*, 17.

67. Bates Gill, Jennifer Chang, and Sarah Palmer, "China's HIV Crisis," *Foreign Affairs* 81, no. 2 (March–April 2002), 97–98.

68. Kaufman, "Turning Points," 77.

69. Kaufman, "Turning Points," 71.

70. Kaufman, "Turning Points," 71.

71. Interview 69.

72. UN Theme Group on HIV/AIDS in China, *HIV/AIDS: China's Titanic Peril*, 12.

73. Wu et al., "Evolution of China's Response," 687.

74. UN Theme Group on HIV/AIDS in China, *HIV/AIDS: China's Titanic Peril*, 13.

75. Juan Shan, "AIDS Deaths Hit 'Peak' as 7700 Die," *China Daily*, 20 April 2011, accessed 1 January 2013, http://www.chinadaily.com.cn/china/2011-04/20/content_12358846.htm.

76. Kaufman, "Turning Points," 71.

77. Anderson and Davis, *AIDS Blood Scandals*, 5.

78. Anderson and Davis, *AIDS Blood Scandals*, 15 fn. 1.

79. Anderson and Davis, *AIDS Blood Scandals*, 15 fn. 1.

80. Shan, "AIDS Deaths Hit 'Peak.'"

81. Zhonghua Renmin Gongheguo Weishengbu, Lianheguo Aizibing Guihuashu, Shijie Weisheng Zuzhi 中华人民共和国卫生部, 联合国艾滋病规划署, 世界卫生组织, *2009 Nian Zhongguo Aizibing Yiqing Guji Gongzuo Baogao* 2009 年中国艾滋病疫情估计工作报告(2009 Estimates for the HIV/AIDS Epidemic in China), Beijing, National Center for AIDS/STD Control and Prevention, China CDC, 2010, 6.

82. State Council AIDS Working Committee [SCAWCO] and the UN Theme Group on AIDS in China [UNAIDS], *A Joint Assessment on HIV/AIDS Prevention, Treatment, and Care in China* (Beijing, 2007), 2 fig. 1.1.

83. Ministry of Health, *2012 China AIDS Response Progress Report*, 25–26. Some researchers dispute the official figures on China's HIV/AIDS epidemic, especially the number of cases that resulted from the blood scandal.

84. Ministry of Health, *2012 China AIDS Response Progress Report*, 6.

85. Ministry of Health, *2012 China AIDS Response Progress Report*, 16.

86. Ministry of Health, *2012 China AIDS Response Progress Report*, 17.

87. Ministry of Health, *China 2010 UNGASS Report (2008-2009)*.

88. Dan He, "Government Vows to Help More AIDS Kids," *China Daily*, 1 June 2011, accessed 24 August 2014, http://www.chinadaily.com.cn/china/2011-06/01/content_12616130.htm.

89. Ministry of Health, *China 2010 UNGASS Report (2008-2009)*, 23.

90. Ministry of Health, *China 2010 UNGASS Report (2008-2009)*, 17.

91. Ministry of Health, *China 2010 UNGASS Report (2008-2009)*, 18–19.

92. Ministry of Health, *2012 China AIDS Response Progress Report*, 15.

93. Economy, *The River Runs Black*; Shapiro, *China's Environmental Challenges*; and Tilt, *The Struggle for Sustainability*, are notable exceptions.

94. Charles R. McElwee, *Environmental Law in China: Mitigating Risk and Ensuring Compliance* (Oxford: Oxford University Press, 2011), 21; Xin Qiu and Honglin Li, "China's Environmental Super Ministry Reform: Background, Challenges, and the Future," *Environmental Law Reporter* 2-2009 (2009).

95. McElwee, *Environmental Law in China*, 8 and 14.

96. Gang Chen, *Politics of China's Environmental Protection: Problems and Prospects* (Singapore: World Scientific, 2009).

97. Jason E. Kelley, "Seeking Justice for Pollution Victims in China: Why China Should Amend the Tort Liability Law to Allow Punitive Damages to Environmental Tort Cases," *Seattle University Law Review* 35 (2012), 539; Srini Sitaraman, "Regulating the Belching Dragon: Rule of Law, Politics of Enforcement, and Pollution Prevention in Post-Mao Industrial China," *Colorado Journal of International Environmental Law and Policy* 18 (Spring 2007), 312.

98. Chen, *Politics of China's Environmental Protection*, 24–25.

99. Alex Wang, "The Search for Sustainable Legitimacy: Environmental Law and Bureaucracy in China," *Harvard Environmental Law Review* 37 (2013), 380.

100. Wang, "The Search for Sustainable Legitimacy."

101. Wang, "The Search for Sustainable Legitimacy."

102. Tilt, *The Struggle for Sustainability*, 40.

103. Elizabeth Economy, *The River Runs Black*, 60.

104. National Bureau of Statistics, *China Statistical Yearbook, 1986* (Beijing: China Statistics Press, 1986), 155.

105. National Bureau of Statistics, *China Statistical Yearbook, 1999* (Beijing: China Statistics Press, 1999), 410.

106. Barry Naughton, *The Chinese Economy: Transitions and Growth* (Cambridge: MIT Press, 2006), 300.

107. Barry Naughton, *The Chinese Economy*, 438–39.

108. McElwee, *Environmental Law in China*, 24.

109. McElwee, *Environmental Law in China*, 26.

110. Chen, *Politics of China's Environmental Protection*, 21.

111. Economy, *The River Runs Black*, 101.

112. Chen, *Politics of China's Environmental Protection*, 24.

113. Abigail R. Jahiel, "The Organization of Environmental Protection in China," *China Quarterly*, no. 149 (1998), 35.

114. Chen, *Politics of China's Environmental Protection*, 26.

115. Genia Kostka, "Environmental Protection Bureau Leadership at the Provincial Level in China," *Journal of Environmental Policy and Planning* 15, no. 1 (2013), 41.

116. Kostka, "Environmental Protection Bureau Leadership," 42.

117. Yu-wai Li, Bo Miao, and Graeme Lang, "The Local Environmental State in China: A Study of County-Level Cities in Suzhou," *China Quarterly*, no. 205 (March 2011), 117.

118. Tilt, *The Struggle for Sustainability*, 70.

119. Interview 77; Jahiel, "The Organization of Environmental Protection in China," 59.

120. Kelley, "Seeking Justice for Pollution Victims," 538.

121. Interview 77.
122. Cited in Marks, *China: Its Environment*, 271.
123. Cited in Marks, *China: Its Environment*, 290.
124. Cited in Marks, *China: Its Environment*, 276.
125. Shapiro, *Mao's War against Nature*, 2.
126. Economy, *The River Runs Black*, 49.
127. Shapiro, *Mao's War against Nature*, 140.
128. Shapiro, *Mao's War against Nature*, 182.
129. Tilt, *The Struggle for Sustainability*, 86.
130. Cited in McElwee, *Environmental Law in China*, 24.
131. *Environmental Protection Law of the People's Republic of China*, adopted 1989 December 26, revised 24 April 2014, and put into effect 1 January 2015.
132. *Environmental Protection Law of the People's Republic of China*, 27.
133. *Environmental Protection Law of the People's Republic of China*, 28.
134. Marks, *China: Its Environment*, 287.
135. Marks, *China: Its Environment*, 288.
136. World Bank and State Environmental Protection Agency, P. R. China (SEPA), *Cost of Pollution in China: Economic Estimates of Physical Damage* (Washington: World Bank, 2007), 1.
137. Carl F. Minzner, "China's Turn against Law," *American Journal of Comparative Law* 59 (2011), 935–84; Elizabeth M. Lynch, "China's Rule of Law Mirage: The Regression of the Legal Profession since the Adoption of the 2007 Lawyers Law," *George Washington International Law Review* 42 (2010), 535–85.
138. Wang, "The Search for Sustainable Legitimacy," 392.
139. McElwee, *Environmental Law in China*, 29.
140. Wang, "The Search for Sustainable Legitimacy," 403–4.
141. Wang, "The Search for Sustainable Legitimacy," 406–7, 410.
142. Wang, "The Search for Sustainable Legitimacy," 409.
143. Wang, "The Search for Sustainable Legitimacy," 417.
144. Wang, "The Search for Sustainable Legitimacy," 375 and passim.

Chapter Four

Civil Society Responses to HIV/AIDS and Environmental Pollution

The development of Chinese environmental and HIV/AIDS crises has revealed the limits of the Chinese state's capacity to control these problems, so for more than a decade authorities have enlisted help from civil society organizations to implement its programs.[1] Both the environmental protection and HIV/AIDS areas of civil society are populated with numerous organizations, and many of the larger organizations enjoy financial support from international funders. Over the last fifteen years, a handful of high-profile civil society organizations have begun to work on legal issues on behalf of HIV/AIDS carriers and pollution victims, entering the realm of advocacy. In sum, civil society development in these two issue areas has become robust and contentious, testing the boundaries of state tolerance. How has China's regime simultaneously allowed the rapid development of civil society and reined in the demands on the regime so that social stability and regime legitimacy have been preserved?

One of the central arguments of this book is that civil society has developed unevenly and that the Chinese regime attempts to subordinate grassroots interests to the state's ideology and organization. There are several reasons for the relative strength of Chinese civil society organizations that focus on AIDS and on the environment. First, the state finds civil society organizations in these two functional areas useful. In the case of HIV/AIDS, the state has difficulty formulating and implementing policies that address at-risk constituencies such as intravenous drug users, MSM, and commercial sex workers. As part of China's turn to a harm-reduction approach to HIV/AIDS in 2003, China's state has looked to nongovernmental organizations (NGOs) to help implement programs for at-risk communities, a policy that has periodically offered AIDS organizations significant scope to operate. The state finds environmental organizations can help the MEP, which is charged with regulating polluters but with inadequate staff and resources (and in some cases, a conflict of interests), to monitor polluting factories. Grassroots NGOs help the MEP to identify and publicize violations by local polluters. Second, the international community has designated prevention and treatment of HIV/AIDS and environmental protection global causes, which has placed pressure on China to address HIV/AIDS and pollution as well as provided funds for Chinese civil society organizations working to address these issues.

China's regime has powerful means to manage civil society in the areas of environmental protection and HIV/AIDS. The regime has attempted to exercise hegemony through its registration procedures, the creation of government-organized NGOs (GONGOs), and selective harassment of civil society organizations and activists who cross "red lines" of acceptable behavior, mainly contentious advocacy for disadvantaged citizens. A focus of this chapter is the regime's measures to control civil society, in this case, civil society organizations working on HIV/AIDS and environmental protection. Essentially, the state uses the above means to subordinate grassroots organizations to the state's interests and public service functional needs and to marginalize overly contentious organizations.

A second focus in this chapter emerges from the state's divergent responses to contentious advocacy pursued by AIDS groups and environmental groups. While civil society organizations in both issue areas have developed legal aid stations and networks of attorneys who provide pro bono services throughout China, some such organizations in the HIV/AIDS area have been targeted for reprisals by the state (along with many other human rights–based legal aid stations) in recent years. In contrast, environmental groups that have taken up legal aid and also pursue rights-based litigation have not been closed down and their attorneys have not been targeted for arbitrary detainment and trial. I argue that the space for civil society growth and the selective attacks on civil society groups arise from political considerations and are mainly rooted in bureaucratic interests, in these cases the interests of the ministries of environmental protection and health. AIDS organizations, especially those providing legal aid, have attracted funding from international organizations that concern the Chinese regime (e.g., the Open Society Institute and the American National Endowment for Democracy). Second, the widespread environmental movement requires the state to address protesters' concerns, and the state has given room to civil society organizations for legal contention. In contrast, there have been fewer protests by AIDS carriers, and the state has pursued administrative measures to avert litigation. Finally, AIDS carriers still carry a social stigma in China which makes them less willing to sustain public contentiousness (and therefore easier for the state to manage) than pollution victims.

THE DEVELOPMENT OF HIV/AIDS ORGANIZATIONS

Although the first Chinese NGO devoted to HIV/AIDS prevention was only established in 1993, a 2010 directory of Chinese civil society organizations and community-based organizations that have programs on HIV/AIDS includes 673 organizations, 35 of which are international or Hong Kong organizations with offices in China.[2] A recent estimate of the number of (more narrowly defined) Chinese AIDS civil society organizations placed the number at nearly 400.[3] What many consider to be the first organization established was, in fact, a GONGO attached to the Chinese Center for Disease Control, called the Chinese Association of STD and AIDS Prevention and Control, and its mission focused primarily on public health and policy formation related to HIV/AIDS. Now, the field of unregistered and even registered organizations working on HIV/AIDS ranges widely. Some NGOs address hard-to-reach groups such as drug addicts, sex workers, and LGBT communities. Others tackle sensitive topics, including needle exchanges, advocating for human rights, and protection during premarital sex. Still others focus on support for people living with HIV/AIDS, education on AIDS transmission, and clinical work on AIDS prevention.

Using the listings in the *2010 China HIV/AIDS CSO/CBO Directory*, which include information on the year that organizations were established, I constructed table 4.1 on the number of organizations by year of their founding. The data only include organizations that still existed in 2010, so early organizations that discontinued operation or that were closed down are not represented. Nevertheless, the figures in the table reveal the rapid proliferation of groups working on AIDS in the period 2004–2010. Prior to 2000, 31 organizations operated AIDS programs, and many of the organizations were groups such as the YMCA or medical units, which do not fit a strict definition of civil society organizations. During the period 2000–2003, on average only 15 organizations with AIDS programs emerged per year. Beginning in 2004, the number of new organizations, however, took off, with 30 new organizations being founded in 2004 and rising to a peak of 104 new organizations in 2007. In 2010, the year of the directory's publication, 86 new organizations were founded. For AIDS organizations, 2003 was a pivotal year because two political opportunities arose that opened space in which they could operate. First, the outbreak of SARS (severe acute respiratory syndrome) and China's poor response to it altered the government's view of public health, leading to an increase in funding and a shake-up of administration. Second, the central government's approach to HIV/AIDS shifted toward a "harm reduction" strategy, punctuated by the unveiling of the "China CARES" (China Comprehensive AIDS Response) policy, which necessitated the help of NGOs. International funding also played a role in the proliferation of Chinese civil society organizations during this period, rising from 335,000 dollars in 2005 to over 5.4 million dollars in 2009.[4]

SARS Crisis

Through 2003, China's government pursued a policy of relatively strict control over NGOs and their activities in the public health field. The turning point in state policy came with the SARS outbreak in China and other parts of Asia.[5] During that epidemic, Chinese officials hid information about the outbreak, which impeded tracking information about the spread of the disease and responding to the crisis. Concerns about the epidemic spreading across borders brought heightened international scrutiny of China's handling of SARS, and China's clampdown on information invited both domestic and international condemnation.[6] The 2003 SARS outbreak revealed that China treated news about epidemics as a "state secret," and some officials threatened retaliation against those who shared information about the outbreak.[7] Domestically, the poor flow of information about SARS thwarted China's diagnosis and response to SARS.[8] Due to international pressure to act openly and transparently, China allowed the WHO, a UN agency, to play a greater part in China's response to the public health crisis.[9]

Table 4.1.   2010 Chinese CSOs/CBOs with AIDS Programs by Year of Founding

Year	Number of Organizations
Prior to 2000	31
2000	9
2001	7
2002	25
2003	19
2004	30
2005	61
2006	87
2007	104
2008	94
2009	73
2010	86
Unknown	47

Calculated from China AIDS Information Network. *2010 China HIV/AIDS CSO/CBO Directory.* Beijing: China AIDS Information Network, 2010.

China's mishandling of information about the SARS outbreak convinced the regime that it needed to reform its information system and approach to civil society. In the years following the outbreak of SARS, China's government responded to epidemics and public health crises by requiring public officials to quickly share information about such outbreaks. The central government underscored its point by forcing the head of the ministry of health and the mayor of Beijing to resign in the aftermath of the SARS outbreak.[10] Civil society organizations and activists, who believed that officials had been complicit in the outbreak and cover-up of the AIDS blood scandal in central China, cheered that officials were being held accountable for their actions during the pandemic. More importantly for civil society, Chinese officials recognized the importance of NGOs in monitoring local conditions in the public health realm (and others).[11] NGOs provided independent information about public health concerns that avoided bureaucratic blockages.

The SARS outbreak and the international complaints about China's response to it caused China's government to give greater attention to public health issues. In retrospect, officials determined that China had neglected its funding for public health. By moving toward decentralization of medical care and calling on the medical field to provide its own resources through fees, central authorities had not provided much state funding for public health programs. The SARS epidemic revealed the weakness of the public health system and spurred spending on public health. The combination of increased spending on public health and greater attention to local monitoring of epidemics created greater space and opportunities for civil society organizations working on HIV/AIDS.

China CARES Program

In 2003, the state rolled out its China CARES program, which called for a rapid expansion of all areas of HIV/AIDS prevention and treatment. To fulfill the ambitious policy goals, government offices had to enlist the support of NGOs, especially to reach out to high-risk populations (intravenous drug users, prostitutes, and MSM).[12] In its Circular on the China CARES Policy, the ministry of health called on the All-China Youth Federation, the All-China Women's Federation, and other social organizations (*shehui tuanti*) attached to the party to help with the policy's outreach programs.[13] The Circular did, however, also call on various ministries and social organizations to solicit volunteers and NGOs to help with the outreach activities, providing an opportunity for grassroots organizations' participation.[14] According to the ministry of health's evaluation of the program, the number of NGOs at the model implementation sites increased from zero in 2003 to 756 in 2008.[15]

LIMITS TO STATE-CENTERED APPROACHES TO HIV/AIDS

An underlying reason for the government's altered approach to AIDS NGOs and the rapid proliferation of NGOs after 2003 is the slow realization that the state needed them to effectively reach high-risk communities. In particular, intravenous drug users and commercial sex workers are fearful of state offi-cials because their activities violate state laws and regulations, while mem-bers of the gay community have been subject to discrimination, harassment, detention, and abuse by some recalcitrant officials. The three groups are important potential agents of HIV transmission, and two groups (intravenous drug users and the gay community) both have very high HIV prevalence rates relative to other categories of the population at risk for HIV in China. Moreover, state-sponsored programs to reduce the likelihood of transmission by the gays and intravenous drug users such as condom use and needle exchange programs have not enjoyed the same level of results as some other HIV prevention programs. The challenges that the state has faced in reaching out to, and gaining compliance from, such groups has caused officials to rethink the role that civil society organizations can play in program develop-ment and implementation.

The state faces a number of policy dilemmas in approaching at-risk groups, including intravenous drug users, commercial sex workers, and MSM. In the case of intravenous drug users, the UNAIDS recommends needle exchange programs, which minimize the risk of spreading infectious diseases—HIV/AIDS and hepatitis—by sharing needles. Intravenous drug users are reluctant to approach state agents for fear of incarceration, but some state agents do not fully support harm reduction programs. The ministry of health's Circular on the China CARES Program points out the conflicting roles that state agents (especially police) must sometimes balance when it states, "In the midst of its strike hard activities against drug trafficking, prostitution, etc., the ministry of public security should support and assist the commerce, family planning, health, and other ministries in their work distrib-uting condoms and putting up posters at clubs."[16]

Needle exchange programs have been shown to be effective in lowering infection rates among intravenous drug users, but other public health pro-grams targeting this population have been less so. In 2009, only 38.5 percent of intravenous drug users surveyed were reached by HIV prevention pro-grams, far less than 74.3 percent of female sex workers and 75.1 percent of MSM reached by such programs. Two related factors have caused programs targeting intravenous drug users to be less effective than for other high-risk communities—persistence of harsh or arbitrary police treatment of intrave-nous drug users and ethnic tensions between public servants and drug users. Public security forces have been known to require urine tests for use of illegal drugs from participants at methadone maintenance clinics and syringe exchange centers. Those who fail the tests are subject to immediate forced detention without access to the methadone maintenance therapy (MMT).[17] Regulations on drugs passed in 2008 authorize the police to require urine tests at any time to check for drug use.[18] Such measures deter intravenous drug users from utilizing programs that reduce the risk of spreading HIV/AIDS through high-risk behavior. Many intravenous drug users are from ethnic minorities in China, including the Dais in Yunnan and the Uyghurs in Xinjiang and scattered throughout China. A study found that only 11.9 percent of Uyghurs were able to participate in MMT programs during the period 2007–2009. The same study of intravenous drug users found that 4.57 percent of Han drug users were HIV positive, while 51.97 percent of Uyghur drug users were HIV positive.[19] The divergent trends among Hans and Uyghurs suggest a potential bias against the Uyghur population, but a related explanation is that tension between minority ethnic groups and state officials makes Uyghurs, Dais, and other ethnic groups reluctant to enter health programs.

Until recently, participation in methadone maintenance programs required documentation from the police on past detention related to drug use.[20] Due to the tense relations with the police, intravenous drug users have been reluctant to go to the police to get authorizing papers to enter methadone maintenance clinics. More generally, fear of detention or harassment keeps intravenous drug users away from government programs that would help to reduce the likelihood of spreading HIV/AIDS. The above examples point to the conflict between the ministries of health and public security. The public health community's harm reduction approach is undermined by the persistence of the public security strike-hard method of dealing with drug users, keeping some drug addicts from approaching the state for treatment and testing.

The state has needed civil society partners to contact high-risk populations and to curb their high-risk behavior, but the ministry of civil affairs has been reluctant to register organizations that work with commercial sex workers, the MSM community, and intravenous drug users. Consequently, very few civil society organizations that work with these populations have existed until recently, and many operate without appropriate registration. Some state officials turn a blind eye toward unofficial NGOs that have either registered surreptitiously as "commercial enterprises" or failed to register at all. Officials in GONGOs or state-affiliated agencies such as local CDCs even solicit the cooperation of unofficial NGOs. For example, an official in the Shanghai CDC explained that when the organization has funding for a project, it puts out notices for all organizations, including unregistered NGOs, to apply. Based on the capacity of the organizations to fulfill the project, the CDC selects partner organizations. Consequently, the CDC has developed mutual understandings and working relations with a number of unregistered NGO partners. [21]

Another area in which grassroots organizations have helped authorities to achieve their AIDS policy goals is by reaching out to commercial sex worker and MSM communities. Initially, China's state, through the CDCs, attempted to approach commercial sex workers, intravenous drug users, and members of the MSM community through direct programs at the site of these groups' activities. To achieve that end in 2004, the national CDC mandated that each level of its organization create an "AIDS prevention team" (*fang'ai gaowei renqun ganyu gongzuodui*, or *gaogandui*, for short) to spread information about HIV/AIDS prevention to high-risk populations. AIDS prevention teams go to sites where intravenous drug users, commercial sex workers, and MSM gather or engage in high-risk behavior, including night clubs, gay bars, and massage parlors where they hold frank information sessions on HIV/AIDS and safe sexual behavior and drug use. The AIDS prevention team model, though, has not been a success. An NGO director sharply criticized the *gaogandui*'s approach in comparison with how NGOs approach people engaged in high-risk behavior: "When we go do our work, we don't look at sex workers as a group that has broken the law. We concern ourselves with whether their profession is following high-risk health practices. . . . We help them to understand how to prevent the spread of AIDS, what they can do in their work." [22] CDC officials complain of having too few personnel and little expertise to undertake such initiatives, [23] while scholars criticize the group for its ineffectiveness due a bland lecturing style and moral conservatism. [24] To relieve some of their workload and to improve the effectiveness of the education programs, CDCs and their AIDS prevention teams in various cities have cooperated with grassroots organizations.

The AIDS prevention team, as part of a state-run agency, the CDC, faces severe challenges in fostering working relations with drug users, sex workers, and members of the MSM community. As a CDC official explained, "These kinds of issues are very sensitive, and NGOs can better come into contact with prostitutes, IDU, and MSM. I have no problems at all with NGOs helping with these kinds of groups." [25] To reach out to sex workers, the CDC in various cities has collaborated with the All-China Women's Federation (another GONGO attached to the Communist Party) and grassroots organizations. Consequently, NGOs that focus on sex workers and MSM communities, in particular, have been granted increased space for operation as well as more responsibility in AIDS prevention. One such organization is Leyi, a Shanghai-based NGO that works closely with commercial (especially male) sex workers and that has registered as a commercial enterprise. Leyi cooperates on projects with the Shanghai CDC to distribute condoms, help with screening for HIV/AIDS, and spread information about the disease. As part of its work, Leyi publishes an online journal about HIV/

AIDS and sex workers that helps to generate sympathy for sex workers and knowledge of AIDS prevention.

INTERNATIONAL EFFORTS TO EMPOWER CHINESE AIDS GROUPS AND THEIR LIMITS

International NGOs (INGOs), foundations, and multilateral organizations have been active in China for three decades and have worked closely with Chinese civil society organizations. The government selectively invited international actors to China in order to draw on international expertise to address specific technical problems that China has faced, as well as to solicit funding to address matters of global concern, including the AIDS epidemic and environmental management. Once inside China, INGOs, foundations, and multilaterals have sought to invigorate Chinese civil society. Many foreign foundations, including the Gates Foundation, Ford Foundation, and the Open Society Foundation have invested significant sums in China to help propel civil society and rule of law development. International funders, however, face the following set of competing goals: (a) working with organizations that have the capacity to address public health and environmental concerns, which leads them to fund GONGOs and state agents; and (b) strengthening grassroots civil society to enhance human rights and citizen participation in governance. These twin goals have led international funding agencies to give most of their funds to GONGOs or state agents (which still is the minority share of GONGOs' funding), while also supplying most of the limited funds available to grassroots groups. [26] International actors' support for grassroots civil society formation, which has been modest, reflects a shift in public policy paradigms. [27] In the past, international society focused on state response to issues such as HIV/AIDS; getting state-funded care and prevention programs was the main concern. International society, however, has increasingly focused on civil society organizations' roles in the policy making and implementation processes. For example, UNAIDS has identified civil society participation as important to ensure that human rights of people living with HIV/AIDS are protected. [28] Beginning around 2005, international organizations have worked with Chinese groups to provide legal aid and litigation to HIV/AIDS carriers, a focus that bridges the goals of advancing human rights and citizen participation.

One of the most important contributions of the international community to China's approach to HIV/AIDS has been the reframing of policies in terms of human rights. In particular, international and multilateral organizations such as UNAIDS and Chinese NGOs have sought to elaborate a new epistemic approach to HIV/AIDS that includes human rights standards as a fundamental consideration. A staff member at a multilateral organization noted that the office has been able to make some progress on human rights with public health officials because "we have managed also to say these things in a way that is not necessarily confrontational and that is not necessarily seen as an arrogant kind of criticism of the Chinese approach. We try to be constructive and to move the limit little by little."[29] A key for multilaterals and international funders is to develop ties to sections of the state who sympathize with such an emphasis on human rights and citizen participation. For example, UNAIDS, which advocates adoption of a rights-based, harm-reduction approach to HIV/AIDS, works with the ministry of health who has accepted that position, while the ministries of public security and propaganda have been resistant to such an approach. For example, the ministry of health has clashed with the ministry of propaganda over public service announcements on condom use and with the ministry of public security over use of condoms and strategies to help intravenous drug users, including needle exchange and methadone maintenance programs.[30]

UNAIDS argues that "protection of human rights is essential to safeguard human dignity in the context of HIV and to ensure an effective, rights-based response to HIV/AIDS."[31] Based on a number of UN, regional, and international statements and agreements on human rights and HIV/AIDS, UNAIDS has produced documents outlining guidelines for human rights for HIV/AIDS carriers. Those rights include access to ART, legal protection from discrimination, and participation in decision making related to HIV/AIDS policies.[32] UNAIDS documents have specifically called on governments to protect vulnerable groups—intravenous drug users, commercial sex workers, MSM, prisoners and detainees, and children orphaned by AIDS—that may also face stigmatization.[33] Chinese civil society groups have used these norms as a basis of advocating for rights and new policies.

Despite the contributions of international organizations, a number of problems have arisen in international support for civil society development in China. First, the goals and interests of INGOs and domestic organizations do not always align well. International funders shift funding opportunities based on their goals rather than Chinese goals, which forces cash-starved Chinese grassroots organizations to shift their objectives in order to gain international funding.[34] Second, the duration of grants offered by INGOs and foundations is too short to adequately help civil society develop and to provide continuous programs. Meng Lin, generally regarded as the oldest living AIDS carrier in China and a leader of several civil society organizations, including Ark of Love, commented, "International funders that try to support Chinese NGOs to participate in addressing social problems have a short-sighted approach. They lack a strategy to support long-term change and civil society development."[35] Typically, international funders will invest in a particular program for a brief amount of time, but they will not cover administrative and personnel costs to run the organization. Civil society development and addressing societal issues related to HIV/AIDS is a long-term process, but cycles of grants that last one year or less and that do not cover administrative costs have limited effectiveness.

As part of a shift toward concern with human rights and citizen participation, beginning in 2004, a small number of Chinese NGOs, with the backing of international organizations and foundations, began to form legal aid stations to better protect the rights and interests of HIV/AIDS carriers. The Ford Foundation has given substantial financial support to Chinese NGOs and other groups that have founded legal aid centers for specific causes, especially related to the environment and HIV/AIDS. The Ford Foundation has designated fighting discrimination against HIV/AIDS carriers and advancing public interest litigation as parts of its human rights program. Such partnerships provide financial resources that are crucial to keeping such legal centers operating.

In major cities such as Beijing and Shanghai, domestic NGOs that work on HIV/AIDS-related issues have established legal aid and information centers. For example, in 2004 Aizhixing, based in Beijing, established a legal aid center to advise HIV/AIDS carriers on their rights and to advocate for them in courts. Aizhixing received substantial foreign funding from the Open Society, Levi-Strauss Foundation, U.S. National Endowment for Democracy, French AIDS Action Organization, and the UN Global Fund, among other sources. In January 2007, Asia Catalyst, based in New York City, working with Li Dan's organization, Orchid, established the Korekata AIDS Law Center to help protect HIV/AIDS carriers' rights, especially in Henan and Yunnan Provinces. In 2009, in Kunming, Yunnan Province, Health Policy Initiative partnered with the Yunnan University legal aid center to establish a new legal aid clinic for HIV/AIDS carriers. Until its grant ended in 2012, the center cooperated with, and was funded by, the USAID's Health Policy Initiative, RTI (Research Triangle Institute), and IDLO (International Development Law Organization). Shanghai's Leyi, a grassroots organization that focuses on HIV/AIDS and sex workers, provides legal information and refers LGBT potential legal cases to a local law firm with technical training on HIV/AIDS, hemophilia, and related issues. Leyi's operating expenses were supported by funding from Oxfam. In Beijing, Shanghai, and other major cities, activist lawyers have received foreign training, often through prominent public interest law programs run at law schools in the United States, Australia, or Europe. The legal aid centers then host training sessions for other lawyers and legal officials to spread knowledge of the laws and regulations governing HIV/AIDS. In each of these legal aid centers, NGO staff and attorneys seek to bring impact litigation cases into the courts for adjudication, which help to define legal standards for the courts on new issue areas.

The NGO-based legal aid centers typically perform three kinds of functions related to spreading the rule of law for HIV/AIDS carriers. First, legal

aid centers provide information about the legal field as it relates to HIV/
AIDS. For example, in 2007 and 2008, NGOs and INGOs assembled legal
scholars and attorneys with expertise on HIV/AIDS in Yunnan to produce
two summaries and analyses of Chinese laws and regulations on HIV/
AIDS.[36] They typically offer a hotline telephone service and/or online message system to answer questions about HIV/AIDS and citizens' legal rights.
Legal aid centers also produce and distribute documents about the legal
system and HIV/AIDS carriers' rights. Second, legal aid centers provide
training to other attorneys, judicial authorities, and officials to help raise
knowledge of HIV/AIDS and relevant laws, as well as how to protect rights.
In 2010, the Yunnan legal aid center operated a training session for seventy-
one lawyers on HIV/AIDS law. Finally, legal aid centers provide legal services—including advocacy, representation in alternative dispute resolution,
and counsel in litigation—to clients. Except for the few attorneys who have
received training by legal aid centers specializing in HIV/AIDS-related law,
lawyers in private law firms generally do not have the expertise (or interest)
to defend HIV/AIDS carriers. Many HIV/AIDS carriers are impoverished, so
the pro bono services offered by the legal aid centers are crucial to retaining
counsel.[37] The emergence of legal aid centers with a focus on HIV/AIDS
demonstrates the fruits of cooperation between international and domestic
civil society groups and the emergence of new forms of advocacy by civil
society activists.

CHINESE GRASSROOTS NGOS—BOUNDED AUTONOMY

The model of state leadership and management of civil society described in
chapter 2 asserts that China's regime is able to shape the contours of civil
society and rein in oppositional activity. In particular, state authorities can
restrict civil society groups from registering and harass advocacy groups that
threaten regime stability. Below I analyze the experiences of a selected representative group of civil society organizations and their relations with the state
to demonstrate how the state attempts to constrain and use civil society
organizations for its own purposes.

AIDS Care China, founded in 2001 by Thomas Cai, exemplifies an organization that has worked closely with international donors and the Chinese
government. Centered in Yunnan Province where China had its earliest outbreak of HIV/AIDS and Guangdong Province, Thomas Cai founded AIDS
Care China to provide support for people living with HIV/AIDS. Cai, who is
HIV positive, has become an advocate for human rights for HIV/AIDS carriers, but his group's programs align with state goals for HIV/AIDS treatment and prevention.

In 2004, AIDS Care China established a community support group for people living with HIV/AIDS in Guangzhou, called "Red Ribbon Societies." By the end of 2009, AIDS Care China had opened thirty-five Red Ribbon Centers in four provinces.[38] The program has proved enormously successful, garnering partnerships and funding from several international sources including the CDC, Pangaea (with funds from the Bill and Melinda Gates Foundation), and the Clinton Health Access Initiative, among others. The Red Ribbon Centers operate in local hospitals to improve HIV/AIDS carriers' care and access to ART. The program has received national recognition because participants in the program enjoy a higher persistence rate in ART and mother-to-child transmission prevention treatments than those who do not participate in the program.[39] After AIDS Care China became involved with the Red Ribbon Centers, on average, the number of new AIDS carriers receiving treatment increased from 4.59 to 8.73 persons per site.[40] At the Red Ribbon Centers, the dropout rate for ART has declined from 3.63 percent to 1.17 percent of participants. At five of the six methadone maintenance treatment centers with which AIDS Care China cooperates to spread information about HIV prevention, a study of HIV-positive rates at the clinics was 12.17 percent, much lower than the 22.33 percent HIV-positive rate among intravenous drug users at other methadone maintenance treatment clinics.[41] AIDS Care China succeeds because (a) it reduces friction between HIV/AIDS patients and doctors, which arises because of the profit-driven nature of doctors and hospitals and the HIV/AIDS patients' lack of resources,[42] and (b) the organization's HIV-positive workers develop positive relations with HIV/AIDS patients.

For its excellent work, AIDS Care China and Thomas Cai have received provincial, national, and international recognition. In 2006, AIDS Care China was recognized by UNAIDS and the UN Development Programme for its contribution to community-based care. In 2008, Thomas Cai was given a special award by the Yunnan provincial government for his work, and in 2009, Premier Wen Jiabao included him in a special seminar on AIDS work in China.[43] China's government lauds AIDS Care China, in part, because it serves the interest of the state in helping to improve its AIDS treatment for high-risk individuals and AIDS carriers who are reluctant to cooperate with authorities. AIDS Care China, too, steers clear of overt political advocacy.

Aizhixing exemplifies an advocacy organization that has been subjected to state harassment. With its first programs starting in March 1994, Aizhixing Research Center was one of China's earliest grassroots organizations to focus on HIV/AIDS, but it was only in September 2002 that Aizhixing finally registered with the commercial bureau as an enterprise. As the first and one of the leading grassroots NGOs, many important figures in China's HIV/AIDS prevention and rights movement have passed through Aizhixing. When the organization registered as an enterprise, it wrote partnership papers among its leaders, Wan Yanhai, Hu Jia, and Zeng Jingyan. Wan Yanhai was an official in the ministry of health who left the ministry over disagreements on policies toward HIV/AIDS. Two others, Jia Ping and Li Dan, played important early roles in the organization and its advocacy work until they left the organization over disagreements with the direction of the organization. After leaving Aizhixing, Jia Ping was elected a representative to China's country coordinating mechanism, which dispenses Global Fund grants to organizations, and later founded China Global Watch. Li Dan, as described below, left the organization to focus his work on orphans left behind by the HIV/AIDS epidemic that ravaged Henan Province.

Since its founding, Aizhixing entered into advocacy work that embroiled it and its leadership in conflict with the government. The organization committed itself to advocate for the rights of disadvantaged segments of society, including commercial sex workers, LGBTs, ethnic minorities, and migrant workers. The organization has recruited a number of staff members from such disadvantaged communities to help with the organization's programs. Around 2004, Wan Yanhai asked Hu Jia (and his wife, Zeng Jingyan) to leave the organization because his democracy advocacy clearly overstepped the perceived boundary of "acceptable political advocacy." Ultimately, Hu was arrested in 2007 and convicted in March 2008 on charges of "inciting subversion to state power," for which he was imprisoned until June 2011.

Since 2005, a new focus of Aizhixing's advocacy work has been provision of legal aid services to AIDS carriers, but their efforts have been thwarted by the courts' resistance to hearing such cases and harassment of the organization and its leaders. Aizhixing's legal advocacy work drew attention and funding from international funders such as George Soros's Open Society Initiative and the American National Endowment for Democracy, organizations which the Chinese government views as potentially trying to destabilize China's regime. Aizhixing fights discrimination against HIV/AIDS carriers, sex workers, and ethnic minorities, as well as exposes officials' involvement in the blood scandal in central China. Wan Yanhai, Aizhixing's leader, worked with Gao Yaojie to initially publicize the scandal, and in the last decade provided advice and legal support to Tian Xi (and other AIDS carriers), a well-known activist who contracted AIDS from a blood transfusion.

Wan Yanhai, too, was detained and questioned by authorities on three occasions. In 2010, Wan and Aizhixing came under severe pressure from the government. The state used rules issued by State Administration of Foreign Exchange (SAFE) in March of 2010 (described in chapter 2), which made it more difficult for grassroots organizations to receive foreign funding, to harass Aizhixing and Wan. In the first half of 2010, officials twice examined the accounting books of Aizhixing, exploring sources of funding and expenditures, especially payment of taxes. Aizhixing is registered as a commercial enterprise and must pay taxes on all revenue. More inexplicable, the fire department went to Aizhixing's office to inspect for fire hazards, an act that confirms Aizhixing was targeted for harassment. Facing financial difficulties and subject to persistent political threat, in May 2010, Wan Yanhai fled China for the United States. [44] Aizhixing continues to operate programs in China, but it has a lowered profile, and individuals who have remained in the organization also have been subjected to arrest or detention.

Li Dan, who worked with Aizhixing in his early days of activism on HIV/ AIDS, went on to found his own organization, Orchid (Dongzhen). In August 2004, Li was detained and beaten by police. On more than one occasion, provincial officials have closed down his organization's programs, specifi- cally a school for orphans left behind by AIDS victims in Henan Province. Additionally, Chinese officials have impeded some efforts to spread litigious methods to NGOs working in the HIV/AIDS area such as the Korekata legal aid station for HIV/AIDS carriers that Orchid operates with Asia Catalyst, a New York–based organization. The Chinese government abruptly canceled a conference scheduled for August 2007 organized by Asia Catalyst and Or- chid, which would have brought together international and Chinese experts on AIDS law with more than two dozen Chinese organizations interested in providing legal aid to HIV/AIDS victims. [45] Without a sponsoring organiza- tion and the accompanying ties to patrons in the party-state, grassroots NGOs registered as commercial enterprises are left vulnerable to political winds in the country and political whims of local officials. When such organizations cross an unknown red line, the leaders and organizations may be harassed or shut down. While forthcoming changes in civil society organizations' regis- tration procedures, which include abandoning the sponsoring organization requirement, may provide greater leeway to organizations to advocate to the government, initial findings suggest that the state will continue to refuse registration to groups that pose a potential threat to the regime's legitimacy.

Another form of advocacy focuses on government policies. For example, the Union of People Living with HIV/AIDS, founded and led by Meng Lin, has worked to secure the right to ART and second-line drugs. Part of that effort has sought to establish Chinese production of ART pharmaceuticals to decrease the costs of drugs, which makes them more accessible to HIV/AIDS carriers. Although China provides free ART to HIV/AIDS carriers, Meng Lin has cautioned people about potential infringement of privacy that comes from registering for ART with the government. Therefore, he has advocated for inexpensive second-line ART drugs to be available for purchase on the market to those who fear exposure of their identity or for other reasons do not wish to register with the government to gain access to ART.

The proliferation of civil society organizations working on HIV/AIDS is impressive, as is the advocacy work that some groups have taken up. Such advocacy, however, comes at a price. The civil affairs bureaucracy is reluc-

tant to register AIDS organizations that strive to advocate forcefully for
people living with HIV/AIDS or for revisions to Chinese policies.[46] In fact, a
survey of AIDS civil society organizations found that only 36.7 percent were
formally registered.[47] Chinese authorities are more interested in cooperating
with organizations such as Thomas Cai's AIDS Care China because it helps
the state to improve delivery of social services to AIDS carriers. In other
words, the state is more willing to register and collaborate with civil society
organizations that are prepared to accept the regime's goals, as opposed to
advocating for changes to the state's policies.

A FRACTURED CIVIL SOCIETY: CHINA'S HIV/AIDS ORGANIZATIONS

Social movements in civil society are strong when the participants enjoy a
unified set of values, knowledge, goals, and methodology. In the case of
HIV/AIDS, Chinese officials, scientists, and NGO activists are deeply divided, undermining their capacity to act as a unified bloc to influence state
policy on HIV/AIDS. Divisions in Chinese civil society result, in part, from
the regulations on registration of civil society organizations. But divisions
also exist because of the personalities that are involved in leading grassroots
organizations. The state is able to exacerbate conflicts among grassroots
AIDS organizations due to its control over a growing share of the scarce
resources available to grassroots groups as international funders have begun
to retreat from China.

At the municipal level, well-placed persons in government units have
been able to overcome factionalism and to serve as central figures of local
activist networks. Such embedded activists can gather input from their com-
patriots in NGOs while also using their contacts with state agents to influence policies. In Shanghai, Xia Guomei, a scholar at the state-run Shanghai
Academy of Social Sciences who researches public health and HIV/AIDS,
has been able to serve as an embedded activist. She has sponsored conferences and workshops that brought together activists and attorneys who are
concerned about HIV/AIDS regulations. She worked with such groups to
help influence the rewriting of Shanghai's AIDS Regulations.[48] In cities with
much larger NGO communities than Shanghai such as Beijing, the local
group of NGOs can be deeply divided.

Beyond local networks, however, NGOs working on HIV/AIDS are split
into rival networks. A staff member in an international organization expressed frustration at their failed efforts to foster a more unified network of
HIV/AIDS groups: "We tried to support and bring together the people working on HIV into one common network. It is not so easy because there are two
large groups and one smaller group that we can't really get to work togeth-

er."[49] In part, organizations in the HIV/AIDS field are driven apart by personalities. The fractures in the movement simmer on a regular basis, but they typically boiled over during elections to the country coordinating mechanism (or CCM) which oversaw dispersion of funds from the UNAIDS fund on HIV/AIDS, Tuberculosis, and Malaria until the Global Fund withdrew from China at the end of 2012. The CCM brought together representatives of China's key organs on HIV/AIDS, multilateral organizations, INGOs and foundations, domestic NGOs, and the community of people living with HIV/AIDS (PLWHA). In order to introduce Chinese organizations to the practice of democracy, UNAIDS coordinates elections for three positions on the CCM—two for all NGOs and one to represent HIV/AIDS carriers. Early elections for Chinese representatives to the CCM generated controversy, including whether GONGOs have the right to vote for representatives and to vie for seats on the CCM. Wan Yanhai and other leaders of grassroots NGOs have charged that GONGOs are essentially appendages of the state, so they should not be able to vote in the NGO elections.[50] In the first two rounds of elections, activists challenged the election results, and the winners (Jia Ping and Wang Shaogang) faced sharp criticism from NGO leaders, especially Wan's faction. Under such criticism, the two elected CCM members—one representing all NGOs and the other representing the PLWHA community—chose to resign rather than continue to endure such condemnation.[51]

The HIV/AIDS sector of Chinese civil society (broadly defined) includes state agents, grassroots NGOs, GONGOs, multilateral organizations, and INGOs and foundations. From this odd admixture of social forces, it is not surprising that conflicting interests and clashes arise. Meng Lin criticized the situation as follows: "I liken the situation of Chinese civil society to a busy Chinese intersection without a traffic light. Everyone is trying to get places, but people run into each other. The government is to blame; the INGOs are to blame; and Chinese NGOs are to blame."[52] Despite UNAIDS' efforts to coordinate international actors with China's state and domestic NGOs, deep divides remain within and between key constituencies.

The growth of civil society organizations focusing on HIV/AIDS and the rise of legal aid stations suggest a vibrancy of civil society, but the authorities also act to restrain civil society advocacy within acceptable boundaries by not registering or harassing organizations that do not subordinate their programs to the regime's interest in social service delivery.[53] A comparison of organizations that thrive and receive government recognition such as Thomas Cai's AIDS Care China to organizations that are subjected to strong political pressure to rein in their advocacy such as Aizhixing reveals how the state can shape civil society and subordinate its development around the goal of improving delivery of social programs to HIV/AIDS carriers and high-risk populations.

ENVIRONMENTAL CIVIL SOCIETY GROUPS

Environmental NGOs comprise one of the most important and strongest sectors of Chinese civil society in terms of development of high-capacity organizations that are affecting state policy making. As seen with the above examples from AIDS civil society groups, China's state has given greater scope to environmental groups as it has confronted a growing environmental crisis and recognized the limits of its capacity to rein in pollution. Also analogous to AIDS organizations, environmental groups have contributed to growing rights-based contention inside and outside the courts. Attorneys pursuing environmental litigation have not been subject to much harassment and intimidation, at least from central authorities, though chapters 6 and 7 detail courts' refusal to hear environmental cases. With a very small number of exceptions, environmental civil society groups and activists have been permitted to operate without threat of being shut down or arrested.

Emergence of Environmental Civil Society Groups

As noted in chapter 2, Chinese civil society development was spurred by China's participation in UN-sponsored conferences, in the case of environmental groups, by the UN Conference on Environment and Development (UNCED), held in Rio in 1992. Chinese official delegates at that conference discovered that China was unique in not having NGOs in their delegation to attend the conference. In reaction to their experience at UNCED and in anticipation of the 1995 UN Conference on Women held in Beijing, China began to encourage the formation of a small number of civil society organizations that were not attached to the regime. In fact, some international environmental NGOs had already worked in China for more than a decade, including the World Wildlife Fund (WWF). In 1979, Chinese authorities invited WWF to China to help to save the panda from extinction. The WWF helped China to establish sanctuaries for the panda population and gradually expanded their mission in China to advocate for sustainable development. Although authorities were quite cautious with regard to INGOs' presence in China, the WWF's initial, narrow focus on preserving an endangered species allowed them to get a foot in the door.

Chinese environmental NGOs began operations with limited goals that did not challenge the state, though their approach has become more contentious over the last two decades. In 1993, the first Chinese environmental civil society organization, Friends of Nature, was formed by Liang Congjie, an academic who hailed from a well-known family. Initially, the National Environmental Protection Agency (NEPA), a precursor to the MEP, encouraged Liang to found the organization as an umbrella group under the NEPA, but Liang decided to found a more autonomous organization on his own.[54] A year later, Global Village Beijing was founded under the leadership of Liao Xiaoyi, a television journalist. The WWF's model of focusing on less-politicized goals and advocacy provided an example of a cautious but politically viable approach for the early development of Chinese environmental civil society groups. Both Friends of Nature and Global Village Beijing initially provided environmental education and advocated for endangered species and the maintenance of biodiversity in China. Friends of Nature sought to save the Tibetan antelope from extinction and to prevent illegal logging in western provinces. Such efforts by civil society groups impeded some economic development efforts, but China also gained international recognition for their preservation work. Many groups, especially university-based environmental groups, helped to spread information about conservation, recycling, and sustainable development. For example, Baike, a student environmental group in Guangzhou, encouraged bicycle riding as a way to lower air pollution. Among its many activities, Grassroots Community in Shanghai helped to organize neighborhood beautification efforts that picked up trash and planted flowers and trees in urban spaces.

Gradually, work to maintain biodiversity or to protect endangered species took on a more overt political tone when civil society organizations challenged major industrial or energy-related projects, some of them backed by national ministries. For example, in 2003 Green Watershed, led by Yu Xiaogang, fought to halt the damming of the Nu, Lancang (Mekong), and Jinsha Rivers in Yunnan Province. The grounds for Green Watershed's advocacy was the preservation of biodiversity and the way of life for the fifty thousand residents who would be displaced in Yunnan, but the effort to halt the dam project was politically charged because it took on major energy interests in China. Yu Xiaogang mobilized communities in the potentially affected areas to argue against the dam projects, a novel approach in China's environmental movement that proved effective.[55] In 2004, Premier Wen Jiabao suspended the Nu dam project for further study. In addition, Green Watershed lobbied banks to deny new credit to factories that violated pollution regulations as part of a "green credit" system. Under the green credit system, Green Watershed monitors and publishes major banks' loans to polluting factories, and the group awards a special prize to the bank with the best environmental record. The green credit project seeks to protect the environment by cutting off funding to China's worst polluters and to foster a more transparent financial system that takes account of environmental sustainability. For his work, Yu Xiaogang won the 2006 Goldman Environmental Prize.

Activism on the environmental protection front has not come without a few activists and civil society organizations suffering from state harassment, especially in the years leading up to the Beijing Olympics in 2008, which was a very tense time in Chinese civil society. Tan Kai owned a computer repair store but became interested in environmental activism after a series of violent environmental protests in his home province of Zhejiang in the mid-2000s. He and five colleagues decided to establish a new organization, Green Watch, to monitor pollution issues. The six members of Green Watch were detained for opening a bank account in the group's name without having registered the group, but only Tan Kai was arrested and tried for "illegally obtaining state secrets." Zhejiang authorities also closed down Green Watch.[56] In 2005, the National People's Congress named Wu Lihong an "environmental warrior" for his decades of individual work monitoring and publicizing chemical factories' pollution being dumped into Lake Tai in Wuxi, Jiangsu Province. Two years later and following harassment, threat, and detention by local authorities, a local court found Wu guilty of extortion, and he was forced to serve three years in jail.[57] More recently, in 2012, Liu Futang was arrested and convicted for "illegal business activities" related to his self-published book on deforestation in Hainan Province, China. In April 2012, Liu had won a prize for his environmental journalism, and the book that he published had been given away for free, so Liu claimed that its publication involved no business activities. A Hainan court convicted him of the charges but issued a suspended three-year sentence.[58]

Despite the above setbacks, environmental civil society groups have proliferated over the last two decades. According to some estimates, by 2012 the number of officially registered Chinese environmental NGOs reached 3,500, and there are likely an equal number of civil society organizations registered as businesses or not registered at all.[59] The large number of civil society organizations evinces the state's, especially the MEP's, tolerance for civil society groups that contribute to environmental education and governance. State tolerance for civil society activities must also be understood against a backdrop of a rising tide of environmental protests, many of them violent. In 2005, Chinese authorities acknowledged an estimated fifty thousand pollution-related protests. From the vantage point of China's state, institutionalized means of addressing pollution such as with the help of civil society groups and environmental litigation are more appealing than protest.

Environmental civil society organizations have become increasingly ambitious and assertive in pursuit of their goals. The efforts of Chinese grassroots organizations have been abetted by their contacts with media—mainly domestic, but also international—and funding from INGOs.[60] As environmental consciousness among Chinese has risen, popular demand for news coverage on environmental issues has grown. Grassroots organizations have successfully used ties to the media to spread stories about environmental disasters, and such coverage, in turn, provides some protection against reprisals by local officials. Many foundations have supplied funding to environmental advocacy groups to cover their expenses, although work can be hampered by the limited duration of programs covered by international funders. The contacts with international bodies and the international recognition that is granted to Chinese environmental activists also makes it more difficult for the state to crack down on environmental groups.

Ma Jun's organization, IPE (Institute of Public and Environmental Affairs), exemplifies a new pattern of environmental activism that draws together policy advocacy, international collaboration, and savvy use of media. A well-known environmental journalist in Hong Kong, Ma Jun wrote the popular book *China's Water Crisis* in 1999, published in China and abroad, which became a clarion call for China to address its water pollution crisis. Ma Jun later collaborated with the Natural Resources Defense Council (NRDC) to begin a pollution monitoring project throughout China. The IPE maintains an online database of air pollution levels in China's major cities, and with the NRDC annually publishes the Pollution Information Transparency Index (PITI). The report ranks each Chinese city against eight indices for levels of transparency on providing information about environmental pollution, including the ease of applying for environmental information from the government and the use of fines against polluters. [61] The goals of the PITI project are to use monitoring and reporting to encourage cities to comply with regulations on pollution, governments to provide environmental information, and authorities to respond to citizen complaints about the environment.

Environmental Legal Aid Groups

In the last two decades, one of the most important developments in China's environmental civil society has been the emergence of NGOs that focus on providing legal services to pollution victims. The leading organization of this type is the Center of Legal Aid for Pollution Victims (CLAPV), which is affiliated with the China University of Political Science and Law in Beijing. CLAPV was established in 1998 and regularly collaborates with international organizations such as the NRDC to provide training courses for environmental lawyers and judges. By 2010, CLAPV had provided training to over six hundred lawyers and three hundred legal officials, thus assembling a legal network throughout China. [62] CLAPV also directly helps pollution victims by operating a hotline for citizens to inform the Center about pollution cases that may warrant legal investigation and filing of complaints. CLAPV is highly regarded in China and abroad, receiving financial support from a number of international organizations and foundations, including the Ford Foundation, the NRDC, and the UN Environment Programme (UNEP). From the many phone calls and other communications that they receive regarding pollution cases, the small cadre of CLAPV lawyers must select only a few cases to investigate and work on in a year. In 2012, however, CLAPV's leader, Wang Canfa, established a new public interest environmental law firm to provide legal aid to pollution victims. With a team of three lawyers, the law firm can handle approximately fifty cases per year.

CLAPV has been granted a fair amount of autonomy to handle cases because their work stays within the parameters of the law and acts in line with the interests of the MEP. As an environmental attorney told me, "The MEP benefits from environmental lawsuits. At the local level, environmental protection bureau officials face a conflict of interests between supporting local businesses and monitoring the environment. Legal cases help to strengthen their roles in monitoring the environment."[63] Although CLAPV attorneys are monitored by local officials during site inspections, they have not been directly threatened, detained, or arrested. Indeed, a former leader of the MEP (then SEPA) and many officials at the MEP have participated in CLAPV-sponsored programs and shared information about new government regulations with CLAPV attorneys.[64]

In recent years, other civil society groups have begun to offer legal assistance to pollution victims. The All-China Environmental Federation (ACEF), a GONGO attached to the MEP, was organized in 2005 to serve as a bridge between the MEP and civil society in the implementation of environmental protection measures and programs. The ACEF has a legal division that investigates pollution cases and offers legal assistance to citizens trying to protect their rights and to halt illegal pollution. As an organization attached to the MEP, the ACEF operates within the parameters of the MEP's interests and enjoys a great deal of authority in conducting its investigations. Like CLAPV, the ACEF also receives significant international backing from groups such as the UNEP to train people in the environmental bureaucracy and the judiciary on environmental laws and regulations. The ACEF has developed a strong network of attorneys throughout China who help ACEF lawyers with environmental cases outside of Beijing.

In addition to the CLAPV and the ACEF, which are the two main environmental legal aid units in China, a small number of legal aid associations and environmental groups have environmental law units. For example, the Center for the Protection of Rights of Disadvantaged Citizens attached to Wuhan University's Law School has an environmental legal aid program. Citizens can receive legal advice and, if warranted, legal representation in litigation from the Center's attorneys. Finally, a small number of environmental civil society organizations have attorneys who provide legal advice and services to pollution victims. For example, Friends of Nature, the first environmental civil society organization founded in China, has a legal aid program as part of its unit working on citizen participation. In 2012, Friends of Nature was able to join with Chongqing Green Volunteers Alliance to represent citizens in a public interest litigation case in Yunnan, which I analyze fully in chapter 7.

THE POLITICS OF CIVIL SOCIETY DEVELOPMENT
AND LEGAL AID

Chinese civil society is opening up, but it remains partly closed and a tenuous place to operate for some organizations. Across the landscape of Chinese civil society, HIV/AIDS and environmental groups have proliferated, and the state grants them more leeway relative to groups working on human rights, religion, or other extremely sensitive issues. The large number of civil society groups working on environmental protection and HIV/AIDS demonstrates state tolerance for such groups, but the HIV/AIDS sector, in particular, shows the fragmentation of civil society caused by the registration rules, many types of participants in civil society, and competition for funding among organizations. While there is growing, widespread societal support for the environmental movement in particular, rules on civil society registration have created a large number of small organizations with very limited capacity. A few large organizations such as IPE, Friends of Nature, and Global Village Beijing have developed, but they are more exceptions than the rule and remain smaller and with less capacity than GONGOs.

Groups working on HIV/AIDS and environmental issues raise human rights concerns, and close analysis of civil society organizations that have emerged to advocate for HIV/AIDS carriers and environmental pollution victims reveals that state authorities attempt to winnow out potentially threatening advocacy groups through registration procedures and selective harassment of organizations. Advocacy can take many forms, and legal advocacy, despite being anchored in laws passed by the state, is an area that can run afoul of the regime's interests. Legal aid stations that are attached to a law school such as the one at Wuhan University and CLAPV at China University of Political Science and Law enjoy a degree of security because of their connection to state-run universities, which can monitor the centers' behavior and litigation efforts. If university administrators believe that the legal aid centers' lawyers are becoming too contentious, the university can cut ties with the legal aid center, as Beijing University did with the Women's Legal Research and Services Center headed by Guo Jianmei. In that case, in 2010 Beijing University officially severed ties with the center, but the center maintains a relationship with Beijing University's law school. CLAPV and the Wuhan University legal aid centers are able to offer services to pollution victims because their work aligns with the interests of the MEP by helping to constrain local polluters.

Legal aid centers that are not attached to a university are far more vulnerable to closure and the associated attorneys to harassment. For example, in 2009 Beijing authorities closed down the Open Constitution Initiative (Gongmeng), which represented a number of human rights activists, after fining it 1.42 million yuan (208,000 dollars) for tax evasion. Authorities shut down the organization shortly after the group organized pro bono lawyers to pursue a class action suit over the sale of milk tainted with melamine. Several lawyers associated with the Open Constitution Initiative have been detained and threatened, and in January 2014 one of the group's organizers, Xu Zhiyong, was sentenced to four years for "assembling a crowd to disrupt public order," a charge stemming from dinner gatherings to discuss Chinese legal issues and the New Citizens' Movement.[65] Legal aid centers that offer services to HIV/AIDS carriers such as Aizhixing and Yirenping and their leaders have been subjected to harassment and incarceration. Aizhixing, which was the first legal aid center to provide services to HIV/AIDS carriers has had a number of its leading members—Wan Yanhai, Hu Jia, Li Xiongbing, and Ilham Tohti—subjected to detention, interrogation, intimidation, and incarceration. Lawyers associated with Yirenping, an organization committed to fighting discrimination against HIV/AIDS carriers and other disadvantaged citizens, have also been detained and interrogated. Li Fangping and Yu Fangqiang, who enjoy high international profiles for their work on AIDS antidiscrimination cases, have been detained and subjected to questioning, while their organizations have also received warnings from local authorities about their groups' operations. Such attempts at intimidation of HIV/AIDS advocacy groups stand out in comparison to the work of environmental legal aid organizations that proceed without direct intervention by the state. Rather than intimidate or shut down environmental activist attorneys such as those at CLAPV or Friends of Nature, the state organized a legal aid station through the state-affiliated ACEF in order to compete with and lead the process of environmental litigation. The MEP and other authorities recognize the need for such litigation, but they seek to modulate its direction, an issue that is addressed fully in chapter 7.

Aizhixing, the Open Constitution Initiative, and Yirenping (a public interest law firm), who all were subjected to closure or harassment by state officials, share a common feature—they all received significant funding from foreign foundations or organizations. In fact, many grassroots NGOs in China receive foreign funding, but as one interview speculated, the state has a triage system of foreign foundations, based on security concerns. The secure (and approved) list of foreign funds includes UN funds; the middle group on the list (requiring closer monitoring) includes the Ford Foundation, Asia Foundation, Gates Foundation, and Clinton Foundation; while the foreign funding from the American National Endowment for Democracy and the Open Society Initiative draws the authorities' close scrutiny.[66] Chinese NGOs that receive funding from foundations and INGOs on the first or second lists have not been subject to government inspections in the same way as NGOs who receive funding from the third list of sources. The AIDS legal aid organizations that have been targeted by the state received funding from the third category of foreign funders.

Chinese authorities have used new regulations from SAFE on international contributions to selectively harass civil society organizations that engage in contentious advocacy. Most grassroots NGOs in China lack more than a few personnel, and their technical and professional qualifications are often lacking, so keeping a sound set of accounting books proves a challenge for most organizations, although international donors have given strong encouragement to greater professionalization of these organizations. In other words, many organizations could be subject to audits and financial penalties, if not closure, were officials to check them. Selective application of the new rules on foreign sources of funding serves two purposes for the government. First, China has been able to curtail the activities of some NGOs that receive funding from sources that the government suspects are motivated by goals of changing China's political system. Second, by targeting a selected group of NGOs for their ties to particular foreign foundations, the government can intimidate other organizations from developing similar ties, an application of the Chinese expression "kill the chicken to scare the monkey." Here again, however, AIDS organizations have been subjected to greater state monitoring and closure than environmental groups, despite rising levels of contentiousness from both sets of civil society organizations.

NOTES

1. Elements of this chapter were originally published in Scott Wilson, "Introduction: Chinese NGOs—International and Online Linkages," *Journal of Contemporary China* 21, no. 76 (July 2012), 551–67. The author wishes to thank the publisher of the journal for permission to reprint those elements here.

2. China AIDS Information Network, *2010 China HIV/AIDS CSO/CBO Directory* (Beijing: China AIDS Information Network, 2010).

3. Hui Li, Nana Taona Kuo, Hui Liu, Christine Korhonen, Ellenie Pound, Haoyan Guo, Liz Smith, Hui Xue, and Jiangping Sun, "From Spectators to Implementers: Civil Society Organizations Involved in AIDS Programmes in China," *International Journal of Epidemiology* 39 (2010), Supplement 2, ii68.

4. Li et al., "From Spectators to Implementers," table 1.

5. Zunyou Wu, Sheena G. Sullivan, Yu Wang, Mary Jane Rotheram, and Roger Detels, "Evolution of China's Response to HIV/AIDS," *Lancet* 369 (24 February 2007), 684; Joan Kaufman, "Turning Points in China's AIDS Response," *China: An International Journal* 8, no. 1 (March 2010), 75–77; Jonathan Schwartz, "The Impact of Crises on Social Service Provision in China: The State and Society Respond to SARS," in *State and Society Responses to Social Welfare Needs in China: Serving the People*, eds. Jonathan Schwartz and Shawn Shieh (London and New York: Routledge, 2009), 135–55.

6. Jacques deLisle, "Atypical Pneumonia and Ambivalent Law and Politics: SARS and the Response to SARS in China," *Temple Law Review*, no. 193, 205–6; Kaufman, "Turning Points," 75–77.

7. deLisle, "Atypical Pneumonia," 209.

8. Cong Cao, "SARS: 'Waterloo' of Chinese Science," *China: An International Journal* 2, no. 2 (September 2004), 262–86.

9. Cao, "SARS: 'Waterloo' of Chinese Science," 209; Wu et al., "Evolution of China's Response," 684.

10. deLisle, "Atypical Pneumonia," 221.

11. Interview 36.

12. Mengjie Han, Qingfeng Chen, Yang Hao, Yifei Hu, Dongmei Wang, Yan Gao, and Marc Bulterys, "Design and Implementation of a China Comprehensive AIDS Response Programme (China CARES), 2003-2008," *International Journal of Epidemiology* 39 (2010), ii149.

13. Weishengbu 卫生部, "*Weishengbu Bangongting Guanyu Yinfa 'Aizibing Zonghe Fangzhi Shifanqu Gongzuo Zhidao Fangan' de Tongzhi* 卫生部办公厅关于印发 '艾滋病综合防治示范区工作指导方案' 的通知 (Circular on the China CARES Policy)," issued 14 May 2004, article 4(5 and 6).

14. Weishengbu, *Circular on the China CARES Policy*, article 4(6(2)).

15. Han et al., ii52.

16. Weishengbu, *Circular on the China CARES Policy*, article 6(8).

17. USAID and Health Policy Initiative, *Assessment of the HIV Legal Environment: Yunnan, China,* (Kunming, China: RTI International, 2008), 2; Talha Khan Burki, "Discrimination against People with HIV Persists in China," *Lancet* 377, 22 January 2011, 287.

18. Yanhai Wan, Ran Hu, Ran Guo, and Linda Arnade, "Discrimination against People with HIV/AIDS in China," *Equal Rights Review* 4, 17.

19. Wan et al., "Discrimination against People with HIV/AIDS," 21.

20. Wan et al., "Discrimination against People with HIV/AIDS," 17.

21. Interview 83.

22. Interview 35.

23. Interviews 69 and 83.

24. Interview 42.

25. Interview 83.

26. Guosheng Deng, "The Decline of Foreign Aid and the Dilemma of Chinese Grassroots NGOs," *Religions and Christianity in Today's China* III, no. 1 (2013), 29.

27. Data on giving to Chinese grassroots civil society groups suggest that international support has been modest, while international funders have given more support to GONGOs and state units. Anthony J. Spires, "US Foundations Boost Chinese Government, Not NGOs," *YaleGlobal*, 28 March 2012, accessed 24 August 2014, http://yaleglobal.yale.edu/content/us-foundations-boost-chinese-government-not-ngos. Yet others have argued that international funding was particularly important in the early stages of grassroots civil society development. Guosheng Deng, "The Decline of Foreign Aid and the Dilemma of Chinese Grassroots NGOs," *Religions and Christianity in Today's China* III, no. 1 (2013), 24–31.

28. UN Theme Group on HIV/AIDS in China, *HIV/AIDS: China's Titanic Peril* (New York: United Nations, June 2002), 25–26.

29. Interview 32.

30. Interviews 2, 19, and 35.

31. Office of the United Nations High Commissioner for Human Rights and the Joint United Nations Programme on HIV/AIDS. 2006. *International Guidelines on HIV/AIDS and Human Rights, 2006 Consolidated Version* (Geneva, Switzerland: UN HCHR and UNAIDS, 2006), 16.

32. Office of the United Nations High Commissioner for Human Rights and the Joint United Nations Programme on HIV/AIDS, *International Guidelines*, 16–18.

33. UNAIDS, *Human Rights and AIDS: Now More than Ever* (New York: Open Society Institute, 2007), 3–4.

34. Interview 35.

35. Interview 67.

36. USAID and Health Policy Initiative, *Assessment of the HIV Legal Environment: Yunnan, China.*

37. Interview 72.

38. Ministry of Health, *China 2010 UNGASS Country Progress Report (2008-2009)* (Beijing: Ministry of Health), 52,http://data.unaids.org/pub/Report/2010/china_2010_country_progress_report_en.pdf.

39. Ministry of Health, *China 2010 UNGASS Report (2008-2009)*, 52.

40. Ministry of Health, *China 2010 UNGASS Report (2008-2009)*, 52.

41. Ministry of Health, *China 2010 UNGASS Report (2008-2009)*, 53.

42. Interview 73.

43. Ministry of Health, *China 2010 UNGASS Report (2008-2009)*, 51.

44. Peter Ford, "Another AIDS Activist, Wan Yanhai, Flees China," *Christian Science Monitor*, 10 May 2010, accessed 12 May 2010,http://www.csmonitor.com/World/Asia-Pacific/2010/0510/Another-AIDS-activist-Wan-Yanhai-flees-China.

45. Daniel Schearf, "Chinese Authorities Prevent Multinational AIDS Rights Conference," *Voice of America News*, 29 July 2007, http://www.voanews.com/english/archive/2007-07/2007-07-29-voa15.cfm.

46. Interview 97.

47. Cited in Li et al., "From Spectators to Implementers," ii65.

48. Interview 46.

49. Interview 32.

50. Ning Rui 宁锐, *"Gongmin Shehui de Suoying—CCM Xuanju Wuhan Huiyi Jishi* 公民社会的缩影—CCM 选举武汉会议记事" (The Microcosm of Civil Society—The Record of the CCM Election at the Wuhan Conference), *Zhongguo Fazhan Jianbao* 中国发展简报 (China Development Brief), December 2006, accessed 24 August 2014, http://www.chinadevelopmentbrief.org.cn/qikanarticleview.php?id=577.

51. Interview 74.

52. Interview 67.

53. Jessica C. Teets, "Let Many Civil Societies Bloom: The Rise of Consultative Authoritarianism in China," *China Quarterly*, no. 213 (March 2013), 19–38, develops a similar argument on the development of civil society and improvements in social service delivery under authoritarianism.

54. Elizabeth Economy, *The River Runs Black: The Environmental Challenge to China's Future* (Ithaca and New York: Cornell University Press, 2004), 154.

55. Economy, *The River Runs Black*, 166–67.

56. Fei Xing幸菲, *"'Luse Guancha' Faqiren Tan Kai Zao Zhonggong Daibu* '绿色观察'发起人谭凯遭中共逮捕" ('Green Watch' Founder, Tan Kai Meets with Chinese Communist Party Arrest), *Da Jiyuan* 大纪元 (Epoch Times), 26 December 2006, accessed 16 August 2014. http://www.epochtimes.com/gb/5/12/26/n1167535.htm

57. Economy, *The River Runs Black*, 177.

58. Keith B. Richburg, "Chinese Environmental Activist Faces Prison Sentence for Publishing Books," *Washington Post*, 12 October 2012, accessed 24 August 2014,http://www.washingtonpost.com/world/chinese-environmental-activist-faces-prison-sentence-for-publishing-books/2012/10/12/86e56f90-145a-11e2-9a39-1f5a7f6fe945_story.html.

59. Sha Liu, "Environmental NGOs Grow across China but Still Struggle for Support," *Global Times*, 12 June 2012, accessed 14 March 2014,http://www.globaltimes.cn/content/714330.shtml.

60. Andrew Mertha, "'Fragmented Authoritarianism 2.0': Political Pluralization in the Chinese Policy Process," *China Quarterly* 200 (December 2009), 997 and *passim*, discusses the positive role of the media in civil society development. Lei Xie, "China's Environmental Activism in the Age of Globalization," Working Papers on Transnational Politics. London: City University of London, 2009, 9, discusses the important role that international NGOs have played in the development of Chinese environmental civil society.

61. Gongzhong Huanjing Yanjiu Zhongxin (IPE) Meiguo Ziran Ziyuan Baohu Weiyuanhui 公众环境研究中心 美国自然资源保护委员会 (NRDC), *Huanjing Xinxi Gongkai Jiannan Pobing* 环境信息公开艰难破冰 (Open Environmental Information: Difficulty Breaking the Ice) (Beijing: IPE and NRDC, 2009), 15.

62. Interview 75.

63. Interview 75.

64. Interview 26.

65. Andrew Jacobs and Chris Buckley, "China Sentences Xu Zhiyong, Legal Activist, to 4 Years in Prison," *New York Times*, 26 January 2014, accessed 20 August 2014,http://www.nytimes.com/2014/01/27/world/asia/china-sentences-xu-zhiyong-to-4-years-for-role-in-protests.html?_r=0.

66. Interviews 70 and 77.

Chapter Five

HIV/AIDS Carriers Settling for Discrimination

Legal efforts to help HIV/AIDS carriers by civil society organizations and activist attorneys present a conundrum: lawyers at specialized legal aid centers have advised many HIV/AIDS carriers on how to protect their rights, but they have represented very few clients in court.[1] Attorneys who advocate for HIV/AIDS carriers have tried just a handful of cases (if any), and, until 2009, they had never litigated in the important area of discrimination. The paucity of legal cases is perplexing in light of the large number of HIV/AIDS victims in China, government culpability during China's blood scandal in the 1990s, and widespread discrimination in the areas of access to health care, education, and employment.[2] Why have the courts tried so few lawsuits involving Chinese HIV/AIDS carriers? This chapter seeks to understand the institutional, political, and societal impediments to legal action by HIV/AIDS carriers in China.

Instead of litigation, legal aid lawyers have employed alternative dispute resolution, primarily negotiating out-of-court settlements. Legal aid stations seek to try impact litigation cases and to change popular attitudes toward HIV/AIDS carriers' legal rights, but they are often forced to negotiate settlements, which are struck without formal legal judgment or society's knowledge. Usually, the settlements provide HIV/AIDS carriers with financial compensation in exchange for instituting discriminatory practices such as restricting an employee's right to work or right to education. To borrow Siri Gloppen's terms, settlement partially succeeds in the "material sense," which "improves the situation of the litigants . . . with regard to the health condition in question" but fails in the "social senses," which would "make the health system more equitable and benefit members of society whose right to health is more at risk."[3] Settlements may address some of the individual complai-

119

nants' material needs without providing benefits to classes of complainants. Such court settlements fall short of a "rights revolution," to use Charles Epp's term, in which courts provide judgments that extend rights to a class of citizens.

In countries with strong rule of law systems, litigation is used to address prejudice, extend rights to new communities of people, and bring actors' everyday practice into closer compliance with the law. In China, civil society organizations and activist attorneys have sought to bring Chinese laws into compliance with international norms on the governance of HIV/AIDS and then to use litigation and legal advocacy to generate social change, namely improvement in the rights and conditions of HIV/AIDS carriers. A Shanghai lawyer whom I interviewed noted that litigation helps to close the gap between the "laws on the books" and the "laws in the streets."[4] Closing that gap has been a difficult task because societal prejudices are deep, institutional interests of government agents strong, and Chinese laws governing AIDS are contradictory and weakly enforced. Confounding matters, Chinese courts have refused to hear many cases related to HIV/AIDS. In countries that adhere to rule of law, courts are able to address social conflicts and create new protections for emerging communities and activists.[5] Although China is making progress toward rule of law, lingering political influence over the courts has limited the work of Chinese citizens, attorneys, and civil society organizations to protect HIV/AIDS carriers' rights.

Litigation and other legal means to pursue justice constitute a potentially important element of governing HIV/AIDS. The right to health is a core element of the UN Universal Declaration on Human Rights that has been elaborated to protect HIV/AIDS carriers. In 1996, the UN Commission on Human Rights "resolved that the term 'or other status' used in several human rights instruments 'should be interpreted to include health status, including HIV/AIDS' and that discrimination on the basis of actual or presumed HIV/AIDS is prohibited," providing a broad extension of human rights to HIV/AIDS carriers.[6] China's government has made significant progress toward adopting international human rights concerns for HIV/AIDS carriers in its laws and policies, but its laws are vaguely defined and poorly enforced by government officials. Litigation offers one avenue to hold the government accountable for its failure to secure health-related rights for citizens.[7] Repeated litigation can increase pressure to secure health-care rights for, and reduce discriminatory practices against, Chinese HIV/AIDS carriers. Litigation encourages related social movements to press forward on their claims for rights to health care and against discrimination.[8] The following pages will explore the types of cases that HIV/AIDS carriers have sought to address through legal means, the reason that most cases have shifted to alternative dispute resolution such as mediation, and a wave of protests, media mobilization, and lawsuits related to antidiscrimination cases brought by HIV/AIDS carriers that began in 2010. The recent wave of mobilized protests and litiga-tion exemplifies AIDS carriers' frustration in trying to get their lawsuits into the courts and the complementary relationship between protest and legal action in China.

LEGAL AND REGULATORY CONTEXT OF HIV/AIDS CARRIERS' RIGHTS

HIV/AIDS is a relatively new disease, and international norms on AIDS-related human rights have formed slowly over the last three decades. The UN General Assembly's Declaration of Commitment on HIV/AIDS provided a nonbinding set of guideposts for international, domestic, and civil society responsibilities for addressing HIV/AIDS.[9] *The Handbook for Legislators on HIV/AIDS, Law and Human Rights*, produced by Inter-Parliamentary Union and UNAIDS, was an important step toward codifying best practices on HIV/AIDS law.[10] To help legislatures bring their national laws and policies into conformity with emerging international norms on human rights, UNAIDS and the Inter-Parliamentary Union constructed a handbook for legislators around the world that synthesized and elaborated the body of human rights norms on HIV/AIDS. The handbook identified ten key human rights for HIV/AIDS carriers, including nondiscrimination and equality before the law; equal access to health; privacy; access to education and information; freedom from inhuman, degrading treatment or punishment; autonomy, liberty, and security of the person; sharing of scientific advancement and its benefits; employment; participation in political and cultural life; and marriage and founding of a family.[11] In addition to enumerating key human rights, the handbook provides a set of guidelines for states to improve their approach to HIV/AIDS, including the following: providing access to medical services and medication at reasonable prices,[12] guaranteeing HIV/AIDS carriers the freedom to express oneself and to form groups,[13] providing legal support services to HIV/AIDS carriers,[14] and addressing discrimination and underly-ing societal prejudices against HIV/AIDS carriers.[15] These recommendations inform advocacy for rights of HIV/AIDS carriers by international non-governmental organizations, multilateral organizations, and, increasingly, Chinese civil society organizations.

Over the last two decades, Chinese laws and regulations have partially moved toward adoption of international norms on HIV/AIDS carriers' rights, including antidiscrimination principles. For example, Article 21 of the Provi-sions for the Monitoring and Control of AIDS stipulates that units and indi-viduals may not discriminate against AIDS carriers and their families, and that AIDS carriers and their families have the right to keep their status private.[16] The Law of the People's Republic of China on the Prevention and

Treatment of Infectious Diseases states that "individuals and work units cannot discriminate against carriers, former carriers, and possible carriers of infectious disease."[17] Article 3 of Regulations on AIDS Prevention and Treatment offers similar protection against discrimination in the areas of education, employment, medical treatment, and marriage for HIV/AIDS carriers and their families.[18] Unfortunately, the loosely written laws and weak enforcement mechanisms in AIDS-related legal instruments have created a significant gap between rights and benefits extended in the letter of the law and the practice of securing rights in society and even the courts. In particular, the antidiscrimination article of the Provisions for the Monitoring and Control of AIDS is quite broad and lacks implementation regulations to define its application.[19] The Provisions outlaw discrimination, but they do not specify that people with HIV/AIDS can file suit if discrimination occurs.[20] While the antidiscrimination articles in Chinese laws may appear strong, without implementation and enforcement guidelines, they lack teeth.

More positively, at the end of 2003, China's government rolled out its "Four Free, One Care" (*simian, yiguan huai*) policy (described in chapter 3), which addressed many AIDS carriers' material needs. The improvement in policies toward, and legal protections for, HIV/AIDS carriers has resulted from collaborative work of transnational advocacy networks linking Chinese civil society organizations with UN agencies, foreign foundations, and international nongovernment organizations. The networks diffuse knowledge of international legal norms and press Chinese officials to come into compliance with such standards.[21] For example, AIDS groups in Shanghai, who were knowledgeable about protocols in foreign countries, have used their ties to academics who serve as policy advisors to the municipal government to press for harm-reduction strategies (such as needle exchanges) in the writing of city regulations on AIDS protection.[22] Legal aid centers in some major cities seek to bring impact litigation cases in the areas of tort, discrimination, and access to information claims into the courts for adjudication in order to defend HIV/AIDS carriers' rights.

STATE ATTEMPTS TO KEEP HIV/AIDS SOCIAL CONFLICT OUT OF THE COURTS

Historically, Chinese citizens have preferred nonlitigious settlement of social conflict.[23] Since 1978, however, Chinese citizens have exhibited a growing interest in using courts to defend their rights, but the state has attempted to channel disputes toward administrative resolutions or alternative dispute resolution. The nonlitigious approach to settling social conflict, which has affected China's administrative response to grievances related to HIV/AIDS, serves the regime's goal of maintaining social stability. The 2003 Four Free,

One Care (*simian, yiguanhuai*) policy, exemplifies the central government's attempt to address HIV/AIDS carriers' basic needs without uncovering officials' roles in the spread of HIV/AIDS. Moreover, the policy helps to resolve several of the immediate and pressing needs of HIV/AIDS carriers, but it does not address a number of potential claims, including the following: loss of wages and employment, punitive damages, psychological and physical suffering, and discrimination. State officials use the policy to stave off litigation, arguing that the state has addressed HIV/AIDS carriers' interests with the policy and, therefore, litigation is not necessary for HIV/AIDS carriers.[24] One attorney flatly stated, "The courts can say there is already the Four Free, One Care policy that gives you [AIDS carriers] free medicine, so you don't really need anything, and we won't take the case."[25] Judges avoid openly using such an excuse for refusing to hear cases, but the policy and political pressure from health bureaus and local governments combine to discourage judges from accepting filings by HIV/AIDS carriers.

In some provinces, courts have accepted cases brought by HIV/AIDS carriers and even found in their favor. For example, a Heilongjiang court awarded a judgment to nineteen HIV/AIDS carriers who were infected by contaminated blood transfusions, and courts in Inner Mongolia, Shanghai, Hebei, and Hubei awarded damages to others infected in China's blood scandal.[26] These cases, however, arose in the early 2000s and in provinces with relatively few HIV/AIDS cases caused by the blood scandal. The provinces with the highest rates of HIV/AIDS infection are also some of China's poorer ones, and some of the provinces such as Henan and Anhui were sites of the illicit blood collection stations.[27] In those provinces very few court cases have been allowed, and since 2006, courts throughout China have tried just a handful of HIV/AIDS cases. In Henan, the courts have been particularly loath to accept cases filed by HIV/AIDS carriers. Chinese courts are not required to accept all filings by citizens, but the Civil Procedure Law requires courts to produce a document stating reasons for rejecting a case, which a citizen may appeal.[28] Lawyers at legal aid stations charge that Chinese judges, however, have rejected HIV/AIDS carriers' complaints without producing such a document, leaving the would-be plaintiff with no legal recourse.[29] Activists, attorneys, and journalists allege that Henan authorities issued a secret order to China's courts not to accept HIV/AIDS filings,[30] and that the courts should not accept filings related to HIV/AIDS infection transmitted by contaminated blood.[31] Indeed, in a 2006 lawsuit related to contraction of AIDS from a blood transfusion, a Henan court discontinued the trial in the middle of the hearing due to instructions from unnamed higher authorities.[32] Pressured by authorities at the local and provincial (if not also, the central) levels, courts refuse to hear cases, which proves a serious stumbling block to AIDS carriers who seek legal redress and which channels many complaints into mediation. The rest of this chapter addresses key legal issues that HIV/AIDS carriers have pursued with the assistance of civil society groups and activist attorneys.

DISCRIMINATION AGAINST HIV/AIDS CARRIERS

In China, popular prejudice against HIV/AIDS carriers runs deep and is concretely expressed in the form of denial of employment to applicants or firing of existing workers, refusal to provide medical treatment, being cast out from schools, and general stigmatization. A survey conducted in Beijing, Kunming, Shanghai, Shenzhen, Wuhan, and Zhengzhou by the China HIV/AIDS Media Partnership found that 47.8 percent of respondents would be unwilling to eat a meal with an HIV/AIDS carrier, 41.3 percent would be unwilling to work in the same place as an HIV/AIDS carrier, and 30 percent did not believe that infected students should attend school with uninfected students. [33] Chinese HIV/AIDS carriers are looked down upon for their perceived sexual promiscuity, same-sex relations, or drug use, despite the fact that nearly one-fourth of Chinese HIV carriers directly contracted HIV from blood donations or transfusions. Chinese who contracted HIV from tainted blood face hostility from members of their community and even their own family. [34] Parents of noninfected children have been known to pressure school principals to force children who contracted HIV through no fault of their own to leave school or dormitories. [35] Many doctors and hospitals effectively have refused to treat AIDS carriers. [36] Employment-based prejudice is particularly troublesome for HIV/AIDS carriers, and bosses and coworkers who discover a person has HIV/AIDS may fail to respect the person's right to privacy and push to remove the employee from the worksite. While popular prejudice is hard to change, in China prejudice has led to infringement on citizens' rights to access health care, education, and employment, all of which are protected by law.

A significant stumbling block to the pursuit of potential antidiscrimination cases brought by HIV/AIDS carriers is the lack of clear statements against discrimination in Chinese law and precedents in AIDS-related cases. China has no overarching antidiscrimination law, and the general legal expressions banning discrimination against HIV/AIDS carriers lack implementing instructions. [37] China does not have a case law system, so judges are also not bound to follow precedent or even permitted to cite precedents as a basis for their rulings, but judges read about court decisions and often follow such verdicts (especially of higher courts) in order to avoid having their decisions overturned by higher courts (and scores on personnel evaluations lowered). [38] According to Bjorn Ahl, prior decisions and "guiding cases" are meant to be consulted and to guide, without "regulating," judges' verdicts, so prior verdicts do not have the same standing as "precedents" in a case law system. [39]

Without model verdicts in HIV/AIDS discrimination cases to emulate or clear implementation guidelines, the courts are reluctant to hear cases involving HIV/AIDS carriers' claims. According to a Chinese attorney trained in AIDS law and who has worked on antidiscrimination cases, China's AIDS Prevention Law does not define "discrimination" and "it does not stipulate what you are to do if someone discriminates against an HIV or AIDS carrier."[40] The vagueness of China's laws and the contradictory statements in laws and regulations impede judges from converting general antidiscrimination principles into awards for HIV/AIDS carriers who encounter discrimination.[41]

The discriminatory practices—denial of access to medical treatment, employment, and education—all violate the spirit, if not the letter, of Chinese laws and regulations governing HIV/AIDS. Thus, they are ripe for legal challenge, but HIV/AIDS carriers have been reluctant to face prejudice that making their HIV-positive status known would generate. An attorney noted that a plaintiff who pursues litigation could request a closed hearing, but the plaintiff must enter a true name (rather than a pseudonym) in court documents, and court documents would include the true name of the plaintiff. When such documents are put into circulation, they effectively reveal the identity of the HIV/AIDS carrier–plaintiff,[42] a problem that the courts have begun to resolve in three recent cases involving alleged discrimination described below. Although Chinese courts have developed procedures to protect the privacy of HIV/AIDS carriers in court proceedings, some infected people have had their cases revealed to the public, which has brought further discrimination.

Rather than risk the exposure that a trial might bring, HIV/AIDS carriers who face discrimination typically turn to alternative dispute resolution (ADR) to seek settlement of their grievances. Additionally, the numerous obstacles to litigating HIV/AIDS-related cases encourage most would-be plaintiffs toward ADR, which has a greater chance of gaining compensation for HIV/AIDS carriers than litigation. A Shanghai lawyer who advocates for HIV/AIDS carriers and the gay community argued that ADR was more useful than litigation in handling employment discrimination for the following reason: "If we don't go to courts and use nonlitigious means, using ADR or petitions, then the government or work unit can make plans, or a hospital or unit can arrange with an individual to resolve the problem. Because our country's laws lack detail, I can only appeal to human sentiment [and not legal rules] to negotiate."[43] Another attorney who specialized in HIV/AIDS made a similar point: "When we have had cases, the mediators and judges have often sympathized with the worker. In some cases, the defendant also sympathizes with the plaintiff. You could say that sentiment (*qingli*) is involved in such settlements."[44] The lawyer concluded, however, that "ADR is good at winning a claim for an individual, but it does not help the rest of society. It does not demonstrate the case for others to see."[45] Moreover, ADR keeps state liability for mishandling the blood supply or denial of access to medical treatment out of the public discourse, which helps to protect the state's reputation.

Discrimination and the Right to Health Care

One of the core human rights is access to health, and UN agencies have articulated the right to health for HIV/AIDS carriers as access to antiretroviral treatment at reasonable costs and medicine to fight opportunistic infections.[46] Chinese legislation and regulations have extended these rights, but interviewees complained about denial of access to medical care for HIV/AIDS carriers, and recent reports have substantiated such claims.[47] A survey conducted in 2005 found that 50 percent of doctors and nurses believed it was permissible to deny medical services to HIV/AIDS carriers.[48] Doctors in Beijing hospitals have turned away patients known to have HIV/AIDS, despite medical ethics and hospital rules to the contrary.[49] The government has designated special hospitals and special quarantined wards for the treatment of HIV/AIDS carriers, but doctors at other hospitals have been known to make excuses to avoid treating HIV/AIDS carriers, until the infected persons, exasperated or reaching a medical crisis without treatment, simply leave. In 2006, sixty-seven AIDS carriers wanted to visit a Shanghai doctor for medical treatment, but the doctor refused treatment, instead asking them to go to another physician to receive treatment. The AIDS carriers approached a lawyer who specializes in AIDS law about the situation, and the attorney sought to take the state-run hospital to court for denying medical treatment and violating the Regulations on AIDS Prevention and Treatment. Ultimately, the AIDS carriers backed away from suing the doctor for fear of publicizing their medical status.[50]

In 2010, the International Labor Organization, Chinese CDC, and the Chinese Alliance of People Living with HIV/AIDS (a grassroots NGO) collaborated on a study and report on hospitals' discrimination against HIV/AIDS carriers. The following year, China's media began to publish stories on hospitals' refusal to provide treatment to people with HIV/AIDS.[51] Those stories have highlighted the particular challenges HIV/AIDS carriers face having surgery performed on them at smaller district hospitals compared to specialized hospitals established to treat HIV/AIDS carriers. To date, no discrimination case based on denial of access to medicine to HIV/AIDS carriers has been reported, but one complaint nearly resulted in a lawsuit against a hospital in Hebei. In 2010, Xiao Chen, an HIV/AIDS carrier, had an accident resulting in a head injury. He went to a hospital for surgery and to receive stitches. According to Chinese medical policy, Xiao Chen had the right to recover in the hospital for a week. During the course of treating Xiao

Chen, the hospital discovered he was HIV positive, so the morning of the second day, he was informed that he had to leave the hospital immediately. He went to the local public health bureau to complain. After mediation by the bureau, Xiao Chen was allowed to return to the hospital for a week.[52] Other HIV/AIDS carriers who are subjected to discrimination in medical treatment simply bear it, fearing to attract attention to their health status.[53]

Discrimination and Health Insurance

HIV/AIDS carriers need access to insurance because the state's Four Free, One Care policy does not cover medical expenses that are unrelated to HIV/AIDS, and some Chinese are either ineligible, or (in order to guard their privacy) choose not to register, for the policy's benefits. Unfortunately, some Chinese insurance policies have excluded HIV/AIDS carriers from coverage. In 2008, Li Wei, a citizen of Kunming, Yunnan Province, tested antidiscrimination protections for HIV/AIDS carriers by challenging his health insurance company's policies. In *Li Wei v. Ping'an Health Insurance Company*, the first legal challenge to discrimination against HIV/AIDS carriers, Li alleged that Ping'an Health Insurance Company discriminated by excluding HIV/AIDS carriers from medical coverage. The policy lumped HIV/AIDS in with health damages caused by warfare, actions of soldiers, bombs, rioting, or the actions of criminals as areas excluded from coverage.[54] Li claimed that such an exclusion against HIV/AIDS, which stood out as a medical condition in a list of violent acts, discriminated against a category of more than seven hundred thousand persons.

On June 25, 2009, a Kunming municipal court heard the complaint but ultimately rejected it. In the trial, the plaintiff raised two main arguments. First, Li's attorney alleged that the insurance coverage did not comply with relevant regulations. Ping'an Insurance retorted that the insurance policy containing the article in question had been written in 1998 and approved by the state's insurance review board (*baojianhui*) in 1999. The attorney representing Li contended that although the policy had been approved in 1999, it violated China's Regulations on AIDS Prevention and Treatment passed in 2006, which included an antidiscrimination clause protecting HIV/AIDS carriers and their families.[55] The insurance company failed to have an attorney ensure that its policies were updated to comply with relevant state law and regulations, and the complainant's claim for coverage occurred after 2006. Ping'an Insurance claimed that it was impossible for it to make calculations about the likelihood and medical costs of a person who contracts HIV/AIDS, so it could not afford to insure against such medical claims. The plaintiff's counsel countered that insurance companies in other countries and even those in Hong Kong, a Chinese territory, have been able to make such calculations.[56] Second, the plaintiff's counsel alleged that the policy discriminated against HIV/AIDS carriers by failing to cover medical claims from an HIV/AIDS carrier that were unrelated to HIV/AIDS. A judge asked the insurance company representative to imagine two people are hit by a car, one infected by HIV/AIDS and the other not—under those circumstances, would the insurance company cover the person not infected by HIV/AIDS but refuse coverage to the HIV/AIDS carrier? The Ping'an Insurance representative stated that the company would deny coverage to the HIV/AIDS carrier.[57] The court found that the article of the insurance policy in question was very convoluted, but determined that the exclusion, on the face of it, did not inherently violate the nondiscrimination article in China's Regulations on AIDS Prevention and Treatment.

Li Wei's case tested new legal principles regarding discrimination, so judges were unable to consult prior verdicts in analogous suits for guidance. The case of *Li Wei v. Ping'an*, though, points to the court's even deeper level of unfamiliarity with the central issues in the case. During the course of the hearing, the plaintiff's attorney provided the judges with a set of materials, including China's Regulations on AIDS Prevention and Treatment (the most basic legal instrument related to HIV/AIDS in China), Yunnan Provincial Regulations on HIV/AIDS Prevention and Treatment, and an edited volume on legal principles related to HIV/AIDS. The judge in the case found the materials very useful and even requested a second set of materials to share with his colleagues on the bench.[58] Given the novelty of the issues raised in the courts, it is likely that judgments, as was the case here, will be rendered by judges with no prior experience in AIDS cases. In this sense, even defeats in court can help to raise the knowledge of the legal community about an issue as well as signal to the state an emerging area of social conflict.

Although the courts did not find that Ping'an Insurance Company had infringed upon Li Wei's right to medical coverage, the Insurance Association of China issued a paper requiring all insurance companies not to exclude HIV/AIDS carriers from health coverage, effective October 1, 2009. The guidelines could remedy the situation that Li Wei encountered with Ping'an Insurance Company, but Li's backers have expressed a cautious approach. Wang Xiaoguang from Daytop Drug Abuse Treatment Center in Kunming, Yunnan, who assisted with Li's case, noted that the paper is not binding and does not have the force of a law.[59]

Employment Discrimination

A 2007 study found that 48.8 percent of the population and 65 percent of business managers surveyed believed that HIV/AIDS carriers should not have equal employment rights.[60] Managers face pressure to discriminate against HIV/AIDS carriers and their families from coworkers who fear working alongside people with the virus. In order to try to keep work units operating, managers try to appease their workers, and it is easier to marginalize one HIV/AIDS carrier who works at a unit, even if it means infringing on his/her rights, than it is to hire all new staff. In some extreme cases, HIV/AIDS carriers, once their medical status was discovered, were fired,[61] while some other business managers either put an employee with HIV/AIDS in a job where the employee works alone, or more commonly asked the person not to show up for work while continuing to pay the person's base salary. Some attorneys negotiate for such a settlement on behalf of HIV/AIDS carriers through ADR.[62] In Yunnan Province, a middle-level manager who contracted HIV/AIDS was asked not to report to work, and his salary was reduced from 100,000 yuan to his base pay of 10,000 yuan.[63] In addition to reducing a worker's pay based on health status, such arrangements are discriminatory in three senses: (1) without opportunities to work at their post, HIV/AIDS carriers cannot earn bonuses or commissions, (2) without work performance evaluations, HIV/AIDS carriers lose opportunities for promotion or salary increases, and (3) by treating HIV/AIDS carriers as unwanted employees in the workplace, managers reproduce, if not legitimize, societal discrimination against HIV/AIDS carriers.[64] One attorney who has helped to broker such pay-not-to-work arrangements described them as "low level discrimination."[65]

Courts have been reluctant to accept employment discrimination cases brought by HIV/AIDS carriers, leading many infected persons to pursue settlements. But on August 26, 2010, the Yingjiang District court in Anqing City, Anhui Province, accepted a case filed by Xiao Wu (a pseudonym), China's first accepted employment antidiscrimination case brought by an HIV/AIDS carrier. Xiao Wu was a student in Anhui Province who upon graduation applied for a teaching position at the Education Bureau and the Personnel Office of Anqing City. In May 2010, Xiao Wu passed a written exam for the position, and in June, his interview qualified him for the job.[66] During a required physical examination, authorities discovered that he was HIV positive, and the school pronounced him unfit for employment.[67] After a period of angry reflection and consultation with lawyers, Xiao Wu filed a case in court in Anqing City, Anhui Province.[68]

Xiao Wu and his lawyer, Yu Fangqiang, from Yirenping, a public interest law firm in Beijing, claimed discrimination based on legal principles found in China's Constitution, Labor Law, Employment Promotion Law, Law of the People's Republic of China on the Prevention and Treatment of Infectious Diseases, and Regulations on AIDS Prevention and Treatment. China's Constitution states, "All citizens have the same right to employment, and any employer or individual may not infringe upon a citizen's equal right to employment."[69] China's Labor Law includes similar protections. The third article of Regulations on AIDS Prevention and Treatment says, "No work unit or individual shall discriminate against HIV/AIDS carriers. HIV/AIDS carriers

and their relatives shall enjoy protection of their rights to marry, work, receive medical treatment, and receive an education".[70] The rules on civil
service employment, however, ran against these general statements against
discrimination in employment. "General Civil Service Recruitment Physical
Examination Standards (Trial Implementation)" flatly states, "[workers with]
HIV/AIDS, inappropriate," and the Handbook on Physical Examinations
Used for Civil Servants notes that "physical examinations cannot be completed once it is discovered that an applicant has HIV."[71]

Xiao Wu's attorney alleged that the defendants—the Anqing municipal
education bureau and the human resources and social security bureau—had
discriminated against Xiao Wu in violation of the above employment rights
of HIV/AIDS carriers. In addition to claiming violation of the legal right to
employment, Xiao Wu believed that teachers should not be subject to special
rules on civil servants.[72] In an interview, Xiao Wu said, "AIDS only can be
transmitted by three means: mother to child, through blood plasma, and
sexual intercourse. Have you met a teacher who must give birth to a child,
exchange blood plasma, or have sex in order to teach? No."[73] The defendants
argued that they acted within the legal guidelines of the relevant regulations,
so the case should be dismissed. The court decided with the defendants in
their lawful use of regulations to deny Xiao Wu employment. Upon appeal,
the courts again denied the plaintiff's claim. One commentator lamented that
the various laws related to discrimination and employment lacked a common
"principle of equality" (*pingdeng yuanze*) and detailed definitions by which
to judge discrimination claims.[74] Implicitly, the courts, by failing to act on
such cases, have indicated that they do not take it upon themselves to help
settle such discrepancies in terminology in legal expressions, instead waiting
for implementing guidelines or instructions from legislative bodies.

At first blush, Xiao Wu's case challenges this chapter's claim that HIV/
AIDS carriers prefer to settle their cases out of fear of exposing their HIV-
positive status and due to judges' reluctance to hear such cases, resulting in
settlements that accept discriminatory practices. One of Xiao Wu's attorneys
in the case explained the unusual circumstances in the Anqing court's acceptance of the case. The court, in fact, initially declined to accept the plaintiff's
filing of the case. Prepared for such a rejection, the plaintiff's attorneys had
spoken with reporters at the *Legal Daily* (Fazhi Ribao), the most important
legal newspaper in China, about the case. The day following the court's
initial action, the paper carried a story about the court's refusal to hear the
antidiscrimination case. The judges at the court immediately called in the
plaintiff's attorneys, paying their airfare to Anqing, to confer about the case.
After the conference, the court reversed itself and accepted the case.[75] The
reversal is suggestive of the way in which attorneys can work with the media
to create pressure on courts to try cases. The example also hints at subtle
ways in which cause lawyers can affect the legal system beyond winning

lawsuits, in this case by publicizing a new area of social conflict to be addressed. Even with media pressure, however, some provinces, Henan in particular, make it very difficult for HIV/AIDS carriers to file lawsuits. Xiao Wu's attorney noted that "Media in every province but Henan covered the HIV/AIDS employment discrimination cases, which did not carry any reports."[76] The news blackout in Henan was an attempt to limit pressure on the court to accept the case.

Following closely on the heels of Xiao Wu's verdict, two other HIV/AIDS carriers brought employment discrimination claims to the courts—one in Sichuan Province, and the other in Guizhou Province. In both cases, the claimants argued that the regulations on civil service employment wrongfully barred them from employment, constituting discrimination in violation of other laws governing HIV/AIDS. As with Xiao Wu's case, the Sichuan court initially refused to accept the case, but after the plaintiff's attorneys spoke with the local media, the court accepted the case. Ultimately, both the plaintiffs in the cases in Anhui and Sichuan lost in the first trial as well as on appeal, thereby ending their pursuit of justice. The court in Guiyang, Guizhou, refused to accept the antiemployment discrimination case, and the plaintiff's lawsuit never made it into the court.[77]

It is difficult to draw conclusions from such a small sample of verdicts (and court refusals to hear cases), but the court's rejection of the plaintiff's allegations of discrimination may discourage future potential plaintiffs from filing suits and encourage settlement out of courts. These cases support some of the arguments advanced here, namely, that the prejudice HIV/AIDS carriers face compels them to remain secretive about their status. Xiao Wu brought his case pseudonymously—he has not even informed his parents of his HIV positive status—out of fear of further discrimination.[78] Significantly, China's courts, at the request of their attorneys, have protected the confidentiality of such plaintiffs. The flurry of lawsuits that followed Xiao Wu's lawsuit may evince growing pressure on the courts to address this important issue.[79] Yet the courts' rulings against HIV/AIDS carriers' claims contrast to a 2009 verdict in favor of a person infected with hepatitis B who alleged employment discrimination.[80] The court's approach to discrimination appears particularly harsh toward HIV/AIDS carriers even within the parameters of health law.

Finally, in November 2012, a Jiangxi court mediated a settlement in a fourth employment discrimination case involving Xiao Qi (a pseudonym), who was denied a teaching position due to his HIV-positive status, and the Jinxian County (Jiangxi Province) education bureau. Xiao Qi filed the case at the Jiangxi court in Nanchang, and the court determined to mediate a settlement, awarding Xiao Qi 45,000 yuan.[81] While the settlement does not leave a clear legal precedent for other courts to follow, the settlement was widely publicized in China and may prove to be a turning point in the government's, if not, the courts', approach to handling HIV employment discrimination cases.

None of the claimants' lawsuits received a positive judgment in the courts, but the lawsuits may have served the grander purpose of highlighting discriminatory employment practices against people with HIV/AIDS. Cases lost by AIDS carriers and even some cases that are never heard by the courts can still contribute to protection of rights in two ways: (1) by highlighting emerging areas of social conflict that the state needs to address, and (2) by portraying causes in a sympathetic light to positively affect public opinion. By this logic, courts are venues for plaintiffs to signal new claims to the state, even when the courts provide no or partial relief to the plaintiffs. In late 2011 signs emerged that government authorities at various levels were beginning to review their public servant employment policies with an eye to revising rules that banned HIV/AIDS carriers from employment. On World AIDS Day, December 1, 2011, former Premier Wen Jiabao announced that the government should review all government policies that might discriminate against HIV/AIDS carriers. [82] According to an activist attorney whom I interviewed, in response to the legal discrimination cases and civil society pressure, the ministry of health scheduled three meetings with the ministry of human resources and social security to discuss a review of state personnel practices and employment discrimination based on health conditions. [83] In 2013, Guangdong Province revised its regulations on public service employment, which entailed a public commentary period on early drafts of legislation prior to adoption by provincial authorities. An early draft of the regulations released in January 2013 excluded HIV/AIDS carriers from employment in state-run schools, causing uproar from activists and civil society groups. [84] Guangdong, however, reversed its position in the final draft, allowing HIV/AIDS carriers to apply for teaching jobs and thus becoming the first province to lift the health-related restriction. [85]

Compensation for Contracting HIV/AIDS from the Mishandling of the Blood Supply

The most politically charged issue that one category of HIV/AIDS carriers has pursued is compensation for contracting the disease through illicit, hazardous collection of blood and use of contaminated blood by hospitals. The issue is politically explosive because it potentially indicts the health-care system, including the ministry of health, and local and provincial authorities where the blood scandal occurred. Two Henan provincial leaders during the mid and late 1990s, the final stages of the initial blood scandal, have ascended the highest levels of China's central government. Li Keqiang, who served as governor of Henan from 1998–2003, in 2013 was named China's premier, and Li Changchun, who was party secretary in Henan from

1993–1997, was the fifth-ranking member on China's standing committee and head of the political (propaganda) office of the CCP from 2002–2012.[86] The fact that two of the leading officials in a province where the blood scandal occurred rose to the highest levels of the central state apparatus has added pressure to address the blood scandal in a quiet manner and outside of the courts. The legal efforts of two persons infected by contaminated blood exemplify the challenges that AIDS carriers face in seeking compensation for the state's gross mismanagement of the blood supply.

On the night of June 23, 1995, Li Xige went to the women and children's hospital in her town in Henan Province, where she received a blood transfusion during the caesarean delivery of her first daughter. The doctor at the local hospital broke from protocol by arranging for three out-of-towners to privately donate blood, for which Li's husband paid 200 yuan (approximately, 25 dollars).[87] Li and her husband went on to have another daughter a few years later. On August 4, 2004, Li and her husband took their older daughter to the hospital, where she received care for six days. At that point, the doctor in charge discovered that the older daughter had AIDS. Tests showed that Li Xige and her younger daughter had also contracted HIV/AIDS, which doctors traced back to a transfusion of contaminated blood during the delivery of Li's first child. Li had infected her two daughters through mother-to-child transmission. At 12:15 a.m. on August 13, 2004, the older daughter died of AIDS at age nine.[88] Thus, Li Xige's fight for justice began.

Having lost one child to AIDS and knowing that she and her remaining daughter could both face the same fate, Li Xige sought compensation and justice for contracting HIV/AIDS. In October 2004, Li and her husband first went to the local people's court to file a case, but the court turned down the case.[89] The court official informed Li, "We have reported the issue to local authorities, and we are not allowing a court case to be established to resolve this problem. The higher authorities have issued an oral order not to accept legal cases related to cases of HIV/AIDS contracted from blood as this will not be the basic method used to resolve the problem."[90] In 2005, Li and her family visited county, provincial, and national authorities to seek redress for her family's loss and continuing struggle with HIV. Her many rounds of petitions at the provincial and national levels solicited letters of support instructing authorities to redress her case, but local officials and courts refused to respond. In one of her attempts to contact the ministry of health, Li was arrested and incarcerated for twenty-one days, charged with "gathering people to assault a state organ."[91]

Li's case attracted national attention from nongovernmental organizations, including Aizhixing, a leading Chinese group that advocates for HIV/AIDS carriers' rights, and from international nongovernmental organizations such as Amnesty International. Li Fangping, one of China's most prominent human rights lawyers, met with Li Xige in late July 2005 to learn about and publicize her situation, as well as to advocate for the urgent protection of HIV/AIDS carriers' rights.[92] Frustrated by the courts' and state officials' unwillingness to help her to resolve her complaint, Li turned to authoring open letters, with the help of Beijing HIV/AIDS activists Wan Yanhai and Hu Jia, to the National People's Congress, President Hu Jintao, and the National People's Political Consultative Congress.[93] In her desperate 2007 letter to President Hu Jintao, Li wrote, "When I look at my older daughter's lingering image and my younger daughter, I want to kill myself. Where is the justice in the laws?!"[94]

Unfortunately, Li Xige's experience in pursuit of justice is more the norm than the exception for HIV/AIDS carriers. To date, no criminal charges have been brought against agents involved in the contaminated blood supply. Ironically, in this drama, Li Xige was the person who ended up in jail, held under house arrest, and kept under surveillance for her pursuit of justice against those responsible for her contracting HIV/AIDS. Like many other HIV/AIDS carriers in their struggle for justice, Li Xige found herself in a labyrinth of bureaucracy reminiscent of Franz Kafka's *The Castle*. Courts told Li Xige, cast in the role of "K," to go to state officials, while officials sent Li back to the courts; local officials waited for instructions from higher authorities, while higher authorities denied there was a significant problem. Some HIV/AIDS carriers have had greater success in pursuing justice in the courts or from government officials than Li Xige, but Li and many others have yet to receive court hearings.

A second, similar case involves Tian Xi, who, in 1996 at the age of nine, suffered a concussion in Henan Province. His parents took him to a local hospital, where a doctor gave him an unnecessary blood transfusion.[95] Later, Tian Xi fell ill with HIV and then AIDS from the transfusion of tainted blood. Out of his legal efforts, Tian has become an AIDS activist, and his efforts were widely publicized and backed by Aizhixing and other civil society organizations. Tian petitioned the government for financial support but initially received nothing from local authorities. In 2010, he went to Beijing to present a film about his life and to speak at a conference sponsored by Aizhixing, a leading AIDS organization in China until 2010, when its leader, Wan Yanhai, fled to the United States due to pressure from Chinese authorities. The conference and film were halted, and authorities from Tian's hometown asked him to return to discuss compensation. In August 2010, failing to get a response from the courts and the local government, Tian Xi went to the hospital where he was infected and to the local authorities to seek compensation. Angered by the intransigence of the hospital and local authorities, he knocked office materials off the hospital director's desk and damaged a fax machine. Rather than being allowed to appear in civil court to sue the local hospital, Tian Xi found himself called into criminal court, which sentenced him to one year of prison for his actions. Tian Xi's case spurred an international and domestic response. Amnesty International circulated an urgent action report claiming that Tian Xi was in danger of torture and denial of his medicine.[96] In August 2011, Tian was released from prison after serving his one-year sentence, and he continues to seek justice for citizens who contracted HIV/AIDS from the blood supply. The courts still refuse to accept Tian's legal filing, arguing that he contracted HIV from a blood transfusion in 1996, while the regulations governing China's blood supplies were only put into force in 1998.[97]

"WE CANNOT CONTROL OUR ANGER ANYMORE"

The above analyses detail the challenges that HIV/AIDS carriers face seeking compensation and protecting their rights through legal means. Advocacy efforts for HIV/AIDS carriers by attorneys and civil society organizations have led to national-level policy responses and some legal changes. While some provincial authorities have helped to secure compensation and some rights for HIV/AIDS carriers, poor provinces in central China where the blood scandal broke out in the mid-1990s have yet to fully implement the policies and laws designed to help HIV/AIDS carriers and their families. After years of contention, including pursuit of their cases through formal legal channels, and government stonewalling, HIV/AIDS carriers' frustration with the regime has begun to boil over into protest. The latest round of anger-induced confrontation between HIV/AIDS carriers and Chinese officials occurred during the period August 2012–February 2013. The protest movement was spurred by a combination of factors, including Henan Province's failure to implement directives from the ministry of civil affairs to help HIV/AIDS carriers and their children, courts refusing to hear AIDS-related lawsuits, and several instances of hospitals denying health care to HIV/AIDS carriers.

On August 27, 2012, more than two hundred HIV/AIDS carriers and their relatives ascended on the Henan provincial government seat in Zhengzhou to protest a host of failures by the provincial government to provide services, resources, and compensation to HIV/AIDS carriers, many of whom had contracted their disease directly or indirectly through the contaminated blood supply. Beginning in 2009, AIDS carriers and their families sought help from the ministry of health and ministry of civil affairs in November 2010, July 2011, and March and July 2012, including medical treatment, welfare subsidies, and compensation for exposure to HIV/AIDS.[98] Angered after being stymied for months and having sat through a torrential rain on August 26, protesters tore down the gates at several government office buildings. The government responded by wielding batons and using some violence against the protestors. Having told protesters in April 2012 that the provincial authorities would roll out their policy within two months, in August 2012 officials asked protesters to wait another two months for an official response. One of the protesters, Gao Yanping, furiously told a reporter, "'Now they are asking us to wait another two months? We cannot control our anger anymore.'"[99]

In February 2013, one hundred AIDS activists from Henan Province again clashed with police, this time in Beijing. After an initial violent confrontation between the police and protesters, the government tried to defuse the situation by sending someone from the petitioners' office to receive the complaint. But one protester recalled how the group rejected the olive branch, "'[W]e didn't want to talk to him, because the complaints office never does anything, so we wanted nothing to do with him.'"[100] Local authorities detained or otherwise barred many activists from attending the protest in Beijing.[101] The Beijing protesters were continuing the earlier efforts to receive promised support from the provincial government. For example, national (and provincial) policy calls for AIDS orphans to receive 600 to 1,000 yuan per month to subsidize their living expenses (or 200 yuan per month if the child lost just one parent to AIDS), but until December of 2012 Henan AIDS carriers only allocated AIDS carriers 20 yuan (little more than 3 dollars) per month to help subsidize their living. In December of 2012, the provincial government raised the subsidy to 200 yuan per month,[102] still too little to support the sixty thousand AIDS carriers who live in Henan and who rarely can find gainful employment due to their ailment and societal discrimination.

The protests grew out of legal efforts to seek government support in compliance with the "The Ministry of Civil Affairs' Opinion on Strengthening the Welfare Protection of Children Affected by AIDS," which addresses the needs of HIV/AIDS carriers and their families,[103] as well as in response to Henan courts' refusal to accept HIV/AIDS carriers' cases calling for compensation for contracting the disease through the blood supply.[104] In the years leading up to the violent protests, Henan AIDS carriers and families have sought to file lawsuits against local authorities in order to secure compensation, but the courts have refused to accept their cases.[105] The wave of protest that has mobilized AIDS carriers in Henan Province is indicative of the necessity of AIDS carriers to use direct political confrontation in order to put pressure on the courts to hear their cases and for the government to protect their rights.

While AIDS carriers throughout China have agitated for improved policies and protection of their rights, some provincial authorities such as those in Henan Province have created more obstacles to AIDS carriers securing their rights than others. For HIV/AIDS carriers in Henan and other central provinces, their animus toward the provincial government is based not just on present policy failures but a history of poor oversight of blood collection agents, often complicit with local authorities, who catalyzed the spread of the epidemic throughout the province. Central and provincial authorities would like to use administrative measures to appease HIV/AIDS carriers and their relatives, but policies like Four Free, One Care and subsidies for children affected by AIDS place the financial burden on provincial and lower authorities to implement. Cash-strapped provinces face challenges in implementing those policies, and they pressure courts not to accept AIDS-related lawsuits out of fear of revealing the blood scandal and the government's responsibility for it in the national press.

CONCLUSION: SETTLING FOR DISCRIMINATION?

Chinese attorneys who wish to press HIV/AIDS carriers' legal claims face a dilemma. In order to establish legal precedents to help advance the rights for all HIV/AIDS carriers, claimants must turn to China's courts, but those courts, especially in central China, are reluctant to hear lawsuits related to mismanagement of the blood supply and discrimination. At the same time, societal discrimination discourages HIV/AIDS carriers from bringing their cases into the courts. Settlement out of court, which may be a more effective approach to redressing individual grievances, leaves no clear legal precedent for other would-be claimants to draw upon. The pattern of using ADR to negotiate for cash settlements that leave discriminatory practices intact may prove cold comfort for HIV/AIDS carriers. Financial settlements impose a small financial penalty on those accused of discrimination against HIV/AIDS carriers or those people whose negligence caused the spread of HIV/AIDS, but they limit the progress of HIV/AIDS carriers to define and protect their legal rights.

Out-of-court settlements of social conflicts such as the ones described above often are not announced. In fact, ADR settlements may stipulate that the details of the settlement cannot be discussed, and they typically do not determine fault. Thus, settlements limit the "demonstration effect" that court cases, which receive media publicity and enjoy the attention of other courts, can have on the legal system and society. Chinese courts are not bound to follow the precedents of earlier rulings, but decisions in publicized impact litigation cases demonstrate the bench's legal reasoning in such cases, which other courts are likely to weigh and even emulate. Equally important, settlements typically provide economic compensation but do not address the alleged underlying discriminatory practices. The persistence of such discriminatory practices does little to change societal prejudice against HIV/AIDS carriers.

In many countries, HIV/AIDS carriers face prejudice, and fear of stigmatization dampens their interest in pursuing litigation to defend their rights. Settling out of court, then, may appear a common or natural course of action.

Yet broad comparisons to other legal systems suggest that China's legal system and its practices pose particular challenges to HIV/AIDS carriers' pursuit of justice. Other countries have encountered blood scandals, including the United States, Japan, France, and Canada. In those countries, the courts heard cases, established precedents, and awarded damages to HIV/AIDS carriers. Interestingly, Japan's legal system, which shares with China a tendency to rely upon administrative measures to keep litigation out of the courts, was more open to hearing AIDS cases than the U.S. courts.[106] In South Africa, a country with a fairly low standard of rule of law, the courts have heard HIV/AIDS cases and established important precedents for other countries to follow, such as the right to antiretroviral therapy.[107] In most countries, early test cases establish a precedent for a new area of litigation, and subsequent would-be plaintiffs seek settlements to avoid legal fees and to speed the process of redress. Defendants are motivated to avoid allegations of negligence or discrimination that would damage their reputation. The courts serve as a backstop for plaintiffs who encounter recalcitrant defendants. The Chinese courts, however, by refusing to hear cases on HIV/AIDS, have shifted the balance in favor of would-be defendants. Potential defendants have little reason to comply with antidiscrimination principles or to eliminate negligence. In the context of discrimination in access to medical treatment, one doctor said, "'Every hospital knows that according to the law they cannot reject HIV patients. . . . Without concrete punishment, hospitals do not consider the law as a restriction on their behavior.'"[108]

Increasingly, scholars and international organizations recognize the importance of litigation to securing the rights of HIV/AIDS carriers.[109] Settling for discrimination limits the capacity for a "rights revolution," to borrow Charles Epp's term.[110] Although some of the organizational conditions—nongovernmental organizations with resources and legal aid centers—are present to help HIV/AIDS carriers in their pursuit of justice, the courts' reluctance to hear such cases and HIV/AIDS carriers' reticence to bring their claims into the courts impede such a rights revolution. In turn, the paucity of litigation constrains the use of legal means to govern AIDS in a way that secures the rights and interests of HIV/AIDS carriers.

Beginning in 2010, the wave of protest by HIV/AIDS carriers, strategic use of media to publicize grievances, and lawsuits brought by HIV/AIDS carriers indicate that HIV/AIDS carriers may no longer be willing to settle for discrimination. The courts' acceptance of lawsuits claiming employment and health insurance discrimination may evince a new trend by the courts to allow discrimination cases against HIV/AIDS carriers to be heard. In fact, in August 2014, a Shenyang court accepted a new antidiscrimination case involving three HIV-positive men who were asked to deboard an airplane due to their health status, which could be another breakthrough in antidiscrimination efforts.[111] Even though none of the discrimination cases resulted in the judgments in favor of the claimants, they instigated reconsideration of state policies that permitted discriminatory practices by state-run schools and private insurance companies. Lawsuits alleging government mismanagement of the blood supply, however, are still politically controversial, too controversial for some provincial courts to accept. Rights revolutions are littered with lost legal cases until plaintiffs begin to gain the courts' favor. Despite the challenges facing HIV/AIDS carriers who seek to redress their grievances, they are rising up in protest and using the media to pressure the courts to accept their lawsuits. The contentiousness in and out of the courts demonstrates both the strong political pressure that state officials bring to bear on courts to refuse to hear lawsuits and the necessity of HIV/AIDS carriers to use protest to compel courts to hear their cases. Rather than politics being played out in the courts, politics is determining what cases, and what types of cases, make it into the courts.

NOTES

1. Elements of this chapter were originally published in Scott Wilson, "Settling for Discrimination: HIV/AIDS Carriers and the Resolution of Legal Claims," special edition on "Governing AIDS" in *International Journal of Asia Pacific Studies* 8, no. 1 (January 2012), 35–55; and Scott Wilson, "Seeking One's Day in Court: Chinese Regime Responsiveness to International Legal Norms on AIDS Carriers' and Pollution Victims' Rights," *Journal of Contemporary China* 21, no. 77 (September 2012), 863–80. The author wishes to thank the publishers of the journals for permission to reprint those elements here.

2. Evan Anderson and Sara Davis, *AIDS Blood Scandals: What China Can Learn from the World's Mistakes* (New York: Asia Catalyst, 2007); Policy Research and Information Division of the National Center for AIDS/STD Control and Prevention, "HIV and AIDS Related Employment Discrimination in China" (ILO Country Office for China and Inner Mongolia, 2011), http://www.ilo.org/wcmsp5/groups/public/---asia/---ro-bangkok/---sro-bangkok/documents/publication/wcms_150386.pdf; and STD and AIDS Prevention and Control Center of the Chinese Center for Disease Control and Prevention and the International Labor Organization, "Discrimination against People Living with HIV within Healthcare Centers in China," International Labor Organization, 2011, http://www.ilo.org/wcmsp5/groups/public/---ed_protect/---protrav/---ilo_aids/documents/publication/wcms_155950.pdf.

3. Siri Gloppen, "Litigation as a Strategy to Hold Governments Accountable for Implementing the Right to Health," *Health and Human Rights* 10, no. 2 (2008), 25.

4. Interview 46.

5. Charles R. Epp, *The Rights Revolution: Lawyers, Activists, and Supreme Courts in Comparative Perspective* (Chicago: University of Chicago Press, 1998); Eric A. Feldman, "Blood Justice: Courts, Conflict, and Compensation in Japan, France, and the United States," *Law and Society Review* 34, no. 3 (2000), 651–701; Gloppen, "Litigation as a Strategy"; and Marius Pieterse, "Health, Social Movements, and Rights-Based Litigation in South Africa," *Journal of Law and Society* 35, no. 3 (September 2008), 364–88.

6. UNAIDS and IPU [Inter-Parliamentary Union], *Handbook for Legislators on HIV/AIDS, Law, and Human Rights* (Geneva, Switzerland: UNAIDS, 1999), 26.

7. Gloppen, "Litigation as a Strategy."

8. Pieterse, "Health, Social Movements, and Rights-Based Litigation."

9. United Nations General Assembly, *Declaration of Commitment on HIV/AIDS*, adopted 27 June 2001 (New York: United Nations, 2001).

10. UNAIDS and IPU [Inter-Parliamentary Union], *Handbook for Legislators.*

11. UNAIDS and IPU [Inter-Parliamentary Union], *Handbook for Legislators*, 26–27.

12. UNAIDS and IPU [Inter-Parliamentary Union], *Handbook for Legislators*, 79.

13. UNAIDS and IPU [Inter-Parliamentary Union], *Handbook for Legislators*, 86.

14. UNAIDS and IPU [Inter-Parliamentary Union], *Handbook for Legislators*, 88.

15. UNAIDS and IPU [Inter-Parliamentary Union], *Handbook for Legislators*, 90 and 98.

16. *Provisions for the Monitoring and Control of AIDS*, approved by the State Council on 26 December 1987, promulgated on 14 January 1988.

17. *Law of the People's Republic of China on the Prevention and Treatment of Infectious Diseases*, passed by the Standing Committee of the National People's Congress on 21 February 1989, revised 28 August 2004, article 16.

18. *Regulations on AIDS Prevention and Treatment*, issued by State Council 29 January 2006 (Document No. 457), put into effect 1 March 2006.

19. *Provisions for the Monitoring and Control of AIDS*, approved by the State Council on 26 December 1987, promulgated on 14 January 1988.

20. John Balzano and Jia Ping, "Coming Out of Denial: An Analysis of AIDS Law and Policy in China," *Loyola University Chicago International Law Review* 3 (Spring 2006), 205.

21. Scott Wilson, "Introduction: Chinese NGOs—International and Online Linkages," *Journal of Contemporary China* 21, no. 76 (July 2012), 551–67.

22. Interview 42.

23. Pitman B. Potter, *The Chinese Legal System: Globalization and Local Legal Culture* (New York: Routledge, 2001), 9 and 12–13.

24. Interview 72.

25. Interview 46; Interview 47; Interview 72.

26. Anderson and Davis, *AIDS Blood Scandals*, 18.

27. According to 2009 data, Henan Province has the third highest number of HIV/AIDS carriers of China's provinces. The six provinces with the most HIV/AIDS carriers in China account for 61.8 percent of China's total number of infected persons. Ministry of Health, *China 2010 UNGASS Country Progress Report (2008-2009)* (Beijing: Ministry of Health, 2010), 23, http://data.unaids.org/pub/Report/2010/china_2010_country_progress_report_en.pdf.

28. *Civil Procedure Law of the People's Republic of China*, promulgated 9 April 1991, promulgated by the president on 9 April 1991, article 85.

29. Interview 46.

30. Interview 47; Interview 72; Zhou, Bin and Huiru Luo 周斌 罗惠如, "*Shuxue Ganran Aizibing Qun Fa Anjian Lvshi Daili Tantao*" 输血感染艾滋病群发案件律师代理探讨 (An Analysis by Attorneys Representing a Group Who Contracted HIV/AIDS from Blood Donations), (New York: Asia Catalyst, no date), 18, accessed 16 July 2014, www.asiacatalyst.org/Blood_transfusion_AIDS_cases.doc.

31. Mark Heywood and Adila Hassim, "Observations and Assessment Arising from a Visit to Beijing and Chengdu, China to Look at Human Rights, Civil Society, and the Government's Response to HIV/AIDS," unpublished report (2009), 16, citing attorney Liu Wei.

32. Haiwei Ma and Yao Wu 马海伟 吴尧, "*Jiangsu Tongshanxian Huanzhe Shuxue Ran Aizi Fayuan Chengshe Ai Anjian bu Shenli* 江苏铜山县患者输血染艾滋法院称涉艾案件不审理" (The Court Refuses to Try Cases Involving AIDS Carriers from Blood Transfusions in Tongshan County, Jiangsu Province), *Jiankang Shibao* 健康时报, 22 November 2006, accessed 24 August 2014, http://news.anhuinews.com/system/2006/11/22/001610749.shtml.

33. CHAMP [China HIV/AIDS Media Partnership] et al., *AIDS-Related Knowledge, Attitudes, Behavior, and Practices: A Survey of 6 Chinese Cities* (Beijing, 2008), 16, http://www.un.org.cn/public/resource/ea0b7baa18b18c711db095673895aeba.pdf.

34. Xiaoshu Li, "The Public Face of AIDS in China," *Global Times*, 3 February 2010, accessed 3 February 2010, http://special.globaltimes.cn/2010-02/503379_3.html.

35. Yanhai Wan, Ran Hu, Ran Guo, and Linda Arnade, "Discrimination against People with HIV/AIDS in China," *Equal Rights Review* 4 (2009), 15–25.

36. Interview 68.

37. Gloppen, "Litigation as a Strategy," notes that health-related and specifically HIV/AIDS-related laws and norms are poorly defined.

38. Bjorn Ahl, "Retaining Judicial Professionalism: The New Guiding Cases Mechanism of the Supreme People's Court," *China Quarterly*, no. 217 (March 2014), 126.

39. Ahl, "Retaining Judicial Professionalism," 126.

40. Interview 78.

41. Balzano and Jia, "Coming Out of Denial."

42. Interview 46.

43. Interview 46.

44. Interview 54.

45. Interview 54.

46. United Nations General Assembly, *Declaration on HIV/AIDS*, article 55.

47. Interview 67; Interview 68; STD and AIDS Prevention and Control Center, "Discrimination against People."

48. STD and AIDS Prevention and Control Center, "Discrimination against People," 7.

49. Agence France Presse, "China Hospital Refused to Treat Woman with HIV: Co-Worker," *Agence France Presse*, 16 July 2010,http://health.asiaone.com/Health/News/Story/A1Story20100716-227326.html.

50. Interview 46.

51. Li Zheng 郑莉, "*Aizibing Ganranzhe Shenxian Jiuyi Qishi Yiyuan Jujue Shouzhi Xianxiang Pubian* 艾滋病感染者深陷就医歧视医院拒绝收治现象普遍" (AIDS Carriers Mired in Access to Healthcare Discrimination, Hospitals' Refusal to Provide Care Is Common), *Gongren Ribao* 工人日报 (Workers Daily), 23 May 2011, accessed 21 August 2014, http://news.xinhuanet.com/health/2011-05/23/c_121445819_3.htm; Qiumeng Li, 李秋萌, "*Baogao Zhi Zhongguo Aizibing Ganranzhe Jiuyi Mianlin 'Shoushu Nan*' 报告指中国艾滋病感染者就医面临'手术难'" (Report Indicates the Access to Medicine Problems Facing HIV/AIDS Carriers in Receiving Surgery), *Jinghua Shibao* 京华时报, 22 May 2011, accessed 16 August 2014, http://news.ifeng.com/mainland/detail_2011_05/22/6545986_0.shtml.

52. Zheng, "*Aizibing Ganranzhe*."

53. Zheng, "*Aizibing Ganranzhe*."

54. Xinhua 新华, "*Aizi Ganranzhe Gao Baoxian Gongsi Qishi Yishen Bohui Yuangao Susong Qingqiu* 艾滋感染者告保险公司歧视一审驳回原告诉讼请求" (Court Rejects AIDS Carrier's Claim in a Discrimination Case against an Insurance Company), *Xinhuawang Zonghe* 新华网综合, 10 July 2009, accessed 21 March 2011, http://news.xinhuanet.com/legal/2009-07/10/content_11685603.htm.

55. *Regulations on AIDS Prevention and Treatment*, issued by State Council 29 January 2006 (Document No. 457), put into effect 1 March 2006

56. Since 2005, China had an insurance policy for HIV/AIDS set up by a small private company in Hubei Province, which had calculated insurance payments and expected payouts, as well as a government-run group insurance policy for select occupations. Yu Zhang, ed. 张渔, *Zhongguo Aizibing Falu Renquan Baogao*中国艾滋病法律人权报告(Chinese AIDS Legal and Human Rights Report), Beijing: *Aizhixing Yanjiusuo*爱知行研究所[Aizhixing Research Unit], May 2009).

57. Interview 78.

58. Interview 78.

59. Quoted in China Daily, "Insurance Fix a Win for HIV Patients," *China Daily*, 15 July 2009, accessed 24 August 2014, http://en.kunming.cn/index/content/2009-07/15/content_1920690.htm.

60. Policy Research and Information Division of the National Center for AIDS/STD Control and Prevention, "HIV and AIDS Related Employment Discrimination," 6.

61. Policy Research and Information Division of the National Center for AIDS/STD Control and Prevention, "HIV and AIDS Related Employment Discrimination," 8; Guomei Xia, *HIV/AIDS in China* (Beijing: Foreign Languages Press, 2004), 82.

62. Interview 27; Interview 42.

63. Xia, *HIV/AIDS*, 152.

64. Interview 42.

65. Interview 46.

66. Guangming Li 李光明, "*Yin Tijian Aizi Yangxing Qiuzhi Beiju Anhui Yi Daxuesheng Qisu Jiaoyu Ju* 因体检艾滋阳性求职被拒安徽一大学生起诉教育局" (An Anhui University Student Sues over His Job Request Being Rejected Based on His HIV Positive Test Result), *Fazhi Ribao* 法制日报 (Legal Daily), 26 August 2010, accessed 13 December 2010,http://www.legaldaily.com.cn/society/content/2010-08/26/content_2261462.htm?node=20771.

67. Li, "*Yin Tijian Aizi Yangxing.*"

68. Jinghua Shibao 京华时报, "*Aizibing Jiuye Qishi Diyi An Dangshiren: Qishi Shi Yi Duqiang* 艾滋病就业歧视第一案当事人：歧视是一堵墙" (Litigant in 'First AIDS Employment Discrimination Case': Discrimination Is a Wall), *Jinghua Shibao*京华时报, 25 October 2010, accessed 13 December 2010, http://www.legaldaily.com.cn/commentary/content/2010-10/25/content_2326576.htm.

69. Quoted in Jinghua Shibao, "*Aizibing Jiuye Qishi.*"

70. *Regulations on AIDS Prevention.*

71. Quoted in Fangping Li 李方平, "'*Wugu Shouhaizhe' de 'Meng Yuan Ru Yu' Ji—Hui Jian Shuxue Ganran HIV—Shouhaizhe Li Xige Nvshi Yougan* 无辜受害者的蒙冤入狱记—会见输血感染HIV受害者李喜阁女士有感" (A Record of a 'Cover-Up of the Unjust Imprisonment' of 'Innocent Victims'— Being Moved by a Meeting with Li Xige, a Person Who Contracted HIV from a Blood Transfusion), report posted to Aizhixing website, 31 July 2006, accessed 15 September 2010, http://www.aizhi.net/view.php?id=204.

72. Quoted in Fangping Li 李方平, "'*Wugu Shouhaizhe' de 'Meng Yuan Ru Yu' Ji—Hui Jian Shuxue Ganran HIV—Shouhaizhe Li Xige Nvshi Yougan* 无辜受害者的蒙冤入狱记—会见输血感染HIV受害者李喜阁女士有感."

73. Jinghua Shibao, "*Aizibing Jiuye Qishi.*"

74. Sheng Lu 鲁生, "*Fan Qishi Xuyao Fangzhi 'Niulan Guanmao'* 反歧视需要防止'牛栏关猫'" (Antidiscrimination Requires Blocking 'the Cattle Gate Closing in the Cat'), *Fazhi Guancha* 法治观察 (Legal Observer), 15 November 2010, accessed 13 December 2010, http://www.legaldaily.com.cn/commentary/content/2010-11/15/content_2350415.htm.

75. Interview 88.

76. Interview 88.

77. Interview 88.

78. Jinghua Shibao, "*Aizibing Jiuye Qishi.*"

79. Zhiling Huang, "HIV-Positive Man Fights in Court for Job," *China Daily*, 17 February 2011, accessed 24 August 2014,http://www.chinadaily.com.cn/china/2011-02/17/content_12029053.htm.

80. China Labour Bulletin, "China's First Successfully Litigated Hepatitis B Employment Discrimination Case," China Labour Bulletin (19 August 2009), accessed 24 August 2014, http://www.china-labour.org.hk/en/node/100542.

81. Xinhua, "China's First Successful AIDS Discrimination Claim," *Xinhua*, 26 January 2013, accessed 20 August 2014,http://english.peopledaily.com.cn/90882/8108798.html.

82. Xinhua, "Chinese Premier Promises to Put More to Help AIDS Patients," *Xinhua*, 1 December 2011, accessed 20 August 2014,http://english.sina.com/china/p/2011/1201/419501.html.

83. Interview 88.

84. Caihong Zheng, "New Draft to Bar HIV/AIDS Carriers from Becoming Teachers in Guangdong," *China Daily*, 9 January 2013, accessed 20 August 2014,http://yourhealth.asiaone.com/content/new-draft-bar-hiv-carriers-becoming-teachers-guangdong.

85. Xinhua, "Cancelling HIV/AIDS Tests for Teachers Sparks Debate," *China Daily*, 29 May 2013, accessed 20 August 2014,http://www.chinadaily.com.cn/china/2013-05/29/content_16544793.htm. Interestingly, lifting the ban on HIV/AIDS carriers to apply to become teachers also stirred controversy among Guangdong citizens.

86. Shar Adams, "PM's Secrecy Protects Chinese Communist Official," *Epoch Times*, 19 September 2010, accessed 20 August 2014,http://www.theepochtimes.com/n2/content/view/14275/.

87. Li, Xige 李喜阁, "*Li Xige Gei Guojia Zhuxi Hu Jintao de Yifeng Gongkaixin* 李喜阁给国家主席胡锦涛的一封公开信" (Li Xige Gives National Secretary Hu Jintao an Open Let-

ter), *Xinwenshe* 新闻社, 12 August 2007, accessed 15 September 2010, http://www. minzhuzhongguo.org/Article/ShowArticle.asp?ArticleID=2268.

88. Li, "Li Xige Gives National Secretary."

89. Li, "Li Xige Gives National Secretary."

90. Quoted in Li, "Li Xige Gives National Secretary."

91. Amnesty International, "UA 217/06: Fear of Torture or Ill-Treatment/Health Concern: Li Xige (F)," PUBLIC AI Index: ASA 17/043/2006 (10 August 2006), accessed 24 August 2014,http://www.amnesty.org/en/library/asset/ASA17/043/2006/en/724cf808-d403-11dd-8743-d305bea2b2c7/asa170432006en.html.

92. Li, "A Record."

93. Li, "Li Xige Gives National Secretary"; and Xige Li and Xi Tian, "Open Letter for NPC Standing Committee Chairman Wu Bangguo and the Chinese People's Consultative Conference/National Committee Chairman Jia Qinglin," AIDS Rights website (31 December 2009), accessed 23 September 2010,http://www.aidsrights.net/bencandy.php?fid=5&id=259. For these and other activism such as calling for democratic reforms, Hu Jia was arrested in 2008 and remains in jail, and Wan Yanhai's group, Aizhixing, was systematically harassed. In April 2010, Wan Yanhai fled China through Hong Kong for the United States.

94. Li, "A Record."

95. Barbara Demick, "Justice Tough to Find for Chinese Who Got HIV/AIDS through Tainted Blood," *Los Angeles Times*, 27 November 2010, accessed 24 August 2014,http://articles.latimes.com/2010/nov/27/world/la-fg-china-blood-20101128.

96. Amnesty International, "UA 190/10: Urgent Action: Chinese HIV/AIDS Activist Risks Torture," AI Index: ASA 17/036/2010, accessed 24 August 2014,http://www.amnesty.org/en/library/asset/ASA17/036/2010/en/f8b17031-e645-40e9-975c-c1f7f21229d6/asa170362010en.pdf.

97. Xincaixian Aizi Fangzhi Gongzuo Weiyuanhui 新蔡县艾滋防治工作委员会, "*Guanyu Tian Xi Youguan Qingkuang de Huibao* 关于田喜有关情况的汇报" (Report Regarding Tian Xi's Situation), issued 1 May 2010, available at Tian Xi's personal blog, accessed 16 August 2014,http://blog.sina.com.cn/aidsguy.

98. Weiquanwang 维权网, "*200 Ming Aizibing Ren Ji Jiashu Dao Henansheng Zhengfu Kangyi* 200 名艾滋病人及家属到河南省政府抗议" (200 AIDS Carriers and Their Relatives Protest at the Henan Provincial Government), *Weiquanwang* 维权网 Blog, 27 August 2012, accessed 26 July 2013,http://wqw2010.blogspot.com/2012/08/400.html.

99. Gillian Wong, "China AIDS Patients Topple Gate of Government Office," *Associated Press*, 27 August 2012, accessed 26 July 2013, http://www.huffingtonpost.com/huff-wires/20120827/as-china-aids-protest/.

100. Yuan Fang, "AIDS Activists Clash with Police in Beijing," *Radio Free Asia*, 27 February 2013, accessed 16 July 2013,http://www.rfa.org/english/news/china/aids-02272013144006.html.

101. Fang, "AIDS Activists Clash."

102. Fang, "AIDS Activists Clash"; and Yazhou Tai 泰亚洲, "*Henan Aizibing Huanzhe Shenghuo Buzhu Tigao Dao 200 Yuan* 河南艾滋病患者生活补助提高到200元" (Living Subsidies for Henan AIDS Carriers Raised to 200 Yuan), *Caixinwang* 财新网, 17 December 2012, accessed 26 July 2013, http://china.caixin.com/2012-12-17/100473348.html.

103. Zhonghua Renmin Gongheguo Minzhengbu 中华人民共和国民政部, *Minzhengbu Guanyu Jinyibu Jiaqiang Shou Aizibing Yingxiang Ertong Fuli Baozhang Gongzuode Yijian* 民政部关于进一步加强受艾滋病影响儿童福利保障工作的意见 (The Ministry of Civil Affairs' Opinion on Strengthening the Welfare Protection of Children Affected by AIDS), issued by the Ministry of Civil Affairs (No. 26), 17 March 2009,http://fss.mca.gov.cn/article/etfl/zcfg/200906/20090600031448.shtml.

104. Yat-yiu Fung, "AIDS Victims Sue for Compensation," *Radio Free Asia*, 4 July 2012, accessed 24 August 2014,http://www.rfa.org/english/news/china/compensation-07042012145508.html; and Yuan Fang, "AIDS Patients Protest in Henan," *Radio Free Asia* (29 August 2012), accessed 24 August 2014,http://www.rfa.org/english/news/china/aids-08292012150012.html.

105. Wong, "China AIDS Patients Topple Gate"; Fang, "AIDS Activists Clash"; and Weiquanwang, "200 AIDS Carriers and Their Relatives Protest."

106. Feldman, "Blood Justice."

107. Heywood and Hassim, "Observations and Assessment."

108. Quoted in STD and AIDS Prevention and Control Center, "Discrimination against People," 14–15.

109. Benjamin Mason Meier and Alicia Ely Yamin, "Right to Health Litigation and HIV/AIDS Policy," *Journal of Law, Medicine & Ethics*, Supplement (Spring 2011), 81–84; Miriam Maluwa, Peter Aggleton, and Richard Parker, "HIV- and AIDS-Related Stigma, Discrimination and Human Rights: A Critical Overview," *Health and Human Rights* 6, no. 1 (2002),12–13; Gloppen, "Litigation as a Strategy," 3; Heywood and Hassim, "Observations and Assessment," 6; UNAIDS, UNDP, and IDLO, *Toolkit: Scaling Up HIV-Related Legal Services* (Rome: International Development Law Organization, 2009), 10; USAID and Health Policy Initiative, *Assessment of the HIV Legal Environment: Yunnan, China* (Kunming, China: RTI International, 2008), 2.

110. Epp, *The Rights Revolution*.

111. BBC, "Passengers with HIV Sue China's Spring Airlines," *BBC News*, 2014 August 15, accessed 2014 August 16.http://www.bbc.com/news/world-asia-china-28804219.

Chapter Six

Litigating for Pollution Victims' Rights

Over the last decade, a rising wave of Chinese environmental protests, some of them violent, have swept across Chinese locales.[1] A retired Communist Party official conservatively estimated that thirty thousand to fifty thousand environmental "mass incidents," usually involving more than ten persons, occurred in China in 2012,[2] while approximately seven hundred thousand petitions were received by the environmental protection bureaucracy.[3] For most of the post-1978 period, citizens have been satisfied with their improving material well-being provided by accelerated economic development. In recent years, however, citizens have developed a critical view of manufacturers that pollute the air that they breathe and ruin the water that they drink or use on their crops. A 2011 Gallup poll conducted in China revealed that 77 percent of Beijing residents value environmental protection over economic growth, and even rural residents who have generally displayed a lower environmental consciousness than urban residents have the same ordering of priorities.[4] Citizens' new environmental consciousness manifests in protests and litigation, and central officials, especially in the ministry of environmental protection (MEP), offer enough encouragement to foster grassroots activism. Increasingly, protesters are complaining about not just polluting factories but government failures to implement environmental regulations. At base, the environmental crisis has called into question the very growth model that has legitimated the post-1978 regime.

How to address environmental pollution divides China's party-state along horizontal and vertical lines. Horizontally, China's officialdom is split between those at the center who wish to adopt a sustainable development model and those at the provincial level and below who seek to continue with a "pollute now, control later" (*xian wuran, hou zhili*) model of development.[5] The environmental issue vertically splits China's state along ministerial

145

lines, especially between the MEP, which seeks to improve China's environmental stewardship, and the ministry of industry and information technology, which dislikes tough environmental regulation. The issue of citizen participation in environmental governance divides the regime along similar vertical and horizontal axes. Local officials more strongly oppose environmental protest and litigation than central officials do. Local officials tend to view manufacturing in terms of providing jobs for constituents, revenue for coffers, and stability for communities. Environmental protest and litigation highlight conflict between the environmental protection bureaucracy and officials charged with promoting industry and commerce.

In the face of persistent protest and civil society agitation, Chinese leaders have sought to find channels for society to express its dissatisfaction without threatening the regime and its legitimacy.[6] The MEP has gone on record supporting the development of civil society groups and environmental litigation. For example, Pan Yue, the former vice minister of the MEP, declared, "'[The MEP] always encourages environmental lawsuits for the public benefit and always tries to act on the recommendations of the public and NGOs.'"[7] Shifting protests out of the streets and into the courts or into administrative offices is one potential means to manage societal conflict related to the environment without imperiling the regime's stability. In their efforts, environmental advocates and plaintiffs enjoy the tacit support of the MEP, who sees most environmental litigation as strengthening the ministry's claims on the importance of environmental protection against those of industrialists.[8] For their part, grassroots and international nongovernmental organizations recognize the value and relative political security of legal challenges to China's state because such challenges accept the state's laws and regulations as given and merely attempt to hold the state to its word.

The courts may appear to be a relatively safe zone for contesting environmental pollution, but officials still see environmental lawsuits as threatening to their legitimacy because of the regime's role in overseeing development and controlling pollution.[9] As Rachel Stern notes, "Although courts defuse conflict and build support for leaders, they can also siphon power and legitimize dissent."[10] More generally, Fu Hualing and Richard Cullen argue that although "the rule of law is a conservative project that stabilizes society and legitimizes regimes," China's regime "has been indifferent or hostile" to rights-based litigation.[11] Carl Minzner argues that Chinese leaders are "turning against law" in the name of maintaining social stability, emphasizing mediation over litigation.[12] Litigation of environmental pollution cases threatens regime legitimacy because it can lay bare violations by enterprises as well as bureaucratic failures to implement regulations. This "ambivalence" of the state toward environmental litigation, which Rachel Stern analyzes in her recent book, stems from fissures in China's regime.[13] Environmental pollution mobilizes opposing political forces—some in support of weak environmental regulation and others in favor of more regulation—that buffet the judiciary, which has been a relatively weak institution and subject to political pressure from party and state officials.

Beginning around 2005, China's regime has tried to develop tools to supervise and lead environmental litigation with the founding of special environmental courts, reliance on criminal charges against polluters, increasing criminal sentences placed on polluters, creating legal aid funds to support pollution victims, inclusion of environmental criteria in cadres' personnel evaluations, and using state agents to represent pollution victims in lawsuits. Such efforts by the state, which I analyze here and in chapter 7, attempt to manage state-society conflict by deflecting anger away from China's state, as well as seek to win back the allegiance of citizens by demonstrating that the regime looks out for society's environmental interests and health. State efforts at deflection, however, are not fully successful because local authorities often attempt to block pollution victims' access to the courts, which is a source of the rising wave of environmental protest. A major difference between the blockage that AIDS victims and pollution victims face in trying to protect their rights is the public support that the MEP offers to pollution victims' legal efforts.

Pollution victims have found it difficult to have their cases tried in China's courts, in part due to local officials' suppression of litigation efforts.[14] Although local officials occasionally use force to intimidate some environmental protesters and would-be plaintiffs, China's state has mainly responded with administrative and legislative efforts to address protesters' concerns and lately has given greater scope to litigation as a means of addressing environmental conflict. A study by the Asian Development Bank noted that during the period 1998–2005 environmental litigation increased approximately 25 percent per year.[15] Another analysis of the 118,779 environmental court cases from 2002–2011, however, shows a much slower rate of growth, 7.66 percent growth in cases per year for the entire period, and 6.24 percent for the final five years of the period.[16] Environmental court cases are on the rise, but their growth rate is slowing, and they represent just a fraction of the total environmental complaints lodged. Despite greater openness to using litigation to resolve environmental matters, state officials place numerous obstacles before would-be plaintiffs in an attempt to discourage litigation. Pollution victims face challenges of finding adequately trained attorneys to represent them, procedural difficulties of collecting evidence, and having a knowledgeable and impartial court hear their case.[17] Additionally, harassment and unlawful arrests of activists, political pressure on courts not to accept filings against local industries, marginalization of local environmental pollution offices, and discouragement of court enforcement of verdicts against polluters are all means of stymying environmental litigation. As with cases brought by HIV/AIDS carriers, the courts have often refused to hear the cases without providing written explanation because "they are afraid that handling such cases will disturb the stability."[18] Indeed, during 2002–2011, a paltry 16.67 percent of the total number of environmental cases heard throughout China's courts were civil lawsuits; 69.86 percent were criminal cases, and the remainder were administrative cases.[19] This chapter explores the politics of pursuing environmental justice in China, including divergent responses from state actors to environmental litigation. What are the obstacles to having courts try environmental cases? In what areas are civil society organizations and attorneys making advances in protecting pollution victims' rights? Analyses of the legal efforts of pollution victims demonstrate that social mobilization and protest, along with media coverage, help complainants to secure a hearing in China's courts, although many cases still languish without the courts' acceptance of lawsuits.[20]

DEVELOPMENT OF CHINESE ENVIRONMENTAL LAWS AND REGULATIONS

The rise of China's environmental litigation would be impossible without a growing body of Chinese laws to govern the environment. By most accounts, China has made impressive gains in developing laws and regulations to govern its environment, even if some of those laws have inherent weaknesses and are weakly enforced.[21] Chinese environmental laws and regulations to an extent frame popular notions of environmental justice and shape the areas of legal contestation. Indeed, the poor enforcement of environmental laws and regulations generates litigation, which helps to close the gap between laws and implementation. The general approach to environmental protection in Chinese laws adheres to the "precautionary principle,"[22] which attempts to halt pollution, even prior to proof of liability. For example, since the Supreme People's Court issued instructions to lower courts in 2001, the burden of proof in environmental pollution cases was shifted to the defendant, whereas in other areas of Chinese civil law, the burden of proof is on the plaintiff.[23] In subsequent years, the burden of proof being placed on defendants was written into laws such as China's Tort Law.[24] The field of environmental laws and regulations also allows environmental protection officials and the courts to impose fines for illegal pollution, albeit the Tort Law does not have a mechanism to impose punitive penalties in environmental cases.[25] According to the Environmental Protection Law and the Civil Procedure Law, courts may only award damages for losses, require cessation of pollution, force restoration of an environment, and eliminate harm.[26] Until the 2014 revision of the Environmental Protection Law significantly raised the fine structure on polluters,[27] the low level of fines imposed on polluters generally covered just a fraction of the costs of remediating damage caused by pollution, and the environmental governance system has been ineffective in imposing abatement measures on factories. Unfortunately, the strong emphasis on the "precautionary principle" in Chinese environmental laws typically lapses into a structure of fines that help fund local environmental protection bureaus without halting illegal pollution or significantly penalizing polluters.

China has also sought to adopt the following three interrelated international norms on environmental management that help to specify concrete steps for ensuring environmental rights and have affected Chinese legal development: (1) the right for citizens to participate in decision making on the environment, (2) the right to access information regarding the environment, and (3) the right to environmental justice (pursued through legal institutions).[28] In 2002, China passed its Environmental Impact Assessment Law, which requires organizations with construction and operation plans to provide an independent environmental impact assessment to the relevant provincial government or, for very large-scale projects, to the national government.[29] The law also requires all other construction and production projects to be evaluated and placed into one of the following three categories: "major impact," "light impact," and "minimal impact."[30] Those projects that are initially designated as having a major impact must produce an environmental impact report filed by a third party—independent of the state and the company—from a list of evaluators approved by the MEP. In the report, the evaluator is required to solicit the views of all "relevant departments, experts, and the public" on the proposed project, and the evaluator must elaborate on why the opinions were accepted or rejected.[31] Projects designated as having a "light" or "minimal" impact require less extensive evaluation, and surveying public opinion is not mandated. Unfortunately, public participation in the evaluation process is often sidestepped or left to post hoc complaints.[32] The initial triaging of projects, notably before an actual assessment has occurred, means that no public participation is guaranteed in the evaluation process for two of three categories. Finally, several cases of environmental pollution catastrophes (analyzed below) reveal that many locales do not fully implement the environmental impact assessment law or that the process is tainted by corruption.

The environmental impact assessment rules allow businesses that initially fail to comply with rules and that begin construction without an environmental impact assessment to later apply for a "make-up environmental impact assessment" without penalty.[33] As Zhao Yuhao points out, businesses that apply for a make-up environmental impact assessment near the end of the construction process or after the construction process is completed are likely to be approved due to the sunk costs, even though the projects may have already inflicted damage to the environment that is difficult to reverse.[34] Such a pattern subverts the environmental impact assessment process and citizen participation in environmental governance. Moreover, an environmental impact assessment report that is found unacceptable by the governing authority does not explicitly bar a construction or production plan from being implemented. [35] The environmental impact assessment law, when implemented well, is an effective tool for regarding environmental concerns in new projects, but it also contains significant shortcomings that provide mechanisms to local authorities and companies to undermine key provisions of the environmental impact assessment process, which has become a source of environmental protest and litigation.

A second international norm that China has begun to adopt relates to the transparency of environmental governance and free flow of information. In 2008, China passed the Regulations of the People's Republic of China on Open Government Information, which provide citizens with legal means to gain access to information to help them to protect their interests and to comply with international norms on environmental governance. [36] The Open Government Information Regulations apply to a number of fields, including public health (see chapter 5), but in Article 10(11) Chinese authorities emphasized the importance of disclosing "information on the supervision and inspection of environmental protection," while Article 11(1-3) calls for providing information on construction, areas of public interest, and land management. [37] China's central leaders have emphasized the importance of open information to environmental governance and its link to citizen participation.

In China, the government is not required to disclose information that might "endanger state security, public security, economic security, and social stability," [38] which officials have used to deny citizens access to information. According to the law, a person requesting information who believes that a government agent has not fulfilled the obligations of the Open Government Information Regulations may appeal to the next higher level of government. [39] The definitions of "open information" and "state secrets," however, remain blurred and a source of contention. According to an attorney with experience seeking information through the Open Government Information Regulations, the State Secrets Bureau "is responsible for making determinations on what constitutes 'state secrets' and what constitutes 'open information,' allowing some requests for information to be filled and others declined." [40] The central MEP has made progress in providing information, but environmental protection bureaus, which are funded by local government, have been less forthcoming with information, hiding behind the cover of not disclosing "state secrets." [41]

A final international norm, legal recourse to environmental justice, has developed slowly in China. China's Civil Procedure Law, Tort Law, and Administrative Litigation Law, among other laws give citizens the right to use the courts to address environmental disputes. Public and private provision of legal aid and encouragement of litigation by citizens in the Revised

Law of the People's Republic of China on the Prevention and Control of Environmental Pollution by Solid Waste and other legal instruments also help citizens to secure the substance of this right. For more than a decade, China has established several environmental courts (discussed below), which provide special venues to enhance access to environmental justice. In mid-2013, China's environmental courts numbered over 130, spread through a number of provinces and centrally administered cities.[42] In some of those environmental courts, plaintiffs are not required to pay court fees, and special legal aid funds have been established to defray the court fees in two other environmental courts. While Chinese laws and legal organizations, especially the environmental courts, have created a legal infrastructure that facilitates environmental litigation, several stumbling blocks to effective use of the courts include opposition to pollution victims' use of the courts from pockets of the regime and citizens' cost-benefit analysis of using the courts (accounting for the high costs of litigation and low likelihood of receiving a significant judgment).

DEVELOPMENT OF ENVIRONMENTAL LITIGATION IN CHINA

Environmental litigation is increasing, but environmental legal action still addresses a small share of environmental disputes in China. Many factors contribute to citizens' uneven access to China's courts, but the primary one is the tight alignment of local government and businesses in China's economic development model. First, local officials' financial dependence on the generation of revenue in the form of taxes and fees pits local government's short-term financial interests against the central government's and pollution victims' long-term interests in sustainability.[43] Xia Jun, a Chinese environmental attorney, has referred to this as "[l]ocal governments' love-affair with GDP growth."[44] Second, at the local level, government forces typically ally with business interests, even going so far as investing in polluting enterprises, which limits local government tolerance for oversight by the environmental protection bureau officials and environmental activists.[45]

Central officials have begun to recognize the importance of using the courts to address pollution and to break up the nexus of local interests that impede environmental litigation. In a 2012 report to a special committee of the National People's Congress, Yang Chaofei, vice chairman of the Chinese Environmental Science Committee, noted that since 1996, mass disturbances related to the environment (*huanjing quntixing shijian*) have gone up 29 percent per year on average, and the courts are only trying environmental cases equal to less than 1 percent of the total number of environmental petitions (*huanjing xinfang*) received.[46] Citing violent environmental protests in Shifan City, Sichuan Province, and Qidong, Jiangsu Province, in 2012 and implying that the protesters were denied legal recourse, Yang called on the courts to play a much greater role in hearing citizens' complaints, which would stave off violent protests and help to build "understanding and trust" between citizens and the government.[47] The following case analyses indicate some of the areas of rising contention, the political forces arrayed for and against plaintiffs, and the challenges and opportunities presented by China's judicial system.

Joint Litigation

Pollution that floats into the air and flows into streams and groundwater rarely affects individuals in isolation; instead, pollution harms groups of people all at once. Therefore, environmental pollution cases naturally lend themselves to joint litigation, more commonly called "class action suits" in the United States. China's Civil Procedure Law provides recourse for joint litigation[48] but grants discretion to the courts to decide whether to accept cases brought by more than one plaintiff as a single filing. Until 2006, judges were primarily evaluated based on the number of cases heard and verdicts rendered rather than on the quality of the decisions.[49] Judges are evaluated poorly if they render judgments that must be overturned,[50] which encourages them to be risk averse in selecting and deciding cases. The evaluation and remuneration system has led judges to prefer to split potential joint litigation cases into multiple lawsuits—even when tried simultaneously—with separate filings by individual plaintiffs.[51] As attorneys and advocates have complained, such handling of cases both adds to the court's time in managing its caseload and duplicates the costs associated with filing suits for plaintiffs.[52] The additional costs of filing multiple lawsuits discourage plaintiffs from litigating. An environmental attorney explained the courts' behavior to me: "I think that the primary rationale for breaking class action suits into individual cases is consideration of social stability. They fear that if there are many cases in which a lot of people are showing up as plaintiffs in suits, that it will upset social stability."[53] By bringing together groups of citizens around rights-based claims, collective action suits join social movements and litigation in a way that the regime fears. Fu Hualing and Richard Cullen note, "A legal action, ironically, catalyzes a movement by framing demands, developing common purpose and forging a common group identity."[54]

Environmental attorneys have sought to overcome these hurdles to protect citizens' rights with joint litigation. Two cases indicate the mixed success of expanding the scope for joint litigation. The case of *Su Zongying et al. v. Shanghai Chinese and Western Medicine Corporation* (1996) involved 231 families of Pengnan Village, Nanhui County, Shanghai, who, in 1996 accused a local pharmaceutical company of discharging chemicals that contaminated local groundwater, causing a decline in rice production.[55] The case had two hearings, and both courts found the defendant liable for damages to crops, totaling 293,562 yuan (approximately 35,800 dollars). Although the 231 families were affected in a similar fashion by the chemical pollution of the groundwater, making them eligible for a joint lawsuit according to China's Civil Procedure Law, the court ordered the families to file 231 separate cases. The court rendered nearly identical verdicts in each of the 231 lawsuits.

The case of *Zhang Changjian v. Rongping Chemical Factory (Xiping Village, Pingnan County, Fujian Province)* (2005), perhaps the most widely studied Chinese environmental lawsuit, marked a modest success in joint environmental litigation.[56] The case involved Rongping Chemical Plant in Pingnan County, Fujian Province, Asia's largest producer of potassium chlorate. The factory dumped its chemical waste—by 2003, nearly sixty thousand tons of it containing hexavalent chromium (Cr +6) and chlorine—outside the factory.[57] In the streams around the factory, aquatic life died, and in fields below the factory, rice and agricultural production had dropped off precipitously—in good years, to 60 percent of average yields, and in bad, to 40 percent or less of average yields.[58] The factory drew both praise and criticism, demonstrated by being both named a "national environmentally advanced industry" and placed on the "list of key environmental pollution problems."[59] By 2001, the villagers decided that they had endured enough damage, so they contacted the MEP, which suggested that the villagers file a complaint.[60] Zhang Changjian, a local "barefoot doctor" who was trained to provide basic medicine to villagers in the countryside, alerted reporters in Beijing to potential pollution damage when he was frightened by very high incidence of dry coughs, sore throats, blisters, dizziness, and vomiting among farmers around the factory. Dr. Zhang initiated a petition drive to stop the plant's production and held a demonstration to attract attention from the media and garner external support. Local authorities beat and tried to intimidate the doctor and organizers of the petition, but he and other villagers persisted with their struggle.[61] Central television crews from Beijing arrived to do an investigative report on the factory, which aired three times in April 2003. Villagers also formed a nongovernmental organization, Pingnan Green Association, to provide an organizational basis to pursue their environmental cause.[62]

When the reporters took a sample of the factory's discharge to the county environmental protection bureau office, they found a staff of ten people but no equipment to conduct diagnostic tests of chemicals in liquid samples.[63] In fact, the environmental protection bureau only received a paltry 5,000 yuan (approximately 600 dollars at the time) from the county government to cover its operation, barely enough to pay phone bills and to purchase office supplies.[64] To test the chemical content of the sample, the team of villagers, reporters, and environmental protection bureau officials had to trek to the provincial capital, Fuzhou, to use equipment at another environmental protection bureau. Analysis of the samples, collected by reporters and villagers at different times, revealed levels of hexavalent chromium that were as high as fifty-four times the central regulatory limit. [65] At a regional environmental protection bureau office, the reporters discovered reports filed by environmental protection agents with analysis of chemical discharge from November 2001 that showed an average level of hexavalent chromium twenty to thirty times the permissible level, [66] but the environmental protection bureau officials took no action to stop the pollution.

The villagers of Xiping in Pingnan County contacted the Center of Legal Aid for Pollution Victims (CLAPV), who helped Zhang Changjian and 1,700 other villagers file a court case, asking the courts to compel the factory to stop harming the local environment, to pay 1.3 million dollars in crop and other damages, to pay 413,316 dollars for mental distress, and to clean up the hazardous pollution that they created. [67] The Intermediate People's Court accepted the case, the largest joint filing in China. The intermediate court decided on behalf of the plaintiffs, and the Fujian Provincial High People's Court upheld the lower court's decision on appeal, but awarded the plaintiffs just 88,000 dollars in property damages and loss of income. The court also ordered the factory to halt its pollution in violation of regulatory standards and asked the defendant to clean up the hexavalent chromium waste. [68] The court refused to award any damages for mental distress. While the monetary compensation fell far short of the requested amount, people praised the court case and verdict, which earned the label of one of the "ten most important court cases of 2005" from the All-China Lawyers Association. That the case even made it into the courts as a joint lawsuit was quite a novelty at the time. The development of the case and its media coverage also evince some central authorities' support for the local plaintiffs' efforts to gain a hearing.

The attorneys from CLAPV described to me how local courts, however, impeded enforcement of the award, dragging out the distribution of compensation for two years. In the aftermath of the joint litigation judgment, the court claimed that it did not know an appropriate means to distribute the compensation funds to so many parties. Rather than devising its own mechanism to do so, the court held the funds in escrow and asked the plaintiffs to develop their own methodology for distributing the award and to have every plaintiff in the case sign a document indicating their approval of the distribution. The lead attorney involved in the case noted that most aspects of the judgment were eventually enforced: the plaintiffs received their compensation and the factory reduced its emissions. [69]

Central and local government officials are wary of the instability that such cases may generate, and local authorities have criticized courts for accepting joint litigation cases. [70] Troubled by a growing number of joint lawsuits in the early 2000s, the All-China Lawyers Association handed down its "Guiding Opinion Regarding Lawyers Handling Cases of a Mass Nature," which made it more difficult for attorneys to take on such cases. [71] The opening statement of the "Guiding Opinion" invokes "constructing a harmonious society" and specifies "environmental pollution" as a common issue for mass (class action or joint litigation) cases and, therefore, a source of concern. [72] The "Guiding Opinion" has a number of stipulations that discourage attorneys from handling "mass cases," defined as involving ten or more plaintiffs. First, three partners in a law firm must discuss and agree to accept such a case. [73] Second, lawyers handling mass action cases are required to report to the local lawyers association [74] and "accept supervision and guidance by judicial administration departments." [75] Third, lawyers involved in such cases are responsible for "safeguarding social stability." [76] Finally, a branch of the lawyers association can punish any lawyer or law firm who takes on mass cases but "does not handle cases . . . in accordance with this 'Opinion,' and thus brings about a negative impact. . . " [77] The above stipulations are intended to intimidate activist lawyers from aggressively using the courts to protect citizens' rights and especially from spawning more social movements. The "Guiding Opinion," combined with recent selective harassment, intimidation, and detention of some high-profile human rights lawyers, has had a somewhat chilling effect on attorneys working in the area of public interest litigation. [78] The "Guiding Opinion" also seeks to contain joint litigation within boundaries acceptable to the local judiciary and officials, thereby protecting the state's interests.

Health Damages

Chinese industries, especially in the countryside, have generated such a volume of pollution that citizens suffer severe health consequences. In rural China 300 to 500 million people lack piped water, subjecting them to a host of waterborne illnesses, including diarrhea, hepatitis, and dysentery as well as liver and other forms of cancer from the chemicals and metals carried by the water. China's cancer rates are well above international norms, and liver cancer has become the leading cause of death in China's countryside. [79] In 2010, an estimated 1.2 million people across China died prematurely due to air pollution. [80] Such hazardous health conditions, one might assume, would lead courts to award health damages to many pollution victims, but, in fact, they have not. In the last fifteen years, attorneys have assisted in many cases in which claimants have attempted to receive medical and property damages caused by pollution, but the courts have been reluctant to award such medical damages, in part because of the difficulty of establishing the causal chain from pollution to health damages. [81] Liu Lican, who investigated twenty Chinese cancer villages, explained why health damages are difficult to collect: "The impact of industrial pollution on crops, livestock, fields, fish, and buildings is easier to identify and determine, while damage to the human body is hidden. Compensation for the economic losses is hard enough to come by—suing for damages to health would be even harder."[82] An environmental attorney explained, "From the court's view, the hardest thing about pollution cases is determining in a scientific way the basis for claims on medical damages caused by pollution that was ingested. . . . The courts are reluctant to hear such cases, then, because they use up a lot of time."[83] In some cases, officials either offer administrative solutions to environmental disputes that provide meager financial compensation for health claims or judges refuse to award health damages. In a 2012 editorial, an environmental attorney, Xia Jun, described his frustration with the courts' refusal to hear health claims in environmental tort cases. He wrote, "In 2004, I represented the plaintiffs in a case against a mining company in Shaodong county, Hunan Province. I tried for three years to get the case heard, ultimately in vain. The court was worried that the case would result in more claims being brought and so opted to ignore it."[84] In such cases, legal considerations are subordinated to political calculations because of pressure on judges not to accept lawsuits.[85]

A Chinese environmental law expert whom I interviewed explained that although the courts have been reluctant to award medical damages, they are anxious to develop a mechanism to do so. The attorney, who is a staff member of an environmental INGO, offered the following explanation for why the courts were reluctant to award health damages:

> The lower courts are worried about rendering a verdict and then others determining that it was incorrect. The judges fear that they may lose their job, so the verdicts that they turn out tend to be very conservative. They will give compensation only for very well recognized, scientifically proven medical damages with a very clear and direct causation from environmental pollution.[86]

The staff member went on to note that at a training session on environmental law hosted by the Natural Resources Defense Council and the American Bar Association, Chinese judges sought guidance from U.S. judges and legal scholars on reaching medical judgments in environmental cases. At present, Chinese judges lack the autonomy, confidence, and expertise to render judgments on medical damages caused by pollution.

The difficulty of proving health damages as an impediment to successful lawsuits is ironic because China's Tort Law places the burden of proof on the defendant to show that its pollution is not responsible for damages.[87] In pollution cases, courts often ignore the burden of proof being placed on the defendants.[88] The bench's tentativeness on this issue and preference for guidance from an administrative organ evince China's historical tendency to shift social conflict away from courts and into administrative channels. Additionally, a number of incentives are built into judges' evaluation system, and exhortations in campaigns call on judges to employ mediation rather than adjudication and to divide potential joint lawsuits into individual claims.[89]

Right to Know

In recent years, NGOs and legal aid centers have sought impact litigation cases to establish precedents for citizens' "right to know" (*zhiqing quan,* in Chinese), based on China's Open Government Information Regulations (2007). In 2009, a citizen in Suzhou, Jiangsu Province, used the Open Government Information Regulations and related rules passed down from the Supreme People's Court to sue Suzhou's environmental protection bureau for information.[90] In the case, *Huang Jianxin v. Suzhou City Environmental Protection Bureau,* the petitioner sought information from the local environmental protection bureau on the effects of a sewage treatment plant located less than sixty meters from the plaintiff's residence. The environmental protection bureau refused to provide the citizen with the environmental impact report, resulting in the lawsuit. The local court, under scrutiny from the Supreme People's Court, accepted the case and compelled the environmental protection bureau to furnish the citizen with the report.[91]

In 2009, Yan Yiming, a Shanghai lawyer, requested information from Anhui Province's environmental protection bureau in the form of a list of the province's factories that violated pollution standards, along with the composition and volume of their discharge. Initially, the provincial environmental protection bureau declined to provide the information, but the MEP in Beijing twice sent written requests to the Anhui authorities to hand over the information.[92] Ultimately, the Anhui environmental protection bureau submitted a list of violating factories without information about the level and type of discharge.[93] The goals of such suits are to gain valuable information about polluters and to demonstrate to average citizens how to exercise their "right to know," which will spur further demand for government transparency.[94] Yan Yiming, who has pursued other high-profile cases based on the Open Government Information Regulations, has personally suffered for his pursuit of such cases. In April 2009, three men brazenly attacked Yan with metal bars and a hammer in his law office's conference room, a criminal act that remains unsolved.[95]

Part of the central government's interest in the Open Government Information Regulations is to create transparency and, therefore, decrease capacity for corruption of government at all levels. Even prior to passing the Open Government Information Regulations, China's State Council called on the governments of provinces, autonomous regions, and municipalities to provide information related to emissions and the status of their local environments "to create conditions for public participation."[96] A Chinese attorney explained that state officials have recognized that "some government public policy formulations require citizen participation" because they are sensitive and need societal backing to propel them forward. Without such opportunities for participation, conflict can erupt between state and society. The attorney explained, "Chinese society now has very many cases arising such as people attacking the police. With some problems, if the state does not give citizens channels to participate, they don't know when issues will arise or how things will go. The Open Government Information Regulations are to allow citizens to have a channel to participate in some public issues or discussions. This is a way of providing people a period of time in which to participate in particularly sensitive issues." [97]

Citizens' demand for information about the environment has been a new line of contentiousness. In 2008, the MEP's central office received 68 requests to provide information through mechanisms set up in response to the Open Government Information Regulations, but by 2010 the number of requests grew to 226. [98] Far more requests for information are made to local government units such as environmental protection offices, where environmental impact assessments and pollution monitoring occur. Citizens may appeal to the courts when officials refuse to provide requested information, but an attorney whom I interviewed noted that the courts are reluctant to hear such appeals. [99] The MEP reports that in 2008, only two legal appeals were brought against the MEP requesting information using the Open Government Information Regulations, while in 2010, twenty-four such cases were brought against the MEP (twenty-three were brought by the same person). [100]

Halting Pollution Violations

One of the ways in which China's environmental legal and regulatory system lacks teeth is the difficulty of compelling polluters to halt their behavior, either through the imposition of compensatory damages, injunctions to halt illegal pollution, or careful environmental impact assessment to prevent illegal polluting practices from starting. Until the 2014 revision of the Environmental Protection Law, the fines that environmental protection bureau officials can levy have been dwarfed by the profits enjoyed by polluting factories. [101] Polluters have dragged out paying fines through a series of appeals, and the courts have been loath to enforce penalties that the environmental protection bureaus impose on polluters. [102] The 2014 Environmental Protection Law, however, permits fines to be levied on a daily basis without limit, greatly increasing the potential size for fines. [103] At the time of writing, it is unclear how the revised fine structure is affecting actual fines imposed by environmental protection officials and courts. In order to halt unlawful polluters and the damage that they inflict on the environment, China's courts will need to employ more drastic fines and injunctions against firms that have not followed environmental impact assessment processes or violate pollution regulations.

Most pollution victims who are able to have their cases heard in the courts have focused on compensation for damages that they have suffered rather than halting pollution. When citizens have requested injunctions against polluters, the courts have been reluctant to grant them.[104] Participants in the environmental governance process, including the courts, environmental protection bureaus, and environmental lawyers, are quite sensitive to the need to sustain industries that supply local government with revenue and local citizens with jobs. Consequently, administrators seek to use their offices to fine firms and offer modest compensation to keep environmental conflict out of the courts. As one attorney argued, "If you try to be unfriendly toward such a business, if the government and the business aren't working in the same direction, then it is a big problem. Many things have to be balanced. You can't just go straight to the courts to settle things."[105] Officials and judges prefer mediation and administrative measures to address the consequences of pollution over litigation, but those methods limit civil society and citizen participation in the process and often allow polluters to continue to operate.

An example of the environmental protection bureaucracy using fines without halting polluting activities involves the Jingquan Spirits Factory, which produces *baijiu*, a type of liquor, in a rural area outside of Muling City, Heilongjiang Province. The factory dumped toxic wastewater into the local water supply, damaging residents' water for drinking and agricultural use. In 2002, after villagers complained about the pollution, the municipal health bureau conducted an on-site investigation and found that the local water was polluted and that the factory's pollution was responsible for damage to the water supply.[106] In 2002, the Muling vice party secretary and vice mayor visited the site of the polluting factory three times and reached a final opinion on how to handle the situation. They concluded that the villagers should not use the groundwater within sixty meters of the factory and that the factory should supply free water or give a subsidy of 30 to 50 yuan (approximately 4 to 6 dollars at the time) to each village household.[107] Such a resolution left untouched the polluter's operations. The villagers were dissatisfied with the administrative decision in this case, so they contacted environmental attorneys at the CLAPV in Beijing. For several years, the center's attorneys have attempted to file a lawsuit on behalf of the villagers, but local courts have refused to accept the case. When the center's attorneys petitioned the intermediate court in Mudangjiang City for help with the problem of the Muling court's refusal to accept the case, the petitioner's office said that it did not have the authority to intervene.[108] To date, the villagers have not been able to secure a hearing for their claim, which permits the factory to continue its operation without addressing the pollution. The case exemplifies the overriding economic interests that local officials share with businesses, preventing enforcement of environmental prevention measures.

Significantly, attorneys at the All-China Environmental Federation (ACEF), a GONGO under the MEP that provides legal services to pollution victims, have had several successful cases in which courts invoked injunctions to have polluters halt their illegal practices. In 2010, Ma Yong, the head of the litigation department of the ACEF, filed a lawsuit against the Dingpa Paper Mill in Wudang District of Guiyang City, which the Qingzhen environmental court accepted. Prior to hearing the case, the environmental court issued an injunction against the paper mill to stop production in order to prevent further damage to the environment. [109] The case is important for the use of an injunction by the court, but it is also noteworthy that the courts responded to requests for injunctions from a GONGO attached to a state ministry, whereas citizen-based organizations are not always able to gain such an injunction.

Ineffective implementation of China's environmental impact assessment regulations also allows new factories to cause environmental damage, giving rise to environmental litigation. In Shutangshan Village, Hunan Province, villagers engaged in a struggle against Hunan Jingtian Technology Industry, LLC, a factory that manufactures allicin, a chemical compound produced from garlic. In September 2001, in a move hastily arranged by local officials, the factory relocated its production to a village factory site that had been vacated by a bankrupt machinery factory earlier that year. [110] The village officials were anxious to recruit Jingtian Company to avoid a loss of more than one hundred jobs in the village due to the machine factory's bankruptcy. [111] In their rush to arrange the move to the village, the new company's leadership skipped the environmental impact assessment process. The county environmental protection bureau, which was in charge of implementing the assessment, told the company that it could begin production and undergo the assessment at a later time, a process that was completed in 2004. [112]

After the factory began operations, workers at the factory and residents near the site experienced health ailments, including headaches, intestinal problems, and cancer. [113] When a heavy rain fell, chemicals from the plant were washed into the water supply, causing crops to wither and livestock to die. The company denied any linkage between its production and the health problems of residents, livestock, and crops. [114] The county environmental protection bureau inspected Jingtian Company and found its pollution exceeded environmental regulations, so they fined the company 5,000 yuan in 2004 and 19,000 yuan in 2006, approximately 600 and 2,300 dollars. [115] As more villagers fell ill, some with cancer, villagers were convinced that the factory's pollution was to blame, and Chen Lifang, an entrepreneurial farmer who lived near the factory and battled illness, began to mobilize her fellow villagers. The villagers petitioned local authorities and environmental protection officials from the county level to the central ministry in Beijing. For her part in mobilizing the petitioners and protests, Chen Lifang was detained on the criminal charge of "assembling a crowd for a disturbance" (*juzhong naoshi*).[116]

In 2009, Chen Lifang and several other villagers filed an administrative lawsuit against the Changsha municipal environmental protection bureau, the Jingtian Company, and the Changsha municipal environmental protection bureau's industrial technology institute, alleging that the three parties had failed to properly implement the rules on environmental impact assessment and had failed to ensure proper management of the regulated discharge at the company. Ultimately, the court returned the complaint, denying that defendants had violated the rules on the environmental impact assessment and noting that the regulatory parties had fined the company for the pollution discharge that exceeded regulatory standards.[117] The court's verdict indicates as much about the lack of teeth in China's Environmental Impact Assessment Law and Tort Law as it does about the timidity of the court. The Environmental Impact Assessment Law has a significant loophole (noted above) that allows for postoperation assessment of environmental impact, which can subvert the goal of preventing hazardous production, as was the case here. China's Tort Law introduces the concept of "punitive" measures, but it does not specify any means to apply them to environmental cases.[118] In the United States and other countries that allow punitive claims in tort cases, Jingtian Company and the environmental protection bureau would have been liable for tort claims because they knowingly allowed—as shown in test samples of emissions and resulting fines—the factory to continue to operate in a way that endangered human, animal, and plant life. Instead, county officials compelled Jingtian to pay minor fines and compensation in exchange for continuing to operate. While the court in the Jingtian case did not back plaintiffs in their complaint about the poor environmental impact assessment process, other courts have used improper environmental impact assessments to halt polluters. In one case lawyers from CLAPV halted construction of an animal-testing laboratory in Beijing and the ACEF temporarily halted use of a site in the Baihua Lake area near Guiyang (discussed in greater detail in chapter 7) due to failures to follow the environmental impact assessment report processes.[119] To date, however, such injunctions are rarely issued.

According to some environmental activists and attorneys, Chinese citizens need to shift their legal consciousness and adjust their tactics in order to halt pollution at the source rather than merely seek compensation for suffering caused by pollution. One instance of such a shift in consciousness occurred in Qiugang *Village*, Anhui Province, a case now documented in the film *Warriors of Qiugang*.[120] In Qiugang Village, located along a tributary to the highly polluted Huai River, several chemical factories discharged their waste into the local waterway, affecting public health, aquatic life, and crops.

In 2005, three factories opened or expanded operations in the village—Jiu-cailuo Chemical Ltd., Haichuan Chemical Ltd., and Zuguang Microchemical Ltd.—and flagrantly violated emission standards. Haichuan Chemical and Zuguang Microchemical had inadequate pollution treatment machinery, while Jiucailuo lacked any filter system to treat its waste, a gross violation of Chinese regulations.[121]

Investigations conducted by Green Anhui, a civil society organization centered in the city of Hefei, Anhui Province, discovered that benzene had been dumped into the groundwater and rivers feeding the Huai River, which they traced back to the factories in Qiugang Village. After two years of the chemical factories' operation, the village developed an extremely high level of cancer (53 persons out of the more than 1,800 in the village) and a high mortality rate (over 80 percent dying from their cancer), affecting all ages, including school-age children.[122] Beginning in 2006, villagers spent three years fighting the polluting factories in the courts with no success at stopping the pollution. As one villager, Zhang Gongli, who filed two lawsuits, re-flected, "I believed that severely polluted areas could use the practice of suing to settle pollution issues, even succeed in the courts, but you are only able to receive monetary compensation, bear witness, and to have matters considered as they stand when protecting environmental rights in the courts."[123] In 2007, villagers used political tactics, including sending a peti-tion to the environmental protection bureau in Bengbu, a nearby city. Initial-ly, the environmental protection bureau refused to act, denying that the facto-ries were in violation of regulations, which resulted in angry village protests and their suppression by local security personnel.[124] Villagers and Green Anhui helped to publicize their circumstances, which caught the attention of provincial and central officials, creating pressure on local leaders and envi-ronmental protection bureau officials to resolve the crisis. The environmental protection bureau slapped light fines on the polluters, called on banks to refuse them loans, threatened to cut off electricity and water, and finally, in 2007, the MEP told the factories to shut down their operations. Brazenly, through the end of 2008, the polluting factories—after closing operations for a few months—restarted production with no change in their pollution man-agement. Finally, in December 2008, the factories were forced to leave the village only to reopen in an industrial zone with proper pollution treatment facilities.[125]

A steady flow of students from a nearby university, sent to do studies of the village and to raise environmental awareness, made villagers conscious of their rights with regard to the polluting factories.[126] Initially, villagers believed that the polluting factories were operating within the law, and the villagers simply sought compensation for their medical suffering and proper-ty damages. The students and Green Anhui worked in the village to help the villagers to realize that the factories had, in fact, violated pollution laws as well as regulations on how close to farms and households factories could operate.[127] One factory operated just over one hundred meters from the local school, which affected students' health and ability to study. A lawyer working for an international nongovernmental organization's legal program described the development of consciousness of these villagers:

> Green Anhui entered and helped villagers to do an investigation, which raised their awareness that the chemical factories were completely violating the law. It wasn't just that their emissions were in violation, but their construction violated regulations. This kind of situation could not be settled with compensation. From here on, the villagers determined, "we don't want money, don't want compensation, we want the factory closed. You can't compensate me for this because it is my life and my family at stake."[128]

Working with Green Anhui and provincial officials, citizens in Qiugang Village succeeded in driving out the polluting factories, but they have failed to receive compensation for the environmental and health disaster left in the wake of the chemical factories. Although the factories have paid for crop damages caused during the factories' operation, the pollution has so damaged farmland that it will not be utilizable for crops for years.[129] The actions of Qiugang Village were a harbinger of a new mode of environmental political action in which advocacy and litigation work in tandem to force greater environmental compliance. Although the Qiugang villagers did not receive compensation through the courts, their efforts and the significant media coverage drew attention to their plight. Such incidents contribute to a widespread rise in environmental consciousness that improves popular understanding of environmental issues, citizens' rights, and how to protect them.

EFFORTS TO IMPROVE IMPLEMENTATION OF ENVIRONMENTAL REGULATIONS

One of the greatest hopes for improving the judiciary's response to environmental petitioners is the development of environmental courts. In 2007, the Supreme People's Court called on local courts to set up environmental courts and to encourage public interest litigation,[130] leading intermediate courts to establish special environmental courts in Guiyang City, Guizhou Province (two); Wuxi City, Jiangsu Province; Kunming City, Yunnan Province; and Yuxi City, Yunnan Province.[131] Other locales soon established their own environmental courts so that by mid-2013, over 130 such courts operated in China. Initially, the municipal governments instituted the environmental courts to overcome grassroots administrative and business opposition to trying environmental cases and to gather expertise for trying such cases. In this sense, the environmental courts are effectively working to overcome the same knowledge gap that the courts faced on trying AIDS-related cases. The emergence of environmental courts also responds to the "State Council Decision on Implementing a Scientific Development Outlook and Strengthening Environmental Protection," issued in 2005, which linked "scientific development"—a concept closely modeled after "sustainable development"—to environmental public interest litigation. [132] More recently created environmental courts, however, were established to burnish local officials' environmental credentials.

The environmental courts are empowered to hear administrative, criminal, civil, and administrative enforcement cases. Surprisingly, in their first years, over 50 percent of the caseload heard by the Kunming and Guiyang environmental courts has been criminal cases, many of them targeting average citizens. [133] The Wuxi environmental court had the heaviest caseload, which was composed primarily of administrative and administrative enforcement cases. [134] From the cases brought by plaintiffs, the environmental courts can select which cases to try, and the judges have chosen some cases with an eye toward hearing new issues and establishing model decisions. Although Chinese courts are not bound by precedents, giving judges flexibility in their decision making, lower courts look to follow model decisions, especially from experts at the environmental courts. These courts, then, hold out the prospect of helping to define new environmental legal reasoning and special procedures for China's judicial system. According to environmental lawyers, however, nonspecialized courts have not altered their practices—refusal to hear most environmental cases and reluctance to enforce judgments—despite the new procedures developed and rulings made by environmental courts. [135] Model decisions have been rendered by environmental courts, but the same pressures from local businesses and officials act on lower courts not to try environmental cases.

The environmental courts may also tighten enforcement of China's environmental regulations. In addition to hearing environmental cases, the environmental courts have been empowered to experiment with a number of new procedures for environmental cases, including hearing public interest lawsuits (discussed in chapter 7), which potentially will give citizens and civil society groups greater access to the participation in environmental governance. Even in their first few years of work, the environmental courts have begun to sketch out new, significant approaches to environmental litigation and enforcement. In addition, in 2013 China's Supreme People's Court and the People's Procuratorate issued an opinion on verdicts that raised the sentences from the previous maximum sentence of seven years for environmental criminal cases, even allowing the death penalty in severe incidents of pollution. [136] These innovations and ratcheting up of sentences hold some promise of giving the environmental regulatory regime stronger teeth.

One area of experimentation has been in the development of new enforcement mechanisms for court decisions, which is a long-standing problem for pollution victims. The Guiyang and Qingzhen environmental courts have led the way in developing new procedures for trying environmental cases and novel means of enforcing verdicts. One of the most important reforms developed by the court is the practice of "follow-up inspections to check on enforcement" (*zhixingde huifang*), which addresses the problem of enforcement of verdicts. The new methodology allows the court to authorize annual inspections to check for compliance with verdicts, determine whether the verdict has resolved the pollution problem, and discover if new conflicts have developed between the litigants. [137] In the case of *The Two Lakes and One Reservoir Management Bureau (Lianghu Yiku Guanliju) v. the Guizhou Tianfeng Chemical Ltd. Company* (discussed in greater detail in chapter 7), the Qingzhen environmental court developed the new mechanism for follow-up monitoring of enforcement, and it has made a substantial difference. When the court enforced its verdict against Tianfeng Chemical Company, the pollution flows from a large dump of phosphogypsum into Hongfeng Lake essentially stopped. By the end of 2009, the level of gypsum pollution in Hongfeng Lake had dropped by 57.2 percent from the level in 2007, the time of the lawsuit brought against Tianfeng Chemical Company. [138]

Another innovation that the environmental courts are advancing is the "polluter pays" principle. The principle calls for the polluter to take responsibility for remedying damage that they do to the environment and people's health. The cases in Qiugang and Shutangshan Villages, where polluting factories have left behind damages caused by their pollution, exemplify why this is a problem. Recent decisions by environmental courts in China have compelled companies to undertake clean-up of their pollution, forming a nascent "polluter pays" principle. [139] Environmental courts have also forced polluting factories to pay court costs in environmental litigation suits. The hope of the polluter pays principle is that raising the costs for violating pollution rules beyond fines to include cleaning up environmental damage will add teeth to China's environmental regulations and alter the calculus of polluters that they will halt unlawful emissions.

A final area of innovation that has occurred alongside the emergence of environmental courts is the creation of special funds to support environmental litigation. The environmental courts have produced some innovations, but many commentators have criticized them for failing to take on a significant caseload. [140] One reason for their light docket is the prohibitive cost of litigating environmental cases. Court fees are just a small component of costs of environmental litigation; gathering evidence and authenticating claims add significantly to the costs. Environmental attorneys and legal scholars in China whom I interviewed asserted that the main reason for the scant number of public interest environmental cases was due to very few cases being filed at the courts, not the courts' rejection of filings. Citizens' calculations of high financial costs against the infrequent and minimal rewards impede environmental and joint litigation lawsuits. [141] NGOs and their sponsored legal aid centers—usually with foreign funding—help to fill this void in protecting citizens' rights.

In response to the low number of environmental protection cases, a fund was set up to help defray the costs of filing public interest environmental lawsuits at the Kunming environmental court. In 2004, the Guiyang government invested 4 million yuan in start-up funds to establish the Two Lakes and One Reservoir Foundation, which, among other activities, supports local environmental legal cases. [142] The funds encourage people to bring forward public interest cases, but it is unclear who can access the funds and whether the funds have spurred environmental litigation at the specialized courts. In the first case supported by the Two Lakes and One Reservoir Fund, the ACEF, a GONGO attached to the MEP, represented the public interest in an environmental lawsuit. [143] There is little or no evidence that private citizens or grassroots civil society organizations have been able to take advantage of such resources. To the contrary, chapter 7 includes analysis of a case in which Friends of Nature, a grassroots organization, has faced financial challenges in a public interest environmental case being tried in Kunming with no support from the fund in that city.

"SCIENTIFIC DEVELOPMENT," "HARMONIOUS SOCIETY," AND LITIGATION

The legal efforts of pollution victims discussed above highlight some of the ways in which Chinese laws are toothless tigers, as well as efforts to give them teeth. In Xiping Village, Shutangshan Village, Qiugang Village, and Wuling City, citizens mobilized to petition, protest, and litigate against polluters to either halt their pollution or to close them down. Their struggles reveal many of the obstacles that pollution victims face in using legal means to protect their interests. In some cases, bureaucratic offices supported pollution victims in their efforts, and that support occasionally tipped the balance so that local authorities or the courts address the environmental dispute. Other times, local authorities and courts ignored instructions from environmental protection offices or higher authorities to resolve the disputes. To stave off litigation, officials such as those in Muling City intervened with administrative solutions that offered modest compensation for pollution victims and minor fines on polluting factories but which failed to resolve the pattern of illegal emissions.

While China has steadily improved its field of environmental laws and regulations, loopholes in the Environmental Impact Assessment Law and

Tort Law provide means for polluters to continue with violations and local officials to avoid proper implementation of the substantive goals of the environmental impact assessment process, including citizen participation. The cases in Shutangshan and Qiugang Villages, among others, point to loopholes that allow officials to subvert citizen participation in, and effective use of, environmental impact assessments. The system of fines assigned by environmental protection officials and lack of measures to impose punitive damages in the Tort Law have given rise to a pattern of environmental officials applying insignificant fines and state officials protecting polluting enterprises to secure jobs and revenue, leaving local citizens to suffer through the effects of pollution.

The role of the courts in handling environmental disputes has been limited, but it is growing. Certainly, not many of the cases of social conflict over environmental pollution find their way into the courts, but some do. Social mobilization involving petitions, protests, and media coverage help pollution victims and civil society backers to press courts to accept cases. Once in the courts, lawyers from CLAPV and other activist attorneys are fairly successful at receiving some compensation for their clients; [144] in a large sample of cases analyzed by legal scholars at Zhongnan University in China, 43 percent of plaintiffs in pollution cases won some compensation in court. [145] The key is gaining access to the courts. But plaintiffs in lawsuits such as Chen Lifang and her fellow villagers from Tangshushan may find that, once in court, China's environmental laws lack teeth. The courts' reticence to consider health claims and the lack of a mechanism to sue for punitive damages dampen the effect of lawsuits on polluters.

The MEP, along with other central authorities, has encouraged use of legal means to address China's growing pollution problem because it lacks resources to monitor and discipline the factories that it regulates. For the MEP, citizen activism in the form of litigation, petitions, and even protests helps to improve the ministry's monitoring of localities and identify particularly egregious polluters. [146] The central ministry has been quite responsive to many of the complaints that have emerged from common citizens and encouraged litigation, even if local environmental protection bureaus have dragged their heels on such agitation. Establishing a hotline for citizens to report environmental pollution violations is just one example of the MEP's efforts to open information flows between citizens and the central ministry. The establishment of the ACEF under the MEP in order to take up environmental litigation is another example of the ministry attempting to exercise leadership over the handling of environmental legal disputes. Citizen participation also allows the central ministry to improve uniformity in the way that the environmental protection officials implement environmental regulations.

China's regime feels threatened by uncontrolled social mobilization that imperils stability and social harmony, as well as lawsuits that expose its failure to protect the environment. To address both of these concerns, central authorities have sought to increase reliance on legal mechanisms, including litigation, to resolve environmental disputes while also allowing agents attached to the state to guide and contain environmental litigation. In the last decade, the regime has tried to guide the development of environmental litigation with a mixture of state-led litigation, institutional innovations, and civil society interventions. The "Guiding Opinion" issued by the All-China Lawyers Association exemplifies the way in which the state can act through civil society organizations to limit, while still permitting, joint litigation lawsuits from activist attorneys. Chinese policy statements on the environment and litigation such as the "Guiding Opinion" and press accounts explicitly relate environmental management, citizen participation, and litigation to the maintenance of "social stability" and a "harmonious society," terms that underscore the importance and sensitivity of these issues.[147] In praising the work of the Qingzhen environmental court (near Guiyang), Wan Exiang, the vice chair of the Supreme People's Court, called for environmental courts "to strengthen their judicial guidance of environmental public interest litigation."[148] The environmental courts were not meant to be mere passive recipients of environmental cases but to exercise leadership over the direction of development of this emerging field of practice.

China's courts do not always respond to environmental complaints—though they do more often than to AIDS-related lawsuits—and judges have tried to steer environmental litigation in line with regime interest. In a report to the standing committee of the National People's Congress in 2012 Yang Chaofei noted that for the period 2006–2010, China's MEP received over 300,000 environmental petitions, but only 980 resulted in administrative lawsuits and just 30 in criminal cases.[149] Moreover, the state has been reluctant to use criminal cases against polluters, instead preferring to levy fines.[150] The low number of administrative lawsuits and criminal cases resulting from the petitions suggest the way in which petitions and complaints are guided away from legal action against government units. The development of China's civil society and environmental legal system reflect regime concerns over containing environmental conflict, but they also evince modest progress due to the pressures of local citizen activism, international nurturing and financing, and the support of the MEP. In recent years, the state has tried to find means to guide the process of environmental litigation in an effort to protect their interests and legitimacy.

The emergence of environmental courts and revisions of the fine system embedded in the 2014 Environmental Protection Law, too, signal important commitments from central and subnational governments to try to improve implementation of environmental laws and regulations. The caseload of some of these courts, however, has been heavily weighted toward criminal cases rather than civil lawsuits, a pattern that mirrors general trends in China's courts. As noted above, during the period 2002–2011, nearly 70 percent of environmental cases accepted by all of China's courts were criminal cases, so the state could exercise control over which polluters were targeted. For the same period, just 16.67 percent of cases were civil lawsuits. Moreover, as I show in chapter 7, many of the civil lawsuits heard in environmental courts are brought by agents of the state or civil society organizations attached to the state such as the ACEF. The 2013 Supreme People's Court opinion that raised the sentencing guidelines on criminal cases related to the environment also indicates that the judiciary and state are trying to increase the pressure on polluters and local officials who violate the environment to change their ways. The environmental courts' case selection and toughening of criminal sentencing for environmental cases allow the state to maintain its position of leadership over environmental litigation while shifting the target of legal action away from the state. The state can marginalize civil society actors and activist attorneys in litigation, which permits the state to minimize its perceived responsibility for pollution and to take some of the credit for addressing environmental conflict.

The issue of how to manage social conflict related to the environment has split the ranks of the state, not just horizontally (between central and local state units) but also vertically (between ministries). While the central officials seek a path of sustainable development, local officials require economic growth to satisfy growing material demands of citizens. If China's reactions to citizen activism and litigation related to the environment—veering from support to repression—sometimes appear contradictory or a case of two steps forward, one step back, it is due to the political disagreements on how to promote and balance social stability that economic growth brings and citizen participation in environmental protection. The central government and the MEP in particular seem to realize the need to rely more on environmental legal institutions to keep protest in check, but they are also trying to lead the process of environmental litigation with an eye to improving their legitimacy and containing environmental litigation to protect the regime's interest.

NOTES

1. Elements of this chapter were originally published in Scott Wilson, "Seeking One's Day in Court: Chinese Regime Responsiveness to International Legal Norms on AIDS Carriers' and Pollution Victims' Rights," *Journal of Contemporary China* 21, no. 77 (September 2012), 863–80. The author wishes to thank the publishers of the journal for permission to reprint those elements here.

2. Quoted in Xin Zhou and Henry Sanderson, "Chinese Anger over Pollution Becomes Main Cause of Social Unrest," *Bloomberg News*, 6 March 2013, accessed 24 August 2014, http://www.bloomberg.com/news/2013-03-06/pollution-passes-land-grievances-as-main-spark-of-china-protests.html.

3. Tun Lin, Cangfa Wang, Yi Chen, Trisa Camacho, and Fen Lin, *Green Benches: What Can the People's Republic of China Learn from Environmental Courts of Other Countries?* (Mandaluyong City, Philippines: Asian Development Bank, 2009).

4. Vera Peneda, "Green Evolution," *Global Times*, 4 July 2012, accessed 24 August 2014, http://www.globaltimes.cn/content/719011.shtml.

5. Elizabeth Economy, *The River Runs Black: The Environmental Challenge to China's Future* (Ithaca and New York: Cornell University Press, 2004); Christine J. Lee, "Comment: 'Pollute First, Control Later' No More: Combatting Environmental Degradation in China through an Approach Based in Public Interest Litigation and Public Participation," *Pacific Rim Law and Policy Journal* 17 (June 2008), 795–823; Xiaoying Ma and Leonard Ortolano, *Environmental Regulation in China: Institutions, Enforcement, and Compliance* (Lanham, MD: Rowman & Littlefield, 2000); and Yu-wai Li, Bo Miao, and Graeme Lang, "The Local Environmental State in China: A Study of County-Level Cities in Suzhou," *China Quarterly*, no. 205 (March 2011), 96–114, argue that local government can be a source of environmental policy experimentation and innovation.

6. Benjamin L. Liebman, "China's Courts: Restricted Reform," *China Quarterly*, no. 191 (September 2007), 622–24. Anna Brettell, "Channeling Dissent: The Institutionalization of Environmental Complaint Resolution," in *China's Embedded Activism: Opportunities and Constraints of a Social Movement*, eds. Peter Ho and Richard Louis Edmonds (London and New York: Routledge, 2007), 111, makes a similar argument about the environmental petitioning system.

7. Fangchao Li, "NGOs in Difficulty, Survey Shows," *China Daily*, 24 April 2006, accessed 24 August 2014, http://www.chinadaily.com.cn/china/2006-04/24/content_574893.htm.

8. Rachel E. Stern, *Environmental Litigation in China: A Study of Political Ambivalence* (Cambridge: Cambridge University Press, 2013), 107.

9. Stern, *Environmental Litigation in China*, 3.

10. Stern, *Environmental Litigation in China*, 100.

11. Hualing Fu and Richard Cullen, "Climbing the *Weiquan* Ladder: A Radicalizing Process for Rights-Protection Lawyers," *China Quarterly*, no. 205 (March 2011), 47.

12. Carl F. Minzner, "China's Turn against Law," *American Journal of Comparative Law* 59 (2011), 938–39 and 943–48.

13. Stern, *Environmental Litigation in China*.

14. Jun Xia, "'China's Courts Fail the Environment,'" *China Dialogue*, 16 January 2012, accessed 13 August 2013, http://www.chinadialogue.net/article/show/single/en/4727--China-s-courts-fail-the-environment-; Lee, "Comment"; Stern, *Environmental Litigation in China*.

15. Lin et al., *Green Benches*.

16. Chunxiang Yuan袁春湘, "*2002 Nian-2011 Nian Quanguo Fayuan Shenli Huanjing Anjian de Qingkuang Fenxi* 2001年—2002 年全国法院审理环境案件的情况分析" (Analysis of Environmental Court Hearings throughout the Country for the Period 2002-2011), *Fazhi Ribao* 法制日报 (Legal Daily), 19 December 2012, accessed 8 August 2013, http://www.legaldaily.com.cn/zbzk/content/2012-12/19/content_4069404.htm?node=25497.

17. Adam Briggs, "China's Pollution Victims: Still Seeking a Dependable Remedy," *Georgetown International Environmental Law Review* 18 (Winter 2006), 326.

18. Interview 53.

19. Yuan, "Analysis of Environmental Court Hearings."

20. Liebman, "China's Courts," 630.

21. Lee, "Comment," 799.

22. Jason E. Kelley, "Seeking Justice for Pollution Victims in China: Why China Should Amend the Tort Liability Law to Allow Punitive Damages to Environmental Tort Cases," *Seattle University Law Review* 35 (2012), 536.

23. Stern, *Environmental Litigation in China*, 111–12.

24. Kelley, "Seeking Justice," 530; Alex Wang, "Environmental Courts and Public Interest Litigation in China," *Chinese Law and Government* 43, no. 6 (November–December 2010), 5.

25. Kelley, "Seeking Justice," 530.

26. Cited in Alex Wang, "The Role of Law in Environmental Protection in China: Recent Developments," *Vermont Journal of Environmental Law* 8 (Spring 2007), 210.

27. Jost Wubbeke, "The Three-Year Battle for China's New Environmental Law," *China Dialogue*, 2014 April 25, accessed August 6, 2014, https://www.chinadialogue.net/article/show/single/en/6938-The-three-year-battle-for-China-s-new-environmental-law.

28. UNEP, "High Level Expert Meeting on the New Future of Human Rights and the Environment: Moving the Global Agenda Forward," United Nations Environment Program webpage, 2009.

29. *Zhonghua Renmin Gongheguo Huanjing Yingxiang Pingjia Fa* 中华人民共和国环境影响评价法 (Environmental Impact Assessment Law), issued on 28 October 2002 by the Standing Committee of the State Council, put into effect 1 September 2003 by the president, http://zfs.mep.gov.cn/fl/200210/t20021028_84000.htm.

30. *Environmental Impact Assessment Law*, article 16.

31. Jesse L. Moorman and Zhang Ge, "Promoting and Strengthening Public Participation in China's Environmental Impact Assessment Process: Comparing China's EIA Law and U.S. NEPA," *Vermont Journal of Environmental Law* 8 (2007), 303.

32. Charles R. McElwee, *Environmental Law in China: Mitigating Risk and Ensuring Compliance* (Oxford: Oxford University Press, 2011).

33. Yuhong Zhao, "Assessing the Environmental Impact of Projects: A Critique of the EIA Legal Regime in China," *Natural Resources Journal* 49 (Spring 2009), 501, 515.

34. Zhao, "Assessing the Environmental Impact," 515.

35. McElwee, *Environmental Law in China*, 129.

36. *Regulations of the People's Republic of China on Open Government Information*, adopted 17 January 2007, effective 1 May 2008.

37. *Open Government Information Regulations*.

38. *Open Government Information Regulations*, article 8.

39. *Open Government Information Regulations*, article 33.

40. Interview 82.

41. Interviews 79 and 82.

42. Guohui Gao and Wang Quan 高国辉 王泉, "*77 Ge Huanbao Fating 'Menting Lengluo'* 77个环保法庭 '门庭冷落'" (Seventy-Seven Environmental Courts 'Give the Cold Shoulder'), *Nanfang Ribao* 南方日报 (Southern Daily), 8 June 2012, accessed 16 August 2014, http://news.163.com/12/0608/09/83FEMCUB00014AED.html.

43. Gang Chen, *Politics of China's Environmental Protection: Problems and Prospects* (Singapore: World Scientific, 2009), 24–26; Ma and Ortolano, *Environmental Regulation in China*, 124–27; Economy, *The River Runs Black*; Srini Sitaraman, "Regulating the Belching Dragon: Rule of Law, Politics of Enforcement, and Pollution Prevention in Post-Mao Industrial China," *Colorado Journal of International Environmental Law and Policy* 18 (Spring 2007), 310.

44. Xia, "'China's Courts Fail the Environment.'"

45. Interview 86; Lee, "Comment," 805; Lin et al., *Green Benches*, 10; Kelley, "Seeking Justice," 535.

46. Xinjingbao新京报, "*Zhongguo Huanjing Qunti Shijian Gaofa Nian Zeng 29%* 中国环境群体事件告发年增29%" (China's Environmental Mass Incidents Increase 29 Percent per Year), *Xinjingbao*新京报, 26 October 2012, accessed 20 August 2013, http://news.sinovision.net/portal.php?mod=view&aid=234077.

47. Xinjingbao 新京报, "*Rang Gengduo Huanjing Jiufen Zai Fating Jiejue* 让更多环境纠纷在法庭解决" (Allow More Environmental Disputes to Be Settled by Courts), *Xinjingbao* 新京报, 28 October 2012, accessed 2 August 2013, http://epaper.bjnews.com.cn/html/2012-10/28/content_383935.htm?div=-1.

48. *Civil Procedure Law of the People's Republic of China*, promulgated 9 April 1991, promulgated by the president on 9 April 1991, revised 2012, articles 53–56.

49. Interviews 31 and 53.

50. Rachel E. Stern, "On the Frontlines: Making Decisions in Chinese Civil Environmental Lawsuits," *Law & Policy* 32, no. 1 (January 2010), 87, 88.

51. Minzner, "China's Turn against Law," 960, notes that current evaluations of judges encourage mediation rather than litigation, affecting the number of cases that judges will try.

52. Jing Hu, "The Case of Compensation for Water Pollution in Nanhui County in Shanghai," CLAPV Case Analysis, 17 December 2003, 9, http://www.clapv.org/new/file/20031217233817_1071675497.pdf.

53. Interview 53.

54. Fu and Cullen, "Climbing the *Weiquan* Ladder," 57.

55. Hu, "The Case of Compensation."

56. Economy, *The River Runs Black*; Stern, *Environmental Litigation in China*; Wang, "The Role of Law," 195–223.

57. "Chemical Factory Endangers Residents," *China Daily*, 21 October 2003, accessed 24 August 2014, http://www.chinadaily.com.cn/en/doc/2003-10/21/content_273872.htm.

58. Hong Chen and Zhang Jie, "*Xipingcun Pangde Huagongchan* 溪坪村旁的化工厂" (The Chemical Factory Next to Xiping Village), Central Television (News Investigation [新闻调查]), report 2/3843, 12 April 2003, accessed 23 October 2009, http://www.clapv.org/new/show.php?id=587.

59. Fei Run 润斐, "*Zongheng Guancha: Baoguang Guo Hou*纵横观察：暴光过后" (Horizontal Inspection: After the Exposure), *Fujian Dianshitai* 福建电视台 (Fujian Television Station), 10 May 2003, accessed 23 October 2009, http://www.pnlszj.ngo.cn/cn/article.php?articleid=80.

60. Shai Oster and Mei Fong, "River of Tears," *Wall Street Journal* (19 July 2006), A1.

61. Oster and Fong, "River of Tears."

62. Melanie Pitkin, "China: Pingnan Green Wins Court Case against Chemical Company," Global Greengrant Fund Profiles, 6 October 2005, accessed 24 August 2014, http://www.greengrants.org/grantstories.php?print=1&news_id=86.

63. Chen and Zhang, "*Xipingcun Pangde Huagongchan.*"

64. Run, "*Zongheng Guancha.*"

65. Chen and Zhang, "*Xipingcun Pangde Huagongchan.*"

66. Chen and Zhang, "*Xipingcun Pangde Huagongchan.*"

67. Wang, "The Role of Law," 213–14.

68. Wang, "The Role of Law," 214.

69. Interview 75.

70. Xia, "'China's Courts Fail the Environment.'"

71. Zhonghua Quanguo Lvshi Xiehui 中华全国律师协会, "*Zhonghua Quanguo Lvshi Xiehui Guanyu Lvshi Banli Quntixing Anjian Zhidao Yijian* 中华全国律师协会关于律师办理群体性案件指导意见" (Guiding Opinion on Lawyers Handling Collective Cases), issued 20 March 2006, accessed 20 January 2010, http://www.chineselawyer.com.cn/pages/2006-5-15/s34852.html.

72. Zhonghua Quanguo Lvshi Xiehui, "Guiding Opinion."

73. Zhonghua Quanguo Lvshi Xiehui, "Guiding Opinion," III, 2.

74. Zhonghua Quanguo Lvshi Xiehui, "Guiding Opinion," III, 1.

75. Zhonghua Quanguo Lvshi Xiehui, "Guiding Opinion," I, 3.

76. Zhonghua Quanguo Lvshi Xiehui, "Guiding Opinion," IV, 4.

77. Zhonghua Quanguo Lvshi Xiehui, "Guiding Opinion," IV, 8.

78. China's Human Rights Lawyers: Current Challenges and Prospects, by James V. Feinerman. 111th Congress, First Session, 10 July 2009.

79. World Bank and State Environmental Protection Agency, P. R. China (SEPA), *Cost of Pollution in China: Economic Estimates of Physical Damage* (Washington: World Bank, 2007), 33–53.

80. Edward Wong, "Air Pollution Linked to 1.2 Million Premature Deaths in China," *New York Times*, 1 April 2010, accessed 24 August 2014, http://www.nytimes.com/2013/04/02/world/asia/air-pollution-linked-to-1-2-million-deaths-in-china.html.

81. Stern "On the Frontlines," 90.

82. Quoted in Yingying Zhang, "The Shadow over Rural China," *China Dialogue*, 10 February 2011, accessed 1 August 2013, http://www.chinadialogue.net/article/show/single/en/4098-The-shadow-over-rural-China.

83. Interview 53.

84. Xia, "'China's Courts Fail the Environment."

85. Lin et al., *Green Benches*, 9; Minzner, "China's Turn against Law," 935–84.

86. Interview 84.

87. Kelley, "Seeking Justice," 542.

88. Wang, "Environmental Courts," 6.

89. Minzner, "China's Turn against Law," 939, 960 and passim, discusses state model judge campaigns and personnel evaluations to encourage mediation over litigation.

90. Weiwei Liu 刘巍巍, "*Suzhou Shouli Shimin Yaoqiu Zhengfu Xinxi Gongkai Guansi Kaida* 苏州首例市民要求政府信息公开官司开打" (A Precedent Court Case of Citizens Suing over Requests for Open Government Information), *Xinhuawang* 新华网(Xinhua News Service), 11 November 2009, accessed 5 March 2010, http://cc.xinhuanet.com/2009-11/11/content_18204135.htm.

91. Liu, "A Precedent Court Case."

92. Yueying Du杜悦英, "*Yige Lvshide Huanjing Xinxi Gongkai Shenqing Zhi Lu*一个律师的环境信息公开申请之路" (One Lawyer's Path to Request Environmental Open Information), *Zhongguo Jingji Shibao* 中国经济时报 (Chinese Economic Times), 29 April 2009, accessed 21 August 2013, http://finance.sina.com.cn/roll/20090429/23312815304.shtml.

93. Interview 80.

94. Interview 80.

95. Louisa Lim, "Rights Lawyers in China Face Growing Threats," *NPR Weekend Edition*, 3 May 2009, accessed 24 August 2014, http://www.npr.org/templates/story/story.php?storyId=103733164.

96. "State Council Decision on Implementing a Scientific Development Outlook and Strengthening Environmental Protection," issued by State Council, 27 December 2005 (Document No. 39), article 27, http://english.mep.gov.cn/Policies_Regulations/policies/Frameworkp1/200712/t20071227_115531.htm.

97. Interview 82.

98. Ministry of Environmental Protection, *The 2008 Year-End Report on the Ministry of Environmental Protection's Open Government Information Work*, Ministry of Environmental Protection Report no. 16 (Beijing: Ministry of Environmental Protection 2009); Ministry of Environmental Protection, *The 2010 Year-End Report on the Ministry of Environmental Protection's Open Government Information Work*, Ministry of Environmental Protection Report no. 16 (Beijing: Ministry of Environmental Protection 2011).

99. Interview 82.

100. Huanjing Baohubu 环境保护部, *Huanjing Baohubu Zhengfu Xinxi Gongkai Gongzuo 2008 Niandu Baogao* 环境保护部政府信息公开工作2008 年度报告 (The 2008 Year-end Report on the Ministry of Environmental Protection's Open Government Information Work), Ministry of Environmental Protection Report no. 16 (Beijing: Ministry of Environmental Protection, 2009); Ministry of Environmental Protection, *Huanjing Baohubu Zhengfu Xinxi Gongkai Gongzuo 2010 Niandu Baogao* 环境保护部政府信息公开工作2010 年度报告 (The 2010 Year-end Report on the Ministry of Environmental Protection's Open Government Information Work), Ministry of Environmental Protection Report no. 16 (Beijing: Ministry of Environmental Protection, 2011).

101. Economy, *The River Runs Black*; Ma and Ortolano, *Environmental Regulation in China*; Chen, *Politics of China's Environmental Protection*; Sitaraman, "Regulating the Belching Dragon," 311–12; Stern, *Environmental Litigation in China*, 35.

102. Interviews 31 and 53.

103. *Environmental Protection Law of the People's Republic of China*, adopted 1989 December 26, revised 2014 April 24, and put into effect January 1, 2015, article 59.

104. Stern, "On the Front Lines."

105. Interview 87.

106. Wuran Shouhaizhe Falv Yuanzhu Zhongxin 污染受害者法律援助中心, "*Heilongjiang Sheng Mulingshi Jingquan Jiuchang You Dufei Shuiwuran An* 黑龙江省穆棱市晶泉酒厂有毒废水污染案" (Jingquan Alcohol Company in Muling Municipality, Heilongjiang Province Is Responsible for Water Pollution), Unpublished case analysis, 2003, accessed 2 August 2013, http://www.clapv.org/ZhiChiAnJian_content.asp?id=70&title=%D6%A7%B3%D6%B0%B8%BC%FE&titlecontent=PD_zhichianjian&lei1=20.

107. Wuran Shouhaizhe Falv Yuanzhu Zhongxin, "Jingquan Alcohol Company."

108. Jinmei Liu, "The Center Sends Lawyers to Heilongjiang to Promote the Civil Lawsuit Brought by Villagers in Muling City against Jingquan Alcohol Company," CLAPV unpublished (2010).

109. Beifangwang北方网, "*Huanjing Minshi Gongyi Susong 'Yangben' Chansheng* 环境民事公益诉讼 '样本' 产生" (Environmental Public Interest Civil Litigation 'Sample Book' Is Published), *Beifangwang* 北方网, 21 January 2011, accessed 23 May 2011, http://news.xinmin.cn/rollnews/2011/01/21/9005109.html.

110. Xiaofeng Wu and Wang Feng 吴晓锋利王峰, "*Zuida Dasuansu Shengchan Qiye Wuran Xiangjiang 7 Nian Cunmin Pin Huan Bingwang* 最大大蒜素生产企业污染湘江 7 年频患病亡" (The Largest Allicin Production Company Pollutes the Xiang River for Seven Years: Villagers Frequently Die of Illnesses), *Xinhuawang* 新华网, 20 July 2008, accessed 5 August 2013, http://news.xinhuanet.com/politics/2008-07/20/content_8578634.htm.

111. Wu and Wang, "*Zuida Dasuansu Shengchan Qiye.*"

112. Wu and Wang, "*Zuida Dasuansu Shengchan Qiye.*"

113. Zhongguo Jingji Shibao 中国经济时报, "*Hunan Cunzhuang Aizheng Bingli Pinfa Cunmin Chengshi Gongchan Wuran Suozhi* 湖南村庄癌症病例频发村民称是工厂污染所致" (Hunan Village Cancer Cases Repeatedly Occur: Villagers Say It Is Caused by Factory's Pollution), *Zhongguo Jingji Shibao* 中国经济时报 (China Economic Times), 31 January 2007, accessed 5 August 2013, http://www.hero.ngo.cn/yntt/165.html#.

114. Wu and Wang, "*Zuida Dasuansu Shengchan Qiye.*"

115. Wu and Wang, "*Zuida Dasuansu Shengchan Qiye.*"

116. Zhongguo Jingji Shibao, "*Hunan Cunzhuang Aizheng Bingli.*"

117. Changshashi Furongqu Renmin Fayuan 长沙市芙蓉区人民法院, "*Yuangao Chen Lifang, Du Qingshan, Yuan Guoxiang, Wen Yunkai, Chen Shunhe, Yuan Jianguo, Hu Lingzhi, Chen Jianhua bu Fu Beigao Changshashi Huanjing Baohu Ju 'Guanyu Hunan Jingtian Keji Shiye Youxian Gongsi 450t/a Siliao Tianjiaji Gongcheng Huanjing Yingxiang Baogaoshu* 原告陈利芳、杜庆珊、袁国祥、文云凯、陈顺和、袁建国、胡灵芝、陈建华不服被告长沙市环境保护局 '关于湖南晶天科技实业有限公司450t/a 饲料添加剂工程环境影响报告书'" (Plaintiffs Chen Lifang, Du Qingshan, Yuan Guoxiang, Wen Yunkai, Chen Shunhe, Yuan Jianguo, Hu Lingzhi, and Chen Jianhua Do not Accept The Hunan Jingtian Technological Industry, LLC 450t/a Fodder Additive Engineering Environmental Impact Assessment Report by the Defendant, Changsha Municipal Environmental Protection Bureau), court verdict issued 30 April 2009, accessed 1 August 2013, http://www.110.com/panli/panli_232363.html.

118. Kelley, "Seeking Justice," 527–57.

119. China Dialogue, "Eight Cases That Mattered," *China Dialogue*, 26 July 2011, accessed 24 August 2014, http://www.chinadialogue.net/article/show/single/en/4429-Eight-cases-that-mattered.

120. Ruby Yang and Thomas Lennon, *Warriors of Qiugang*, online film directed by Ruby Yang (Thomas Lennon and Chang Ai Media Projects, 2010).

121. Yao Lu 卢尧, "*Anhui Bengbu Qiye Weigui Paiwu Cunmin Pinpin Siyu Guai Bing* 安徽蚌埠企业违规排污村民频频死于怪病" (Anhui's Bengbu Factory Illegally Pollutes, Villagers Repeatedly Die of a Mysterious Illness), *Xinhuawang* 新华网 (Xinhua Net), 4 August 2007, accessed 6 June 2010, http://xzj.2000y.net/mb/2/ReadNews.asp?NewsID=523336.

122. Gongli Zhang张功利, "*Ruhe Zuohao Huanjing Weiquan* 如何做好环境威权" (How to Succeed in Safeguarding Environmental Rights), *Wangyi Tansuo* 网易探索 (NetEase Explorations), 12 October 2009, accessed 10 August 2010, http://www.green-anhui.org/guanyuwomen/meitibaodao/2010-01-15/256.html.

123. Zhang, "Safeguarding Environmental Rights."

124. Yang and Lennon, *Warriors of Qiugang*.

125. Lei Xiang 项磊, "*Cunmin Sannian Ganzou Wuran Gongchang* 村民三年赶走污染工厂"" (Villagers' Three Years of Pushing Out Polluting Factories), *Zhongan Zaixian Yi Xin An Wanbao* 中安在线—新安晚报(Central Anhui Online—New Anhui Evening Report), 24 December 2008, accessed 10 August 2010, http://www.green-anhui.org/guanyuwomen/meitibaodao/2010-01-15/252.html.

126. Interview 95; Hai Gong 龚海, "*Qiugang Baowei Zhan* 仇岗保卫战" (Battle to Protect Qiugang), *Qilu Wanbao* 齐鲁晚报, 25 April 2011, accessed 21 August 2014, http://sjb.qlwb.com.cn/html/2011-04/25/content_117202.htm?div=-1&jdfwkey=c1mdx1.

127. Gong, "Qiugang Battle."

128. Interview 77.

129. Zhang "Safeguarding Environmental Rights."

130. Beifangwang, "*Huanjing Minshi Gongyi Susong 'Yangben.'*"

131. In 1989, Wuhan City established a special environment court, but the Supreme People's Court disbanded it. The high court also struck down other attempts to establish environmental courts in the 1990s. Alex Wang and Jie Gao, "Environmental Courts and the Development of Environmental Public Interest Litigation in China," *Journal of Court Innovation* 3, no. 1 (2010), fn. 4.

132. Jie Gao高洁, "*Huanjing Gongyi Susong Yu Huanbao Fating de Shengmingli—Zhongguo Huanbao Fating de Fazhan Yu Weilai* 环境公益诉讼与环保法庭的生命力—中国环保法庭的发展与未来" (Environmental Public Interest Litigation and Environmental Courts' Vitality: China's Environmental Courts' Development and Future), NRDC (no date).

133. Rachel E. Stern, "Poor Rural Residents in China Seen as Easy Target for Environmental Lawsuits," *China Dialogue*, 24 April 2013, accessed 20 August 2014, https://www.chinadialogue.net/article/show/single/en/5937-Poor-rural-residents-in-China-seen-as-easy-target-for-environmental-lawsuits, notes that many of the criminal cases brought to the Guiyang environmental court target average citizens rather than significant polluters, a type of redirection of the courts from their intended purpose.

134. Gao, "Environmental Public Interest Litigation."

135. Interviews 85, 86, 101, and 102.

136. Ben Blanchard, "China Threatens Death Penalty for Serious Polluters," *Reuters*, 19 June 2013, accessed 20 August 2014, http://www.reuters.com/article/2013/06/19/us-china-pollution-idUSBRE95I10D20130619; and Yan Zhang, "'Legal Weapons' against Pollution Offenses," *China Daily*, 5 August 2013, accessed 20 August 2014, http://www.chinadaily.com.cn/cndy/2013-06/19/content_16635612.htm.

137. Guiyang Ribao 贵阳日报, "*Guiyang Qingzhen Fayuan Huanbao Fating Jinnian Qi Tuixing Anjian Huifang Zhi* 贵阳清镇法院环保法庭今年起推行案件回访制" (This Year the Guiyang Qingzhen Court's Environmental Tribunal Uses a Return Investigation System to Push Through Cases), *Guiyang Ribao* 贵阳日报, 20 April 2009, accessed 16 August 2013, http://www.anquan.com.cn/html/greenpeace/news/2009/0420/56078.html; Jing Jin,金晶. "*Guizhou Huanbao Fating Qingshan Lushuide Shouhu Shen* 贵州环保法庭青山绿水的守护神" (Guizhou's Environmental Court Becomes Qingshan Green Water's Patron Saint), *Renmin Fayuan Bao* 人民法院报 (People's Court Reporter), 25 June 2010, accessed 18 May 2011, http://www.chinacourt.org/html/article/201006/25/415529.shtml.

138. Yazhou Tai, Wang Li, Yang Yimiao, and Liu Xiaoyi 泰亚洲 王丽 杨一苗 刘晓莉, "*Zhongguo Yunyong Huanbao Fating 'Zhiliao' Wuran Wanji* 中国运用环保法庭'治疗'污染顽疾" (China Uses Environmental Courts as "Medicine" against the Scourge of Pollution), *Xinhuawang* 新华网, 30 July 2010, accessed 7 July 2010, http://news.xinhuanet.com/environment/2010-06/22/c_12247458.htm; Guiyangshi Lianghu Yiku Guanli Ju 贵阳市两湖一库管理局, "*Anli Si: Guizhou Tianfeng Huagong Youxian Zeren Gongsi Huanjing Qinquan An* 案例四：贵州天峰化工有限责任公司环境侵权案" (Case Four: Guizhou Tianfeng Chemical, LLC Environmental Tort Case), *Guiyangshi Lianghu Yiku Wangzhan* 贵阳市两湖一库网站(Guiyang Municipality Two Lakes One Reservoir Network), 8 May 2009, accessed 3 August 2010, http://lhyk.gygov.gov.cn/lhyk/74872343805034496/20090508/187211.html.

139. Asia Water Project, "Regulatory Trends: Litigation," Report on the Asia Water Project website, 2010, accessed 30 July 2010, http://www.asiawaterproject.org/regulatory-trends/litigation/.

140. Chaohui Jiang蒋朝晖, "*Huanjing Gongyi Susong Gao Chengben Rang Bushao Ren Wanger Quebu Shei Lai Wei Gongyi Susong Maidan* 环境公益诉讼高成本让不少人望而却步谁来为公益诉讼埋单" (The High Costs of Public Interest Environmental Litigation Allows Few People to Pursue It), *Huanjing Pindao* 环境频道, 1 June 2010, accessed 30 July 2010, http://www.022net.com/2010/6-1/434748112783746.html.

141. Jun Xie and Lijuan Sun, "Access to Collective Litigations in China: A Tough Work," *Journal of Politics and Law* 3, no. 1 (March 2010), 49.

142. Guizhousheng Guiyangshi Lianghu Yiku Huanjing Baohu Jijinhui 贵州省贵阳市两湖 一库环境保护基金会, "*Jijinhui Jianjie* 基金会简介" (Foundation Introduction), Foundation website, accessed 25 August 2010, http://www.lhyk.org.cn/web_info.aspx?id=2.

143. Beifangwang, "*Huanjing Minshi Gongyi Susong*"; Zhiqiu Wang王志球, "*Huanjing Guansi Chengben Gao Shei Maidan? Shouhai Qunzhong 'Gan Nu Er Gan Gao'* 环境官司成 本高谁埋单？受害群众敢怒而敢告" (Who Will Cover the High Cost of Environmental Litigation? Masses of Pollution Victims Have to Suppress Their Rage), *Renmin Ribao* 人民日报 (People's Daily), 17 February 2011, accessed 13 August 2013, http://env.people.com.cn/GB/ 13937591.html.

144. The Center of Legal Aid for Pollution Victims wins approximately 30 percent of its cases, loses 25 percent, with the remainder waiting consideration from the courts. Interview 86.

145. Stern, *Environmental Litigation in China,* 10.

146. Brettell, "Channeling Dissent," 131.

147. Zhonghua Quanguo Lvshi Xiehui, "Guiding Opinion."

148. Jin, "*Guizhou Huanbao Fating.*"

149. Xinjingbao, "*Zhongguo Huanjing Qunti Shijian.*"

150. Lee, "Comment," 804.

Chapter Seven

Who May Defend the "Public Interest"?

The preceding two chapters addressed legal developments and litigation related to HIV/AIDS and environmental pollution. Nearly all of the cases discussed in those chapters involve complaints by private citizens with the support of grassroots organizations or private attorneys in pursuit of protecting personal interests. Chinese authorities have begun to assert themselves in environmental legal disputes by taking up the mantle of environmental public interest litigation, the focus of this chapter. In public interest litigation, plaintiffs act on the behalf of citizens in suing polluters or other legal persons who harm the public's interest. In most countries, public interest litigation is defined by nongovernmental organizations leading the effort to litigate public interest lawsuits because they are independent of the government's interest and, therefore, can provide a check on the state with lawsuits.[1] Chinese grassroots organizations are also vying with state-backed civil society groups over who may defend the public's interest, and this chapter reveals the political and legal struggles between the two sets of groups.

Although the state has a number of levers with which to affect pollution levels in China, including personnel reviews of local officials, fines and criminal charges against polluters, and policy making, central officials have been thwarted by two obstacles in their pollution abatement efforts. First, central authorities have had difficulty piercing through the tightly knit interests of local authorities and businesses, and second, personnel reviews only weigh environmental criteria next to other factors and, in any case, are slow to reverse the cumulative effects of pollution. Citizens on the frontlines of pollution problems are not likely to halt protests with the promise of lowering pay for local officials, some of whom may receive payments from polluters to ignore pollution regulations. State agents have pursued environmental

177

public interest litigation for the following two reasons: to contend for leadership with grassroots activists and lawyers in this new front in the struggle against pollution and because other bureaucratic mechanisms have not proved very effective or been viewed as satisfactory by citizens.

The development of environmental public interest litigation in China reveals that civil society is an arena of contention between state-backed and grassroots organizations who vie for leadership and legitimacy in the eyes of citizens. The ministry of environmental protection has founded a GONGO, the All-China Environmental Federation (ACEF), with a legal aid department to argue environmental public interest litigation cases in the courts and to work on its behalf in civil society. In recent years, some grassroots civil society organizations such as Friends of Nature (Beijing) and Green Volunteers Union (Chongqing) have also sought to represent the public interest in environmental litigation. In pursuing environmental public interest litigation, state officials and their agents in civil society must balance the twin goals of leading litigation that protects society from pollution and shielding the state from societal opprobrium for its failure to avert environmental disasters. From the perspective of China's regime, the delicate balance required to simultaneously address these goals is politically dangerous, so the regime wants to limit the participation of grassroots civil society organizations, who might undermine the regime's legitimacy. The overarching goal of the ACEF's litigation efforts is to respond to and quell civil society complaints about the growing environmental crisis.

The struggle among grassroots organizations, the ACEF, and the state over environmental public interest litigation lends support to a Gramscian, rather than a liberal, framework for analyzing Chinese civil society. As discussed in chapter 2, Gramsci viewed civil society as an arena of conflict among actors vying to support or attack the ruling class's power.[2] Within civil society, some groups and intellectual leaders articulate and defend the regime's and the ruling class's interests.[3] According to Gramsci, the state and ruling elites use organizations in civil society to spread, and thereby construct consent to, their hegemonic ideology. When subordinated classes' consent to the ideology falters, state coercion serves as a backing force to maintain elite and state rule. In Chinese civil society, some groups such as the ACEF, a GONGO under the ministry of environmental protection, represent the state and its interests, while others seek to maintain greater autonomy and criticism of the state, its ideology, and its policies. Although many grassroots civil society organizations in China work alongside state authorities, as well as receive authorization and funding from the state, civil society is also an arena in which forces compete with one another, contest state policies, and protect citizens' rights and interests.

Gramsci also points to a particular strategy used to foster ideological leadership to society: appearing to transcend attachment to a particular class or ruling group. One technique that the state and ascendant groups use to undermine opposition is to articulate an ideology that proffers a harmony of interests among all groups in society. [4] Although in comparison to the era of Mao Zedong (1949–1976), ideology has receded in importance in China, the previous administrations of Jiang Zemin and Hu Jintao moved China's Communist Party away from its original defense of the working class toward a more universal representation of societal interests. Jiang Zemin's "three represents" was an ideological construct that called for the Chinese Communist Party to represent the "vast majority of society," [5] and Hu Jintao's construction of a "harmonious society" called for the Chinese Communist Party to strengthen its leadership and to address problems that help society cohere economically, socially, and culturally. [6] The last two generations of leaders in China have emphasized the importance of maintaining stability (*weiwen*) as part of the ideology of constructing a "harmonious society" (*hexie shehui*), an appeal to avoid fragmentation. Any disruption of the unity of interests and social harmony, therefore, is framed as a danger to society. Public interest litigation, which takes up social conflict that threatens social fabric, offers an opportunity to the state or civil society groups to lead the process of defending societal interests.

The MEP is attempting to maintain social stability through the ACEF, which provides legal services to pollution victims and litigates environmental public interest lawsuits. The MEP hopes to manage conflict over environmental pollution and to lead civil society efforts to protect citizens' rights and interests related to the environment. By doing so, the MEP can advance its own bureaucratic interests by gaining more power for itself while also legitimating the party-state as a whole and deflecting criticism away from the regime's responsibility for a development model that has generated an environmental crisis.

THE LEGAL BASIS OF CHINESE ENVIRONMENTAL PUBLIC INTEREST LITIGATION

Public interest litigation was late to arrive in China because existing laws such as the Civil Procedure Law, Tort Law, and Administrative Litigation Law lacked any provisions for public interest litigation. But the growing problem of environmental pollution and the steady discussion of environmental public interest litigation at conferences and training programs sponsored by international organizations led China's state to recognize the importance of developing a means to advance public interest litigation. The Guiyang and Kunming environmental courts were encouraged to experiment with new rules on environmental public interest litigation in order to help find a path for promoting public interest litigation to protect the environment. "Public interest litigation" is a term that has been much used and infrequently defined in China, but its core element is litigation pursued by a plaintiff or set of plaintiffs to alter public policies, advance a social cause, or provide a public benefit, especially to disadvantaged members of society.[7] For example, public interest litigation in the environmental realm might involve a citizen-based organization's attempt to halt construction of a factory that mars a scenic landscape or that threatens to pollute a river. Public interest litigation is a means of addressing crucial environmental issues such as pollution abatement and environmental restoration, which transcend the interests of a single individual or group of individuals. Environmental public interest litigation can be quite expensive to undertake, which may make such lawsuits beyond the financial reach of a local group of citizens.

The pressure on China's state to develop public interest environmental litigation increased in response to the November 13, 2005, petrochemical factory explosion that dumped benzene, aniline, and nitrobenzene into the Songhua River.[8] The Songhua River incident marked an important turning point in China's approach to environmental civil society organizations and litigation. The chemical spill raised the levels of benzene in the Songhua River to more than thirty-five times the regulatory limit,[9] affecting the population's water supply along the river, but no one person had the resources, or would sufficiently benefit from court action, to sue the company responsible for the spill. Public interest litigation, not yet developed in China at the time, might have been an effective means to pursue court remedies.

China's central government, especially the State Council and the ministry of environmental protection have been active proponents of environmental public interest litigation since the Songhua River chemical spill. In fact, the State Council explicitly began promoting environmental public interest litigation in late December 2005, just weeks after the chemical spill.[10] Exemplifying the central government's supportive attitude toward environmental litigation, Pan Yue, the vice minister of the MEP, announced, "'The [MEP] always encourages environmental lawsuits for the public benefit and always tries to act on the recommendations of the public and NGOs.'"[11] Nevertheless, in its existing laws and regulations, the central government did not define rules or procedures for hearing environmental public interest litigation cases including basic issues such as "Who has standing as a legal person to file public interest claims and enforcement procedures?" Until the end of 2012, such issues had been left primarily to the environmental courts to iron out in their experimental trial regulations. The rules for environmental public interest litigation, especially who may stand as plaintiffs in public interest lawsuits and thereby define and defend the public's interest, became a point of debate in the 2012 revision of China's Civil Procedure Law and the subsequent revision of the Environmental Protection Law. Since Jiang Zemin's "three represents theory" was introduced, the party has clung to an ideology that calls for it to represent universal interests of society,[12] so the regime has been reluctant to surrender authority to nongovernmental organizations (the typical leaders of public interest litigation in other countries) who might challenge the regime's leadership of society and protection of societal interests. China's party-state has worked through its state-backed civil society organizations, especially the ACEF, to try to protect its domination over environmental public interest litigation and to maintain legitimacy by defending the public interest. The ACEF, for its part, seeks to protect particular citizens from environmental problems while shielding the state from fallout over environmental pollution.

THE SLOW DEVELOPMENT OF ENVIRONMENTAL PUBLIC INTEREST LITIGATION

In the first few years of their operation, the environmental courts heard very few public interest litigation cases. Kunming's environmental court, which was established to help promote public interest litigation, heard no such cases from its founding in 2008 through July 2010. Journalists and environmental groups rightly decried the failure of the court to hear any public interest cases,[13] which created pressure on the court and the provincial government to respond to the criticism. In an interview, an expert in Chinese environmental law suggested that the court needed to hear a number of cases in order to legitimate the creation of the environmental court, or it would have to face the unpleasant prospect of this significant environmental reform being phased out.[14] The Qingzhen environmental court in Guiyang City, Guizhou Province, has been more active in promoting public interest cases, including developing rules that gave the broadest number of types of organizations standing as plaintiffs in such cases.

After the Qingzhen and Kunming environmental courts developed rules authorizing public interest litigation, a fundamental obstacle to public interest litigation had been removed, at least in these specialized courts, but cases were slow to emerge. One explanation for the scant number of such cases coming before the environmental courts is the restrictions placed on civil society organizations and regulations on plaintiffs' standing in public interest litigation. In addition, the rules on NGO registration have given rise to a large number of civil society organizations with very limited geographical scope of operations, financial resources, and qualified personnel, which limits their capacity to take up public interest litigation. International foundations have extended funding to some environmental groups such as the Center of Legal Aid to Pollution Victims (CLAPV) in order to help the organizations pursue environmental rights-based litigation, but the resources do not often directly underwrite lawsuits. Instead, international organizations have used conferences and capacity-raising training programs to diffuse knowledge of environmental law and litigation to civil society organizations throughout China, what Rachel Stern calls "soft support."[15]

The regulatory restrictions and financial limitations on civil society organizations combine to constrict the opportunities for such lawsuits filed by grassroots organizations, leaving a gaping space for state offices and GONGOs, which have significant resources and national scope to lead the process of developing environmental public interest litigation. It is not surprising that government agents and organizations under the direct supervision of the government served as the plaintiffs in early public interest litigation, a pattern revealed by the below analyzed cases. Currently, state offices such as the procuratorate and GONGOs such as the ACEF are vying to lead environmental public interest litigation, thereby limiting grassroots organizations' access to the courts in public interest litigation cases. As the environmental public interest litigation cases show, even the courts have somewhat impeded grassroots organizations from championing public interest litigation.

Since the end of 2007, a handful of landmark cases have been heard by environmental courts, which have contributed to defining plaintiffs' standing in public interest environmental cases. A brief examination of public interest cases illuminates both the shifts in plaintiffs' standing in such cases and the state's attempts to exercise leadership in this type of case. In a very important breakthrough in December 2007, the Qingzhen environmental court in Guiyang accepted a case, *The Two Lakes and One Reservoir Management Bureau (Lianghu Yiku Guanliju) v. the Guizhou Tianfeng Chemical Ltd. Company.* In that case, Tianfeng Chemical was found for years to have stockpiled phosphogypsum waste along the shore of Hongfeng Lake, one of the three main water sources for the region (Hongfeng Lake, Baihua Lake, and Aha Reservoir), which then seeped into and contaminated the lake. Due to the pollution from Tianfeng Chemical and similar companies in the region, the water quality in those three sources had been rendered unfit for consumption, despite the local environmental protection bureau persistently leveling fines on Tianfeng Chemical. The company, unafraid of toothless Chinese laws, found it more economical to pay the insubstantial fines and continue polluting than to halt their contaminating the reservoirs. The case broke from the previous standard of the court and the version of the Civil Procedure Law in effect at that time, which required a plaintiff to have a direct interest in the filing of a claim.[16] The Qingzhen environmental court ordered the polluting company, within three months, to build a new chemical waste containment facility that would remedy the seepage problem. Unlike previous fines levied by the environmental protection bureau, the Qingzhen court threatened Tianfeng Chemical's owner with criminal prosecution if he failed to comply, which changed the owner's calculus on continuing to pollute.[17]

The case was significant for three reasons. First, the court accepted a case filed by a government agent—in this case, a special bureau established to oversee the water quality in the two lakes and one reservoir—on behalf of citizens, which helped establish a precedent that government agencies could file claims in environmental public interest litigation.[18] Other cases followed with government offices and local procuratorates standing as plaintiffs in environmental public interest lawsuits. Second, the court's verdict issued injunctions against the factory not to pollute the lakes and reservoir, a significant step up from the minor fines slapped on polluters by the environmental protection bureau agents. Third, the court created mechanisms for monitoring of the company's level of compliance with the court order.[19] The court employed a practice called "follow-up investigation on enforcement" (*zhixing huifang*), which is permitted under the "Guiyang Regulations on Setting Up and Promoting a Civilized Habitat."[20]

In 2008 and 2009, the Guangzhou Maritime Court heard two environmental public interest litigation cases with local procuratorates serving as plaintiffs. Procuratorates (*jianchayuan*) are bodies charged with exercising supervision over legal affairs, and they may become involved in cases, especially in the criminal realm, that are threatening to the regime or otherwise sensitive. According to the website of the Supreme People's Court in China, one of the purposes of the procuratorate is "to safeguard the unity of the country,"[21] a point directly related to this chapter's emphasis on China's state seeking to defend the public's universal interests to maintain harmony. In November 2008, the first lawsuit was brought by the Haizhu District procuratorate in Guangzhou City, Guangdong Province, against a privately owned laundry facility (Xin Zhong Xing Laundry) and its owner, Chen Zhongming. The laundry facility opened in 2007 without a valid business license and pollution permit. In the process of their operations, the laundry used soaps and detergents, and the facility discharged the untreated water from the laundering process directly into the Shi Liu Gang River.[22] In response to citizen complaints, rather than simply fine the laundry, which might have opted to pay the fine without changing their operations, the environmental protection bureau contacted the district procuratorate. The latter office investigated the situation and decided to file a civil enforcement lawsuit against Chen and his laundry facility in the Guangdong Maritime Court.[23] The court heard the case in December 2008 and rendered a judgment of 117,289 yuan against Chen, which was handed over to the national treasury in a fund solely for cleaning up the affected river.[24]

The *Haizhu Procuratorate v. Chen Zhongming* case was significant for a number of reasons. First, the judges in the maritime court attempted to provide a legal rationale for the procuratorate's standing in the case, which had no basis in the letter of national or Guangdong provincial law.[25] The judges reasoned that according to the Water Law of the People's Republic of China, water is a national resource, and according to Article 73 of the General Principles of the Civil Law of the People's Republic of China, the procuratorate acts for the country in supervising the law in civil and administrative cases. Hence, the procuratorate had the right to represent the country's interest in overseeing the law in this civil enforcement case.[26] Second, the case pursued an emerging legal path, civil enforcement, to seek an injunction against the polluter, as well as compensation for damages.[27] Previous efforts to use fines had little effect on polluters' behavior because of the insignificant size of the fines levied. Finally, it is worth noting that the lawsuit was filed against a small private business, rather than a large state-owned industry. It would have been more politically difficult to engineer agreement on the court accepting a lawsuit targeting a state-owned enterprise than a small private enterprise. In fact, the local procuratorate discussed the case with the maritime court prior to filing the lawsuit to get approval for its action,[28] which underscores the need to receive political approval for the courts to even accept new, controversial cases.

Following on the heels of the Haizhu Procuratorate lawsuit, the procuratorate of Panyu District, Guangzhou City, Guangdong Province, filed a similar civil enforcement lawsuit against a privately owned leather and dye factory. In this case, the Panyu Procuratorate alleged that the factory illicitly dumped fifty-five tons of chemicals into the Xia Dong Yong, a small river, affecting the water quality and aquatic life in the river.[29] The factory had diverted their wastewater so that it would not go through a purification process but be directly discharged into the water.[30] The district environmental protection bureau and procuratorate collaborated in collecting and verifying evidence in the case. The procuratorate stood as the plaintiff in the lawsuit against Lu Pingzhang, owner of the Yong Dong Tai Leather and Dye Factory. As in *Haizhu Procuratorate v. Chen Zhongming*, the Panyu Procuratorate sought damages on behalf of those harmed by the polluted river and an injunction against the factory. The Guangzhou Maritime Court heard the case and decided on behalf of the plaintiffs, awarding them 62,500 yuan.[31]

The two district-level procuratorates sought to develop examples for other courts and enforcement agents to follow, as well as send a signal to local factories that they would need to improve their compliance with pollution standards. The two cases seem to have been effective in propelling public interest litigation, though the effect on polluters is much more difficult to gauge. In the wake of the Panyu Procuratorate verdict, however, a private entrepreneur said, "Times have changed. In the past, if you discharged pollution, the worst that would happen is the environmental protection bureau would slap a fine on you. I would never have thought that now the procuratorate would make a big deal and sue a company."[32] In addition, the two successful lawsuits spawned a number of similar cases argued in basic people's courts in Guangdong.[33]

In July 2009, two cases brought by the ACEF also expanded the scope for legal standing to include civil society organizations (*shehui tuanti*) in public interest environmental lawsuits.[34] The Wuxi environmental court and the Qingzhen environmental court accepted separate cases brought by the ACEF. In the case handled by the Qingzhen court, ACEF sued a private company, which, in 1994, had sublet land on an island in Baihua Lake to a third party. Over ten years later and in violation of the land contract and environmental impact assessment regulations, the third party failed to conduct the impact assessment and to follow through with applications for land management permits. The local land management office also failed to enforce its own procedures. The ACEF filed suit against the company with the contract to the land because of runoff pollution from the site into the lake as well as damage to the ecosystem. Within hours of meeting in court, the defendant agreed to correct its errors and halt the cause of the pollution, causing the ACEF to withdraw its suit.[35] Without a formal verdict of the court, the standing of civil society organizations in environmental public interest lawsuits still was not fully affirmed. In the case, the ACEF also could have named the land management office as a defendant for its failure to follow its procedures, but the ACEF chose not to bring suit against a government office. The selection of plaintiffs conforms to what some claim is a pattern of the ACEF's approach to filing lawsuits. One environmental lawyer charged that the ACEF's selection of defendants indicates the underlying bias of the ACEF, to protect state interests by avoiding filing suits against state offices.[36]

On July 6, 2009, the ACEF joined with Zhu Zhengmao, a Jiangyin City resident, in an environmental public interest case, *Zhu Zhengmao and ACEF v. Jiangyin Container, LLC*, tried in the Wuxi Intermediate Court. The plaintiffs alleged that the defendant, the Jiangyin Port Packaging Company, Ltd., had failed to go through the environmental impact assessment process and receive approval to operate.[37] According to the complaint, the company produced dust pollution that affected the surrounding environment, as well as discharged a red liquid that contained iron ore particles into the waterway.[38] In response to public outcry, the municipal government investigated the situation, and the company developed a plan to address the pollution problem, but the plan failed to fully resolve the pollution issue. The court investigated the complaint and ordered the company to halt its activities that infringed on surrounding citizens' rights.[39] The ACEF-backed plaintiff then negotiated a settlement, which the court supported, to have the company successfully go through the environmental impact assessment and licensing process within ninety days and to halt their polluting activities. The case was a victory for the ACEF and the pollution victims in the sense of addressing the particular claim, but the case also resulted in a settlement and, thus, no legal decision that could affect other courts and future plaintiffs.

In 2010, acting on a tip from a caller in Guizhou to their environmental law hotline, the ACEF investigated and became party to another important suit in the Qingzhen environmental court. In this case, the ACEF attorneys filed a lawsuit against a Guiyang paper company that dumped pollution into a local river, turning it black. The ACEF worked with a local environmental organization, Guiyang Public Environmental Education Center, to file a public interest lawsuit against the paper mill. Between the time of this and an earlier lawsuit that the Qingzhen environmental court heard, the Guiyang government had passed and put into effect the "Guiyang Regulations on Setting Up and Promoting a Civilized Habitat." Article 23 of those regulations stipulated that "the procuratorate, environmental protection administrative organs, and environmental protection public interest organizations (*huanbao gongyi zuzhi*) may serve as plaintiffs" in public interest lawsuits at the Guiyang environmental court.[40] The regulations authorized "environmental protection public interest organizations," a category of organizations that was not legally defined, to represent the public interest in such lawsuits. The rules for the Yunnan environmental courts allowed the procuratorate, state organs, and "relevant social organizations (*youguan shehui tuanti*)" to serve as plaintiffs in public interest lawsuits.[41] As noted in chapter 1, the term "social organization" (*shehui tuanti*) is a specific category of NGOs that register with the ministry of civil affairs, and it is mostly populated with GONGOs. In the Qingzhen court case, the responsible party for the paper factory admitted to dumping waste into the river from 7:00 p.m. to 7:00 a.m. each day.[42] An investigation by the court confirmed the dumping of waste in violation of the regulatory limits of chemical by-products.[43] Concerned that the paper factory would drag out the proceedings and continue to harm the environment, the ACEF sought and received from the Qingzhen court an injunction to halt the factory's production.[44] The case was novel in one further respect: in order to help finance the suit, local residents and the ACEF were able to draw funds from the Two Lakes and One Reservoir Protection Foundation (Lianghu Yiku Baohu Jijinhui), a fund established to support plaintiffs in environmental public interest litigation cases because of the high costs of undertaking such lawsuits.

As a GONGO under the ministry of environmental protection, the ACEF constituted a civil society organization, so their representation of the public interest was an important breakthrough, but their status as a GONGO meant that they were still closely attached to the state. When the Wuxi and Qingzhen environmental courts accepted lawsuits filed by the ACEF, they established precedents for civil society organizations (and not just state offices) to act as plaintiffs in such cases.[45] If the courts interpreted the filing of these cases by the ACEF as a general acceptance of civil society organizations having standing in environmental public interest litigation cases, then potentially many more cases with civil society organizations as plaintiffs could emerge. Organizations, especially those that cooperate with international NGOs and foundations, could muster resources to sustain environmental litigation, which average citizens typically lack.

Environmental public interest litigation is still in its early stages with many procedural issues still being resolved, but a subtle trend emerges from a close examination of the first public interest lawsuits and the rules of the environmental courts. Nearly all of the public interest lawsuits have been brought either by (a) agents of the state such as local procuratorates or environmental protection bureaus or (b) the ACEF, a GONGO directly tied to the MEP. This pattern reflects the central state's interest in advancing litigation to protect the public interest but also a degree of insecurity in trusting grassroots civil society organizations and activist lawyers to fight in the courts. Using the ACEF and the procuratorates allows the state to moderate and to contain the development of environmental public interest. The pattern of public interest litigation hews to the Hu Jintao–Wen Jiabao leadership's emphasis on "harmonious society" (*hexie shehui*); the state and its ancillary groups gained legitimacy for protecting the public interest while limiting the unpredictable pursuit of public interest causes by civil society organizations.

The emerging model of public interest lawsuits headed up by organizations such as ACEF and procurators remains quite controversial. Some officials would like to have investigatory units (procuratorates) and environmental management units, which represent societal interests and are state agents, rather than civil society organizations, take the lead in public interest lawsuits. Such an approach would keep representation of the public interests in environmental litigation safely in the hands of state officials. But others such as Wang Canfa, head of CLAPV, argue that it is important to separate litigation from legal enforcement functions, allowing civil society to bring public interest lawsuits to the courts.[46] A conflict of interest could surface, for example, in a case in which a potential public interest lawsuit would implicate the local environmental protection office for failure to enforce environmental regulations, perhaps due to bribery or incompetence. In such a (not so) hypothetical case, if the environmental protection office is also responsible for instigating and arguing public interest litigation cases, it might be reluctant to do so. In an important 2010 opinion, China's Supreme People's Court threw its weight behind the Guiyang and Qingzhen environmental courts' efforts to expand public interest litigation to include civil society organizations, although what types of organizations would be included was not clear because of the vague wording on qualifications for standing as a plaintiff in the environmental courts' trial regulations on environmental public interest litigation.[47]

The issue of allowing grassroots organizations the right to stand as plaintiffs in environmental public interest lawsuits came to a head in late 2011. In

November 2011, the environmental court of the Qujing (Yunnan Province) Intermediate People's Court accepted an environmental public interest lawsuit against two chemical factories in Luliang County, Yunnan Province, *Beijing Friends of Nature, Chongqing Green Volunteers Union, and Qujing, Yunnan Environmental Protection Bureau v. Yunnan Province Lulang Chemical Company, LLC and Yunnan Province Lulang Peaceful Technology, LLC.*[48] The plaintiffs allege that the two factories are responsible for unlawfully storing and emitting heavy chromium and hexavalent chromium into the water supply. After initially founding their companies in 1988, the two companies expanded, which required environmental impact assessments and construction and siting in compliance with China's environmental regulations. The defendants violated instructions of their 2004 environmental impact assessment report, which warned against unlawful disposal and storage of chromium near local water supplies. The factories, in fact, built a storage facility with only a single containment wall for chromium waste on the banks of the local section of the Nanpan River and in proximity to a spring that supplied water to local agricultural fields. Chromium is soluble, and in this case, rainfall caused the chromium to dissolve and flow around the containment wall into the river and to seep into the soil. During the period 1988–2011, the two chemical factories had cumulatively produced 440,000 tons of chromium residue, a by-product of their manufacturing of ferrous and nonferrous metals and chromium salt. In 2011, the chemical factories' leadership could not account for 300,000 tons of the chromium residue, claiming that it had "been used in synthetic processes."[49] In mid-May 2011, Lu Guoliang, the party secretary of Zhangjiaying Village, located outside of Qujing City, came across five trucks—four with empty beds and one loaded with some substance—backed up to the local water reservoir. Lu Guoliang tried to stop the fifth truck from dumping its load in the water, but could not do so, and the five trucks raced away.[50] Villagers suspect that the five trucks dumped loads of chromium residue into the water supply. Later investigations found that the two chemical companies had ordered their chromium waste removed and dumped in other locales, some as far away as Guizhou, a neighboring province.[51] Villagers noticed a problem with their water supply on June 11, 2011, when their livestock (over thirty sheep, a cow, and a horse) drank at a local reservoir and suddenly died later that day.[52] Villagers in rural areas surrounding the industrial park where the chemical factories are located also claimed that they suffered from an inordinately high rate of cancer, an allegation that has been a source of controversy in reporting on the matter. While a local government official has called the list of cancer victims false, a reporter visited the site and verified that forty people in an affected village had contracted cancer.[53] Greenpeace, which has branches in China including one in nearby Kunming, the capital of Yunnan Province, took samples from the groundwater, water in streams, and in rice paddies of two affected villages to test for levels of heavy chromium and hexavalent chromium. The samples indicated that chromium levels in the villages' groundwater reached as high as 242 times the statutory limit, and water in the rice paddies found concentrations of chromium 126 times over the limit.[54] The Qujing environmental protection bureau sent investigators to take water samples in September 2011, and they found that in one part of the affected waterway, hexavalent chromium exceeded the statutory limit, but in other parts, the water samples were within standard II water quality for hexavalent chromium. The authorities explained the significant discrepancy by noting that they had sampled dissimilar areas of the bodies of water on different days than Greenpeace.[55] The participation of Greenpeace in the documentation of evidence, however, created pressure from an outside force to take this case seriously and for the local environmental protection bureau to justify the results from its water samples.

Unfortunately, the fact that chromium emissions may have created another cancer village in China is not what makes this case stand out. Rather, the fact that the environmental court accepted a public interest lawsuit filed by a grassroots NGO, Friends of Nature (Beijing) joined by Green Volunteers Union of Chongqing, an organization registered as a social organization, or *shetuan*, made this case unprecedented. All earlier public interest environmental cases had been filed by government organs or the government-backed ACEF. The court's acceptance of the case has been widely hailed in China's press and legal circles as a breakthrough for grassroots NGOs to participate in public interest litigation. The development of the case demonstrates the distinct approach that the grassroots NGOs would like to take to public interest cases in contrast to the ACEF and government bureaus that file such cases, as well as the great challenges that NGOs face in the judicial system.

After receiving the legal brief from the two NGOs acting as plaintiffs, the court strongly argued that Friends of Nature and Green Volunteers Union should include the Qujing environmental protection bureau as a plaintiff.[56] According to attorneys in the case, if they failed to include the Qujing environmental protection bureau as a plaintiff, the environmental court would not set up a trial.[57] The local environmental protection bureau, which was responsible for overseeing and monitoring the factories that were named as defendants, also could have been named as a defendant for failing to carry out their regulatory duties, so the court's action appears to have been an attempt to shield the local officials from allegations or exposure of their ineptitude. Including the Qujing environmental protection bureau as a plaintiff also allowed a state agent to monitor and temper the development of the case. During the process of gathering evidence and building a case, the lawyers representing the NGOs found the local bureau officials uncooperative and anxious to have the case mediated rather than litigated by the courts.

An environmental attorney who is knowledgeable of the Qujing case said, "From the start of the case, the Qujing EPB has been a bit opposed (*dichu*) to litigation. The EPB was saying, 'This kind of matter can be settled calmly. Why should it be litigated?' From their perspective, they wanted to be very passive." [58] The officials have an interest in avoiding litigation, which could expose the environmental protection bureau's behavior leading up to the environmental disaster, while the lawyers for the NGOs want to litigate in order to establish a precedent for grassroots NGOs to represent the public interest, as well as to issue a verdict with the court's legal reasoning. Attorneys also acknowledged, however, that the local environmental protection bureau, after it became a plaintiff, was helpful in building evidence against the companies in the case. [59]

Since accepting the case filing, the environmental court created a substantial obstacle to proceeding. After hearing the evidence in a preliminary hearing, the court ordered the plaintiffs to hire a court-approved authority to provide a verified estimation of damages caused by the chromium spill. [60] Few such scientific experts exist in China, and still fewer have been authorized by the courts to file legal documents estimating damages. Xia Jun, a lawyer for the plaintiffs, told reporters that this specialized area of environmental science is essentially a "monopoly in the hands of the environmental protection bureaus, but the EPB's environmental science unit has chosen not to become involved in this case." [61] A scientific organization in Fujian Province that is authorized to submit assessments to the courts offered to file an estimate of damages but sought a fee of nearly 7 million yuan (over 1.1 million dollars), which exceeded the entire 2011 budget of Friends of Nature by 2 million yuan. [62] Facing a potentially insurmountable obstacle, one of the attorneys admitted willingness to have a court-mediated settlement despite the legal team's desire for litigating the dispute, so long as the defendants agreed to admit fault and take responsibility for restoring the environment. [63] Moreover, according to Xia Jun, the judges are pressuring the attorneys to allow the court to mediate the case. [64] If the case is mediated, then no formal verdict will be rendered, and no precedent for grassroots civil society organizations protecting the public interest will be left behind.

Given the court's disposition and the high costs of substantiating the damage claims, the case seemed likely to be mediated by the courts. In fact, on December 28, 2012, the court mediated between the two sides, who reached an agreement to settle the dispute. The settlement called for the accused factories to take responsibility for restoring the environment from the pollution caused by the chromium spill; that the plaintiffs would stipulate a time for the cleanup, which would include citizen oversight of the progress; and that a public fund would be set up for the costs of the cleanup. [65] Although both sides agreed to the settlement, the polluting factories very quickly began to argue for exemptions from the settlement, and on April 18, 2013, the factories formally canceled the agreement.[66] At that point, the Qujing Environmental Court announced the cancellation of the settlement and that the case would move to trial.[67] At time of writing, the case is still pending in the courts.

LAW REVISIONS AND ENVIRONMENTAL PUBLIC INTEREST LITIGATION

The Qujing case may prove a breakthrough if it is, in fact, litigated rather than mediated. It has the potential to become a nonbinding precedent that greatly expands the scope of average citizens through grassroots organizations to participate in environmental governance. Some attorneys feared, however, that the window for grassroots NGOs to file public interest environmental lawsuits would close almost as soon as it was opened. As one attorney sardonically noted, "The first environmental public interest lawsuit argued by a grassroots organization may also be the last."[68] During the period 2012–2014, the possibility of grassroots organizations bringing future public interest lawsuits hung in the balance as the courts and the National People's Congress interpreted revisions to laws that address the right to represent the public interest in environmental litigation. Clarification of standing in laws and regulations provides a stronger legal basis for civil society to participate in public interest litigation than the outcome of the Qujing case, given the nonbinding nature of prior legal decisions.

In recent years, China's National People's Congress has piqued the interest of lawyers and activists by taking up revisions to a number of laws relevant to environmental public interest litigation. In 2012, the National People's Congress completed its revision of the 2007 Civil Procedure Law, and the revised law includes a newly inserted article that: (a) authorizes environmental public interest litigation and (b) designates the legal persons who may stand as plaintiffs in environmental public interest litigation to include "government units (*jiguan*) and relevant organizations (*youguan zu-zhi*)."[69] At the time of passage, Article 55 in the revised Civil Procedure Law seemed to be the breakthrough that grassroots organizations need to secure standing in environmental public interest litigation cases.

The process of reaching this final version of the law was filled with controversy and political intrigue. China's process for revising laws includes draft resolutions that are open to public inspection and written commentary. The first two draft resolutions for the law defined the groups with standing in environmental public interest litigation as "government units (*jiguan*) and relevant social organizations (*youguan shehui tuanti*)." The early drafts of the revised article would effectively have clarified and broadened current judicial definitions of standing in civil litigation cases because the law prior to revision lacked any article on public interest environmental regulation, but the number and types of authorized organizations would have been severely limited. The key term in the drafts of the article in question was "social organization" (*shehui tuanti*), a clearly defined type of organization in the regulations used to register civil society organizations with the ministry of civil affairs. "Social organization" has long been the most difficult status for an NGO to obtain through registration, and many of the registered *shehui tuanti* are GONGOs, groups that are backed and overseen by a government or party unit. Defining standing in environmental public interest litigation cases to include just government organs and social organizations (*shehui tuanti*) would have authorized the ACEF to continue its work on such cases, but Friends of Nature, a grassroots NGO, registered as a "popular nonenterprise unit" (*minban feiqiye danwei*), would have been excluded. If the National People's Congress had adopted the first two draft resolutions of the law with the inserted article on public interest environmental litigation, then presumably, Friends of Nature and all other similar grassroots NGOs would have been defined outside the parameters of permissible plaintiffs in public interest litigation lawsuits. In the period for public commentary on the draft resolutions of the law, environmental lawyers and organizations argued on behalf of changing the revised article's key term from "social organization" (*shehui tuanti*) to "organization" (*zuzhi*). Interestingly, the terminology on standing in the article on environmental public interest litigation in the first two draft resolutions departed from the language in the trial regulations used by the Guiyang and Kunming environmental courts, which had been interpreted to permit grassroots NGOs to have standing in environmental public interest litigation, but the language in the final revision followed the Guiyang court's regulations. The Guiyang rules allow "investigatory government offices, environmental protection management offices, and environmental protection public interest groups (*huanbao gongyi zuzhi*)" to serve as plaintiffs.[70] The Guiyang regulations left unanswered what constitutes a "public interest organization." Interestingly, Zhao Jun, the head of the Guiyang Intermediate Court, called for a relatively strict interpretation of the regulation to include just "citizen and environmental social organizations" (*gongmin, huanbao tuanti*). Zhao justified the restrictive interpretation by saying, "The reason to strictly control the qualification [as plaintiffs] in environmental public interest litigation is to avoid having many citizens coming forth as plaintiffs, resulting in the spread of litigation."[71]

Many legal scholars and civil society advocates hailed the final draft revisions of the Civil Procedure Law and its inclusion of "organizations" among those with standing in environmental public interest litigation cases.[72] While the article is a breakthrough for civil society organizations, there is a great deal of ambiguity about the significance of giving legal standing to "organizations"—not a legally defined term in regulations governing civil society organizations—in environmental public interest litigation. For that reason, activists and attorneys noted that the Supreme People's Court or the National People's Congress will likely need to issue instructions on or explanations of the article that define the term "organization" in order to determine whether it includes groups such as Friends of Nature.[73] In fact, on 1 October 2014, the Supreme People's Court issued an opinion on the revised Environmental Protection Law, which explained that organizations registered at the district level of directly administered cities, such as Friends of Nature, do have standing in environmental public interest lawsuits.[74]

While activists and environmental attorneys praised the revised Civil Procedure Law for clarifying the legality of environmental public interest litigation and expanding the standing of organizations in such cases, the courts essentially refused to hear any environmental public interest cases until the standing issue was resolved either by procedural instructions from the National People's Congress or Supreme People's Court or through a clarification in the revision of the Environmental Protection Law.[75] During the public commentary period, attorneys and activists were disappointed with the first three draft revisions of the Environmental Protection Law. Lawyers and civil society organizations criticized the first draft revision of the Environmental Protection Law because it lacked any article addressing environmental public interest litigation.[76] The second draft of the revised law acknowledged environmental public interest litigation but called for only the ACEF, along with state offices, to be permitted to have standing as a defender of the public interest in environmental lawsuits. The second draft unleashed scores of complaints from civil society organizations, environmental attorneys, and business leaders.[77] Even an official at the ministry of environmental protection, Bie Tao, questioned whether the ACEF's small staff could take on such a duty alone, saying, "I think that specifying only one organization [will not] meet the nation's legal demands in tackling environmental grievances. . . . The scope [of public interest claimants] could be expanded . . . and legally registered environmental groups could also have the right to sue."[78] The potential role of the ACEF in leading the charge for environmental litigation was undermined by discovery of the fact that its governing board includes industrial companies, some of which are heavy polluters.[79] The third draft revision of the law stipulated the following organizations had the right to represent the public interest: "organizations that are legally registered with the ministry of public affairs, have at least five years of specialized and continuous activities in the area of environmental protectionism, and have a good reputation" (*yifa zai guowuyuan minzheng bumen dengji, zhuanmen congshi huanjing baohu gongyi huodong lianxu wunian yishang qie xinyanghao de quanguoxing shehui zuzhi*). Lawyers, activists, and government officials criticized the third draft of the revised legislation, in part for the vague and restrictive wording on standing of plaintiffs in public interest lawsuits.[80]

According to one scholar, only three organizations in all of China—all of them GONGOs—could qualify under the third draft's proposed provisions.[81] The National People's Congress refused to vote on the third draft, a surprising move in light of most revised laws receiving approval by their third reading.

On April 24, 2014, the issue of standing was finally settled when the National People's Congress passed the fourth draft of the Environmental Protection Law. In the revised law, environmental public interest litigation was upheld and civil society organizations registered with bureaus of civil affairs at the municipal level or above, a level of registration that is much lower than the third draft's registration requirement with the ministry of civil affairs at the national level. Passage of the revised law gives legal authorization to a much greater number of civil society groups than activists and attorneys expected would be the case after the law's first three drafts. The multistage revision process is instructive about the state's attitude toward civil society and public interest litigation in two senses. First, the state's starting position in the revision process strictly avoided citizen participation in environmental public interest litigation, leaving it to state agents to lead such litigation. With each subsequent draft, the state softened its position, but the state clearly sought to limit grassroots civil society organizations' access to the courts. Second, the mobilization of civil society complaints during the public commentary period convinced the legislators of the need to allow more public participation in environmental litigation.[82] The revision process illustrated the state's tendency to oppose grassroots participation but also its responsiveness to sustained protest against excluding civil society.

GONGO LEADERSHIP OF PUBLIC INTEREST LITIGATION AND SOCIETAL QUIESCENCE

Determining who may stand as plaintiffs in environmental public interest litigation cases has important ramifications for the participation of average citizens in environmental governance and the way in which environmental cases are prosecuted. According to some environmental attorneys, one of the salient differences between the handling of pollution cases by lawyers working for grassroots NGOs and GONGOs such as the ACEF is the latter organization seeks to avoid direct challenges to state offices and, relatedly, has a tendency to mediate conflicts. One environmental attorney suggested that cases selected by the ACEF must go through several filters, including "not stirring up trouble (*bu re mafan*)" and selection criteria created by a government office.[83] "Not stirring up trouble" entails a general concern for maintaining stability and avoiding criticism from government units, including the ministry of environmental protection. The ACEF has litigated public interest environmental lawsuits as well as compensation cases for pollution victims who approach their legal aid center, but, according to some environmental lawyers, the ACEF is quick to mediate.[84] Unlike litigation, mediation receives little publicity (sometimes the parties must agree not to publicize the results of mediation) and attempts to maintain harmony in society. Such pressure is consistent with an ongoing "model judge" campaign that calls on judges to use mediation rather than litigation to settle conflicts and maintain social stability.[85]

An environmental attorney who is familiar with the litigation team at the ACEF questioned the appropriateness of having a GONGO take up public interest litigation:

> I've always argued that the ACEF cannot be responsible for environmental public interest litigation . . . because they are a governmental unit. Their leader is a retired state council member. The courts accept more of their cases not because they are committed to using litigation to protect the environment but because they want to guard the rights of the ministry of environmental protection. . . . I think that the ACEF sometimes more represents the government's interests and considers environmental problems from their own vantage point rather than the public's.[86]

The attorney saw a similar tendency to mediate and avoid open airing of environmental disputes in a 2008 environmental disaster at Yangzong Hai, a large lake in Yunnan Province.

> In 2009, the ACEF came to discuss the disaster with us. After discussing the case with us, they said that we could not litigate it. They did not say so directly to us, but I was conscious that we could not. We asked, "Why?" because we wanted to litigate it. We could not because the main mine responsible produced more than 10 million yuan in revenue. They said we had to consider the effect on the government. . . . The ACEF wants to mediate everything.[87]

The environmental attorney lays bare the ACEF's political commitments, which call for it to balance protecting people's rights and interests against the need to protect the state's interests. The ACEF's direct ties to the MEP potentially compromise its ability to challenge state offices that may be negligent in dispatching their duties as agents charged to protect the environment.

In fact, the ACEF has, on occasion, prosecuted state offices in its work. For example, in pursuit of a public interest case against a polluting milk processing company in Xiuwen County, Guizhou Province, the ACEF needed supporting documents that the local environmental protection bureau was responsible for collecting and filing. Based on the Open Government Information Regulations, the ACEF filed a formal request for documents with the environmental protection bureau, and when the latter refused to respond within the allotted time, the ACEF went to the court to compel the environmental protection bureau to hand over the documents. The court ordered the environmental protection bureau to comply with the ACEF's request.[88] In a personal interview, litigators for the ACEF told me that they were "most proud of this case" because of "the important legal precedent that it upheld" and its "contribution to the development of rule of law" in the environmental realm.[89] The case stands out because of the ACEF's willingness, in this instance, to file suit against a state agent.

In leading the process of environmental public interest litigation, GONGOs such as ACEF, though, are constrained by their lack of autonomy from state ministries and their reluctance to challenge local state officials to enforce environmental laws and regulations, which has been a persistent problem in China's environmental crisis. An official at the ACEF claimed that, when addressing a group of MEP officials, he argued,

> If I file public interest lawsuits against environmental protection bureaus, then it really helps them in their work. If I am a local environmental protection bureau, then I would go to my local government and tell them that I have to comply with environmental regulations. It is my responsibility. Public interest litigation really is on the side of protecting the environment and on the side of the environmental protection bureau. Lawsuits filed against the environmental protection bureaus really help them to raise their power or to give them more strength. . . . Unfortunately, the local environmental protection officials have not reached that level of consciousness, and they still engage in local protectionism, valuing local industries and tax revenues over the environment.[90]

According to this logic, public interest litigation is a way of breaking up local protectionism and relieving the pressure that local authorities and enterprises bring to bear on local environmental protection units to ignore environmental rules. Until the local environmental protection bureaus accept such an enlightened view, however, the ACEF will likely continue to avoid direct conflicts with the MEP and offices under their control.

An environmental attorney agreed that the MEP has conflicting interests in litigation brought against state units, especially local environmental protection bureaus:

> I sense that the MEP likes litigation as long as it targets other government units. But there has been an evolution in their thinking. I remember the legal affairs office telling me that if we were to work together to sue a unit in the MEP, it would raise the legal affairs office's clout. . . . If the MEP does not take the lead in dealing with cases, then it cannot present their work on these cases to the State Council. At the same time, they do not want to be sued; they do not have any interest in that.[91]

In a sense, the ACEF and activist environmental attorneys working with grassroots NGOs have a common belief in the use of litigation to strengthen the hand of environmental protection officials in enforcing environmental laws and regulations. The difference between the two sides hinges on their willingness in practice to hold officials accountable for pollution problems in the process of litigation. The ACEF can select cases that target private companies or steer cases in the direction of suing private businesses rather than government units, whereas grassroots organizations may wish to target local officials alongside polluters. When a state office must be challenged, the ACEF, by some accounts, prefers to use the authority vested in it by the MEP to pressure state offices to do a better job of complying with environmental regulations without open disclosure of violations, through litigation.[92] The ACEF's approach, which relies more on mediation and negotiation than litigation, can resolve the particular problem for pollution victims without creating a great deal of publicity against the state, an obvious advantage from the state's perspective.

COURTS AND THE POLITICS OF ENVIRONMENTAL ADJUDICATION

Not only are the actions of groups like the ACEF colored by political considerations on how to handle cases, but China's judiciary also is subject to political pressure. In general, environmental courts have greater autonomy and authority than regular courts. Part of that autonomy is due to judges in environmental courts having higher levels of legal training on environmental issues than the rest of China's bench, which gives environmental courts more capacity to hear difficult cases and render judgments against the state. The Qujing case, however, indicates the subtle ways that the environmental court can press for mediation in cases that might be embarrassing to local officials. An attorney claimed that the Qujing environmental court required the Qujing environmental protection bureau to serve as a plaintiff not only to help defray some of the costs of litigation and to gather evidence for the case but more importantly, "to control the situation (*kongzhi jumian*), to control the NGOs' lawyers."[93] The attorney went on to argue that courts are subject to pressure at every step of the judicial process:

> After the court accepts a case, the judges have the right to independently render their decision. But court cases receive a lot of pressure from the government on how to render judgments, and the decisions reflect the attitude of the government. The government will determine whether or not it supports a case. From the start, if the government doesn't support a case, then it is able to contact the courts to let them know. The court then will not set up the case. If

they take the case, then the court can solicit the views of the government or their advice. The government can interfere (*ganshe*) a lot in such cases. [94]

Another lawyer who has worked for a GONGO confirmed that the courts were subject to such political considerations, especially at the crucial stage of accepting cases: "Before any case is accepted, it will certainly be subject to internal review, discussion, and decision processes within the judiciary. Of course the judiciary also has a channel to the government through the political and legal affairs committee (*zhengfa weiyuanhui*). Generally speaking, the courts won't accept any case that they don't have to accept (*neng bushou-li jiu bushouli*)."[95] The lawyer's comments underscore the courts' recent turn toward a conservative approach to enhancing their own power and autonomy. Fearful of rendering an inappropriate decision that could derail their careers, judges prefer to limit the types of cases they handle and render noncontroversial opinions. Indeed, as Carl Minzner shows, judges have begun to be evaluated and paid according to the numbers of cases settled through mediation (rather than litigation) or dropped by plaintiffs, both of which discourage litigation. [96]

Politics has influenced the handling of the above chromium case in the Qujing environmental court. In that case, strong pressure from the judges and a letter from the ACEF compelled the local environmental protection bureau to act as a plaintiff and Friends of Nature and Green Volunteers Union to accept the environmental protection bureau as a plaintiff. [97] Political pressure guided the courts and plaintiffs toward a lawsuit that protected local government offices from potential embarrassment about their (mis-) handling of regulations on the chromium by-product.

While the autonomy of GONGOs such as the ACEF may be compromised by their ties to the state, those same ties empower them to challenge and bring pressure to bear on state officials. The authority that the ACEF has is most readily seen in the fact that it has a relatively easy time having its lawsuits accepted in the environmental courts, while the courts often refuse cases filed by grassroots NGOs and private attorneys. [98] All environmental attorneys whom I interviewed in 2012, including some with ties to the ACEF, agreed that the courts were more open to hearing cases from the ACEF than from grassroots organizations and private attorneys due the ACEF's status as a social organization attached to the MEP. [99] One environmental attorney neatly summarized the matter in an interview: "Their status as a unit under the ministry of environmental protection is useful in advancing litigation and filing lawsuits. Local governments and courts are likely to pay close attention and be friendlier to the ACEF because it represents the ministry of environmental protection than they would be toward grassroots organizations."[100]

More subtly, the ACEF can receive responses to its interventions and requests for information that grassroots organizations cannot. An attorney explained how the ACEF weighed in on a case as a third party to pressure local officials to solve a serious case of water pollution:

> As third parties, we went to represent the ACEF in order to meet with the government, the Party committee, the political and legal affairs committee in order to put some pressure on them. In the course of our discussions, we were able to discover that the government had different views on the matter. There was one very high placed person representing the government who said, "How can you, the court, accept this case? What are you going to do after you accept the case? If you don't take on this case, you can just clock out of work. If you don't do anything, then it's no big deal."[101]

In this case, the participation of the ACEF helped compel the courts to pay attention to the case and mediate it with an out-of-court settlement. If the ACEF is partly hamstrung in handling cases by its ties to the MEP, those same ties give it leverage in pressuring local businesses and officials to address environmental pollution problems.

An activist environmental attorney explained two kinds of political constraints that discourage the courts from accepting environmental lawsuits filed by grassroots groups. First, if lawsuits from pollution victims may drive a business into bankruptcy by winning their claims, "the local government is likely to go and look for the judges. They encourage the courts to avoid such cases by sometimes not accepting a filing by pollution victims." Second, courts decide against plaintiffs not based on legal principles but to avoid further litigation. "The courts will not give a legal victory to the pollution victims, but they will resolve some of the problems of pollution victims. . . . The courts protect the enterprises. So, the courts allow a person to sue and lose, but they resolve some of the problems of the plaintiff. Other parties see that the person doesn't win, so they don't want to sue."[102]

In rendering their decisions, the courts seek to balance a number of competing principles. First, the courts must balance commitments to local citizens' health against considerations of economic development. Second, the courts seek to balance commitments to social harmony and developing rule of law. Third and more interestingly, the courts seek to help plaintiffs but also guard the interests of the state. To meet these competing principles, the courts must try to help address environmental concerns through mediation, which minimizes negative publicity while helping to address some of the plaintiffs' environmental concerns. Mediation has the added benefit of helping the court to avoid rendering an opinion that affects the personnel evaluations of judges. These constraints on the courts are part of a larger pattern that subordinates environmental concerns to financial and economic consid-

erations, which is the underlying problem that gives rise to the need for
environmental public interest litigation.

REPRESENTING THE PUBLIC INTEREST: CITIZEN-STATE STRUGGLES IN CIVIL SOCIETY

The struggle over who can serve as plaintiffs in environmental public interest
litigation is emblematic of contestation between forces allied with the state
and grassroots organizations in civil society. In that struggle, both grassroots
organizations and GONGOs have a shared concern for protecting pollution
victims' rights and encouraging pollution abatement, but the "government
wants to dominate public interest litigation,"[103] presumably in order to steer
litigation toward mediation and away from naming state agents as defendants. The state uses the tentacles that it has extended into civil society with
state-backed organizations to try to indirectly manage controversial matters,
including public interest litigation. GONGOs such as the ACEF serve at least
two political functions for the Chinese state. First, they provide leadership in
civil society, helping to direct and restrain the development of forces that
might align against the state. The ACEF's penchant for mediation, which
hews closely to the regime's emphasis on "social harmony," simultaneously
addresses and contains upheaval over environmental concerns. An environmental attorney pithily charged that China's state has substituted "protecting
stability (*weiwen*)" for "protecting rights (*weiquan*)."[104] Quiescence is the
prime motivation of China's state, and the ACEF helps to keep in check
social conflict generated by environmental pollution by working on behalf of
the state to guard the public interest.

Second, the ACEF as a state-backed organization allows the state to take
credit for representing all of society through public interest litigation. Bor-
rowing from Gramsci's analysis of civil society, the state and ruling interests
must attempt to appear to represent universal interests in society rather than
just those of dominant classes.[105] China's regime—at the central and local
levels—is prone to criticism from disadvantaged segments of society that
state policy represents and advances elite interests and advances economic
development at the expense of the public's health; environmental degradation is the by-product of such a constellation of interests and development
policies. Litigation by GONGOs such as ACEF allows the government to
articulate and protect universal interests, expressed in the form of the "public
interest," which rises above any particular class or segment of society. Public
interest litigation carried out by GONGOs and state offices helps to legitimate the state by demonstrating that it and its civil society allies strive to
serve the people. Somewhat ironically, many of the generators of pollution
are state-run enterprises or recently privatized enterprises (albeit with some

official investment). In many cases, state agents in the environmental protection offices or local government officials could also be sued. So the state and its agents are culpable in many pollution disasters, but the ACEF helps to deflect attention away from administrative offices responsible for the problems and appears to be an antidote.

The ACEF and the environmental courts have the capacity to break down doors that have kept citizens and grassroots organizations out of the courts to defend the public interest and to participate in environmental governance. Unfortunately, the work of the ACEF and the environmental courts has had very little impact on the space available to grassroots organizations and common citizens to advance their roles in environmental governance. Rather than the ACEF working in tandem with other civil society organizations to expand the latter groups' role in environmental public interest litigation, the ACEF and grassroots civil society organizations are in a state of tension and competition with one another over who can represent the public's interest. Courts have provided little support for grassroots organizations to take up this mantle. The revised Civil Procedure Law and Environmental Protection Law establish a firm legal basis for greater citizen participation through grassroots organizations in environmental public interest litigation, but the practical effects of the revisions remain to be seen.

Finally, the cases analyzed here underscore the limited autonomy that China's courts have relative to other nondemocratic countries where judicialization of politics has occurred.[106] In other countries, the courts attempt to assert their independence and advance their interests by taking on cases that demonstrate the judges' expertise and legitimacy. As do most courts in China, the environmental courts, despite the superior training of judges and relative autonomy from state officials (in comparison to regular basic courts in the judicial system), still closely follow the party line.[107] The courts prefer not to hear some types of cases, and they push for mediation rather than litigation. The pattern of the courts' conduct underscores the pressure that the regime can bring to bear on judges to help maintain social harmony. Even cases of protecting the public interest are constrained to guard the legitimacy of the state.

NOTES

1. James A. Goldston, "Public Interest Litigation in Central and Eastern Europe: Roots, Prospects, and Challenges," *Human Rights Quarterly* 28, no. 2 (May 2006), 492–527.

2. Joseph A. Buttigieg, "Gramsci on Civil Society," *boundary 2* 22 (1995), 7.

3. Kate Crehan, *Gramsci, Culture, and Anthropology* (Berkeley: University of California Press, 2002), 137–41.

4. Buttigieg, "Gramsci on Civil Society," 11–12; Robert Fatton, "Gramsci and the Legitimization of the State: The Case of the Senegalese Passive Revolution," *Canadian Journal of Political Science* 19 (1986), 730.

5. Xinhua, "The 'Three Represents' Theory," *Xinhuanet*, 25 June 2001, accessed 24 August 2014, http://news.xinhuanet.com/english/20010625/422678.htm.

6. Jintao Hu, "Hold High the Great Banner of Socialism with Chinese Characteristics and Strive for New Victories in Building a Moderately Prosperous Society in All Respects," Report to Seventeenth National Congress of the Communist Party of China, 15 October 2007, accessed 24 August 2014, http://news.xinhuanet.com/english/2007-10/24/content_6938749.htm.

7. Yiyi Lu, *Public Interest Litigation and Political Activism in China* (Montreal: Rights and Democracy, 2008), 9.

8. Beifangwang北方网, "*Huanjing Minshi Gongyi Susong 'Yangben' Chansheng* 环境民事公益诉讼'样本'产生" (Environmental Public Interest Civil Litigation 'Sample Book' Is Published), *Beifangwang* 北方网, 21 January 2011, accessed 23 May 2011, http://news.xinmin.cn/rollnews/2011/01/21/9005109.html.

9. UNEP, "The Songhua River Spill," Beijing: Field Report (December 2005).

10. "State Council Decision on Implementing a Scientific Development Outlook and Strengthening Environmental Protection," issued by State Council 27 December 2005 (Document No. 39), accessed 4 August 2010, http://english.mep.gov.cn/Policies_Regulations/policies/Frameworkp1/200712/t20071227_115531.htm.

11. Quoted in Yingling Liu, "SEPA Releases New Measure on Public Participation in Environmental Impact Assessment Process," *China Watch*, 24 February 2006, accessed 24 August 2014, http://www.worldwatch.org/node/3886.

12. Xinhua, "The 'Three Represents' Theory."

13. Chaohui Jiang蒋朝晖, "*Huanjing Gongyi Susong Gao Chengben Rang Bushao Ren Wanger Quebu Shei Lai Wei Gongyi Susong Maidan* 环境公益诉讼高成本让不少人望而却步谁来为公益诉讼埋单" (The High Costs of Public Interest Environmental Litigation Allows Few People to Pursue It), *Huanjing Pindao* 环境频道, 1 June 2010, accessed 30 July 2010, http://www.022net.com/2010/6-1/434748112783746.html.

14. Interview 81.

15. Rachel E. Stern, *Environmental Litigation in China: A Study of Political Ambivalence* (Cambridge: Cambridge University Press, 2013).

16. *Civil Procedure Law of the People's Republic of China*, promulgated by the president on 9 April 1991, revised October 28, 2007, and August 31, 2012, put into effect January 1, 2013, article 108.

17. Xinhua, "Environmental Tribunals Hammer Polluters with Legal Accountability," *People's Daily Online*, 15 July 2010, accessed 24 August 2014, http://english.people.com.cn/90001/90776/90882/7067902.html.

18. Gao, Jie 高洁, "*Huanjing Gongyi Susong Yu Huanbao Fating de Shengmingli—Zhongguo Huanbao Fating de Fazhan Yu Weilai* 环境公益诉讼与环保法庭的生命力—中国环保法庭的发展与未来" (Environmental Public Interest Litigation and Environmental Courts' Vitality: China's Environmental Courts' Development and Future), NRDC (no date).

19. Asia Water Project, "Regulatory Trends: Litigation," Report on the Asia Water Project website, 2010, accessed 30 July 2010, http://www.asiawaterproject.org/regulatory-trends/litigation/.

20. Guiyangshi Shengtai Wenming Weiyuanhui 贵阳市生态文明委员会, *Guiyangshi Cujin Shengtai Wenming Jianshe Tiaoli* 贵阳市促进生态文明建设条例 (Guiyang Regulations on Setting Up and Promoting a Civilized Habitat). Issued by the Twelfth Meeting of the Standing Committee of the Guizhou Eleventh People's Congress, 8 January 2010, accessed 16 August 2014, http://www.ghb.gov.cn/doc/201029/52054307.shtml; Asia Water Project, "Regulatory Trends: Litigation."

21. Supreme People's Court of China, website, http://en.chinacourt.org/public/detail.php?id=44.

22. Xinjian Deng 邓新建, "*Guangzhoushi Jianchayuan Chutai Minshi Gongyi Susong Zhidao Yijian Pojie Huanjing Baohu Weiquan Sidao Nanti* 广州市检察院出台民事公益诉讼指导意见破解环境保护威权四道难题" (Guangzhou Procuratorate Promulgates Civil Public Interest Litigation Opinion to Break through the Four Difficulties of Protecting Environmental Rights), *Fazhi Ribao* 法制日报 (Legal Daily), 27 August 2009, accessed 13 June 2013, http://news.sohu.com/20090827/n266266573.shtml.

23. Huiling Deng 邓慧玲, "*Guangdong Shouli Huanjing Gongyi Susong Huosheng Gao Dao Wuran Qiye* 广东首例环境公益诉讼获胜告倒污染企业" (Guangdong's First Environmental Public Interest Lawsuit Wins a Victory: The Case Closes Down the Polluting Factory), *Zhongguo Huanjing Bao* 中国环境报 (China Environmental Report), 21 January 2009, accessed 12 June 2013, http://lvse.sohu.com/20090121/n261878394.shtml.

24. Jingjing Liu, "China's Procuratorate in Environmental Civil Enforcement: Practice, Challenges and Implications for China's Environmental Governance," *Vermont Journal of Environmental Law* 13 (2011), 41–68.

25. At the time of the cases, some local governments, but not Guangzhou's, had issued announcements on government offices having standing as plaintiffs in environmental public interest litigation cases. For example, the procuratorate and environmental protection bureau of Nanhu District, Jiaxing City, Zhejiang Province, issued rules that allowed the procuratorate to represent the public interest in environmental litigation. Liu, "China's Procuratorate," 54.

26. Deng, "Guangdong's First Environmental Public Interest Lawsuit."

27. Deng, "*Guanghoushi Jianchayuan.*"

28. Liu, "China's Procuratorate in Environmental Civil Enforcement," 61–62.

29. Lin Tan 谭林, "*Gongchang Wuran Heyong Zao Jianchayuan Suopei* 工厂污染河涌遭检察院索赔" (Factory Pollutes River, Meets with Procuratorate's Demand for Compensation), *Nanfang Dushibao* 南方都市报, 14 July 2009, accessed 12 June 2013, http://gcontent.oeeee.com/4/fa/4fa53be91b4933d5/Blog/5ff/85c96a.html.

30. Tan, "*Gongchang Wuran*"; Guangzhou Haishi Fayuan 广州海事法院, "*Guangzhoushi Panyuqu Renmin Jianchayuan yu Lupingzhang Shuiyu Wuran Sunhai Peichang Jiufen Panjueshu* 广州市番禺区人民检察院与卢平章水域污染损害赔偿纠纷判决书" (Civil Judgment in Procuratorate of Panyu District, Guangzhou City v. Lu Pingzhang Water Pollution Damage Compensation Lawsuit), *Guanghaifa Chuzi Di 247 Hao* 广海法初字第247号(Guangzhou Court Verdict No. 247), 2009, accessed 13 June 2013, http://ahlawyers.fyfz.cn/b/152938.

31. Tan, "*Gongchang Wuran*"; Guangzhou Haishi Fayuan, *Guangzhoushi Panyuqu Renmin Jianchayuan.*

32. Quoted in Tan, "*Gongchang Wuran.*"

33. Liu, "China's Procuratorate in Environmental Civil Enforcement," 59.

34. Lin, "Development of Environmental Public Interest Litigations."

35. Ming Yi佚名, "Zhonghua Huanbao Lianhehui Tiqi de Woguo Diyi Li Huanjing Gongyi Xingzheng Susong Huo Lian 中华环保联合会提起的我国第一例环境公益行政诉讼获立案" (ACEF Succeeds in Setting Up Our Country's First Environmental Public Interest Litigation Case), ACEF website, 28 July 2009, accessed 3 August 2010, http://www.acef.com.cn/html/hjflfw/wqdt/3361.html; and Qianru Hu 胡倩茹, "*Quanguo Shouli Shetuan Zuzhi Huanjing Xingzheng Gongyi Susong Guiyang Kaishen* 全国首例社团组织环境行政公益诉讼贵阳开审" (The Country's First Case of the Guiyang Court Hearing an Environmental Administrative Public Interest Litigation Brought by a Societal Organization), *Guiyang Ribao* 贵阳日报, 2 September 2009, accessed 3 August 2010, http://www.gz.xinhuanet.com/2008htm/xwzx/2009-09/02/content_17581899.htm.

36. Interview 91.

37. Xudong Tai 泰旭东, "*Quanguo Shouli Huanjing Gongyi Minshi Susong Yi Tiaojie Jiean* 全国首例环境公益民事诉讼以调解结案" (The Country's First Environmental Public Interest Civil Litigation Case Is Settled by Mediation), *Caijingwang* 财经网 (24 September 2009), accessed 3 August 2010, http://www.caijing.com.cn/2009-09-24/110260142.html.

38. Tai, "*Quanguo Shouli Huanjing Gongyi Minshi Susong.*"

39. Tai, "*Quanguo Shouli Huanjing Gongyi Minshi Susong.*"

40. Cited in Gao, "Environmental Public Interest Litigation."

41. Kunmingshi Zhongji Renmin Fayuan, Kunmingshi Renmin Jianchayuan, Kunmingshi Gonganju, Kunmingshi Huanjing Baohuju 昆明市中级人民法院, 昆明市人民检察院, 昆明市公安局, 昆明市环境保护局, "*Guanyu Jianli Huanjing Baohu Zhifa Xietiao Jizhide Shishi Yijian* 关于建立环境保护执法协调机制的实施意见" (Trial Opinion on Establishing Environmental Protection Law Enforcement Coordination Mechanism), jointly issued on 5 November 2008, accessed 27 July 2012, http://www.kmepb.gov.cn/kmhbj/75157117316628480/20081106/11030.html.

42. Beifangwang, "*Huanjing Minshi Gongyi Susong 'Yangben.'*"

43. Beifangwang, "*Huanjing Minshi Gongyi Susong 'Yangben.'*"

44. Beifangwang, "*Huanjing Minshi Gongyi Susong 'Yangben.'*"

45. Gao, "Environmental Public Interest Litigation," 6.

46. Zhongguo Jingying Bao 中国经营报, "*Huanjing Gongyi Susong Poju Daqiye Ren Nan-han* 环境公益诉讼破局大企业仍难撼" (Environmental Public Interest Litigation Break-through: Large Enterprise Is Difficult to Shake), *Zhongguo Jingying Bao*中国经营报 (China Management Reporter), 22 January 2011, accessed 23 May 2011, http://vnetcj.jrj.com.cn/2011/01/2216399054001-1.shtml.

47. Beifangwang, "*Huanjing Minshi Gongyi Susong 'Yangben'*"; and Jing Jin 金晶, "*Gui-zhou Huanbao Fating Qingshan Lushuide Shouhu Shen* 贵州环保法庭青山绿水的守护神" (Guizhou's Environmental Court Becomes Qingshan Green Water's Patron Saint), *Renmin Fayuan Bao* 人民法院报 (People's Court Reporter), 25 June 2010, accessed 18 May 2011, http://www.chinacourt.org/html/article/201006/25/415529.shtml.

48. Ziran Zhiyou et al. 自然之友, "*Huanjing Gongyi Minshi Qisu Zhuang* 环境公益民事起诉状" (Environmental Public Interest Lawsuit Brief), filed with Yunnansheng Qujingshi Zhongji Renmin Fayuan 云南省曲靖市中级人民法院, 28 November 2011.

49. Guangshou Li,黎光寿, "*30 Wandun Gezha Xiaoshi, Luliang Huagong Gongxian 23 Nian Heise GDP* 30万吨铬渣消失陆良化工贡献23年黑色GDP" (300,000 Tons of Chromium Sediment Disappears: Luliang Chemical's Twenty-Three-Year Contribution to Black GDP), *Meiri Jingji Xinwen* 每日经济新闻 (Everyday Economic News), 25 August 2011, accessed 16 July 2012, http://old.nbd.com.cn/newshtml/20110825/20110825093303525.html.

50. Li, "300,000 Tons of Chromium Sediment Disappears."

51. Li, "300,000 Tons of Chromium Sediment Disappears."

52. Li, "300,000 Tons of Chromium Sediment Disappears"; Interview No. 96.

53. Li, "300,000 Tons of Chromium Sediment Disappears"; Gang Zhao, Heng Tang, and Yuan Zeng 赵岗 汤恒 曾苑, "*Guanfang Cheng Yunnan Qujing Cunmin Huan Ai yu Gezha Wuguan* 官方称云南曲靖村民患癌与铬渣无关" (State Calls Qujing, Yunnan Villagers' Can-cer and Chromium Sediment 'Unrelated'), *Yunnan Wang* 云南网 (Yunnan Network), 5 Sep-tember 2011, accessed 16 July 2012, http://news.163.com/11/0905/04/7D5MLRNV0001124J.html.

54. Renminwang 人民网, "*Yunnan Luliang Ge Wuran Shijian: Dixia Shui Ge Chaobiao 242 Bei* 云南陆良铬污染事件: 地下水铬超标242 倍" (Yunnan Lulang Chromium Sediment Case: Groundwater Chromium Levels 242 Times over Limit), *Renminwang* 人民网点(Peo-ple's Network), 1 September 2011, accessed 16 July 2012, http://news.163.com/11/0901/09/7CRV0IF100014JB6.html.

55. Zhao, Tang, and Zeng, "*Guanfang Cheng Yunnan Qujing Cunmin.*"

56. Lei Chen 陈磊, "*Zuigao Fayuan Weituo Zhuanjia Qicao Huanjingfa Sifa Jieshi Wei Huanbao Gongyi Susong Songbang* 最高法院委托专家起草环境法司法解释为环保公益诉讼松绑" (Supreme People's Court Entrusts Specialists to Draft Environmental Law: Judicial Interpretation Loosens Environmental Public Interest Litigation), *Fazhi Zhoumo* 法治周末 (Legal Weekend), 26 June 2012, accessed 11 July 2012, http://news.hexun.com/2012-06-26/142874179.html.

57. Interviews 96 and 102.

58. Interview 96.

59. Interview 96.

60. Chen, "*Zuigao Fayuan Weituo Zhuanjia.*"

61. Quoted in Chen, "*Zuigao Fayuan Weituo Zhuanjia.*"

62. Chen, "*Zuigao Fayuan Weituo Zhuanjia.*"

63. Interview 96.

64. Chen, "*Zuigao Fayuan Weituo Zhuanjia.*"

65. Ping Lin 林平, "*Yunnan Gezha Gongyi Susong An Tiaojie Shibai Yin Beigao Danfang-mian Fanhui* 云南铬渣公益诉讼案调解失败因被告单方面反悔" (Effort to Mediate the Yun-nan Chromium Public Interest Litigation Suit Fails Because the Defendants Single-Handedly Go Back on Their Word), *Zhongguo Ribao* 中国日报, 19 April 2013, accessed 14 June 2013, http://www.chinadaily.com.cn/hqgj/jryw/2013-04-19/content_8809533.html.

66. Xi Huo获悉, "*Yunnan Gezha Gongyi Susong An Tiaojie Shibai Yin Beigao Danfang-mian Fanhui* 云南铬渣公益诉讼案调解失败因被告单方面反悔" (Mediation Fails in Yunan Chromium Public Interest Lawsuit Because the Defendant's Side Goes Back on Its Word), *Zhengyiwang* 正义网 (Justice Network), 19 April 2013, accessed 14 June 2013, http://www. chinadaily.com.cn/hqgj/jryw/2013-04-19/content_8809533.html.

67. Lin, "*Yunnan Gezha Gongyi Susong An.*"

68. Interview 96.

69. *Civil Procedure Law of the People's Republic of China.* Promulgated by the president on 9 April 1991, revised October 28, 2007, and August 31, 2012, put into effect January 1, 2013.

70. Guiyangshi Shengtai Wenming Weiyuanhui, *Guiyangshi Cujin Shengtai*, Article 23.

71. Quoted in Jun Zhang张俊, "*Sifa zai Jiejue Shuiwuran Zhong Gai Ruhe Zuowei* 司法在解决水污染中如何作为?"(What Role Should the Judiciary Play in Settling Water Pollution?) *Zhongguo Huanjingbao* 中国环境报 (China Environmental Report), 4 July 2008, accessed 3 August 2010, http://www.cenews.com.cn/xwzx/fz/qt/200807/t20080703_587559.html.

72. Huimin Li, "China's Public Interest Litigation Gate Is Half Open," *New York Times* (Chinese Version), 17 September 2012, accessed 10 October 2012, http://cn.nytimes.com/ china/20120917/cc17lihuimin/, quotes Wang Canfa and Xia Jun among others on the surprising final version of the revised law.

73. Jun Zhao 赵俊, "*Wanshan Huanjing Gongyi Susong Zhidu bu Neng Zai Tuole* 完善环境公益诉讼制度不能再拖了" (Perfect the Environmental Public Interest Litigation System and Do Not Delay It Again), *Dongfang Ribao* 东方日报, 26 February 2013, accessed 4 March 2013, http://www.dfdaily.com/html/63/2013/2/26/925142.shtml; Interviews 101 and 102; and Stern, *Environmental Litigation in China.*

74. Wei Wang王玮, "*Zuigao Fayuan Huanjing Minshi Gongyi Susong Anjian Sifa Jieshi Zhengqiu Yijian* 最高法院环境民事公益诉讼案件司法解释征求意见" (The Supreme People's Court's Solicitation of Opinions on the Judicial Interpretation of Environmental Public Interest Litigation Cases), *Zhongguo Huanjing Bao Zonghe* 中国环境报综合 (China Environmental Report Summary), 15 October 2014, accessed 18 October 2014, http://fj.people.com.cn/ changting/n/2014/1015/c355602-22612085.html.

75. Yongqi Hu and Wencong Wu, "A Bumpy Road for Environmental Courts," *China Daily*, 30 October 2013, accessed 19 June 2014, http://usa.chinadaily.com.cn/china/2013-10/ 30/content_17070049.htm.

76. Huanjing Baohubu 环境保护部, "*Guanyu Baosong Dui 'Huanjing Baohu Fa Xiuzheng An (Caoan)' Yijian he Jianyi de Han* 关于报送对'环境保护法修正案（草案）意见和建议的函" (Letter Regarding Ideas and Criticism in Response to the "Draft Resolution of Revisions to Environmental Protection Law"), Ministry of Environmental Protection, Document No. 284, 2012, accessed 16 August 2014, http://www.mep.gov.cn/gkml/hbb/bh/201210/t20121031_ 240778.htm.

77. Jianqiang Liu, "New Environmental Protection Law Would Exacerbate Pollution in China," *China Dialogue*, 2 July 2013, accessed 18 June 2014, https://www.chinadialogue.net/ blog/6171-China-s-Environmental-Federation-in-danger-of-becoming-a-new-Lin-Biao/en; Jing Li, "Tycoons Join Activists in Call to Scrap Limit on Lawsuits against Polluters," *South China Morning Post*, 14 August 2013, http://www.scmp.com/news/china/article/1296565/tycoons-join-activists-call-scrap-limit-lawsuits-against-polluters.

78. Quoted in Jing Li, "Green Law Change Would Limit Lawsuits," *South China Morning Post*, 27 June 2013, http://www.scmp.com/news/china/article/1269766/green-law-change-would-limit-lawsuits.

79. China Daily, "The ACEF Needs to Clean House," *China Daily*, 3 July 2013, accessed 8 July 2013, http://usa.chinadaily.com.cn/opinion/2013-07/03/content_16719657.htm.

80. Ke Zhang 章轲, "*Huanbao Fa Xiuding Caoan Sanshen Gongyi Susong Zhuti Beizhi Guodu Xianding* 环保法修订草案三审公益诉讼主体被指过度限定" (The Third Draft Revision of the Environmental Protection Law's Provision on Standing in Public Interest Suits Is Determined to Be Excessively Prescribed), *Diyi Caijing Shibao* 第一财经时报, 23 October 2013, accessed 16 August 2014, http://news.sohu.com/20131023/n388711561.shtml.

81. Zhang, "*Huanbao Fa Xiuding Caoan.*"

82. Jost Wubbeke, "The Three-Year Battle for China's New Environmental Law," *China Dialogue*, 2014 April 25, accessed August 6, 2014, https://www.chinadialogue.net/article/show/single/en/6938-The-three-year-battle-for-China-s-new-environmental-law.

83. Interview 102.

84. Intervews 91 and 102.

85. Carl F. Minzner, "China's Turn against Law," *American Journal of Comparative Law* 59 (2011), 939.

86. Interview 91.

87. Interview 91.

88. Jianrong Qie 郄建荣. "*Shouli Huanjing Xinxi Gongkai Gongyi Susong An Zhonghua Huanbao Lianhehui Shengsu* 首例环境信息公开公益诉讼案中华环保联合会胜诉" (First Case of Environmental Open Government Information Public Interest Lawsuit: The All-China Environmental Federations Wins), *Fazhi Ribao* 法制日报 (Legal Daily), 6 April 2012, accessed 16 August 2014, http://www.legaldaily.com.cn/legal_case/content/2012-04/06/content_3481295.htm?node=33809.

89. Interview 101.

90. Interview 101.

91. Interview 91.

92. Interview 102.

93. Interview 96.

94. Interview 96.

95. Interview 87.

96. Minzner, "China's Turn against Law," 960.

97. Interview 102.

98. Christine J. Lee, "Comment: 'Pollute First, Control Later' No More: Combatting Environmental Degradation in China through an Approach Based in Public Interest Litigation and Public Participation," *Pacific Rim Law and Policy Journal* 17 (June 2008), 815.

99. Interviews 85, 86, 87, 91, 96, 101.

100. Interview 102.

101. Interview 87.

102. Interview 86.

103. Interview 102.

104. Interview 102.

105. Buttigieg, "Gramsci on Civil Society," 10 and 11; Fatton, "Gramsci and the Legitimization of the State," 730.

106. Tamir Moustafa, *The Struggle for Constitutional Power: Law, Politics, and Economic Development in Egypt* (Cambridge: Cambridge University Press, 2009).

107. Minzner, "China's Turn against Law," 935–84, discusses the lack of autonomy that China's courts have in applying the law.

Chapter Eight

Conclusion:
Helping Tigers Grow Teeth

This book began with an attorney's description of Chinese laws as "tigers without teeth." Chinese laws and regulations often lack "bite," rendering them ineffective instruments for protecting rights within China's legal system. Seven chapters later, it is appropriate to reflect on what forces can help Chinese laws to grow "teeth." In this conclusion, I first examine the agents and activities propelling rights protection by the legal system. Next, I turn to an analysis of structural constraints on a breakthrough in rights protection, focusing on the uneven development and fragmented nature of Chinese civil society and the decentralized and fractured administrative and judicial bureaucracy. I conclude with a discussion of the prospects for civil society and rights-based contention under the regime's ideology of harmonious society and social stability.

FACTORS PROPELLING RIGHTS PROTECTION IN CHINA

The efforts of pollution victims and AIDS carriers to use China's courts to protect their rights shed light on the uneven advancement of rights-based claims. One of the key findings of *Tigers without Teeth* has been the way the social and political contexts outside of courts affect the actions of courts. Advancing rights-based claims requires material and political resources, so civil society development must be considered alongside the efforts of rights lawyers and their clients. Based on examples from the preceding chapters, the following four factors help Chinese laws and propel rights protection to develop "teeth": (1) international funding and diffusion of norms, (2) mobilization by Chinese protesters and media, (3) litigation that pushes the boundaries of prevailing rights considerations, and (4) allies within the regime that support rights-based claims brought by activists.

International Funding and Linkages

Several Chinese attorneys and civil society activists whom I interviewed complained that international funders and partners provided limited benefit to their work to advance rights-based claims related to environmental pollution and AIDS.[1] International funders only provide short-term assistance to civil society organizations, but international actors raised the capacity of Chinese organizations and activist attorneys through collaboration, primarily training programs and funding. Such contributions have been significant, especially in the early stages of civil society organizations' development.[2] Some of the highest profile and, in a few cases, most adversarial organizations in China's civil society have included Friends of Nature, Global Village Beijing, Green Watershed (Kunming), Daytop (Kunming), and AIDS Care China, along with legal aid centers started by CLAPV, Yirenping (and affiliates), Orchid (Dongzhen) and Aizhixing. All of the above organizations have received significant technical and financial assistance from international groups. Moreover, all of the legal aid centers and several of the civil society organizations have used resources to press for better protection of citizen rights related to the environment and AIDS. As this book has shown, progress in protecting rights has been uneven and inconsistent, but international support for Chinese activist organizations and attorneys has helped to sustain rights-based claimants' challenges to violations of state laws and regulations.

International actors have also played an important role in diffusing norms about rights-based claims and public interest protections related to particular causes. Many, though by no means all, public interest and cause attorneys have participated in training programs on public interest law abroad or sponsored by international groups in China. The same is true of civil society activists, some of whom have attended UN conferences with the help of international partners or have participated in "public intellectual" programs sponsored by foreign universities. For example, Asia Catalyst, a New York–based civil society organization, raised funds to send personnel from their Chinese partner organization, Orchid, to UN conferences on AIDS. Through contact with international organizations, activists and attorneys gain information and conceptual frames related to their causes and form networks that help advance their efforts. In some cases, technical and financial resources are very important in Chinese activists' pursuit of sensitive objectives, including nondiscrimination policies for HIV/AIDS carriers and reporting of air quality. Chinese civil society organizations' foreign ties and funding enhance autonomy from China's state and improve their capacity to offer criticism of state policies and practices. Through conferences and technical exchanges, international groups' interactions with Chinese activists and lawyers have diffused a new vocabulary and encouraged practices that enhance rights protection. Activists and attorneys are using those new frameworks to press for policy changes and claim rights, compelling the regime to respond with new policies and hear lawsuits. Antidiscrimination cases and environmental public interest litigation are two such examples. Rachel Stern has noted, however, that a low percentage of participants in the CLAPV environmental law training programs, run collaboratively with the Natural Resources Defense Council, have gone on to work on environmental lawsuits.[3] The fact that few of the lawyers trained in environmental law programs persist in litigating environmental cases does not negate the contention that many lawyers who argue environmental and other rights-based cases have received some form of training in public interest law supplied or funded by international organizations. In addition, the CLAPV-NRDC training programs work with judges and environmental officials who can contribute to improved environmental governance and better protection of rights.

The importance of international funders is revealed by their recent partial withdrawal from Chinese civil society. Beginning around 2008, the withdrawal of many international AIDS organizations and funders from China and the declining level of international resources available to Chinese organizations highlighted the important role that international groups have played in China.[4] The withdrawal of foreign funding from the HIV/AIDS sector has left Chinese grassroots civil society organizations susceptible to political pressure from China's state not to challenge the regime's authority. (In contrast, foreign funding for China's environmental governance has remained fairly consistent, helping civil society organizations and environmental legal aid centers to maintain their operations.) At the time of writing, the effects of the international funders' partial disengagement from the AIDS sector of China's civil society are still being discerned, but the situation in Yunnan Province may be instructive. Chinese AIDS groups in Yunnan have suffered from the early departure of international collaborating partners and funders after the province implemented restrictive new regulations on the registration of organizations and programs in 2010.[5] For example, a law and policy program funded by RTI and HPI (two U.S.-based international nongovernmental organizations) was discontinued in 2012, and the related AIDS legal aid center at Yunnan University was closed because its international funding expired and sponsors withdrew from China. Fortunately, administrators of the AIDS law and policy program negotiated with the UN Development Programme to continue funding of a legal aid center for AIDS carriers run out of Daytop, a Kunming-based organization that focuses on AIDS services and rehabilitation programs for drug addicts. The legal aid center, which did not enjoy the support of the regime, would likely have been discontinued (rather than funded) by the state if international funding had stopped.

Mobilization of Protest and Media

Most of this book's pages have focused on formal legal efforts to advance pollution victims' and AIDS carriers' rights and interests, but the case material has also shown that legal contention is closely linked to mobilization of protests and media. As Kevin O'Brien and Lianjiang Li assert in their study of administrative litigation, average citizens' success in the courts depends on combinations of official support, media allies, and "collective action, or the threat of it."[6] Social mobilization and media reports affect whether courts hear specific cases and, potentially, the outcome of such cases, as well as public opinion on emergent social conflict. As AIDS employment discrimination cases and several environmental pollution cases (e.g., Qiugang and Rongping) revealed, savvy rights-based attorneys took advantage of collective action or media coverage to press their arguments in the public realm. When claimants drew the attention of provincial or regional authorities, local officials and courts found themselves on the defensive and were more willing to hear complaints than when social and media mobilization were absent.[7] Chinese officials also increased their focus on discrimination against HIV/AIDS carriers, especially denial of access to schools and medical treatment, when AIDS carriers mobilized several violent protests in 2012.[8] The protests attracted regional and national officials' attention as well as international scrutiny, which increased officials' interest in addressing AIDS carriers' concerns.

Environmental protests in China are frequent, and they increase pressure on officials to respond to citizens' complaints. Not-in-my-backyard (NIMBY) protests against paraxylene chemical factories, for example, have closed down or halted plans to open facilities in Kunming, Dalian, and Xiamen. The rising wave of environmental protests has changed the context of officials' decisions on environmental policy making and enforcement. Consequently, courts are turning more attention to addressing environmental cases. In summer 2014, the Supreme People's Court established an environmental court under its supervision, which can provide guidance to lower courts on hearing environmental cases. In addition, the state has included environmental criteria in the personnel evaluation system in order to improve local compliance with central environmental regulations. As Alex Wang shows, environmental disturbances in an official's locale can significantly reduce his/her pay.[9] Such a lever allows the state to create pressure on local officials to avoid environmental protests and improve compliance with environmental regulations. Finally, specific environmental lawsuits such as the Qiugang and Rongping cases were propelled by national media coverage and protest. Such attentiveness by the judiciary and the bureaucracy to address pollution and maintain stability is hard to imagine without the high levels of ongoing mobilization by environmental protesters.

In contrast, AIDS carriers have tended to avoid protests because of lingering social stigma and discrimination against AIDS carriers, and their legal efforts have suffered as a consequence. The 2010–2012 wave of protests by AIDS carriers was exceptional (though perhaps a bellwether of growing assertiveness) and a result of denial of access to medical care and adequate financial support as promised by the "Four Free, One Care" policy.[10] The protests highlighted continued material struggles by AIDS carriers as well as asserted areas of Chinese policies and private business practices that discriminated against AIDS carriers. A Shenyang court's acceptance of a lawsuit brought by three AIDS carriers who were denied boarding on a flight is the latest example of the fruits of such mobilization.[11] Mobilization in civil society raises the political stakes of managing emerging social conflict along with specific cases of complaints. Failure to successfully handle protests threatens stability and regime legitimacy. Media reports and social movements serve to highlight the importance of social problems and shift popular opinion on the issues, which have long-term consequences for rights-based contention. So long as officials create pressure on courts to apply political criteria (rather than solely legal criteria) in determining court dockets and judgments, rights-based plaintiffs and attorneys will need to appeal to political as much as legal authorities. In China, social movements and rights-based litigation are fundamentally linked and mutually supportive.

Litigation

Rights-based litigation addresses the concerns of individual plaintiffs, but it can have a positive effect on the broader development of rule of law and legal protection of rights. As the above chapters have shown, AIDS and pollution victims have pursued personal claims, affecting not just their own cases but also policies. Courts have not been fully responsive to citizens' legal petitions; courts turn down many, if not most, lawsuits over pollution- or AIDS-related causes without trial. Moreover, in cases heard by courts, judgments often favor defendants, provide plaintiffs with little compensation, and, in some cases, are not enforced. Despite such limited personal rewards for pursuing legal claims, claimants can advance protection of rights just by having their cases tried. Some court losses have been followed by policy victories for disadvantaged groups. For example, AIDS carriers have challenged discriminatory aspects of civil servant employment, access to health care, and health insurance policies, but they have not won court judgments (though one employment case resulted in a settlement). Yet those legal cases instigated review of discriminatory hiring, access to hospital care, and insurance policies.

In environmental pollution cases, many judgments provide (at best) partial victories in the form of compensation for plaintiffs, but recent litigation and public mobilization have also created pressure to add teeth to China's laws. The addition of environmental criteria in the personnel evaluation system is one such example. The revision of environmental regulations, including the Environmental Protection Law, is another way in which mobilization of public opinion and litigation have improved opportunities for citizen participation in environmental governance and increased the punishment for violating pollution regulations. After four rounds of draft revisions of the above law—an inordinately large number of drafts that indicates a very high level of public interest in the revision—the National People's Congress passed a revised version that greatly increased the level of fines to be levied on polluters and provided recourse for some civil society organizations (beyond *shehui tuanti*) to engage in environmental public interest litigation. [12] The revised law has significantly improved the teeth in China's environmental regulations by strengthening enforcement measures and civil society participation in litigation. Such improvements likely would not have been adopted in the revised law without substantial public pressure in the form of collective and legal action focused on environmental issues and widespread criticism of earlier drafts of the law. Analogously, officials addressed discriminatory practices against HIV/AIDS carriers because legal cases and civil society mobilization raised the issue. The effect of these policy and regulatory changes was to strengthen enforcement of existing laws and regulations, giving the laws teeth.

Regime Allies

Supportive state agents or state-backed organizations can be particularly instrumental in helping civil society groups to convince cautious courts to try cases involving new types of social conflict. Judges in basic-level people's courts and tribunals are reluctant to hear cases without a signal from the regime that they may take up a new line of litigation or the direction that the courts' judgments should lean out of fear of rendering judgments that are struck down or violate the regime's interests. Grassroots activists are frequently turned away from courts by judges who refuse to hear their cases, but when state organs or state-backed civil society groups serve as plaintiffs, such as the ACEF in environmental pollution cases, the state sends a message to the courts that (at least) pockets of the state support judges trying such cases. As noted in chapter 7, the ACEF has much greater access to the courts than other civil society organizations, especially in the vital emerging area of environmental public interest litigation, because the ACEF carries the authority of the ministry of environmental protection when it petitions the courts to hear a lawsuit. Grassroots civil society organizations face more obstacles in gaining access to the courts on emerging social conflict.

In contrast to the recent advances of environmental public interest litigation, state organs and GONGOs that work on AIDS issues have not served as, or represented, plaintiffs in AIDS-related lawsuits. Would-be plaintiffs wish to charge state organs as defendants in lawsuits alleging discrimination or health damages due to poor administrative oversight of the blood supply. The lack of state agents who back AIDS-related litigation signals to the courts that they should exercise caution in accepting such lawsuits, which explains the paucity of AIDS cases that the courts have tried. On some occasions and in some provinces analyzed in chapter 5, officials specifically told local courts not to try AIDS-related cases. Indeed, the courts have been loath to hear AIDS-related lawsuits, preferring to have administrative resolutions to such social conflict. Li Xige's long, quixotic attempt to receive compensation in the courts for her infection by HIV-contaminated blood exemplifies the courts' tentativeness to take up controversial cases without clear signals from the state to hear such lawsuits.

Varied access to courts is one of the core features of what I have termed the "politics of justice" in China, and access to courts is influenced by the interests of state agents. I have argued in this book that the interests of the ministry of health are opposed to most AIDS-related litigation while the interests of ministry of environmental protection are advanced by environmental litigation. The ministry of health is likely to be found directly or indirectly culpable in many of the likely lawsuits brought by victims of HIV/AIDS, so it has sought to find bureaucratic responses to the needs of HIV/AIDS carriers in order to avoid public scrutiny of its mismanagement. Policy changes may address some of the material concerns of AIDS carriers and, occasionally, AIDS carriers' rights concerns. The state may offer administrative resolutions in the form of policies, but they may protect the interests of AIDS carriers without extending to them rights that can be protected in courts. AIDS carriers' legal contention over rights is circumscribed by the lack of state supporters of rights-based litigation related to HIV/AIDS. In contrast, the MEP has supported environmental pollution victims litigating against local polluters because it strengthens the ministry's hand in bureaucratic struggles with other ministries or with local officials. A comparison of pollution victims' and AIDS carriers' pursuit of justice shows that rights-based litigation advances when pockets of the state support such litigation. This book's comparison of civil society groups and legal efforts that focus on AIDS and pollution victims, including their legal complaints that courts refuse to hear, reveals the politics of justice in civil society and courts.

OBSTACLES TO RIGHTS-BASED CONTENTION

While the preceding section highlighted forces that are helping to propel rights-based contention, this section turns to the constraints that are impeding such progress. Even when social movements and rights-based attorneys receive domestic and international support, a number of factors can slow progress on rights-based contention. This section analyzes two such factors—the uneven and fragmented nature of Chinese civil society and the decentralized and fractured character of the judicial system.

Uneven and Fragmented Civil Society

Rights-based movements rely on the strength of civil society organizations, so China's regime has sought to modulate, shape, and even lead civil society development. The contour of civil society development is a by-product of politics, especially the regime's interests toward particular causes. Chinese authorities have responded in divergent fashion to the efforts of HIV/AIDS activists and environmental pollution victims who have sought to form civil society organizations or take their cases into the courts. The regime's differentiated responses to civil society organizations—suppressing strident activist groups and attorneys who work on behalf of AIDS victims, while giving greater leeway to those fighting for pollution victims—renders a topography of civil society that has peaks (including environmental protection and social service organizations) and valleys (e.g., religious organizations). Some pockets of civil society are stronger than others because the authorities grant them more freedom to operate and Chinese citizens and international organizations provide sustained support for their activities.

China has a large number of environmental protection– and AIDS-related civil society organizations, making these two of China's stronger sectors of civil society. While some environmental activists have been subjected to intimidation, few environmental civil society organizations have been closed down. In comparison, several activists who work on issues related to HIV/AIDS carriers, including discrimination and management of China's blood supply, have been harassed and their organizations closed down. State authorities have attempted to subordinate the missions and activities of AIDS civil society organizations to those of the state social service delivery system. Some AIDS organizations have ventured into more open advocacy such as Aizhixing, but their efforts have run afoul of authorities.

The relative strength of various Chinese rights-based movements is also conditioned by societal attitudes toward the causes advanced by civil society organizations, which helps to explain the divergence of pollution victims' and AIDS carriers' pursuit of justice. Chinese AIDS organizations have enjoyed a great deal of international support, which has propelled AIDS activism and proliferated a large number of AIDS organizations, but the movement is held back by lingering societal and state discrimination. Societal and state discrimination mutually reinforce one another; the state persists with some discriminatory policies because society, until recently, has not pressed hard for removal of discrimination, and society continues with discriminatory attitudes because the state does not clearly articulate and enforce nondiscrimination principles. Societal attitudes affect the threat level of rights-based movements and contention to state authorities. If a cause is widely supported by society, then the state must respond with great care, whereas a less popular cause gives the state a freer hand to repress or benignly ignore those claiming rights.

In China, environmental consciousness has greatly advanced in the last decade, such that polls of citizens (even in rural areas where environmental consciousness has lagged behind urban areas) now prioritize pollution abatement over development.[13] While AIDS organizations, with the help of central leaders and national publicity campaigns, have contributed to a decrease in societal stigmatization of AIDS and raised awareness of AIDS transmission, polls suggest that Chinese citizens retain lingering prejudice against HIV/AIDS carriers.[14] The different levels of societal consciousness of environmental and AIDS causes affect support for civil society movements and state reaction to rights-based claims.

Most importantly, China's state has sought to keep civil society deeply divided and render it dependent on official authorization in order to limit its capacity to challenge the regime's authority.[15] In part, splintering of Chinese civil society is induced by state policies that circumscribe the geographic operations of civil society groups and limit access to resources. Designed to prevent the emergence of national organizations that could challenge the authority of social organizations attached to the Communist Party, as well as the power of the Communist Party itself, the registration regulations have effectively given rise to a highly fragmented civil society composed of micro-organizations with limited capacity.[16] As international funding has declined, a higher percentage of funding for civil society organizations' programs is channeled through China's state, which allows authorities to pit groups against one another, thereby limiting cooperation among groups. A staff member at a UN agency in Beijing argued, "These divisions really undermine the NGOs' ability to have a strong voice. It really plays into the hands of the government, and the government exploits these differences. If NGOs want to have a say in policies, they need to speak as one."[17]

Chinese civil society registration procedures give local authorities significant scope to choose which organizations to register, creating geographic areas in China where civil society is more robust than in other locales, as well as some sectors of civil society that flourish while others fail to thrive.[18] AIDS organizations have developed more fruitfully in some locales such as

Yunnan Province and Beijing, while they have faced opposition from authorities in other locales including Henan Province and been subordinated to the
state's interests in places such as Shanghai. The registration rules for civil
society organizations and the 2011 State Administration of Foreign Exchange (SAFE) regulations on access to foreign funds have reduced civil
society organizations' capacity to knit together national networks. The 2011
SAFE rules on organizations' access to foreign funds have attempted to
distance local civil society groups from international organizations and
funders who have the potential to spin webs of civil society networks across
China. Internet-based communications, however, have lowered the costs of
networking activities and partially offset the effect of the above regulations.[19]

International financial support for Chinese civil society organizations has
been in decline for nearly six years, spurred in part by SAFE's new regulations on foreign support for civil society and the announcement that the
Global Fund would not provide funding for members of the G20 except
South Africa. These shifts have forced some civil society organizations to
close and pushed others to depend more on state funding, compromising their
ability to oppose state policies. In this new context, China's state may be
altering the direction of the AIDS sector of Chinese civil society away from
advocacy and toward social service delivery. As one leader of an international organization noted, "I don't see a lot of government resources going to
capacity-building, going to the more advocacy-based work at all. It is purely
going to be service delivery."[20] In addition, regulations on fund-raising
strictly bar civil society organizations from soliciting gifts, while organizations registered as nonprofit enterprises are unable to offer any tax advantages to donors.[21] The tenuous nature of support from Chinese citizens and
the state have resulted in competition among AIDS organizations for funding
and sharp divisions among factions of civil society working on AIDS-related
issues. China's environmental organizations have enjoyed steadier funding
and technical assistance from foreign sources as well as widespread domestic
support from citizens. As a consequence of these rules, few civil society
organizations (other than GONGOs) have reliable resources, including personnel and funding, to carry out sustained work on rights-based litigation.

Decentralized and Fractured Bureaucracy and Judiciary

A second impediment to rights-based movements in China is the decentralized and fractured nature of China's administration and judiciary. *Tigers
without Teeth* has highlighted some of the vertical (between ministries and
agencies) and horizontal (between center and locality) fractures and rivalries
that exist within China's state and judiciary. Such fissures undermine effective implementation of policies and protection of citizens' rights. The chal-

lenges of implementing China's environmental regulations exemplify the tension between central and local authorities, while the mishandling of China's blood supply and persistence of discriminatory practices against HIV/AIDS carriers also demonstrate the difficulties that the central government faces in implementing its regulations and policies at the local level. Additionally, China's administrative bureaucracy is riven by vertical fractures, especially between ministries. The MEP's rivalries with the ministry industry and information technology and with the National Development and Reform Commission have hampered its environmental protection efforts, just as the ministry of health's conflict with the department of propaganda and the ministry of public security has led to an inconsistent use of harm reduction strategies advocated by the ministry of health and pursuit of criminalization approaches to HIV/AIDS and high-risk behaviors that the ministry of public security favors.

At first blush, such fissures and the varied interests within China's regime may seem an opportunity for activists to find allies within the regime to protect their activities. Kevin O'Brien and Lianjiang Li's path-breaking work on "rightful resistance," for example, shows how "resisters" take advantage of patrons and political fissures to advance their claims. [22] The decentralized, fragmented organization of China's party-state structure (often called the "*tiao-tiao, kuai-kuai*" system) undermines state cohesiveness and has created political opportunities for activist lawyers and civil society groups by fostering allies in some quarters of the regime. [23] To effectively carry out their work, the environmental protection and health bureaucracies need help from civil society, which has been the basis of partnership between state agents and civil society organizations.

Political fissures in states and assertiveness of courts can create opportunities for activists; however, China's cellular organizational structure geographically circumscribes opportunities for rights-based movements. [24] Under China's decentralized court system, local courts vary in their willingness to hear cases involving AIDS carriers and pollution victims. In China, local courts are subject to perhaps greater influence from horizontal ties to local administrative bodies than supervision from higher courts in the vertical legal bureaucracy. In part, the courts' willingness to hear lawsuits on controversial subject matters is a function of local authorities' calculations on political fallout from litigation (especially if local officials or administrators are culpable), as well as local resources available to meet the needs of complainants. In locales with few resources to pay potential judgments to plaintiffs, authorities press the courts not to accept lawsuits. An additional consideration is the types of plaintiffs (and issues) that come before courts. Environmental cases wind their way into the courts more frequently than AIDS-related cases, and attorneys who work on the environment have been subjected to less harassment and intimidation than those working with AIDS victims.[25] The courts have been affected by politicization, which pressures judges to accept some types of cases but not others and even to render judgments on behalf of particular parties in cases. Such politicization of the judiciary has created uneven access to courts, and AIDS carriers face more judicial obstacles than environmental pollution victims in their pursuit of justice. The judiciary's decentralized organization allows for a great deal of variance in legal outcomes and, therefore, substantive justice, across China. The gap in access to justice is less noticeable in the form of varied verdicts, however, than it is in courts' willingness to hear cases. For example, courts in areas affected by the blood scandal, especially in Henan Province, have thwarted efforts by AIDS carriers to bring lawsuits to the courts over medical malpractice and administrative incompetence in managing China's blood collection and distribution. The uneven access to China's courts and inconsistent judgments rendered reveal the politics of justice in China.

China's development of rights protection is also held back by the fact that legal practice does not follow a common law system, but also does not constitute a well-developed (continental) civil law system. In China's courts, judges pay attention to, but are not bound to follow, precedents. To the detriment of activists seeking to break ground in emerging legal areas such as environmental and AIDS law, Chinese judges in lower courts are reluctant to accept legal cases until a precedent, or more likely, a government policy determination, has been issued on a particular type of case. For example, until 2008 China's state lacked a hard, clear position on domestic violence, but in that year, authorities produced a "Bench Book" on court procedures to handle such cases. In the first fifteen months of the circulation of the non-binding guidelines on domestic violence, courts issued over one hundred protection orders.[26] Since 2010, the Supreme People's Court has begun to publish "guiding cases" to try to help lower courts render more consistent decisions and to strengthen and professionalize the judiciary, although the courts are not bound to follow the guiding cases.[27] With only a few guiding cases being published each year and none in the AIDS or environmental realm so far, courts remain tentative in taking on such cases. In addition to the problem of setting precedents without a common law system, Chinese laws do not provide a solid base for strong civil law determinations because they include vague language and have inconsistent, if not contradictory, expressions. The cumulative effects of the above factors—decentralized courts, a conservative bench, and lack of a common law tradition—are twofold: judges in lower courts enjoy a great deal of autonomy to decide cases without regard to precedent (or to simply refuse cases), and courts are rendered susceptible to pressure from local officials to give greater weight to political calculations than commitments to rule of law in their work.[28]

Typically, breakthroughs in rights-based litigation occur when a court sets a precedent by hearing a new issue or by offering novel reasoning in a decision on an existing area of litigation. Often, such verdicts are rendered by high courts through an appeals process, or when a high court settles a conflict between lower courts' conflicting decisions on the same subject. China's courts have not proven fruitful venues for either pattern of precedent-setting litigation. In one well-publicized case, a judge in a Henan court struck down provincial regulations on seed prices on the grounds that they conflicted with national laws, only to have her judgment overturned and to suffer professionally.[29] Hence, judges have hesitated to take up new subject areas and have often refused to issue written explanations for their rejection of court filings, which violates the Civil Procedure Law.[30] By doing so, courts have also closed off the appeals process to potential plaintiffs. China's decentralized judiciary and lack of a common law tradition renders a single positive verdict less powerful to a rights-based movement than it would in a country with a common law tradition. In sum, as Rachel Stern points out, "Chinese courts lack two of the lynchpins of judicial influence: judicial review and binding precedent."[31]

Works on breakthroughs in rights protection begin with the assumption of judicial independence from executive authorities, which hinges on judges' financial autonomy and tenure.[32] As we have seen, China's courts remain dependent on state budgets, and judges are evaluated by state officials, from the same level of the administrative hierarchy. The judiciary lacks autonomy (and much assertiveness) typically found in cases of judicialization of politics under authoritarian regimes. In China's case, the regime has a number of direct and indirect means to influence what cases the courts try and the types of judgments they render. Rather than speaking of the "judicialization of politics," it is more appropriate in China's case to speak of the politicization of the judiciary. In other words, rights-based contention is not only restrained by the lack of judicial autonomy but also by the decentralized, fragmented court system that is susceptible to politicization. Local courts are under pressure and have scope to deny to claimants access to justice, so a breakthrough in rights-based movements in the form of constructing and spreading precedents throughout the judicial system likely necessitates greater central judicial control rather than more decentralization. Attempts to centralize and improve the legitimacy of the judiciary have had mixed results. While the judge qualification system has improved the quality of the bench, guiding decisions have met with resistance from other institutions and are nonbinding.[33]

IS A RIGHTS REVOLUTION INCOMPATIBLE WITH REGIME MAINTENANCE?

An underlying theme of this book is that China's regime seeks to balance citizen participation in governance (including rights-based litigation) with its desire to maintain stability. The above chapters have shown that concern for regime stability has been a brake on some areas of litigation and judicial autonomy. Can rights protection improve under such conditions? A careful (and perhaps hopeful) reading of the evidence presented here suggests that rights protection can advance under such conditions, albeit slowly, inconsistently, and unevenly across the range of rights-based claims, and improvements in rights protection may not occur through court victories but other forms of activism.

The state's varied responses to environmental pollution and AIDS victims reflect different means of containing and alleviating social conflict. As shown in the above chapters, state officials are more likely to allow litigation to proceed when pockets of the state support such litigation, and impede litigation when it imperils the regime's interests. The regime may be discovering, however, that denying would-be plaintiffs access to the courts to settle social conflict can escalate problems. Several of the environmental pollution cases discussed in this book spawned protest activities when courts refused to hear lawsuits. Speaking on the subject of environmental litigation, Wang Canfa of CLAPV said, "[I]f the courts continue to reject lawsuits, it will result in many people seeking other ways (to make their case heard), such as petitioning or staging sit-ins outside government offices."[34] Similarly, the 2012 wave of violent protests in Henan by AIDS carriers was a reaction to courts refusing to try lawsuits from AIDS carriers suing Henan authorities for not supplying subsidies that the central government recommended for AIDS victims. Politicization of courts, especially over acceptance or refusal of cases, has created incentives for protests to occur alongside litigation, in order to persuade courts to hear cases.

Channeling social conflict into the courts may provide a better path to social stability than responding with a mixture of repression, policy measures, and denial of justice. Xi Jinping's 2012 speech to the Central Committee of the Communist Party on the desirability of judicial autonomy and legal transparency is suggestive of a potentially enhanced role for courts in settling conflict in the coming years.[35] However, Xi's statement has not yet been backed by institutional reforms, and the speech was made in the context of a (ongoing) severe crackdown on rights-based lawyers. It appears that the regime will allow the legal system only limited autonomy; if judges have more independence and the courts greater transparency, then attorneys' freedom to litigate rights-based cases will be curtailed. In theory, the regime can maintain more control over judges than rights-based attorneys because of the regime's direct and indirect means of influencing courts, so it is preferable to grant the former limited autonomy.

In order to understand the prospects for a breakthrough in protecting citizens' rights, we need to refine our assumptions about how China's courts operate in terms of balancing regime legitimacy and commitment to rule of law. Rather than thinking of courts solely as autonomous arenas for contestation and settlement of social conflict, China's courts are also venues for the communication of grievances to the regime.[36] The courts have become even more important in this regard as petitioning offices, which traditionally filled such a communication function, have become less responsive to complaints of common citizens since 2006.[37] While courts may not provide adequate settlement for the citizens involved in particular pollution or AIDS cases, evidence presented in chapters 5 and 6 suggests that the state gathers information from lawsuits related to new areas of social conflict and sometimes responds with bureaucratic remedies. Lawsuits alleging discrimination against AIDS carriers who could not gain access to medical insurance coverage and who could not be employed as public officials resulted in the state's reviewing and rewriting regulations to better protect AIDS carriers' interests. Courts also denied claims of discrimination embodied in health insurance policies, but the regime had the Insurance Association of China revise its guidelines to secure health insurance coverage for AIDS carriers. Significantly, none of the small handful of lawsuits in these issue areas led to legal victories for the plaintiffs, but the cases signaled to the regime a new area of social conflict and the need for legal redress or extension of new protections. The regime responded not with legal victories but policy measures, crafted by the hands of politically reliable officials.

Rather than a breakthrough on rights protection emerging from judgments of the courts, the regime prefers to attend to the interests of disadvantaged groups through policies and bureaucratic mechanisms. Such an approach allows citizens to engage in rights-based contention while the regime responds with moderate improvements in laws, regulations, and policies to protect interests. The process is not fully controlled by the state but it is also not left to litigants in the courts to determine the course of rights protection. From the state's perspective, bureaucratic remedies also prevent the emergence of courts as a strong independent voice of authority in Chinese politics. The state gets to claim that it has protected the interests of disadvantaged groups rather than citizens winning the rights from the state in court. Such a pattern is likely appealing to the Chinese regime because protection of interest also fits well with the tradition of Communist parties defending citizens' interests, whereas citizens' defense of their rights is rooted in the tradition of liberal politics.

Rights protection also is likely to advance in China through collaboration between civil society organizations and the state with help from media and the courts. Even in the face of the regime's "turn against the law" and attacks on rights-based (*weiquan*) attorneys, China has improved environmental protection and advanced AIDS carriers' interests. Such advances have been made by state officials and administrative agents working with civil society organizations to improve on policy formulation and implementation. Further collaboration is likely to occur and may be necessitated by the partial retraction of international support for Chinese civil society development. Although collaboration between state and civil society can result in fruitful policies that better protect average citizens, China's regime has been reluctant to surrender control over the process and it often responds more to collective action (or its threat) than policy proposals from civil society groups. Again, protest and the ensuing media coverage help civil society activists and attorneys to gain traction for rights-based claims from the state and courts.

The synergy between protest, media coverage, and rights-based litigation poses a significant threat to China's regime legitimacy and its conceptualization of social stability. China's regime has responded to this threat by developing a sophisticated approach to managing and engaging civil society, a central point of Gramscian theory and a core argument in *Tigers without Teeth*. Rather than passively responding to demands from autonomous groups and activist attorneys in civil society, the state has attempted to shape the political orientation of civil society through its registration procedures and lead civil society with state-backed organizations. Unlike China's attempts to manage civil society, the role of authorities in managing legal contention has been less widely discussed and is an important new development of regime maintenance and legitimation.[38] Authorities have reined in some rights-based lawyers by intimidating activist attorneys with the threat of harassment and construction of regulations on lawyers and lawyers' associations, which give the threat of disbarment an air of legal legitimacy.[39] Attorneys and legal centers that work on AIDS and discrimination issues have faced a great deal of pressure from the state not to cross vague boundaries of acceptable behavior. In case areas where some state officials see a need for legal action such as environmental pollution, the state is willing to take the lead in supplying legal advocacy for citizens, as it has with the law section of the ACEF. China's regime will continue to attempt to moderate and, to the extent possible, lead the development of litigation to retain its legitimacy just as it has used administrative responses to civil society initiatives to develop measured remedies to social conflict.

Despite state attempts to lead legal efforts related to sensitive areas of social conflict and marginalize autonomous activist attorneys in the process, international groups and Chinese civil society have called for room for autonomous organizations to play a prominent role in defending citizens' rights. The multidraft revision process of the Environmental Protection Law is an example of state legislative authors attempting to use laws to restrict civil society participation in the sensitive area of public interest litigation. The second and third drafts of the Environmental Protection Law attempted to restrict civil society participation in environmental public interest litigation by limiting standing in such cases to state organs and the ACEF, an indication of law writers' distrust of grassroots activism and leadership in environmental litigation. In the face of strong criticism from civil society groups and attorneys and even leaders in the MEP that early drafts of the revised law were too restrictive on civil society organizations' role in environmental public interest litigation, authorities compromised by allowing some autonomous civil society organizations to have standing as plaintiffs in environmental public interest litigation.

For the foreseeable future, the politics of justice in China will be molded by the varied interests of China's state forces who support or oppose specific rights-based movements and civil society activists who seek greater rights protection. China's regime has developed a number of tools to improve protection of citizens' rights including personnel review procedures, policy making in response to social conflict, and dispute settlement processes that include litigation and petitioning. Rights-based movements have also developed a repertoire of actions—protest, civil society organization, media mobilization, and litigation—to advance their claims, which, when combined, can prove a formidable force. The fragmented nature of Chinese civil society and China's administration and judiciary will circumscribe rights advancement to local victories; national breakthroughs will likely occur as a result of local legal and policy experiments that the center then adopts. The varied interests within pockets of the regime and the uneven development of sectors of civil society will continue to provide divergent opportunities for protecting and advancing rights in China. Some rights-based claims, such as those advanced by religious organizations, will founder due to the regime's ardent opposition, while rights-based claims related to public health and the environment, which the regime must address, will advance in fits and starts. The environmental rights movements will continue to advance more quickly, including gaining access to courts for litigation, than AIDS carriers' rights because the former has stronger support from quarters of the state as well as civil society. AIDS carriers can advance protection of their interests and rights, but activists will face limited access to courts and international funding, rendering them more dependent on collaboration with the regime to advance their rights and interests.

NOTES

1. Interviews 67, 85, 86, 102.
2. Guosheng Deng, "The Decline of Foreign Aid and the Dilemma of Chinese Grassroots NGOs," *Religions and Christianity in Today's China* III, no. 1 (2013), 30.

3. Rachel E. Stern, *Environmental Litigation in China: A Study of Political Ambivalence* (Cambridge: Cambridge University Press, 2013), 195–98.

4. Deng, "The Decline of Foreign Aid," 30.

5. Jessica C. Teets, "The Evolution of Civil Society in Yunnan: Contending Models of Civil Society Management in China," *Journal of Contemporary China* (forthcoming).

6. Kevin O'Brien and Li Lianjiang, "Suing the Local State: Administrative Litigation in Rural China," *China Journal*, no. 51 (January 2004), 93.

7. O'Brien and Li also note that local officials go to great ends to suppress activists and thwart their pursuit of justice in the courts. "Suing the Local State," 79 and 82–84.

8. Economist, "Bad Blood: In Central China AIDS Activists Step up Pressure on the Government," *Economist*, 8 September 2012, accessed 1 January 2013,http://www.economist. com/node/21562241/pri; Gillian Wong, "China AIDS Patients Topple Gate of Government Office," Associated Press, 27 August 2012.

9. Alex Wang, "The Search for Sustainable Legitimacy: Environmental Law and Bureaucracy in China," *Harvard Environmental Law Review* 37 (2013), 381.

10. BBC, "*Henan Aizibing Huanzhe Kangyi Caizheng Yuanzhu bu Duixian* 河南艾滋病患者抗议财政援助不兑现" (Henan AIDS Carriers Protest Failure to Fulfill Commitment of Financial Support), *BBC Zhongwenwang* BBC 中文网 (BBC Chinese Network), 27 August 2012, accessed 25 July 2014,http://www.bbc.co.uk/zhongwen/simp/chinese_news/2012/08/120827_china_aids_henan.shtml.

11. BBC, "Passengers with HIV Sue China's Spring Airlines," BBC News, 15 August 2014, accessed 16 August 2014,http://www.bbc.com/news/world-asia-china-28804219.

12. Jost Wubbeke, "The Three-Year Battle for China's New Environmental Law," *China Dialogue*, 2014 April 25, accessed August 6, 2014,https://www.chinadialogue.net/article/show/single/en/6938-The-three-year-battle-for-China-s-new-environmental-law.

13. Daniela Yu and Anita Pugliese, "Majority of Chinese Prioritize Environment over Economy," *Gallup*, 2012 June 8, accessed 2014 July 24, http://www.gallup.com/poll/155102/majority-chinese-prioritize-environment-economy.aspx?version=print.

14. China Daily, "Parade of Prostitutes Lands Shenzhen Police in Hot Water," *China Daily*, 7 December 2006, accessed 24 August 2014,http://www.china.org.cn/english/China/191491.htm.

15. Guosheng Deng, "The Hidden Rules Governing China's Unregistered NGOs: Management and Consequences," *China Review* 10, no. 1 (Spring 2010), 194.

16. Deng, "Hidden Rules," 199. Anthony J. Spires, "Contingent Symbiosis and Civil Society in an Authoritarian State: Understanding the Survival of China's Grassroots NGOs," *American Journal of Sociology* 117, no. 1 (July 2011), 12, argues that organizations remain small (with limited capacity) in order to evade state registration rules and monitoring.

17. Interview 74.

18. Deng, "Hidden Rules," 191.

19. Guobin Yang, "The Co-evolution of the Internet and Civil Society in China," *Asian Survey* 43, no. 3 (May–June 2003), 405–22, discusses the positive relationship between Internet and civil society development in China.

20. Interview 97.

21. Karla W. Simon, *Civil Society in China: The Legal Framework from Ancient Times to the 'New Reform Era'* (Oxford and New York: Oxford University Press, 2013), 286.

22. Kevin O'Brien and Li Lianjiang, *Rightful Resistance in Rural China* (Cambridge: Cambridge University Press, 2006), 28 and 38.

23. Scholars in the China field have long noted the fragmentary nature of China's state structure, which is divided along vertical lines (*tiao*) as well as horizontal space (*kuai*). Some of the more noteworthy works that use the fragmentary state model to explain aspects of Chinese politics include the following: Kenneth Lieberthal and Michel Oksenberg, *Policy Making in China: Leaders, Structures, and Processes* (Princeton: Princeton University Press, 1988); Vivienne Shue, *The Reach of the State: Sketches of the Chinese Body Politic* (Stanford, CA: Stanford University Press, 1988); Andrew Mertha, "'Fragmented Authoritarianism 2.0': Political Pluralization in the Chinese Policy Process," *China Quarterly* 200 (December 2009), 995–1012.

24. Shue, *Reach of the State*, discusses how Chinese administrative structure has been affected by the cellular nature of Chinese (especially rural) society.

25. Congressional-Executive Commission on China, *China's Human Rights Lawyers: Current Challenges and Prospects*, by James V. Feinerman, 111th Congress, First Session, 10 July 2009, 8–9, notes that attorneys advancing HIV/AIDS carriers rights have been subject to detainment and harassment.

26. Robin R. Runge, "An American Concept with Distinctly Chinese Characteristics: The Introduction of the Civil Protection Order in China," *North Dakota Law Review* 88 (2012), 886.

27. Bjorn Ahl, "Retaining Judicial Professionalism: The New Guiding Cases Mechanism of the Supreme People's Court," *China Quarterly*, no. 217 (March 2014), 126.

28. O'Brien and Li, "Suing the Local State," 81.

29. Benjamin L. Liebman, "China's Courts: Restricted Reform," *China Quarterly*, no. 191 (September 2007), 631–32.

30. Liebman, "China's Courts," 620–38, finds that judges have been allowed to innovate and increase their hearing of rights-based litigation. His findings, however, are from the period prior to 2007, when other analysts argue that China's regime "turned against the law." Elizabeth M. Lynch, "China's Rule of Law Mirage: The Regression of the Legal Profession since the Adoption of the 2007 Lawyers Law," *George Washington International Law Review* 42, (2010), 535–85; Carl F. Minzner, "China's Turn against Law," *American Journal of Comparative Law* 59 (2011), 935–84.

31. Stern, *Environmental Litigation in China*, 214.

32. Tamir Moustafa and Tom Ginsburg, "Introduction: The Functions of Courts in Authoritarian Politics," in *Rule by Law: The Politics of Courts in Authoritarian Regimes*, eds. Tom Ginsburg and Tamir Moustafa (Cambridge: Cambridge University Press, 2008), 12–13; Charles R. Epp, *The Rights Revolution: Lawyers, Activists, and Supreme Courts in Comparative Perspective* (Chicago: University of Chicago Press, 1998), 11; Tamir Moustafa, *The Struggle for Constitutional Power: Law, Politics, and Economic Development in Egypt* (Cambridge: Cambridge University Press, 2009), 32 and passim.

33. Ahl, "Retaining Judicial Professionalism," 127.

34. Quoted in Sui-Lee Wee, "Chinese Court Dismisses Water Pollution Lawsuit," *Reuters*, 15 April 2014, accessed 19 June 2014, http://www.reuters.com/assets/print?aid=USBREA3E05P20140415.

35. Jinping Xi 习近平, "*Xi Jinping: Guanyu 'Zhonggong Zhongyang Guanyu Quanmian Shenhua Gaige Ruogan Zhongda Wenti de Jueding' de Shuoming* 习近平：关于'中共中央关于全面深化改革若干重大问题的决定'的说明" (Xi Jinping: Explanation Related to 'The Central Committee Decision on Major Problems Related to All-around Deepening of Reforms'), *Xinhuawang* 新华网 (News Network), 2013 November 15.

36. Gal Dor, "Litigation as Public Participation," *Israel Studies* 11, no. 2 (Summer 2006), 131–57.

37. Lianjiang Li, Mingxing Liu, and Kevin J. O'Brien, "Petitioning Beijing: The High Tide of 2003-2006," *China Quarterly*, no. 210 (June 2012), 313–34.

38. Hualing Fu, "Challenging Authoritarianism through Law: Potentials and Limit," *National Taiwan University Law Review* 6, no. 1 (2011), 339–65; Benjamin L. Liebman, "China's Courts," 620–38; Lynch, "China's Rule of Law Mirage," 535–85; Minzner, "China's Turn against Law," 935–84; Pitman Potter, "The Chinese Legal System: Continuing Commitment to the Primacy of State Power," *China Quarterly*, no. 159 (September 1999), 673–83; and Wang, "The Search for Sustainable Legitimacy," 365–440, represent works that examine the politics of China's courts.

39. Lynch, "China's Rule of Law Mirage," 535–85.

Interview List

Interview 1: Director of Shanghai-based international business organization, interview by author, Shanghai, 28 September 2007.

Interview 2: Director of Shanghai office of Hong Kong AIDS NGO, interview by author, Shanghai, 12 October 2007.

Interview 3: Communications director of international business organization, phone interview by author, Washington, DC, 17 October 2007.

Interview 4: Director of Shanghai office of U.S. environmental NGO, interview by author, Shanghai, 19 October 2007.

Interview 5: Corporate social responsibility officer of international business organization, interview by author, Shanghai, 2 November 2007.

Interview 6: Director of NGO in Shanghai, interview by author, Shanghai, 6 November 2007.

Interview 7: Professors at Shanghai Communist Party School, interview by author, Shanghai, 8 November 2007.

Interview 8: Attorney in the United States, phone interview by author, Washington, DC, 9 November 2007.

Interview 9: Marketing manager for environmental INGO, interview by author, Shanghai, 14 November 2007.

Interview 10: Officer for educational INGO, interview by author, Shanghai, 14 November 2007.

Interview 11: Director of INGO, interview by author, Shanghai, 19 November 2007.

Interview 12: Legal aid volunteers, interview by author, Shanghai, 23 November 2007.

Interview 13: Corporate social responsibility employee of U.S. multinational corporation, interview by author, Shanghai, 23 November 2007.

Interview 14: Acting director of Chinese labor rights NGO, phone interview by author, Beijing, 29 November 2007.

Interview 15: Supervisor of Shanghai state-run legal aid station, interview by author, Shanghai, 6 December 2007.

Interview 16: Officer of Chinese NGO with legal aid station, interview by author, Shanghai, 10 December 2007.

Interview 17: Foreign affairs officer of Shanghai charity foundation, interview by author, Shanghai, 11 December 2007.

Interview 18: Associate general secretary of Chinese service NGO with legal aid center, interview by author, Nanjing, 12 December 2007.

Interview 19: Chairman of U.S.-based foundation, interview by author, Nanjing, 12 December 2007.

Interview 20: Director of former Chinese LGBT and HIV/AIDS NGO, interview by author, Shanghai, 31 December 2007.

Interview 21: Head of labor branch of a legal aid center, interview by author, Shanghai, 2 January 2008.

Interview 22: Deputy director of HIV/AIDS research center, interview by author, Shanghai, 10 January 2008.

Interview 23: Vice president of microcredit INGO, interview by author, Beijing, 14 January 2008.

Interview 24: Director of Chinese NGO, interview by author, Beijing, 14 January 2008.

Interview 25: Director of Chinese HIV/AIDS NGO, interview by author, Beijing, 14 January 2008.

Interview 26: Research director of legal aid center, interview by author, Beijing, 15 January 2008.

Interview 27: Head and legal officer of Chinese HIV/AIDS NGO with legal aid center, interview by author, Beijing, 15 January 2008.

Interview 28: Director and officers of Chinese legal aid center, interview by author, Beijing, 15 January 2008.

Interview 29: Political activist, interview by author, Beijing, 16 January 2008.

Interview 30: Director of office for environmental INGO, interview by author, Beijing, 16 January 2008.

Interview 31: Officer of legal INGO, interview by author, Beijing, 16 January 2008.

Interview 32: Officer of HIV/AIDS INGO, interview by author, Beijing, 17 January 2008.

Interview 33: Officer of Chinese HIV/AIDS NGO, interview by author, Beijing, 17 January 2008.

Interview 34: Program director of Chinese environmental NGO, interview by author, Beijing, 17 January 2008.

Interview 35: Director of Chinese HIV/AIDS NGO, interview by author, Shanghai, 22 February 2008.

Interview 36: Director of Chinese public health NGO, interview by author, Shanghai, 29 February 2008.

Interview 37: Legal aid recipient, interview by author, Shanghai, 17 March 2008.

Interview 38: Legal aid recipient, interview by author, Shanghai, 17 March 2008.

Interview 39: Legal aid recipient, interview by author, Shanghai, 18 March 2008.

Interview 40: Associate director of Chinese public health NGO, interview by author, Shanghai, 27 March 2008.

Interview 41: Executive director of Chinese environmental NGO, interview by author, Shanghai, 31 March 2008.

Interview 42: Professor of public health and expert on HIV/AIDS, interview by author, Shanghai, 8 April 2008.

Interview 43: Head of Chinese environmental NGO, interview by author, Nanjing, 9 April 2008.

Interview 44: Secretary general of Chinese environmental NGO, interview by author, Nanjing, 9 April 2008.

Interview 45: Founder and executive director of legal INGO, phone interview by author, New York City, 10 April 2008.

Interview 46: Attorneys and legal aid workers, interview by author, Shanghai, 15 April 2008.

Interview 47: Leader of Chinese HIV/AIDS NGO, interview by author, Beijing, 5 May 2008.

Interview 48: Director of office for legal INGO, interview by author, Beijing, 5 May 2008.

Interview 49: Director of office for legal INGO, interview by author, Beijing, 6 May 2008.

Interview 50: Program manager for Chinese environmental NGO, interview by author, Beijing, 6 May 2008.

Interview 51: Director of Chinese HIV/AIDS NGO, interview by author, Beijing, 6 May 2008.

Interview 52: President of Chinese HIV/AIDS NGO, interview by author, Beijing, 7 May 2008.

Interview 53: Lawyer for Chinese environmental legal aid center and for environmental INGO, interview by author, Beijing, 7 May 2008.

Interview 54: Lawyer for Chinese HIV/AIDS NGO and legal aid center, interview by author, Beijing, 8 May 2008.

Interview 55: Acting director of Chinese environmental NGO, interview by author, Beijing, 8 May 2008.

Interview 56: Lawyer and head of Chinese HIV/AIDS NGO, interview by author, Beijing, 9 May 2008.

Interview 57: Lawyer and legal aid volunteer, interview by author, Shanghai, 15 May 2008.

Interview 58: Professor of environmental law, interview by author, Shanghai, 20 May 2008.

Interview 59: Professor of environmental law, interview by author, Wuhan, 10 June 2008.

Interview 60: Attorney at legal aid center, interview by author, Wuhan, 10 June 2008.

Interview 61: Director of Chinese environmental NGO, interview by author, Kunming, 11 June 2008.

Interview 62: Officer of Chinese environmental NGO, interview by author, Kunming, 11 June 2008.

Interview 63: Director of Chinese environmental NGO, interview by author, Kunming, 12 June 2008.

Interview 64: Director of Chinese HIV/AIDS NGO, interview by author, Kunming, 12 June 2008.

Interview 65: Director of Chinese HIV/AIDS NGO, interview by author, Kunming, 12 June 2008.

Interview 66: U.S. environmental lawyer in Shanghai office of international law firm, interview by author, Shanghai, 19 June 2008.

Interview 67: Director, Chinese HIV/AIDS NGO, interview by author, Beijing, 21 May 2010.

Interview 68: Associate director, Chinese HIV/AIDS NGO, interview by author, Beijing. 21 May 2010.

Interview 69: Director, Chinese HIV/AIDS NGO, interview by author, Beijing, 23 May 2010.

Interview 70: Attorney with environmental INGO, interview by author, Beijing, 25 May 2010.

Interview 71: Professor with expertise on HIV/AIDS and environmental NGOs, interview by author, Beijing, 26 May 2010.

Interview 72: Director, Chinese HIV/AIDS NGO, interview by author, Beijing, 27 May 2010.

Interview 73: Associate director HIV/AIDS INGO, interview by author, Beijing, 27 May 2010.

Interview 74: Associate director HIV/AIDS INGO, interview by author, Beijing, 28 May 2010.

Interview 75: Attorney with environmental NGO, interview by author, Beijing, 28 May 2010.

Interview 76: Associate director HIV/AIDS multilateral organization, interview by author, Beijing, 31 May 2010.

Interview 77: Attorney with INGO, interview by author, Beijing, 31 May 2010.

Interview 78: Attorney with expertise on AIDS law, interview by author, Kunming, 2 June 2010.

Interview 79: Attorney with expertise on environmental law, phone interview by author, Wuhan, 2 June 2010.

Interview 80: Project manager Chinese HIV/AIDS NGO, interview by author, Kunming, 4 June 2010.

Interview 81: Attorney at legal aid center, interview by author, Kunming, 5 June 2010.

Interview 82: Attorney, interview by author, Shanghai, 7 June 2010.

Interview 83: Associate director government AIDS work unit, interview by author, Shanghai, 7 June 2010.

Interview 84: Attorney with expertise on HIV/AIDS law, interview by author, Shanghai, 9 June 2010.

Interview 85: Attorney with environmental INGO, phone interview by author, Beijing, 9 June 2010.

Interview 86: Attorney with public interest NGO, interview by author, Beijing, 4 June 2012.

Interview 87: Attorney with environmental legal aid center, interview by author, Beijing, 4 June 2012.

Interview 88: Environmental attorney, interview by author, Beijing, 5 June 2012.

Interview 89: Attorney with human rights NGO, interview by author, Nanjing, 6 June 2012.

Interview 90: Attorney with AIDS INGO, interview by author, Shanghai, 9 June 2012.

Interview 91: Former project manager with AIDS INGO, interview by author, Kunming, 11 June 2012.

Interview 92: Environmental attorney, interview by author, Kunming, 12 June 2012.

Interview 93: Worker AIDS NGO, phone interview by author, Zhengzhou, 15 June 2012.

Interview 94: Worker AIDS NGO, interview by author, Guangzhou, 17 June 2012.

Interview 95: Worker AIDS NGO, interview by author, Guangzhou, 18 June 2012.

Interview 96: Worker environmental NGO, interview by author, Guangzhou, 19 June 2012.

Interview 97: Attorney with environmental NGO, interview by author, Beijing, 20 June 2012.

Interview 98: Program head, multilateral organization, interview by author, Beijing, 21 June 2012.

Interview 99: Program head, multilateral organization, interview by author, Beijing, 22 June 2012.

Interview 100: Program head, AIDS NGO, interview by author, Beijing, 25 June 2012.

Interview 101: Head of AIDS NGO, interview by author, Beijing, 25 June 2012.

Interview 102: Attorney, environmental legal aid center, Beijing, 26 June 2012.

Interview 103: Environmental attorney, personal communication with author, Beijing, 4 August 2012.

Bibliography

Adams, Shar. "PM's Secrecy Protects Chinese Communist Official." *Epoch Times*, 19 September 2010. Accessed 20 August 2014. http://www.theepochtimes.com/n2/content/view/14275/

Agence France Presse. "China AIDS Campaigner Detained: Activists." Agence France Presse, 21 August 2010. http://www.google.com/hostednews/afp/article/ALeqM5i0DSDtEISxTCWgRZEoL7aXXQBIUg

——— "China Hospital Refused to Treat Woman with HIV: Co-Worker." *Agence France Presse*, 16 July 2010. http://health.asiaone.com/Health/News/Story/A1Story20100716-227326.html

Ahl, Bjorn. "Retaining Judicial Professionalism: The New Guiding Cases Mechanism of the Supreme People's Court." *China Quarterly*, no. 217 (March 2014): 121–39.

Alpermann, Bjorn. "State and Society in China's Environmental Politics." In *China's Environmental Crisis*, eds. Joel Jay Kassiola and Sujian Guo, 123–51. Houndsmill, Basingstroke: Palgrave McMillan, 2010.

Amnesty International. "UA 217/06: Fear of Torture or Ill-Treatment/Health Concern: Li Xige (F)," PUBLIC AI Index: ASA 17/043/2006, 10 August 2006. Accessed 24 August 2014. http://www.amnesty.org/en/library/asset/ASA17/043/2006/en/724cf808-d403-11dd-8743-d305bea2b2c7/asa170432006en.html

———. "UA 190/10: Urgent Action: Chinese HIV/AIDS Activist Risks Torture," AI Index: ASA 17/036/2010. http://www.amnesty.org/en/library/asset/ASA17/036/2010/en/f8b17031-e645-40e9-975c-c1f7f21229d6/asa170362010en.pdf

Anderson, Evan and Sara Davis. *AIDS Blood Scandals: What China Can Learn from the World's Mistakes*. New York: Asia Catalyst, 2007.

Armstrong, E. A. "From Struggle to Settlement." In *Social Movements and Organization Theory*, eds. G. E. Davis, D. McAdam, W. R. Scott, and M. N. Zald, 161–87. Cambridge University Press, 2005.

Asia Water Project. "Regulatory Trends: Litigation," Report on the Asia Water Project website, 2010. Accessed 30 July 2010. http://www.asiawaterproject.org/regulatory-trends/litigation/

Balzano, John and Jia Ping. "Coming Out of Denial: An Analysis of AIDS Law and Policy in China." *Loyola University Chicago International Law Review* 3 (Spring 2006): 187–212.

BBC. "Passengers with HIV Sue China's Spring Airlines." BBC News, 15 August 2014. Accessed 16 August 2014. http://www.bbc.com/news/world-asia-china-28804219

Bignami-Van Assche, Simona. "Estimates and Projections of HIV/AIDS for Yunnan Province, China." *Population Review* 43, no. 2 (2004): 70–87.

Blanchard, Ben. "China Threatens Death Penalty for Serious Polluters." *Reuters*, 19 June 2013. Accessed 20 August 2014. http://www.reuters.com/article/2013/06/19/us-china-pollution-idUSBRE95I10D20130619

Brettell, Anna. "Channeling Dissent: The Institutionalization of Environmental Complaint Resolution." In *China's Embedded Activism: Opportunities and Constraints of a Social Movement*, eds. Peter Ho and Richard Louis Edmonds, 111–50. London and New York: Routledge, 2007.

Briggs, Adam. "China's Pollution Victims: Still Seeking a Dependable Remedy." *Georgetown International Environmental Law Review* 18 (Winter 2006): 305–33.

Brook, Timothy and B. Michael Frolic. "The Ambiguous Challenge of Civil Society." In *Civil Society in China*, eds. Timothy Brook and B. Michael Frolic, 3–16. Armonk, NY: East Gate Books, 1997.

Brown, Lester. *Who Will Feed China? Wake-Up Call for a Small Planet*. New York: Norton, 1995.

Brown-Nagin, Tomiko. "Elites, Social Movements, and the Law: The Case of Affirmative Action." *Columbia Law Review* 105, no. 5 (June 2005): 1436–528.

Burki, Talha Khan. "Discrimination against People with HIV Persists in China." *Lancet* 377 (22 January 2011), 286–87.

Buttigieg, Joseph A. "Gramsci on Civil Society." *boundary 2* (1995): 22:1–32.

Cai, John. "Turning Away from Dependence on the Economic System: Looking Forward and Back on the Reform of China's Health Care System." In *Economic Transitions with Chinese Characteristics*, eds. Arthur Sweetman and Jun Zhang, 135–47. Montreal and Kingston: McGill-Queen's University Press, 2009.

Cai, Yongshun. "Managed Participation in China." *Political Science Quarterly* 119, no. 3 (Fall 2004): 425–51.

Cao, Cong. "SARS: 'Waterloo' of Chinese Science." *China: An International Journal* 2, no. 2 (September 2004): 262–86.

Cao, Kai. "NGOs' Participation Help China Fight AIDS." *Xinhua*, 30 November 2012. Accessed 23 August 2014. http://news.xinhuanet.com/english/china/2012-11/30/c_132009780.htm

Carothers, T. and M. Ottaway. "The Burgeoning World of Civil Society Aid." In *Funding Virtue*, eds. M. Ottaway and T. Carothers, 3–17. Washington: Carnegie Endowment for International Peace, 2000.

CHAMP [China HIV/AIDS Media Partnership] et al. *AIDS-Related Knowledge, Attitudes, Behavior, and Practices: A Survey of 6 Chinese Cities*, 2008. http://www.un.org.cn/public/resource/ea0b7baa18b18c711db095673895aeba.pdf

Chan, Kin-Man. "Harmonious Society." In *International Encyclopedia of Civil Society*, eds. Helmut K. Anheier and Stefan Toepler, 121–25. Springer US, 2010.

"Chemical Factory Endangers Residents." *China Daily*, 21 October 2003. Accessed 24 August 2014. http://www.chinadaily.com.cn/en/doc/2003-10/21/content_273872.htm

Chen, Albert. "The Limits of Official Tolerance: The Case of Aizhixing." *China Rights Forum*, no. 3 (2003): 51–55. http://www.hrichina.org/sites/default/files/PDFs/CRF.3.2003/Albert_Chen.pdf

Chen, Gang. *Politics of China's Environmental Protection: Problems and Prospects*. Singapore: World Scientific, 2009.

Chen, Guangyao. "China's Non-Governmental Organizations: Status, Government Policies, and Prospects for Further Development." *International Journal of Not-for-Profit Law* 3, no. 3 (March 2001).

Chen, Jie. "The NGO Community in China: Expanding Linkages with Transnational Civil Society and Their Democratic Implications." *China Perspectives*, no. 68 (November-December 2006): 2–15.

Chen, Titus C. "China's Reaction to the Color Revolutions: Adaptive Authoritarianism in Full Swing." *Asian Perspectives* 34, no. 2 (2010): 5–51.

China AIDS Information Network. *2010 China HIV/AIDS CSO/CBO Directory*. Beijing: China AIDS Information Network, 2010.

China Daily. "Parade of Prostitutes Lands Shenzhen Police in Hot Water." *China Daily*, 7 December 2006. Accessed 24 August 2014. http://www.china.org.cn/english/China/191491. htm

———. "Discrimination against AIDS Patients Still Serious: Survey." *China Daily*, 8 July 2009. Accessed 24 July 2014. http://www.china.org.cn/china/news/2009-07/08/content_ 18092947.htm

———. "Insurance Fix a Win for HIV Patients." *China Daily*, 15 July 2009. Accessed 24 August 2014. http://en.kunming.cn/index/content/2009-07/15/content_1920690.htm

———. "The ACEF Needs to Clean House." *China Daily*, 3 July 2013. Accessed 8 July 2013. http://usa.chinadaily.com.cn/opinion/2013-07/03/content_16719657.htm

China Dialogue. "Eight Cases That Mattered." *China Dialogue*, 26 July 2011. Accessed 24 August 2014. http://www.chinadialogue.net/article/show/single/en/4429-Eight-cases-that-mattered

China Labour Bulletin. "China's First Successfully Litigated Hepatitis B Employment Discrimination Case." *China Labour Bulletin*, 19 August 2009. Accessed 24 August 2014. http://www.china-labour.org.hk/en/node/100542

China's Human Rights Lawyers: Current Challenges and Prospects, by James V. Feinerman. 111th Congress, First Session, 10 July 2009.

Civil Procedure Law of the People's Republic of China. Promulgated 9 April 1991, promulgated by the president on 9 April 1991.

Civil Procedure Law of the People's Republic of China. Promulgated by the president on 9 April 1991, revised 28 October 2007 and 31 August 2012, put into effect 1 January 2013.

Claeson, Mariam, Hong Wang, and Shanlian Hu. "A Critical Review of Public Health in China." Unpublished paper, August 2004. Accessed 19 August 2014. http://siteresources.worldbank.org/INTEAPREGTOPHEANUT/Resources/publichealth,09-13-04.pdf

Coglianese, Cary. "Social Movements, Law, and Society: The Institutionalization of the Environmental Movement." *University of Pennsylvania Law Review* 150, no. 1 (November 2001): 85–118.

Coleman, Christopher, Laurence D. Nee, and Leonard S. Rubinowitz. "Social Movements and Social-Change Litigation: Synergy in the Montgomery Bus Protest." *Law and Social Inquiry* 30, no. 4 (Autumn 2005): 663–736.

Congressional-Executive Commission on China. "Statement to Congressional-Executive Commission on China," testimony by Carol Lee Hamrin. 24 March 2003.

———. "Clearing the Air: The Human Rights and Legal Dimensions of China's Environmental Dilemma," testimony by Brian Rohan. 27 January 2003. http://www.cecc.gov/events/roundtables/clearing-the-air-the-human-rights-and-legal-dimensions-of-chinas-environmental

———. Roundtable on HIV/AIDS. "China's HIV/AIDS Crisis: Implications for Human Rights, the Rule of Law and U.S.-China Relations," testimony by Bates Gill, 9 September 2002.

Constitution of the People's Republic of China. Adopted 4 December 1982, last amended 14 March 2004.

Crehan, Kate. *Gramsci, Culture, and Anthropology*. Berkeley: University of California Press, 2002.

Criminal Law of the People's Republic of China. Adopted by the National People's Congress on 1 July 1979, revised 14 March 1997, and promulgated by Order No. 83 of the president on 14 March 1997.

Decision by the State Council Regarding Revision of "The Detailed Instructions on Procedures for Foreigners Entering and Exiting China." Issued by the State Council on 19 April 2010. http://www.chinaaids.cn/n16/n1193/n4073/380299.html

deLisle, Jacques. "Atypical Pneumonia and Ambivalent Law and Politics: SARS and the Response to SARS in China." *Temple Law Review*, no. 193 (2004): 193–245.

Demick, Barbara. "Justice Tough to Find for Chinese Who Got HIV/AIDS through Tainted Blood." *Los Angeles Times*, 27 November 2010. Accessed 24 August 2014. http://articles.latimes.com/2010/nov/27/world/la-fg-china-blood-20101128

Deng, Guosheng. "The Hidden Rules Governing China's Unregistered NGOs: Management and Consequences." *China Review* 10, no. 1 (Spring 2010): 183–206.

———. "The Decline of Foreign Aid and the Dilemma of Chinese Grassroots NGOs." *Religions and Christianity in Today's China* III, no. 1 (2013): 24–31.

Deng, Yanhua and Guobin Yang. "Pollution and Protest in China: Environmental Mobilization in Context." *China Quarterly*, no. 214 (June 2013): 321–36.

Deng, Zhenglai and Yuejin Jing. "The Construction of the Chinese Civil Society." In *State and Civil Society: The Chinese Perspective*, ed. Zhenglai Deng, 25–46. New Jersey: World Scientific, 2010.

Diamant, Neil J., Stanley B. Lubman, and Kevin J. O'Brien. "Law and Society in the People's Republic of China." In *Engaging the Law in China: State, Society, and Possibilities of Justice*, eds. Neil J. Diamant, Stanley B. Lubman, and Kevin J. O'Brien, 3–27. Stanford, CA: Stanford University Press, 2005.

Ding, X. L. "Institutional Amphibiousness and the Transition from Communism: The Case of China." *British Journal of Political Science* 24, no. 3 (July 1994): 293–318.

Dor, Gal. "Litigation as Public Participation." *Israel Studies* 11, no. 2 (Summer 2006): 131–57.

Economist. "Bad Blood: In Central China AIDS Activists Step Up Pressure on the Government." *Economist*, 8 September 2012. Accessed 1 January 2013. http://www.economist.com/node/21562241/print

Economy, Elizabeth. *The River Runs Black: The Environmental Challenge to China's Future*. Ithaca and New York: Cornell University Press, 2004.

Edwards, Bob and Michael W. Foley. "Civil Society and Social Capital: A Primer." In *Beyond Tocqueville: Civil Society and the Social Capital Debate in Contemporary Perspective*, eds. Bob Edwards, Michael W. Foley, and Mario Diani, 1–14. Hanover, NH: Tufts University and University Press of New England, 2001.

Eggleston, Karen. "Health Care for 1.3 Billion: An Overview of China's Health System." Asia Health Policy Program working paper no. 28. Stanford: Stanford University, Walter H. Shorenstein Asia-Pacific Research Center, 2012.

Environmental Protection Law of the People's Republic of China. Adopted 26 December 1989, revised 24 April 2014, and put into effect 1 January 2015.

Epp, Charles R. *The Rights Revolution: Lawyers, Activists, and Supreme Courts in Comparative Perspective*. Chicago: University of Chicago Press, 1998.

Fang, Yuan. "AIDS Patients Protest in Henan." *Radio Free Asia*, 29 August 2012. Accessed 26 July 2013. Accessed 24 August 2014. http://www.rfa.org/english/news/china/aids-08292012150012.html

———. "AIDS Activists Clash with Police in Beijing." *Radio Free Asia*, 27 February 2013. Accessed 16 July 2013. http://www.rfa.org/english/news/china/aids-02272013144006.html

Fatton, R. "Gramsci and the Legitimization of the State: The Case of the Senegalese Passive Revolution." *Canadian Journal of Political Science* 19 (1986): 729–50.

Feldman, Eric A. "Blood Justice: Courts, Conflict, and Compensation in Japan, France, and the United States." *Law and Society Review* 34, no. 3 (2000): 651–701.

Ferris Jr., Richard J. "Reaching Out to the Rule of Law: China's Continuing Efforts to Develop an Effective Environmental Law Regime." *William and Mary Bill of Rights Journal* 11 (2003): 569–602.

Fitzgerald, John. "A Response." *YaleGlobal Online*, 28 March 2012. Accessed 24 August 2014. http://yaleglobal.yale.edu/content/us-foundations-boost-chinese-government-not-ngos

Ford, Peter. "Another AIDS Activist, Wan Yanhai, Flees China." *Christian Science Monitor*, 10 May 2010. Accessed 12 May 2010. http://www.csmonitor.com/World/Asia-Pacific/2010/0510/Another-AIDS-activist-Wan-Yanhai-flees-China

Frolic, B. Michael. "State-Led Civil Society." In *Civil Society in China*, eds. Timothy Brook and B. Michael Frolic, 46–67. Armonk, NY: East Gate Books 1997.

Fu, Hualing. "Challenging Authoritarianism through Law: Potentials and Limit." *National Taiwan University Law Review* 6, no. 1 (2011): 339–65.

Fu, Hualing and Richard Cullen. "Climbing the *Weiquan* Ladder: A Radicalizing Process for Rights-Protection Lawyers." *China Quarterly*, no. 205 (March 2011): 40–59.

Fung, Yat-yiu. "AIDS Victims Sue for Compensation." *Radio Free Asia*, 4 July 2012. Accessed 24 August 2014. http://www.rfa.org/english/news/china/compensation-07042012145508.html

Gallagher, Mary E. "'Use the Law as Your Weapon!' Institutional Change and Legal Mobilization in China." In *Engaging the Law in China: State, Society, and Possibilities for Justice*, eds. Neil J. Diamant, Stanley B. Lubman, and Kevin J. O'Brien, 54–83. Stanford: Stanford University Press, 2005.

General Principles of the Civil Law of the People's Republic of China. Adopted by the National People's Congress on 12 April 1986, promulgated by Order No. 37 of the president on 12 April 1986.

Gil, Vincent E. "Sinic Conundrum: A History of HIV/AIDS in the People's Republic of China." *Journal of Sex Research* 31, no. 3 (1994): 211–17.

Gill, Bates, Jennifer Chang, and Sarah Palmer. "China's HIV Crisis." *Foreign Affairs* 81, no. 2 (March-April 2002): 96–110.

Ginsburg, Tom and Tamir Moustafa. *Rule by Law: The Politics of Courts in Authoritarian Regimes*. Cambridge: Cambridge University Press, 2008.

Gloppen, Siri. "Litigation as a Strategy to Hold Governments Accountable for Implementing the Right to Health." *Health and Human Rights* 10, no. 2 (2008): 21–36.

Goldston, James A. "Public Interest Litigation in Central and Eastern Europe: Roots, Prospects, and Challenges." *Human Rights Quarterly* 28, no. 2 (May 2006): 492–527.

Golub, S. "Democracy as Development: A Case for Civil Society Assistance in Asia." In *Funding Virtue: Civil Society Aid and Democracy Promotion*, eds. Marina Ottaway and Thomas Carothers, 135–58. Washington, DC: Carnegie Endowment for International Peace, 2000.

Gramsci, Antonio. *Selections from the Prison Notebooks*. Trans. and ed. by Q. Hoare and G. Smith. New York: International Publishers, 1971.

Han, Mengjie, Qingfeng Chen, Yang Hao, Yifei Hu, Dongmei Wang, Yan Gao, and Marc Bulterys. "Design and Implementation of a China Comprehensive AIDS Response Programme (China Cares), 2003–2008." *International Journal of Epidemiology* 39 (2010): ii47–ii55.

He, Baogang. "The Making of a Nascent Civil Society." In *Civil Society in Asia*, eds. David C. Schak and Wayne Hudson, 114–39. Farnham, Surrey: Ashgate, 2003.

He, Dan. "Government Vows to Help More AIDS Kids." *China Daily*, 1 June 2011. Accessed 24 August 2014. http://www.chinadaily.com.cn/china/2011-06/01/content_12616130.htm

He, Xin. "Judicial Innovation and Local Politics: Judicialization of Administrative Governance in East China." *China Journal*, no. 69 (January 2013): 20–42.

He, Zengke. "Institutional Barriers to the Development of Civil Society in China." In *China's Opening Society*, eds. Zheng Yongnian and Joseph Fewsmith, 161–73. Abingdon and New York: Routledge, 2008.

Heywood, Mark and Adila Hassim. "Observations and Assessment Arising from a Visit to Beijing and Chengdu, China to Look at Human Rights, Civil Society, and the Government's Response to HIV/AIDS." Unpublished report, 2009.

Hildebrandt, Timothy. "Development and Division: The Effect of Transnational Linkages and Local Politics on LGBT Activism in China." *Journal of Contemporary China* 21, no. 77 (September 2012): 845–62.

Hildebrandt, Timothy. *Social Organizations and the Authoritarian State in China*. Cambridge: Cambridge University Press, 2013.

Hildebrandt, Timothy and Jennifer Turner. "Greening Activism? Reassessing the Role of Environmental NGOs in China." In *State and Society Responses to Social Welfare Needs in China: Serving the People*, eds. Jonathan Schwartz and Shawn Shieh, 89–110. London and New York: Routledge, 2009.

Ho, Peter. "Introduction: Embedded Activism and Political Change in a Semi-Authoritarian Context." In *China's Embedded Activism: Opportunities and Constraints of a Social Movement*, eds. Peter Ho and Richard Louis Edmonds, 1–19. London and New York: Routledge, 2008.

Howell, Jude. "Prospects for NGOs in China." *Development in Practice* 5, no. 1 (February 1995): 5–15.
———. "Seizing Spaces, Challenging Marginalization and Claiming Voice." In *Exploring Civil Society: Political and Cultural Contexts*, eds. Marlies Glasius, David Lewis, and Hakan Seckinelgin, 121–29. Abingdon and New York: Routledge Press, 2004.
Hsu, Carolyn. "Chinese NGOs and the State: Institutional Interdependence Rather Than Civil Society." Unpublished paper presented at the annual meeting of the American Sociological Association Annual Meeting, Hilton San Francisco, San Francisco, 2009, CAOnline. Accessed 18 August 2014. http://citation.allacademic.com/meta/p305261_index.html
———. "An Institutional Approach to Chinese NGOs: State Alliance versus State Avoidance Resource Strategies." *China Quarterly* (forthcoming).
Hsu, Jennifer Y. J. and Reza Hasmath. "Local Corporatist State and NGO Relations in China." *Journal of Contemporary China* 23 (2014): 516–34.
Hu, Jing. "The Case of Compensation for Water Pollution in Nanhui County in Shanghai." CLAPV Case Analysis, 17 December 2003. http://www.clapv.org/new/file/20031217233817_1071675497.pdf
Hu, Jintao. "Hold High the Great Banner of Socialism with Chinese Characteristics and Strive for New Victories in Building a Moderately Prosperous Society in All Respects." Report to Seventeenth National Congress of the Communist Party of China, 15 October 2007. Accessed 24 August 2014. http://news.xinhuanet.com/english/2007-10/24/content_6938749.htm
Hu, Yongqi and Wencong Wu. "A Bumpy Road for Environmental Courts." *China Daily*, 30 October 2013. Accessed 19 June 2014. http://usa.chinadaily.com.cn/china/2013-10/30/content_17070049.htm
Huang, Zhiling. "HIV-Positive Man Fights in Court for Job." *China Daily*, 17 February 2011. Accessed 24 August 2014. http://www.chinadaily.com.cn/china/2011-02/17/content_12029053.htm
Human Rights Watch. "Locked Doors: The Human Rights of People Living with HIV/AIDS in China." *Human Rights Watch* 15, no. 7(C): 1–95.
Hyde, Sandra Teresa. *Eating Spring Rice: The Cultural Politics of AIDS in Southeast China*. Berkeley: University of California Press, 2007.
International Center for Non-Profit Law. *NGO Law Monitor: China*, 6 June 2013. Accessed 24 August 2014. http://www.icnl.org/research/monitor/china.html
Jacobs, Andrew and Chris Buckley. "China Sentences Xu Zhiyong, Legal Activist, to 4 Years in Prison." *New York Times*, 26 January 2014. Accessed 20 August 2014. http://www.nytimes.com/2014/01/27/world/asia/china-sentences-xu-zhiyong-to-4-years-for-role-in-protests.html?_r=0
Jahiel, Abigail R. "The Organization of Environmental Protection in China." *China Quarterly*, no. 149 (1998): 33–63.
Judges Law. Issued on 28 February 1995 by the Standing Committee of the National People's Congress, put into effect 1 July 1995. (Chinese version available at http://news.sina.com.cn/c/290364.html.)
Kaufman, Joan. "The Role of NGOs in China's AIDS Crisis: Challenges and Possibilities." In *State and Society Responses to Social Welfare Needs in China: Serving the People*, eds. Jonathan Schwartz and Shawn Shieh, 156–73. London and New York: Routledge, 2009.
———. "Turning Points in China's AIDS Response." *China: An International Journal* 8, no. 1 (March 2010): 63–84.
———. "Global Women's Movement." *Journal of Contemporary China* (July 2012): 585–602.
Kelley, Jason E. "Seeking Justice for Pollution Victims in China: Why China Should Amend the Tort Liability Law to Allow Punitive Damages to Environmental Tort Cases." *Seattle University Law Review* 35 (2012): 527–57.
Kostka, Genia. "Environmental Protection Bureau Leadership at the Provincial Level in China." *Journal of Environmental Policy and Planning* 15, no. 1 (2013): 41–63.
Kutcher, Norman. "To Speak the Unspeakable: AIDS, Culture, and the Rule of Law in China." *Syracuse Journal of International Law and Commerce* 30, no. 271 (Summer 2003): 271–86.

Labor Law of the People's Republic of China. Promulgated by the president on 5 July 1994.

LaFraniere, Sharon. "AIDS Funds Frozen for China in Grant Dispute." *New York Times*, 20 May 2011. Accessed 18 August 2014. http://www.nytimes.com/2011/05/21/world/asia/21china.html?_r=1&hp

Landry, Pierre. "The Institutional Diffusion of Courts in China: Evidence from Survey Data." In *Rule by Law: The Politics of Courts in Authoritarian Regimes*, eds. Tom Ginsburg and Tamir Moustafa, 207–34. Cambridge: Cambridge University Press, 2008.

Langfitt, Frank. "China's Inaction Carries AIDS Toll." *Baltimore Sun*, 30 August 2001. Accessed 24 August 2014. http://articles.baltimoresun.com/2001-08-30/news/0108300116_1_infected-henan-aids-education

Larson, Christina. "China's Pollution Revolution." *Washington Monthly* (December 2007). Accessed 2 August 2013. http://www.washingtonmonthly.com/features/2007/0712.larson2.html

Law of the People's Republic on Blood Donation. Adopted on 29 December 1997 by the Standing Committee of the National People's Congress, promulgated as Order No. 93 by the president on 1 October 1998.

Law of the People's Republic of China on Lawyers. Adopted on 28 October 2007, promulgated and put into effect on 1 June 2008.

Law of the People's Republic of China on Penalties for Administration of Public Security. Passed by the Standing Committee of the National People's Congress on 28 August 2005, put into effect 1 March 2006.

Law of the People's Republic of China on the Prevention and Control of Environmental Pollution by Solid Waste. Adopted by the Standing Committee of the National People's Congress on 30 October 1995, revised and promulgated by Order No. 31 of the president on 29 December 2004.

Law of the People's Republic of China on the Prevention and Treatment of Infectious Diseases. Passed by the Standing Committee of the National People's Congress on 21 February 1989, revised 28 August 2004.

Law of the People's Republic of China on the Promotion of Employment. Adopted by the Standing Committee of the National People's Congress on 30 August 2007, promulgated 1 January 2008.

Lee, Christine J. "Comment: 'Pollute First, Control Later' No More: Combatting Environmental Degradation in China through an Approach Based in Public Interest Litigation and Public Participation." *Pacific Rim Law and Policy Journal* 17 (June 2008): 795–823.

Levitsky, Sandra R. "To Lead with Law: Reassessing the Influence of Legal Advocacy Organizations in Social Movements." In *Cause Lawyers and Social Movements*, eds. Austin Sarat and Stuart Scheingold, 145–63. Stanford, CA: Stanford University Press, 2006.

Li, Fangchao. "NGOs in Difficulty, Survey Shows." *China Daily*, 24 April 2006. Accessed 24 August 2014. http://www.chinadaily.com.cn/china/2006-04/24/content_574893.htm

Li, Hui, Nana Taona Kuo, Hui Liu, Christine Korhonen, Ellenie Pound, Haoyan Guo, Liz Smith, Hui Xue, and Jiangping Sun. "From Spectators to Implementers: Civil Society Organizations Involved in AIDS Programmes in China." *International Journal of Epidemiology* 39 (2010, Supplement 2): ii65–ii71.

Li, Huimin. "China's Public Interest Litigation Gate Is Half Open." *New York Times* (Chinese Version), 17 September 2012. Accessed 10 October 2012. http://cn.nytimes.com/china/20120917/cc17lihuimin/

Li, Jing. "Green Law Change Would Limit Lawsuits." *South China Morning Post*, 27 June 2013. http://www.scmp.com/news/china/article/1269766/green-law-change-would-limit-lawsuits

———. "Tycoons Join Activists in Call to Scrap Limit on Lawsuits against Polluters." *South China Morning Post*, 14 August 2013. http://www.scmp.com/news/china/article/1296565/tycoons-join-activists-call-scrap-limit-lawsuits-against-polluters

Li, Lianjiang, Mingxing Liu and Kevin J. O'Brien. "Petitioning Beijing: The High Tide of 2003-2006." *China Quarterly*, no. 210 (June 2012): 313–34.

Li, Qian. "Health Funding Freeze Shows NGO Dilemma." *Global Times*, 25 May 2011. http://china.globaltimes.cn/society/2011-05/658765.html

Li, Xiaoshu. "The Public Face of AIDS in China." *Global Times*, 3 February 2010. Accessed 3 February 2010. http://special.globaltimes.cn/2010-02/503379_3.html

Li, Xige and Tian Xi. "Open Letter for NPC Standing Committee Chairman Wu Bangguo and the Chinese People's Consultative Conference/National Committee Chairman Jia Qinglin," AIDS Rights website, 31 December 2009. Accessed 23 September 2010. http://www.aidsrights.net/bencandy.php?fid=5&id=259

Li, Yu-wai, Bo Miao, and Graeme Lang. "The Local Environmental State in China: A Study of County-Level Cities in Suzhou." *China Quarterly*, no. 205 (March 2011): 115–32.

Lieberthal, Kenneth and Michel Oksenberg. *Policy Making in China: Leaders, Structures, and Processes*. Princeton: Princeton University Press, 1988.

Liebman, Benjamin L. "China's Courts: Restricted Reform." *China Quarterly*, no. 191 (September 2007): 620–38.

Lim, Louisa. "Rights Lawyers in China Face Growing Threats," *NPR Weekend Edition*, 3 May 2009. Accessed 24 August 2014. http://www.npr.org/templates/story/story.php?storyId=103733164

Lin, Tun, Cangfa Wang, Yi Chen, Trisa Camacho, and Fen Lin. *Green Benches: What Can the People's Republic of China Learn from Environmental Courts of Other Countries?* Mandaluyong City, Philippines: Asian Development Bank, 2009.

Lin, Yanmei. "Development of Environmental Public Interest Litigations in China: Seven Experimental Cases." In *The China Environment Yearbook, Volume 5*, eds. Dongping Yang and Friends of Nature, 107–20. Leiden and Boston: Brill, 2011.

Liu, Jianqiang. "New Environmental Protection Law Would Exacerbate Pollution in China." *China Dialogue*, 2 July 2013. Accessed 18 June 2014. https://www.chinadialogue.net/blog/6171-China-s-Environmental-Federation-in-danger-of-becoming-a-new-Lin-Biao/en

———. "China's New Environmental Law Looks Good on Paper." The Third Pole, 28 April 2014. Accessed 18 June 2014. http://www.thethirdpole.net/chinas-new-environmental-law-looks-good-on-paper/

Liu, Jingjing. "China's Procuratorate in Environmental Civil Enforcement: Practice, Challenges and Implications for China's Environmental Governance." *Vermont Journal of Environmental Law* 13 (2011): 41–68.

Liu, Jinmei. "The Center Sends Lawyers to Heilongjiang to Promote the Civil Lawsuit Brought by Villagers in Muling Municipality against Jingquan Alcohol Company." CLAPV unpublished case analysis, 2010.

Liu, Sha. "Environmental NGOs Grow across China but Still Struggle for Support." *Global Times*, 12 June 2012. Accessed 14 March 2014. http://www.globaltimes.cn/content/714330.shtml

Liu, Xingzhu and Junle Wang. "An Introduction to China's Health Care System." *Journal of Public Health Policy* 12, no. 1 (Spring 1991): 104–16.

Liu, Yingling. "SEPA Releases New Measure on Public Participation in Environmental Impact Assessment Process." *China Watch*, 24 February 2006. Accessed 24 August 2014. http://www.worldwatch.org/node/3886

Lu, Yiyi. "NGOs in China: Development Dynamics and Challenges." In *China's Opening Society: The Non-State Sector and Governance*, eds. Zheng Yongnian and Joseph Fewsmith, 89–105. London and New York: Routledge, 2008.

———. *Public Interest Litigation and Political Activism in China*. Montreal: Rights and Democracy, 2008.

Lubman, Stanley. "Civil Litigation Being Quietly 'Harmonized.'" China Real Time Report, *Wall Street Journal*, 31 May 2011. http://blogs.wsj.com/chinarealtime/2011/05/31/civil-litigation-being-quietly-harmonized/

Lynch, Elizabeth M. "China's Rule of Law Mirage: The Regression of the Legal Profession since the Adoption of the 2007 Lawyers Law." *George Washington International Law Review* 42 (2010): 535–85.

Ma, Hua. "The Situation and Predicament of Guangdong's New Government-Issued Regulations on Registration of Social Organizations." *China Development Brief* blog post, 4 September 2013. Accessed 24 August 2014. http://www.chinadevelopmentbrief.org.cn/qikanarticleview.php?id=1400

Ma, Jin, Mingshan Lu, and Hude Quan. "From a National, Centrally Planned Health System to a System Based on the Market: Lessons from China." *Health Affairs* 27, no. 4 (July/August 2008): 937–48.

Ma, Jun. *China's Water Crisis*. Pacific Century Press, 2004.

Ma, Lie. "Chinese Hospital to Pay $60,400 in Transfusion AIDS Case." *China Daily*, 22 April 2014. Accessed 19 June 2014. http://yourhealth.asiaone.com/print/content/chinese-hospital-pay-60400-transfusion-aids-case

Ma, Xiaoying and Leonard Ortolano. *Environmental Regulation in China: Institutions, Enforcement, and Compliance*. Lanham, MD: Rowman & Littlefield, 2000.

Maluwa, Miriam, Peter Aggleton, and Richard Parker. "HIV- and AIDS-Related Stigma, Discrimination and Human Rights: A Critical Overview." *Health and Human Rights* 6, no. 1 (2002): 1–18.

Marks, Robert B. *China: Its Environment and History*. Lanham, MD: Rowman and Littlefield, 2011.

Marriage Law of the People's Republic of China. Passed by the National People's Congress on 10 September 1980, revised by the Standing Committee of the National People's Congress on 28 April 2001.

McCann, Michael W. "Interests, Ideas, and Institutions in Comparative Analysis of Judicial Power." *Political Research Quarterly* 62, no. 4 (December 2009): 834–39.

McCutcheon, Aubrey. "Contributing to Legal Reform in China." In *Many Roads to Justice: The Law and Related Work of Ford Foundation Grantees around the World*, eds. Mary McClymont and Stephen Golub, 159–96. New York: The Ford Foundation, 2000.

McElwee, Charles R. *Environmental Law in China: Mitigating Risk and Ensuring Compliance*. Oxford: Oxford University Press, 2011.

Meier, Benjamin Mason and Alicia Ely Yamin. "Right to Health Litigation and HIV/AIDS Policy." *Journal of Law, Medicine & Ethics*, supplement (Spring 2011): 81–84.

Meili, Stephen E. "Consumer Cause Lawyers in the United States: Lawyers for the Movement or a Movement Unto Themselves." In *Cause Lawyers and Social Movements*, eds. Austin Sarat and Stuart Scheingold, 253–77. Stanford: Stanford University Press, 2006.

Mertha, Andrew. "'Fragmented Authoritarianism 2.0': Political Pluralization in the Chinese Policy Process." *China Quarterly* 200 (December 2009): 995–1012.

Michels, Ingo Ilja, Yu-xia Fang, Dong Zhao, Li-yan Zhao, Lin Liu. "Comparison of Drug Abuse in Germany and China." *Acta Pharmacologica Sinica* 2007, no. 10 (October): 1505–18.

Migdal, Joel S. "The State in Society: An Approach to Struggles for Domination." In *State Power and Social Forces*, eds. Joel S. Migdal, Atul Kohli, and Vivienne Shue, 5–34. New York: Cambridge University Press, 1994.

Ministry of Environmental Protection. *China Environmental Statistical Yearbook*, 2006. Beijing: National Bureau of Statistics, 2006. http://english.mep.gov.cn/standards_reports/EnvironmentalStatistics/yearbook2006/

Ministry of Health. *China 2010 UNGASS Country Progress Report (2008-2009)*. Beijing: Ministry of Health, 2010. Accessed 20 August 2014. http://data.unaids.org/pub/Report/2010/china_2010_country_progress_report_en.pdf

———. *2012 China AIDS Response Progress Report*. Beijing: Ministry of Health, 2012. Accessed 20 August 2014. http://www.unaids.org/en/dataanalysis/knowyourresponse/countryprogressreports/2012countries/ce_CN_Narrative_Report%5B1%5D.pdf

Ministry of Health and General Office of Customs of China. *Notice on Banning Importing Factor III and Other Blood Products*. Issued 1986. Beijing, 1986.

Ministry of Health et al. "Education Principles Related to the Spread of AIDS." Issued on 8 January 1998 by the Ministry of Health, Central Party Propaganda Ministry, National Education Committee, Ministry of Public Security, Ministry of Justice, Ministry of Culture, Ministry of Cinematic Broadcasting, National Reproductive Planning Committee, and News Broadcasters. Beijing, 1998.

Minzner, Carl F. "China's Turn against Law." *American Journal of Comparative Law* 59 (2011): 935–84.

Moorman, Jesse L. and Zhang Ge. "Promoting and Strengthening Public Participation in China's Environmental Impact Assessment Process: Comparing China's EIA Law and U.S. NEPA." *Vermont Journal of Environmental Law* 8 (2007): 282–312.

Morton, Katherine. "Transnational Advocacy at the Grassroots: Benefits and Risks of International Cooperation." In *China's Embedded Activism: Opportunities and Constraints of a Social Movement*, eds. Peter Ho and Richard Louis Edmonds, 195–215. London and New York: Routledge, 2008.

Moustafa, Tamir. *The Struggle for Constitutional Power: Law, Politics, and Economic Development in Egypt*. Cambridge: Cambridge University Press, 2009.

Moustafa, Tamir and Tom Ginsburg. "Introduction: The Functions of Courts in Authoritarian Politics." In *Rule by Law: The Politics of Courts in Authoritarian Regimes*, eds. Tom Ginsburg and Tamir Moustafa, 1–22. Cambridge: Cambridge University Press, 2008.

National Bureau of Statistics. *China Statistical Yearbook*. Beijing: China Statistics Press, various years.

Naughton, Barry. *The Chinese Economy: Transitions and Growth*. Cambridge: MIT Press, 2006.

O'Brien, Kevin and Li Lianjiang. "Suing the Local State: Administrative Litigation in Rural China." *China Journal*, no. 51 (January 2004): 75–96.

———. *Rightful Resistance in Rural China*. Cambridge: Cambridge University Press, 2006.

Office of the United Nations High Commissioner for Human Rights and the Joint United Nations Programme on HIV/AIDS. *International Guidelines on HIV/AIDS and Human Rights, 2006 Consolidated Version*. Geneva, Switzerland: UN HCHR and UNAIDS, 2006.

Oster, Shai and Mei Fong. "River of Tears." *Wall Street Journal*. 19 July 2006, A1.

Pan, Suiming, Huang Yingying, and Li Dun. "Analyses of the 'Problem' of AIDS in China." Originally published in *China Social Science*, no. 1 (2006).

Pearson, Margaret M. *China's New Business Elite: The Political Consequences of Economic Reform*. Berkeley: University of California Press, 1997.

Peerenboom, Randall. *China's Long March toward Rule of Law*. Cambridge: Cambridge University Press, 2003.

———. *China Modernizes: Threat to the West or Model for the Rest?* Oxford: Oxford University Press, 2007.

Peneda, Vera. "Green Evolution." *Global Times*, 4 July 2012. Accessed 24 August 2014. http://www.globaltimes.cn/content/719011.shtml

Pieterse, Marius. "Health, Social Movements, and Rights-Based Litigation in South Africa." *Journal of Law and Society* 35, no. 3 (September 2008): 364–88.

Pitkin, Melanie. "China: Pingnan Green Wins Court Case against Chemical Company." Global Greengrant Fund Profiles (6 October 2005). Accessed 24 August 2014. http://www.greengrants.org/grantstories.php?print=1&news_id=86

Policy Research and Information Division of the National Center for AIDS/STD Control and Prevention. China CDC. "HIV and AIDS Related Employment Discrimination in China." ILO Country Office for China and Inner Mongolia: 2011. http://www.ilo.org/wcmsp5/groups/public/---asia/---ro-bangkok/---sro-bangkok/documents/publication/wcms_150386.pdf

Potter, Pitman. "The Chinese Legal System: Continuing Commitment to the Primacy of State Power." *China Quarterly*, no. 159 (September 1999): 673–83.

———. *The Chinese Legal System: Globalization and Local Legal Culture*. New York: Routledge, 2001.

———. "*Guanxi* and the PRC Legal System: From Contradiction to Complementarity." In *Social Connections in China: Institutions, Culture, and the Changing Nature of Guanxi*, eds. Thomas Gold, Doug Guthrie, and David Wank, 179–96. Cambridge: Cambridge University Press, 2002.

Provisional Regulations on the Registration and Management of Civil, Non-Commercial Enterprises. Issued on 25 October 1998 by the State Council, decree number 251.

Provisions for the Monitoring and Control of AIDS. Approved by the State Council on 26 December 1987, promulgated on 14 January 1988.

Putnam, Robert D. *Bowling Alone: The Collapse and Revival of American Community*. Simon and Schuster, 2001.

Qiu, Xin and Honglin Li. "China's Environmental Super Ministry Reform: Background, Challenges, and the Future." *Environmental Law Reporter* 2-2009 (2009).

Regulations of the People's Republic of China on Open Government Information. Adopted 17 January 2007 by the State Council, effective 1 May 2008.

Regulations on AIDS Prevention and Treatment. Issued by State Council 29 January 2006 (Document No. 457), put into effect 1 March 2006.

Regulations on the Registration and Management of Social Organizations. Issued by the State Council on 25 October 1998, decree number 250.

Reiman, Kim D. "A View from the Top: International Politics, Norms and the Worldwide Growth of NGOs." *International Studies Quarterly* 50 (2006): 45–67.

Renwick, Neil. "The 'Nameless Fever': The HIV/AIDS Pandemic and China's Women." *Third World Quarterly* 23, no. 2 (April 2002): 377–93.

Richburg, Keith B. "Chinese Environmental Activist Faces Prison Sentence for Publishing Books." *Washington Post*, 12 October 2012. Accessed 24 August 2014. http://www.washingtonpost.com/world/chinese-environmental-activist-faces-prison-sentence-for-publishing-books/2012/10/12/86e56f90-145a-11e2-9a39-1f5a7f6fe945_story.html

Rosenberg, Gerard N. *The Hollow Hope: Can Courts Bring About Social Change?* Chicago: University of Chicago Press, 1991.

Ru, Jiang and Leonardo Ortolano. "Corporatist Control over Environmental Non-Governmental Organizations." In *China's Embedded Activism: Opportunities and Constraints of a Social Movement*, eds. Peter Ho and Richard Louis Edmonds, 44–68. London and New York: Routledge, 2008.

Rules for the Implementation of the Law of the People's Republic of China Governing the Administration of Entry and Exit for Foreigners. Approved 3 December 1986 by the State Council, promulgated 27 December 1986.

Runge, Robin R. "An American Concept with Distinctly Chinese Characteristics: The Introduction of the Civil Protection Order in China." *North Dakota Law Review* 88 (2012): 871–905.

Saich, Tony. "Negotiating the State: The Development of Social Organizations in China." *China Quarterly*, no. 161 (March 2000): 124–41.

Sarat, Austin and Stuart Scheingold. "What Cause Lawyers Do *For*, and *To*, Social Movements." In *Cause Lawyers and Social Movements*, eds. Austin Sarat and Stuart Scheingold, 1–34. Stanford, CA: Stanford University Press, 2006.

Schearf, Daniel. "Chinese Authorities Prevent Multinational AIDS Rights Conference." *Voice of America News*, 29 July 2007. http://www.voanews.com/english/archive/2007-07/2007-07-29-voa15.cfm

Schwartz, Jonathan. "The Impact of Crises on Social Service Provision in China: The State and Society Respond to SARS." In *State and Society Responses to Social Welfare Needs in China: Serving the People*, eds. Jonathan Schwartz and Shawn Shieh, 135–55. London and New York: Routledge, 2009.

Schwartz, Jonathan and Shawn Shieh, eds. *State and Society Responses to Social Welfare Needs in China: Serving the People*. London and New York: Routledge, 2009.

———. "Serving the People? The Changing Roles of the State and Social Organizations in Social Service Provision." In *State and Society Responses to Social Welfare Needs in China: Serving the People*, eds. Jonathan Schwartz and Shawn Shieh, 177–88. London and New York: Routledge, 2009.

Seligson, M. "Exporting Democracy: Does It Work?" In *Is Democracy Exportable?*, eds. Z. Barany and R. Moser, 222–41. Cambridge: Cambridge University Press, 2009.

Settle, Edmund. *AIDS in China: An Annotated Chronology 1985-2003*. Monterey, CA: China AIDS Survey, 2003.

Shan, Juan. "AIDS Deaths Hit 'Peak' as 7700 Die." *China Daily*, 20 April 2011. Accessed 1 January 2013. http://www.chinadaily.com.cn/china/2011-04/20/content_12358846.htm

Shapiro, Judith. *Mao's War against Nature: Politics and the Environment in Revolutionary China*. Cambridge: Cambridge University Press, 2001.

————. *China's Environmental Challenges.* Cambridge: Polity Press, 2012.

Shirk, Susan. *China: Fragile Superpower.* New York: Oxford University Press, 2008.

Shue, Vivienne. *The Reach of the State: Sketches of the Chinese Body Politic* (Stanford: Stanford University Press, 1988).

Sikkink, Kathryn. "Patterns of Dynamic Multilevel Governance and the Insider-Outsider Coalition." In *Transnational Protest and Global Activism,* eds. Donatella della Porta and Sidney Tarrow, 151–73. Lanham, MD: Rowman & Littlefield, 2005.

Simon, Karla W. *Civil Society in China: The Legal Framework from Ancient Times to the "New Reform Era."* Oxford and New York: Oxford University Press, 2013.

Sitaraman, Srini. "Regulating the Belching Dragon: Rule of Law, Politics of Enforcement, and Pollution Prevention in Post-Mao Industrial China." *Colorado Journal of International Environmental Law and Policy* 18 (Spring 2007): 267–335.

Smil, Vaclav. *China's Environmental Crisis: An Inquiry into the Limits of National Development.* Armonk, NY: M. E. Sharpe, Inc., 1993.

Spires, Anthony J. "Contingent Symbiosis and Civil Society in an Authoritarian State: Understanding the Survival of China's Grassroots NGOs." *American Journal of Sociology* 117, no. 1 (July 2011): 1–45.

————. "US Foundations Boost Chinese Government, Not NGOs." *YaleGlobal,* 28 March 2012. Accessed 15 October 2012. http://yaleglobal.yale.edu/content/us-foundations-boost-chinese-government-not-ngos

Spires, Anthony J., Lin Tao, and Kin-man Chan. "Societal Support for China's Grass-Roots NGOs: Evidence from Yunnan, Guangdong, and Beijing." *China Journal,* no. 71 (January 2014): 65–90.

State Administration of Foreign Exchange, People's Republic of China. "Notice of the State Administration of Foreign Exchange on Issues Concerning the Administration of Foreign Exchange Donated to or by Domestic Institutions." Issued 25 December 2009, effective 1 March 2010.

State Council AIDS Working Committee [SCAWCO] and the UN Theme Group on AIDS in China [UNAIDS]. "A Joint Assessment on HIV/AIDS Prevention, Treatment, and Care in China." Beijing, 2007.

"State Council Decision on Implementing a Scientific Development Outlook and Strengthening Environmental Protection." Issued by State Council 27 December 2005 (Document No. 39). Accessed 4 August 2010. http://english.mep.gov.cn/Policies_Regulations/policies/Frameworkp1/200712/t20071227_115531.htm

State Environmental Protection Agency. "Tentative Measures for Public Participation in Environmental Impact Assessments." Promulgated 14 February 2006 and effective 18 March 2006.

STD and AIDS Prevention and Control Center of the Chinese Center for Disease Control and Prevention and the International Labor Organization. "Discrimination against People Living with HIV within Healthcare Centers in China." International Labor Organization, 2011. http://www.ilo.org/wcmsp5/groups/public/---ed_protect/---protrav/---ilo_aids/documents/publication/wcms_155950.pdf

Stern, Rachel E. "On the Frontlines: Making Decisions in Chinese Civil Environmental Lawsuits." *Law & Policy* 32, no. 1 (January 2010): 79–103.

————. *Environmental Litigation in China: A Study of Political Ambivalence.* Cambridge: Cambridge University Press, 2013.

————. "Poor Rural Residents in China Seen as Easy Target for Environmental Lawsuits." *China Dialogue,* 24 April 2013. Accessed 20 August 2014. https://www.chinadialogue.net/article/show/single/en/5937-Poor-rural-residents-in-China-seen-as-easy-target-for-environmental-lawsuits

Supreme People's Court of China. Website. Accessed 24 August 2014. http://en.chinacourt.org/public/detail.php?id=44

Tarrow, Sidney. *Power in the Movement.* Cambridge: Cambridge University Press, 1998.

Teets, Jessica C. "Let Many Civil Societies Bloom: The Rise of Consultative Authoritarianism in China." *China Quarterly,* no. 213 (March 2013): 19–38.

———. "The Evolution of Civil Society in Yunnan: Contending Models of Civil Society Management in China." *Journal of Contemporary China* (2014).

Tilt, Bryan. *The Struggle for Sustainability in Rural China: Environmental Values and Civil Society.* New York: Columbia University Press, 2010.

de Tocqueville, Alexis. *Democracy in America,* translated by George Lawrence and edited by J. P. Mayer. Garden City, NY: Anchor Books, 1969.

Tort Law of the People's Republic of China. Adopted by the National People's Congress on 9 April 1991, revised 28 October 2007 and 31 August 2012.

UNAIDS. *Human Rights and AIDS: Now More than Ever.* New York: Open Society Institute, 2007.

UNAIDS and IPU [Inter-Parliamentary Union]. *Handbook for Legislators on HIV/AIDS, Law, and Human Rights.* Geneva, Switzerland: UNAIDS, 1999.

UNAIDS, UNDP, and IDLO. *Toolkit: Scaling Up HIV-Related Legal Services.* Rome: International Development Law Organization, 2009.

Unger, Jonathan and Anita Chan. "China, Corporatism, and the East Asian Model." *Australian Journal of Chinese Affairs,* no. 33 (January 1995): 29–53.

United Nations Environment Program. "The Songhua River Spill." Beijing: Field Report (December 2005).

———. "High Level Expert Meeting on the New Future of Human Rights and the Environment: Moving the Global Agenda Forward." United Nations Environment Program webpage, 2009. http://www.unep.org/environmentalgovernance/Events/HumanRightsandEnvironment/tabid/2046/language/en-US/Default.aspx

United Nations General Assembly. *Declaration of Commitment on HIV/AIDS,* adopted 27 June 2001. New York: United Nations, 2001.

United Nations Theme Group on HIV/AIDS in China. *HIV/AIDS: China's Titanic Peril.* New York: United Nations, June 2002.

USAID and Health Policy Initiative. *Assessment of the HIV Legal Environment: Yunnan, China.* Kunming, China: RTI International, 2008.

Wan, Yanhai, Hu Ran, Guo Ran, and Linda Arnade. "Discrimination against People with HIV/AIDS in China." *Equal Rights Review* 4 (2009): 15–25.

Wang, Alex. "The Role of Law in Environmental Protection in China: Recent Developments." *Vermont Journal of Environmental Law* 8 (Spring 2007): 195–223.

———. "Environmental Courts and Public Interest Litigation in China." *Chinese Law and Government* 43, no. 6 (November-December 2010): 4–17.

———. "The Search for Sustainable Legitimacy: Environmental Law and Bureaucracy in China." *Harvard Environmental Law Review* 37 (2013): 365–440.

Wang, Alex and Jie Gao. "Environmental Courts and the Development of Environmental Public Interest Litigation in China." *Journal of Court Innovation* 3, no. 1 (2010): 37–50.

Wang, Hui. "Grassroots NGOs Use Special Accounts to Raise Funds." China Development Brief (15 June 2011). Accessed 29 July 2014. http://chinadevelopmentbrief.com/articles/grassroots-ngos-use-special-accounts-to-raise-funds/

Wang, Shaoguang and Jianyu He. "Training Ground for Democracy: Associational Life in China." In *State and Civil Society: The Chinese Perspective,* ed. Zhenglai Deng. New Jersey, London: World Scientific, 2010, 271–310.

Water Law of the People's Republic of China. Adopted by the Standing Committee of the National People's Congress on 29 August 2002, promulgated 1 October 2002.

Wee, Sui-Lee. "Chinese Court Dismisses Water Pollution Lawsuit." *Reuters,* 15 April 2014. Accessed 19 June 2014. http://www.reuters.com/assets/print?aid=USBREA3E05P20140415

Weigel, Marcia A. and Jim Butterfield. "Civil Society in Reforming Communist Regimes: The Logic of Emergence." *Comparative Politics* 25, no. 1 (October 1992): 1–23.

White, Gordon. "Prospects for Civil Society in China: A Case Study of Xiaoshan City." *Australian Journal of Chinese Affairs* 29 (1993): 63–87.

White, Gordon, Jude Howell, and Shang Xiaoyuan. *In Search of Civil Society.* Oxford: Clarendon Press, 1996.

Whyte, Martin King and Zhongxin Sun. "The Impact of China's Market Reforms on the Health of Chinese Citizens: Examining Two Puzzles." *China: An International Journal* 8, no. 1 (March 2010): 1–32.

Wilson, Jeanne. "Colour Revolutions: The View from Moscow and Beijing." *Journal of Communist Studies and Transition Politics* 25, nos. 2 and 3 (June 2009): 369–95.

Wilson, Scott. "Law *Guanxi*: Multinational Corporations, State Actors, and Rule of Law in China." *Journal of Contemporary China* 17, no. 54 (February 2008): 25–51.

———. *Remade in China: Foreign Investors and Institutional Change*. New York and Oxford: Oxford University Press, 2009.

———. "Settling for Discrimination: HIV/AIDS Carriers and the Resolution of Legal Claims." Special edition on "Governing AIDS" in *International Journal of Asia Pacific Studies* 8, no. 1 (January 2012): 35–55.

———. "Introduction: Chinese NGOs—International and Online Linkages." *Journal of Contemporary China* 21, no. 76 (July 2012): 551–67.

———. "Seeking One's Day in Court: Chinese Regime Responsiveness to International Legal Norms on AIDS Carriers' and Pollution Victims' Rights." *Journal of Contemporary China* 21, no. 77 (September 2012): 863–80.

———. "China's State in the Trenches: A Gramscian Analysis of Civil Society and Rule of Law Development." *Protosociology* 29 (2012): 57–76.

Wong, Edward. "AIDS Activist Leaves China for U.S., Citing Pressure." *New York Times*, 10 May 2010. http://www.nytimes.com/2010/05/11/world/asia/11beijing.html?_r=1

———. "Air Pollution Linked to 1.2 Million Premature Deaths in China." *New York Times*, 1 April 2010. Accessed 24 August 2014. http://www.nytimes.com/2013/04/02/world/asia/air-pollution-linked-to-1-2-million-deaths-in-china.html

Wong, Gillian. "China AIDS Patients Topple Gate of Government Office." *Associated Press*, 27 August 2012. Accessed 26 July 2013. http://www.huffingtonpost.com/huff-wires/20120827/as-china-aids-protest/

World Bank and State Environmental Protection Agency, P. R. China (SEPA). *Cost of Pollution in China: Economic Estimates of Physical Damage*. Washington: World Bank, 2007.

Wu, Fengshi. "Environmental GONGO Autonomy: Unintended Consequences of State Strategies in China." *Good Society* 12, no. 1 (2003): 35–45.

Wu, Zunyou, Sheena G. Sullivan, Yu Wang, Mary Jane Rotheram, and Roger Detels. "Evolution of China's Response to HIV/AIDS." *Lancet* 369 (24 February 2007): 679–90.

Wu, Zunyou, Sheena G. Sullivan, Yu Wang, Mary Jane Rotheram, and Roger Detels. "The Evolving Response to HIV/AIDS." In *Chinese Social Policy in a Time of Transition*, eds. Douglas Besharov and Karen Baehler, 270–96. Oxford Scholarship Online, 2014.

Wubbeke, Jost. "The Three-Year Battle for China's New Environmental Law." *China Dialogue*, 25 April 2014. Accessed 6 August 2014. https://www.chinadialogue.net/article/show/single/en/6938-The-three-year-battle-for-China-s-new-environmental-law

Xia, Guomei. *HIV/AIDS in China*. Beijing: Foreign Languages Press, 2004.

Xia, Jun. "'China's Courts Fail the Environment.'" *China Dialogue*, 16 January 2012. Accessed 13 August 2013. http://www.chinadialogue.net/article/show/single/en/4727--China-s-courts-fail-the-environment-

Xie, Jun and Lijuan Sun. "Access to Collective Litigations in China: A Tough Work." *Journal of Politics and Law* 3, no. 1 (March 2010): 45–55.

Xie, Lei. "China's Environmental Activism in the Age of Globalization." Working Papers on Transnational Politics. London: City University of London, 2009.

———. *Environmental Activism in China*. Abingdon: Routledge, 2009.

Xinhua. "The 'Three Represents' Theory." *Xinhuanet*, 25 June 2001. Accessed 24 August 2014. http://news.xinhuanet.com/english/20010625/422678.htm

———. "China Launches New Campaign against Illegal Blood Collection." *People's Daily Online*, 8 June 2007. http://english.peopledaily.com.cn/200706/08/eng20070608_382451.html

———. "Condoms No Longer Proof of Prostitution." *Xinhua*, 1 December 2007. Accessed 20 August 2014. http://www.chinadaily.com.cn/china/2007-12/01/content_6292045.htm

———. "HIV-Related Employment Discrimination in China Highlighted by Report." *Xinhua*, 30 November 2010. http://news.xinhuanet.com/english2010/china/2010-11/30/c_13629251.htm

———. "Environmental Tribunals Hammer Polluters with Legal Accountability." *People's Daily Online*, 15 July 2010. Accessed 24 August 2014. http://english.people.com.cn/90001/90776/90882/7067902.html

———. "China's 'Floating Population' Exceeds 221 Million." *Xinhua*, 1 March 2011. Accessed 20 August 2014. http://www.china.org.cn/china/2011-03/01/content_22025827.htm

———. "Chinese Premier Promises to Put More to Help AIDS Patients." *Xinhua*, 1 December 2011. Accessed 20 August 2014. http://english.sina.com/china/p/2011/1201/419501.html

———. "28,000 Die of HIV/AIDS in China in 2011." *China Daily*, 21 January 2012. Accessed 23 August 2014. http://www.chinadaily.com.cn/china/2012-01/21/content_14488896.htm

———. "Number of NGOs in China Grows to Nearly 500,000." *China Daily*, 20 March 2012. Accessed 24 August 2014. http://www.chinadaily.com.cn/china/2012-03/20/content_14875389.htm

———. "China's First Successful AIDS Discrimination Claim." *Xinhua*, 26 January 2013. Accessed 2013 January 28. Last accessed 20 August 2014. http://english.peopledaily.com.cn/90882/8108798.html

———. "Cancelling HIV/AIDS Tests for Teachers Sparks Debate." *China Daily*, 29 May 2013. Accessed 20 August 2014. http://www.chinadaily.com.cn/china/2013-05/29/content_16544793.htm

———. "China's Registered Drug Users Top 2 Mln." *Xinhua*, 25 June 2013. Accessed 24 August 2014. http://news.xinhuanet.com/english/china/2013-06/25/c_132485980.htm

Yang, David Da-hua. "Civil Society as an Analytical Lens for Contemporary China." *China: An International Journal* 2, no. 1 (2004): 1–27.

Yang, Guobin. "The Co-evolution of the Internet and Civil Society in China." *Asian Survey* 43, no. 3 (May–June 2003): 405–22.

Yang, Ruby and Thomas Lennon. *Warriors of Qiugang*. Online film. Directed by Ruby Yang. Thomas Lennon and Chang Ai Media Projects, 2010.

Yu, Daniela and Anita Pugliese. "Majority of Chinese Prioritize Environment over Economy." *Gallup*, 8 June 2012. Accessed 24 July 2014. http://www.gallup.com/poll/155102/majority-chinese-prioritize-environment-economy.aspx?version=print

Yu, Elena S. H., Qiyi Xie, Konglai Zhang, Ping Lu, and Lillian L. Chan. "HIV Infection and AIDS in China, 1985 through 1994." *American Journal of Public Health* 86, no. 8 (August 1996): 1116–22.

Yu, Xin. "AIDS Patients' Call for Justice." *Radio Free Asia*, 1 December 2008. Accessed 6 September 2010. http://www.rfa.org/english/news/china/aids-12012008100742.html

Yunnan Provincial Regulations on HIV/AIDS Prevention and Treatment. Issued 20 January 2004 by the Yunnan Provincial Government, effective 1 March 2004.

Zhai, Keith. "Communist Party Committees Are Meddling Less in Courtrooms: Judges." *South China Morning Post*, 12 December 2013. Accessed 24 August 2014. http://www.scmp.com/news/china/article/1378830/party-committees-are-meddling-less-courtrooms-judges

Zhang, Yan. "'Legal Weapons' against Pollution Offenses." *China Daily*, 5 August 2013. Accessed 20 August 2014. http://www.chinadaily.com.cn/cndy/2013-06/19/content_16635612.htm

Zhang, Yingying. "The Shadow over Rural China." *China Dialogue*, 10 February 2011. Accessed 1 August 2013. http://www.chinadialogue.net/article/show/single/en/4098-The-shadow-over-rural-China

Zhao, Yuhong. "Assessing the Environmental Impact of Projects: A Critique of the EIA Legal Regime in China." *Natural Resources Journal* 49 (Spring 2009): 485–524.

Zheng, Caihong. "New Draft to Bar HIV/AIDS Carriers from Becoming Teachers in Guangdong." *China Daily*, 9 January 2013. Accessed 20 August 2014. http://yourhealth.asiaone.com/content/new-draft-bar-hiv-carriers-becoming-teachers-guangdong

Zhou, Xin and Henry Sanderson. "Chinese Anger over Pollution Becomes Main Cause of Social Unrest." *Bloomberg News*, 6 March 2013. Accessed 24 August 2014. http://www.

bloomberg.com/news/2013-03-06/pollution-passes-land-grievances-as-main-spark-of-
china-protests.html

CHINESE LANGUAGE SOURCES

BBC. *"Henan Aizibing Huanzhe Kangyi Caizheng Yuanzhu bu Duixian* 河南艾滋病患者抗议
财政援助不兑现" (Henan AIDS Carriers Protest Failure to Fulfill Commitment of Financial Support). *BBC Zhongwenwang* BBC 中文网 (BBC Chinese Network), 27 August 2012.
Accessed 25 July 2014. http://www.bbc.co.uk/zhongwen/simp/chinese_news/2012/08/
120827_china_aids_henan.shtml

Beifangwang北方网. *"Huanjing Minshi Gongyi Susong 'Yangben' Chansheng* 环境民事公益
诉讼'样本'产生" (Environmental Public Interest Civil Litigation 'Sample Book' Is Published). *Beifangwang* 北方网, 21 January 2011. Accessed 23 May 2011. http://news.xinmin.
cn/rollnews/2011/01/21/9005109.html

Cai, Chu 蔡楚. *"Shuxuehou Ganran Aizibing Susong Anjian Ershen Daili Ci* 输血后感染爱滋
病诉讼案件二审代理词" (Report from Counsel in Legal Case Regarding Contraction of
AIDS after Donating Blood). *Boxun* 博讯, 1 August 2007. Accessed 14 July 2014. http://
news.boxun.com/news/gb/china/2007/08/200708011241.shtml

Changshashi Furongqu Renmin Fayuan 长沙市芙蓉区人民法院. *"Yuangao Chen Lifang, Du
Qingshan, Yuan Guoxiang, Wen Yunkai, Chen Shunhe, Yuan Jianguo, Hu Lingzhi, Chen
Jianhua bu Fu Beigao Changshashi Huanjing Baohu Ju 'Guanyu Hunan Jingtian Keji Shiye
Youxian Gongsi 450t/a Siliao Tianjiaji Gongcheng Huanjing Yingxiang Baogaoshu* 原告陈
利芳、杜庆珊、袁国祥、文云凯、陈顺和、袁建国、胡灵芝、陈建华不服被告长沙
市环境保护局'关于湖南晶天科技实业有限公司450t/a 饲料添加剂工程环境影响报告
书" (Plaintiffs Chen Lifang, Du Qingshan, Yuan Guoxiang, Wen Yunkai, Chen Shunhe,
Yuan Jianguo, Hu Lingzhi, and Chen Jianhua Do Not Accept The Hunan Jingtian Technological Industry, LLC 450t/a Fodder Additive Engineering Environmental Impact Assessment Report by the Defendant, Changsha Municipal Environmental Protection Bureau).
Court verdict issued 30 April 2009. Accessed 1 August 2013. http://www.110.com/panli/
panli_232363.html

Chen, Hong and Zhang Jie. *"Xipingcun Pangde Huagongchan* 溪坪村旁的化工厂" (The
Chemical Factory Next to Xiping Village). Central Television (News Investigation [新闻调
查]), report 2/3843, 12 April 2003. Accessed 23 October 2009. Available at http://www.
clapv.org/new/show.php?id=587

Chen, Lei 陈磊. *"Zuigao Fayuan Weituo Zhuanjia Qicao Huanjingfa Sifa Jieshi Wei Huanbao
Gongyi Susong Songbang* 最高法院委托专家起草环境法司法解释为环保公益诉讼松
绑" (Supreme People's Court Entrusts Specialists to Draft Environmental Law: Judicial
Interpretation Loosens Environmental Public Interest Litigation). *Fazhi Zhoumo* 法治周末
(Legal Weekend), 26 June 2012. Accessed 11 July 2012. http://news.hexun.com/2012-06-
26/142874179.html

Chu, Wanzhong and Shi Huaiji 储皖中 施怀基. *"Kunming Aizibing Ren Su Baoxian Gongsi
Qishi An Yishen Baisu* 昆明爱滋病人诉保险公司歧视案一审败诉" (A Losing Verdict for
a Kunming AIDS Carrier's Discrimination Case against an Insurance Company). *Fazhi
Ribao* 法制日报 (Legal Daily), 10 July 2009. Accessed 31 January 2010. http://www.
chinacourt.org/html/article/200907/10/365004.shtml

Deng, Huiling 邓慧玲. *"Guangdong Shouli Huanjing Gongyi Susong Huosheng Gao Dao
Wuran Qiye* 广东首例环境公益诉讼获胜告倒污染企业" (Guangdong's First Environ-
mental Public Interest Lawsuit Wins a Victory: The Case Closes Down the Polluting Factory). *Zhongguo Huanjing Bao* 中国环境报 (China Environmental Report), 21 January 2009.
Accessed 12 June 2013. http://lvse.sohu.com/20090121/n261878394.shtml

Deng, Xinjian 邓新建. *"Guanghoushi Jianchayuan Chutai Minshi Gongyi Susong Zhidao
Yijian Pojie Huanjing Baohu Weiquan Sidao Nanti* 广州市检察院出台民事公益诉讼指导
意见破解环境保护威权四道难题" (Guangzhou Procuratorate Promulgates Civil Public
Interest Litigation Opinion to Break Through the Four Difficulties of Protecting Environ-

mental Rights). *Fazhi Ribao* 法制日报 (Legal Daily), 27 August 2009. Accessed 13 June 2013. http://news.sohu.com/20090827/n266266573.shtml

Du, Yueying 杜悦英. "*Yige Lvshide Huanjing Xinxi Gongkai Shenqing Zhi Lu* 一个律师的环境信息公开申请之路" (One Lawyer's Path to Request Environmental Open Information). *Zhongguo Jingji Shibao* 中国经济时报 (Chinese Economic Times), 29 April 2009. Accessed 21 August 2013. http://finance.sina.com.cn/roll/20090429/23312815304.shtml

Gao, Guohui and Wang Quan 高国辉 王泉. "*77 Ge Huanbao Fating 'Menting Lengluo'* 77 个环保法庭 '门庭冷落'" (Seventy-Seven Environmental Courts 'Give the Cold Shoulder'). *Nanfang Ribao* 南方日报 (Southern Daily), 8 June 2012. Accessed 16 August 2014. http://news.163.com/12/0608/09/83FEMCUB00014AED.html

Gao, Jie 高洁. "*Huanjing Gongyi Susong Yu Huanbao Fating de Shengmingli – Zhongguo Huanbao Fating de Fazhan Yu Weilai* 环境公益诉讼与环保法庭的生命力 – 中国环保法庭的发展与未来" (Environmental Public Interest Litigation and Environmental Courts' Vitality: China's Environmental Courts' Development and Future). NRDC (no date).

Gao, Yuan 高原. "*Minjian Zuzhi Zhijie Zhuce Zhangai Weichu* 民间组织直接注册障碍未除" (Popular Organizations' Registration Barriers Still Not Removed). *Fazhi Zhoumou* 法治周末 (Legal Weekend), 13 July 2011. Accessed 16 August 2014. http://www.legaldaily.com.cn/zmbm/content/2011-07/12/content_2791219.htm?node=7570

Gong, Hai 龚海. "*Qiugang Baowei Zhan* 仇岗保卫战" (Battle to Protect Qiugang). *Qilu Wanbao* 齐鲁晚报, 25 April 2011. Accessed 21 August 2014. http://sjb.qlwb.com.cn/html/2011-04/25/content_117202.htm?div=-1&jdfwkey=c1mdx1

Gongren Ribao 工人日报. "*Aizibing Ganranzhe Shenxian Jiuyi Qishi, Yiyuan Jujue Shouzhi Xianxiang Pubian* 艾滋病感染者深陷就医歧视医院拒绝收治现象普遍" (AIDS Carrier Mired in Discriminatory Denial of Medicine, Hospital Refusal to Treat Patients Is Common). *Gongren Ribao* 工人日报 (Workers Daily), 23 May 2011. Accessed 27 June 2011. http://news.xinhuanet.com/health/2011-05/23/c_121445819.htm

"*Gongwuyuan Luyong Tijian Tongyong Biaozhun (Shixing)* 公务员录用体检通用标准（试行）(General Civil Service Recruitment Physical Examination Standards [Trial Implementation]). Adopted 23 October 2007.

Gongzhong Huanjing Yanjiu Zhongxin (IPE) Meiguo Ziran Ziyuan Baohu Weiyuanhui 公众环境研究中心 美国自然资源保护委员会 (NRDC). *Huanjing Xinxi Gongkai Jiannan Pobing* 环境信息公开艰难破冰 (Open Environmental Information: Difficulty Breaking the Ice). Beijing: IPE and NRDC, 2009.

Guangzhou Haishi Fayuan 广州海事法院. "*Guangzhoushi Panyuqu Renmin Jianchayuan yu Lupingzhang Shuiyu Wuran Sunhai Peichang Jiufen Panjueshu* 广州市番禺区人民检察院与卢平章水域污染损害赔偿纠纷判决书" (Civil Judgment in Procuratorate of Panyu District, Guangzhou City v. Lu Pingzhang Water Pollution Damage Compensation Lawsuit). *Guanghaifa Chuzi Di 247 Hao* 广海法初字第247号(Guangzhou Court Verdict No. 247), 2009. Accessed 13 June 2013. http://ahlawyers.fyfz.cn/b/152938

Guiyang Ribao 贵阳日报. "*Guiyang Qingzhen Fayuan Huanbao Fating Jinnian Qi Tuixing Anjian Huifang Zhi* 贵阳清镇法院环保法庭今年起推行案件回访制" (This Year the Guiyang Qingzhen Court's Environmental Tribunal Uses a Return Investigation System to Push Through Cases). *Guiyang Ribao* 贵阳日报, 20 April 2009. Accessed 16 August 2013. http://www.anquan.com.cn/html/greenpeace/news/2009/0420/56078.html

Guiyangshi Shengtai Wenming Weiyuanhui 贵阳市生态文明委员会. *Guiyangshi Cujin Shengtai Wenming Jianshe Tiaoli* 贵阳市促进生态文明建设条例 (Guiyang Regulations on Setting up and Promoting a Civilized Habitat). Issued by the Twelfth Meeting of the Standing Committee of the Guizhou Eleventh People's Congress, 8 January 2010. Accessed 16 August 2014. http://www.ghb.gov.cn/doc/201029/52054307.shtml

Guiyangshi Lianghu Yiku Guanli Ju 贵阳市两湖一库管理局. "*Anli Si: Guizhou Tianfeng Huagong Youxian Zeren Gongsi Huanjing Qinquan An* 案例四：贵州天峰化工有限责任公司环境侵权案" (Case Four: Guizhou Tianfeng Chemical, LLC Environmental Tort Case). *Guiyangshi Lianghu Yiku Wangzhan* 贵阳市两湖一库网站(Guiyang Municipality Two Lakes One Reservoir Network), 8 May 2009. Accessed 3 August 2010. http://lhyk.gygov.gov.cn/lhyk/74872343805034496/20090508/187211.html

Guizhousheng Guiyangshi Lianghu Yiku Huanjing Baohu Jijinhui 贵州省贵阳市两湖一库环境保护基金会. "*Jijinhui Jianjie* 基金会简介" (Foundation Introduction). Foundation Website. Accessed 25 August 2010. http://www.lhyk.org.cn/web_info.aspx?id=2

Hu, Qianru 胡倩茹. "*Quanguo Shouli Shetuan Zuzhi Huanjing Xingzheng Gongyi Susong Guiyang Kaishen* 全国首例社团组织环境行政公益诉讼贵阳开审" (The Country's First Case of the Guiyang Court Hearing an Environmental Administrative Public Interest Litigation Brought by a Societal Organization). *Guiyang Ribao* 贵阳日报, 2 September 2009. Accessed 3 August 2010. http://www.gz.xinhuanet.com/2008htm/xwzx/2009-09/02/content_17581899.htm

Huanjing Baohubu 环境保护部. *Huanjing Baohubu Zhengfu Xinxi Gongkai Gongzuo 2008 Niandu Baogao* 环境保护部政府信息公开工作2008 年度报告 (The 2008 Year-End Report on the Ministry of Environmental Protection's Open Government Information Work). Ministry of Environmental Protection Report no. 16. Beijing: Ministry of Environmental Protection 2009.

———. *Huanjing Baohubu Zhengfu Xinxi Gongkai Gongzuo 2010 Niandu Baogao* 环境保护部政府信息公开工作2010 年度报告 (The 2010 Year-End Report on the Ministry of Environmental Protection's Open Government Information Work). Ministry of Environmental Protection Report no. 16. Beijing: Ministry of Environmental Protection 2011.

———. *Huanjing Baohubu Zhengfu Xinxi Gongkai Gongzuo 2011 Niandu Baogao* 环境保护部政府信息公开工作2010 年度报告 (2010 Report on the State of the Environment in China). Beijing: Environmental Information Center, 2011.

———. "*Guanyu Baosong Dui 'Huanjing Baohu Fa Xiuzheng An (Caoan)' Yijian he Jianyi de Han* 关于报送对'环境保护法修正案（草案）意见和建议的函" (Letter Regarding Ideas and Criticism in Response to the "Draft Resolution of Revisions to Environmental Protection Law"). Ministry of Environmental Protection, Document No. 284, 2012. Accessed 16 August 2014. http://www.mep.gov.cn/gkml/hbb/bh/201210/t20121031_240778.htm

Huo Xi 获悉. "*Yunnan Gezha Gongyi Susong An Tiaojie Shibai Yin Beigao Danfangmian Fanhui* 云南铬渣公益诉讼案调解失败因被告单方面反悔" (Mediation Fails in Yunan Chromium Public Interest Lawsuit Because the Defendant's Side Goes Back on Its Word). *Zhengyiwang* 正义网 (Justice Network), 19 April 2013. Accessed 14 June 2013. http://www.chinadaily.com.cn/hqgj/jryw/2013-04-19/content_8809533.html

Jiang, Chaohui 蒋朝晖. "*Huanjing Gongyi Susong Gao Chengben Rang Bushao Ren Wanger Quebu Shei Lai Wei Gongyi Susong Maidan* 环境公益诉讼高成本让不少人望而却步谁来为公益诉讼埋单" (The High Costs of Public Interest Environmental Litigation Allows Few People to Pursue It). *Huanjing Pindao* 环境频道, 1 June 2010. Accessed 30 July 2010. http://www.022net.com/2010/6-1/434748112783746.html

Jiang, Hua 江华. "*Aizibing Weihe Manyan? Henan Guanyuan Buzai Chenmo* 艾滋病为何蔓延？河南官员不再沉默" (Why Is AIDS Spreading? A Henan Official Won't Stay Silent). *Nanfang Zhoumo* 南方周末 (Southern Weekend), 4 December 2001. Accessed 2 May 2010. http://news.eastday.com/epublish/gb/paper148/20011204/class014800009/hxz551708.htm

Jin, Jing 金晶. "*Guizhou Huanbao Fating Qingshan Lushuide Shouhu Shen* 贵州环保法庭青山绿水的守护神" (Guizhou's Environmental Court Becomes Qingshan Green Water's Patron Saint). *Renmin Fayuan Bao* 人民法院报 (People's Court Reporter), 25 June 2010. Accessed 18 May 2011. http://www.chinacourt.org/html/article/201006/25/415529.shtml

Jinghua Shibao 京华时报. "*Aizibing Jiuye Qishi Diyi An Dangshiren: Qishi Shi Yi Duqiang* 艾滋病就业歧视第一案当事人：歧视是一堵墙" (Litigant in 'First AIDS Employment Discrimination Case': Discrimination Is a Wall). *Jinghua Shibao* 京华时报, 25 October 2010. Accessed 13 December 2010. http://www.legaldaily.com.cn/commentary/content/2010-10/25/content_2326576.htm

Kunmingshi Zhongji Renmin Fayuan, Kunmingshi Renmin Jianchayuan, Kunmingshi Gonganju, Kunmingshi Huanjing Baohuju 昆明市中级人民法院、昆明市人民检察院、昆明市公安局、昆明市环境保护局. "*Guanyu Jianli Huanjing Baohu Zhifa Xietiao Jizhide Shishi Yijian* 关于建立环境保护执法协调机制的实施意见" (Trial Opinion on Establishing Environmental Protection Law Enforcement Coordination Mechanism). Jointly issued on 5 November 2008. Accessed 27 July 2012. http://www.kmepb.gov.cn/kmhbj/75157117316628480/20081106/11030.html

Li, Fangping 李方平. "'*Wugu Shouhaizhe' de 'Meng Yuan Ru Yu' Ji – Hui Jian Shuxue Ganran HIV Shouhaizhe Li Xige Nvshi Yougan* 无辜受害者的蒙冤入狱记—会见输血感染HIV受害者李喜阁女士有感" (A Record of a 'Cover up of the Unjust Imprisonment' of 'Innocent Victims' – Being Moved by a Meeting with Li Xige, a Person Who Contracted HIV from a Blood Transfusion). Report posted to Aizhixing website, 31 July 2006. Accessed 15 September 2010. http://www.aizhi.net/view.php?id=204

————. "*Li Fangping: Shuxue Ganran HIV Shouhaizhe Tian Xi de Weiquan Gushi* 李方平：输血感染HIV受害者田喜的威权故事" (Li Fangping: The Story of Tian Xi, an HIV Victim Caused by Blood Transfusion). *Da Jiyuan* 大纪元 (Epoch Times), 19 September 2010. Accessed 5 July 2011. http://www.epochtimes.com/gb/10/9/20/n3029938p.htm

Li, Guangming 李光明. "*Yin Tijian Aizi Yangxing Qiuzhi Beiju Anhui Yi Daxuesheng Qisu Jiaoyu Ju* 因体检艾滋阳性求职被拒安徽一大学生起诉教育局" (An Anhui University Student Sues over His Job Request Being Rejected Based on His HIV Positive Test Result). *Fazhi Ribao* 法制日报 (Legal Daily), 26 August 2010. Accessed 13 December 2010. http://www.legaldaily.com.cn/society/content/2010-08/26/content_2261462.htm?node=20771

————. "*Woguo Shouli Aizi Jiuye Qishi Bei'an Jinri Yishen Xuanpan Yuangao Baisu* 我国首例艾滋就业歧视被案今日一审宣判原告败诉" (Today, the Court Returns a Verdict in the Country's First Employment Discrimination Due to AIDS: The Plaintiff Loses). *Fazhiwang* 法制网 (Legal Network), 12 November 2010. Accessed 13 December 2010. http://www.legaldaily.com.cn/zfzz/content/2010-11/12/content_2349410.htm

Li, Guangshou 黎光寿. "*30 Wandun Gezha Xiaoshi, Luliang Huagong Gongxian 23 Nian Heise GDP* 30万吨铬渣消失陆良化工贡献23年黑色GDP" (300,000 Tons of Chromium Sediment Disappears: Luliang Chemical's Twenty-Three-Year Contribution to Black GDP). *Meiri Jingji Xinwen* 每日经济新闻 (Everyday Economic News), 25 August 2011. Accessed 16 July 2012. http://old.nbd.com.cn/newshtml/20110825/20110825093303525.html

Li, Qiumeng 李秋萌. "*Baogao Zhi Zhongguo Aizibing Ganranzhe Jiuyi Mianlin 'Shoushu Nan'* 报告指中国艾滋病感染者就医面临'手术难'" (Report Indicates the Access to Medicine Problems Facing HIV/AIDS Carriers in Receiving Surgery). *Jinghua Shibao* 京华时报, 22 May 2011. Accessed 16 August 2014. http://news.ifeng.com/mainland/detail_2011_05/22/6545986_0.shtml

Li, Xige 李喜阁. "*Li Xige Gei Guojia Zhuxi Hu Jintao de Yifeng Gongkaixin* 李喜阁给国家主席胡锦涛的一封公开信" (Li Xige Gives National Secretary Hu Jintao an Open Letter). *Xinwenshe* 新闻社, 12 August 2007. Accessed 15 September 2010. http://www.minzhuzhongguo.org/Article/ShowArticle.asp?ArticleID=2268

Li, Yutong 李禹潼. "*Aizibing Du Xiedaizhe Qisu Juzhen Yiyuan Cengwei Shoushu Yinman Bingqing* 艾滋病毒携带者起诉拒诊医院曾为手术隐瞒病情" (AIDS Carriers File a Lawsuit against Hospitals That Refuse to Examine the State of Patients Who Have Had Surgeries to Conceal Their Medical Condition). *Xinjing Baoxun* 新京报讯, 4 March 2013. Accessed 3 July 2013. http://news.qq.com/a/20130304/000254.htm

Lin, Ping 林平. "*Yunnan Gezha Gongyi Susong An Tiaojie Shibai Yin Beigao Danfangmian Fanhui* 云南铬渣公益诉讼案调解失败因被告单方面反悔" (Effort To Mediate the Yunnan Chromium Public Interest Litigation Suit Fails Because the Defendants Single-Handedly Go Back on Their Word). *Zhongguo Ribao* 中国日报, 19 April 2013. Accessed 14 June 2013. http://www.chinadaily.com.cn/hqgj/jryw/2013-04-19/content_8809533.html

Liu, Weiwei 刘巍巍. "*Suzhou Shouli Shimin Yaoqiu Zhengfu Xinxi Gongkai Guansi Kaida* 苏州首例市民要求政府信息公开官司开打" (A Precedent Court Case of Citizens Suing over Requests for Open Government Information). *Xinhuawang* 新华网(Xinhua News Service), 11 November 2009. Accessed 5 March 2010. http://cc.xinhuanet.com/2009-11/11/content_18204135.htm

Lu, Sheng 鲁生. "*Fan Qishi Xuyao Fangzhi 'Niulan Guanmao'* 反歧视需要防止'牛栏关猫'" (Anti-Discrimination Requires Blocking 'the Cattle Gate Closing in the Cat'). *Fazhi Guancha* 法治观察 (Legal Observer), 15 November 2010. Accessed 13 December 2010. http://www.legaldaily.com.cn/commentary/content/2010-11/15/content_2350415.htm

Lu, Yao 卢尧, "*Anhui Bengbu Qiye Weigui Paiwu Cunmin Pinpin Siyu Guai Bing* 安徽蚌埠企业违规排污村民频频死于怪病" (Anhui's Bengbu Factory Illegally Pollutes, Villagers Repeatedly Die of a Mysterious Illness). *Xinhuawang* 新华网 (Xinhua Net), 4 August 2007. Accessed 6 June 2010. http://xzj.2000y.net/mb/2/ReadNews.asp?NewsID=523336

Luo, Daohai 罗道海. "*Yunnan Gezha Wuran Zeren Gongchang Zao Gongyi Susong An Shangwu Kaishen* 云南铬渣污染责任工厂遭公益诉讼案上午开审" (The Factory Responsible for the Yunnan Chromium Sediment Pollution Encounters Opening Arguments of Public Interest Lawsuit). *Huaxi Dushibao* 华西都市报 (West China Capital Reporter), 11 July 2012. Accessed 11 July 2012. http://green.sina.com.cn/news/roll/2012-05-23/035924461122.shtml

Ma, Haiwei and Wu Yao 马海伟 吴尧. "*Jiangsu Tongshanxian Huanzhe Shuxue Ran Aizi Fayuan Chengshe Ai Anjian bu Shenli* 江苏铜山县患者输血染艾滋法院称涉艾案件不审理" (The Court Refuses to Try Cases Involving AIDS Carriers from Blood Transfusions in Tongshan County, Jiangsu Province). *Jiankang Shibao* 健康时报, 22 November 2006. Accessed 24 August 2014. http://news.anhuinews.com/system/2006/11/22/001610749.shtml.

Ma, Hua 马骅. "*Guangdong Xin Zhengxia Shehui Zuzhi Zhuce de Xianzhuang yu Kunjing*" 广东新政下社会组织注册的现状与困境 (The Situation and Predicament of Guangdong's New Government-Issued Regulations on Registration of Social Organizations). *Zhongguo Fazhan Jianbao* 中国发展简报 (China Development Brief) blog post, 4 September 2013. Accessed 17 September 2013. http://www.chinadevelopmentbrief.org.cn/qikanarticleview.php?id=1400

Minzheng Bu 民政部 (Ministry of Civil Affairs). "*Minzheng Bu Guanyu Jinyibu Jiaqiang Aizibing Yingxiang Ertong Fuli Baoxian Gongzuo de Yijian*" 民政部关于进一步加强艾滋病儿童福利保险工作的意见 (The Ministry of Civil Affairs' Opinion on Strengthening the Welfare Protection of Children Affected by AIDS). Issued by the Ministry of Civil Affairs (No. 26) on 17 March 2009. Accessed 16 August 2014. http://fss.mca.gov.cn/article/etfl/zcfg/200906/20090600031448.shtml

Mo Jingqing 莫静清. "*Jin 8 Nian Gongwuyuan Jiuye Qishi Weiquan Shaoyou Shengsu* 近8年公务员就业歧视维权少有胜诉" (In the Last Eight Years Attempts to Combat Discriminatory Hiring Practices for Public Servants Have Had Few Legal Victories). *Fazhi Zhoumo* 法治周末 (Legal Weekend), 8 December 2010. Accessed 14 January 2011. http://www.legaldaily.com.cn/zmbm/content/2010-12/16/content_2398082.htm

Nanfang Zhoumo 南方周末. "*Xin Baoxian Tiaokuan Zaibu Qishi Aizibing Ren*" 新保险条款再不歧视艾滋病人 (New Insurance Clause Again Does not Discriminate against AIDS Carriers). *Nanfang Zhoumo* 南方周末 (Southern Weekend), 2009 July 18. Accessed 16 August 2014. http://discover.news.163.com/09/0718/09/5EGBJHSU000125LI.html

Qie, Jianrong 郄建荣. "*Shouli Huanjing Xinxi Gongkai Gongyi Susong An Zhonghua Huanbao Lianhehui Shengsu* 首例环境信息公开公益诉讼案中华环保联合会胜诉" (First Case of Environmental Open Government Information Public Interest Lawsuit: The All-China Environmental Federations Wins). *Fazhi Ribao* 法制日报 (Legal Daily), 6 April 2012. Accessed 16 August 2014. http://www.legaldaily.com.cn/legal_case/content/2012-04/06/content_3481295.htm?node=33809

Ren, Lei 任雷. "*Zhuanranbing Huanzhe Jiuye Quan Pinzao Qinhai Falv Guiding bu Qingxi Bei Zhi Shi Zhuyin* 传染病患者就业权频侵害法律规定不清晰被指是主因" (HIV Carrier Continually Encounters Damages and the Lack of Clear Direction of Laws and Regulations Are a Main Cause). *Fazhi Ribao* 法制日报(Legal Daily), 18 November 2010. Accessed 13 December 2010. http://www.legaldaily.com.cn/index/content/2010-11/18/content_2356218.htm

Renminwang 人民网. "*Yunnan Luliang Ge Wuran Shijian: Dixia Shui Ge Chaobiao 242 Bei* 云南陆良铬污染事件: 地下水铬超标242 倍" (Yunnan Lulang Chromium Sediment Case: Groundwater Chromium Levels 242 Times over Limit). *Renminwang* 人民网点(People's Network), 1 September 2011. Accessed 16 July 2012. http://news.163.com/11/0901/09/7CRV0IF100014JB6.html

Rui, Ning锐宁, "*Gongmin Shehui de Suoying—CCM Xuanju Wuhan Huiyi Jishi* 公民社会的缩影—CCM 选举武汉会议记事" (The Microcosm of Civil Society—The Record of the CCM Election at the Wuhan Conference). *Zhongguo Fazhan Jianbao* 中国发展简报 (China Development Brief) (December 2006). Accessed 24 August 2014. http://www.chinadevelopmentbrief.org.cn/qikanarticleview.php?id=577

Run, Fei 润斐. "*Zongheng Guancha: Baoguang Guo Hou*纵横观察：暴光过后" (Horizontal Inspection: After the Exposure), *Fujian Dianshitai* 福建电视台 (Fujian Television Station) (10 May 2003). Accessed 23 October 2009. http://www.pnlszj.ngo.cn/cn/article.php?articleid=80

Tai, Xudong 泰旭东. "*Quanguo Shouli Huanjing Gongyi Minshi Susong Yi Tiaojie Jiean* 全国首例环境公益民事诉讼以调解结案" (The Country's First Environmental Public Interest Civil Litigation Case Is Settled by Mediation), *Caijingwang* 财经网 (24 September 2009). Accessed 3 August 2010. http://www.caijing.com.cn/2009-09-24/110260142.html

Tai, Yazhou, Wang Li, Yang Yimiao, and Liu Xiaoyi 泰亚洲 王丽 杨一苗 刘晓莉. "*Zhongguo Yunyong Huanbao Fating 'Zhiliao' Wuran Wanji* 中国运用环保法庭'治疗'污染顽疾" (China Uses Environmental Courts as "Medicine" against the Scourge of Pollution). *Xinhuawang* 新华网, 30 July 2010. Accessed 7 July 2010. http://news.xinhuanet.com/environment/2010-06/22/c_12247458.htm

Tai, Yazhou泰亚洲. "*Henan Aizibing Huanzhe Shenghuo Buzhu Tigao Dao 200 Yuan* 河南艾滋病患者生活补助提高到200元" (Living Subsidies for Henan AIDS Carriers Raised to 200 Yuan). *Caixinwang* 财新网, 17 December 2012. Accessed 26 July 2013. http://china.caixin.com/2012-12-17/100473348.html

Tan, Lin 谭林. "*Gongchang Wuran Heyong Zao Jianchayuan Suopei* 工厂污染河涌遭检察院索赔" (Factory Pollutes River, Meets with Procuratorate's Demand for Compensation). *Nanfang Dushibao* 南方都市报, 14 July 2009. Accessed 12 June 2013. http://gcontent.oeeee.com/4/fa/4fa53be91b4933d5/Blog/5ff/85c96a.html

Tian, Xi 田喜. "*Lianheguo Aizibing Guihua Shu Yinggai Huiying Shuxue Ganran Aizibing Renshi de Husheng* 联合国艾滋病规划署应该回应输血感染艾滋病人士的呼声" (United Nations AIDS Plan Should Respond to the Cry of Persons Who Contracted AIDS from Blood Transfusion). Beijing Aizhixing Yanjiusuo blog post, 5 December 2009. Accessed 8 January 2010. http://blog.sina.com.cn/s/blog_4b87e3950100fw4j.html

Wan, Xingya 万兴亚. "*Zuigao Fayuan Yanjin Renmin Fating Canyu Difang Xingzheng Zhifa Huodong* 最高法院严禁人民法庭参与地方行政执法活动" (Supreme People's Court Strictly Forbids People's Courts from Participating in Local Administration Execution of Laws). *Zhongguo Qingnian Bao* 中国青年报 (China Youth Daily), 29 September 2005. Accessed 3 August 2013. http://www.chinalawinfo.com/fzdt/NewsContent.aspx?id=15184

Wan, Yanhai 万延海. "*Mai Xue Chuanbo Aizibing he Guojia Jimi* 卖血传播艾滋病和国家机密" (The Transmission of AIDS through Blood Sales and National Secrets). Aizhi Action Project press release, 28 December 2002. Accessed 15 August 2014. http://www.peacehall.com/news/gb/pubvp/2002/12/200212290253.shtml

Wang, Wei 王玮. "*Zuigao Fayuan Huanjing Minshi Gongyi Susong Anjian Sifa Jieshi Zhengqiu Yijian* 最高法院环境民事公益诉讼案件司法解释征求意见" (The Supreme People's Court's Solicitation of Opinions on the Judicial Interpretation of Environmental Public Interest Litigation Cases). *Zhongguo Huanjing Bao Zonghe* 中国环境报综合 (China Environmental Report Summary), 15 October 2014. Accessed 18 October 2014. http://fj.people.com.cn/changting/n/2014/1015/c355602-22612085.html

Wang, Zhiqiu 王志球. "*Huanjing Guansi Chengben Gao Shei Maidan? Shouhai Qunzhong 'Gan Nu Er Gan Gao'* 环境官司成本高谁埋单？受害群众敢怒而敢告" (Who Will Cover the High Cost of Environmental Litigation? Masses of Pollution Victims Have to Suppress Their Rage). *Renmin Ribao* 人民日报 (People's Daily), 17 February 2011. Accessed 13 August 2013. http://env.people.com.cn/GB/13937591.html

Weiquanwang 维权网. "*200 Ming Aizibing Ren Ji Jiashu Dao Henansheng Zhengfu Kangyi* 200 名艾滋病人及家属到河南省政府抗议" (200 AIDS Carriers and Their Relatives Protest at the Henan Provincial Government). *Weiquanwang* 维权网 blog, 27 August 2012. Accessed 26 July 2013. http://wqw2010.blogspot.com/2012/08/400.html

Weishengbu 卫生部. "*Weishengbu Bangongting Guanyu Yinfa 'Aizibing Zonghe Fangzhi Shifanqu Gongzuo Zhidao Fangan' de Tongzhi* 卫生部办公厅关于印发'艾滋病综合防治示范区工作指导方案'的通知." (Circular on the China Cares Policy). Issued 14 May 2004.

Wuran Shouhaizhe Falyu Yuanzhu Zhongxin 污染受害者法律援助中心. "*Heilongjiang Sheng Mulingshi Jingquan Jiuchang You Dufei Shuiwuran An* 黑龙江省穆棱市晶泉酒厂有毒废水污染案" (Jingquan Alcohol Company in Muling Municipality, Heilongjiang

Province Is Responsible for Water Pollution). Unpublished case analysis, 2003. Accessed 2 August 2013. http://www.clapv.org/ZhiChiAnJian_content.asp?id=70&title=%D6%A7%B3%D6%B0%B8%BC%FE&titlecontent=PD_zhichianjian&lei1=20

Wu, Xiaofeng and Wang Feng 吴晓锋利王峰. "*Zuida Dasuansu Shengchan Qiye Wuran Xiangjiang 7 Nian Cunmin Pin Huan Bingwang* 最大大蒜素生产企业污染湘江 7 年频患病亡" (The Largest Allicin Production Company Pollutes the Xiang River for Seven Years: Villagers Frequently Die of Illnesses). *Xinhuawang* 新华网, 20 July 2008. Accessed 5 August 2013. http://news.xinhuanet.com/politics/2008-07/20/content_8578634.htm

Xi, Jinping 习近平. "*Xi Jinping: Guanyu 'Zhonggong Zhongyang Guanyu Quanmian Shenhua Gaige Ruogan Zhongda Wenti de Jueding' de Shuoming* 习近平：关于'中共中央关于全面深化改革若干重大问题的决定'的说明" (Xi Jinping: Explanation Related to 'The Central Committee Decision on Major Problems Related to All-Around Deepening of Reforms'). *Xinhuawang* 新华网 (News Network), 15 November 2013. Accessed 18 July 2014. http://news.xinhuanet.com/politics/2013-11/15/c_118164294.htm

Xiang, Lei 项磊. "*Cunmin Sannian Ganzou Wuran Gongchang* 村民三年赶走污染工厂" (Villagers' Three Years of Pushing Out Polluting Factories). *Zhongan Zaixian Yi Xin An Wanbao* 中安在线—新安晚报(Central Anhui Online—New Anhui Evening Report), 24 December 2008. Accessed 10 August 2010. http://www.green-anhui.org/guanyuwomen/meitibaodao/2010-01-15/252.html

Xincaixian Aizi Fangzhi Gongzuo Weiyuanhui 新蔡县艾滋防治工作委员会. "*Guanyu Tian Xi Youguan Qingkuang de Huibao* 关于田喜有关情况的汇报" (Report Regarding Tian Xi's Situation). Issued 1 May 2010. Available at Tian Xi's personal blog. Accessed 16 August 2014. http://blog.sina.com.cn/aidsguy

Xing, Fei 幸菲. "*'Luse Guancha' Faqiren Tan Kai Zao Zhonggong Daibu* '绿色观察'发起人谭凯遭中共逮捕" ('Green Watch' Founder, Tan Kai Meets with Chinese Communist Party Arrest). *Da Jiyuan* 大纪元 (Epoch Times), 26 December 2006. Accessed 16 August 2014. http://www.epochtimes.com/gb/5/12/26/n1167535.htm

Xinhua 新华. "*Aizi Ganranzhe Gao Baoxian Gongsi Qishi Yishen Bohui Yuangao Susong Qingqiu* 艾滋感染者告保险公司歧视一审驳回原告诉讼请求" (Court Rejects AIDS Carrier's Claim in a Discrimination Case against an Insurance Company). *Xinhuawang Zonghe* 新华网综合, 10 July 2009. Accessed 21 March 2011. http://news.xinhuanet.com/legal/2009-07/10/content_11685603.htm

Xinjingbao 新京报. "*Rang Gengduo Huanjing Jiufen Zai Fating Jiejue* 让更多环境纠纷在法庭解决" (Allow More Environmental Disputes to Be Settled by Courts). *Xinjingbao* 新京报, 28 October 2012. Accessed 2 August 2013. http://epaper.bjnews.com.cn/html/2012-10/28/content_383935.htm?div=-1

———. "*Zhongguo Huanjing Qunti Shijian Gaofa Nian Zeng 29%* 中国环境群体事件告发年增29%" (China's Environmental Mass Incidents Increase 29 Percent per Year). *Xinjingbao* 新京报, 26 October 2012. Accessed 20 August 2013. http://news.sinovision.net/portal.php?mod=view&aid=234077

Xu, Yingyan 徐盈雁. "*Wang Tianhai Daibiao: Mingque Jiancha Jiguan Huanjing Gongyi Susong Yuangao Zige* 王田海代表：明确检察机关环境公益诉讼原告资格" (Wang Tianhai: Clarify Procuracy Organs' Plaintiff Standing in Environmental *Public* Interest Litigation). *Jiancha Ribao* 检察日报, 10 March 2011. Accessed 23 May 2011. http://news.jcrb.com/jxsw/201103/t20110309_509043.html

Yi, Ming 佚名. "*Zhonghua Huanbao Lianhehui Tiqi de Woguo Diyi Li Huanjing Gongyi Xingzheng Susong Huo Lian* 中华环保联合会提起的我国第一例环境公益行政诉讼获立案" (ACEF Succeeds in Setting Up Our Country's First Environmental Public Interest Litigation Case). ACEF website, 28 July 2009. Accessed 3 August 2010. http://www.acef.com.cn/html/hjflfw/wqdt/3361.html

———. "*Henan Tian Xi 'Huihuai Caiwu' An Zhongshen Weichi Yuanpan* 河南田喜'毁坏财务'案终审维持原判" (The Final Verdict in Henan's Tian Xi's "Damaged Goods" Case Upholds Earlier Decision). *BBC*, 23 April 2011, reprinted in *Xinshiwang* 新时网. Accessed 16 August 2011. http://www.newcenturynews.com/Article/china/201104/20110423002159.html

Yuan, Chunxiang 袁春湘. "*2002 Nian-2011 Nian Quanguo Fayuan Shenli Huanjing Anjian de Qingkuang Fenxi* 2001年—2002 年全国法院审理环境案件的情况分析" (Analysis of Environmental Court Hearings throughout the Country for the Period 2002–2011). *Fazhi Ribao* 法制日报 (Legal Daily), 19 December 2012. Accessed 8 August 2013. http://www.legaldaily.com.cn/zbzk/content/2012-12/19/content_4069404.htm?node=25497

Yunnansheng Aizibing Fangzhi Banfa云南省艾滋病防治办法 (Yunnan Province AIDS Prevention Regulations), 2004.

Zhang, Gongli 张功利. "*Ruhe Zuohao Huanjing Weiquan* 如何做好环境威权" (How to Succeed in Safeguarding Environmental Rights). *Wangyi Tansuo* 网易探索 (NetEase Explorations), 12 October 2009. Accessed 10 August 2010. http://www.green-anhui.org/guanyuwomen/meitibaodao/2010-01-15/256.html

Zhang, Jun 张俊. "Sifa zai Jiejue Shuiwuran Zhong Gai Ruhe Zuowei 司法在解决水污染中如何作为?"(What Role Should the Judiciary Play in Settling Water Pollution?) *Zhongguo Huanjingbao* 中国环境报 (China Environmental Report), 4 July 2008. Accessed 3 August 2010. http://www.cenews.com.cn/xwzx/fz/qt/200807/t20080703_587559.html

Zhang, Ke 章轲. "*Huanbao Fa Xiuding Caoan Sanshen Gongyi Susong Zhuti Beizhi Guodu Xianding* 环保法修订草案三审公益诉讼主体被指过度限定" (The Third Draft Revision of the Environmental Protection Law's Provision on Standing in Public Interest Suits Is Determined to Be Excessively Prescribed). *Diyi Caijing Shibao* 第一财经时报 , 23 October 2013. Accessed 16 August 2014. http://news.sohu.com/20131023/n388711561.shtml

Zhang, Yu, ed. 张渔. *Zhongguo Aizibing Falv Renquan Baogao*中国艾滋病法律人权报告(Chinese AIDS Legal and Human Rights Report). Beijing: *Aizhixing Yanjiusuo*爱知行研究所[Aizhixing Research Unit], May 2009).

Zhao, Gang, Heng Tang, and Yuan Zeng 赵岗 汤恒 曾苑. "*Guanfang Cheng Yunnan Qujing Cunmin Huan Ai yu Gezha Wuguan* 官方称云南曲靖村民患癌与铬渣无关" (State Calls Qujing, Yunnan Villagers' Cancer and Chromium Sediment 'Unrelated'). *Yunnan Wang* 云南网 (Yunnan Network), 5 September 2011. Accessed 16 July 2012. http://news.163.com/11/0905/04/7D5MLRNV0001124J.html

Zhao, Jun 赵俊. "*Wanshan Huanjing Gongyi Susong Zhidu bu Neng Zai Tuole* 完善环境公益诉讼制度不能再拖了" (Perfect the Environmental Public Interest Litigation System and Do Not Delay It Again). *Dongfang Ribao* 东方日报 , 26 February 2013. Accessed 4 March 2013. http://www.dfdaily.com/html/63/2013/2/26/925142.shtml

Zheng, Li 郑莉. "*Aizibing Ganranzhe Shenxian Jiuyi Qishi Yiyuan Jujue Shouzhi Xianxiang Pubian* 艾滋病感染者深陷就医歧视医院拒绝收治现象普遍" (AIDS Carriers Mired in Access to Health-Care Discrimination, Hospitals' Refusal to Provide Care Is Common). *Gongren Ribao* 工人日报 (Workers Daily), 23 May 2011. Accessed 21 August 2014. http://news.xinhuanet.com/health/2011-05/23/c_121445819_3.htm

Zhong, Xinxuan 钟新轩. "*Rongping Huagong Wuran Kaiting Zhizheng* 榕屏化工污染开庭质证" (The Court Opens Hearing of Material Evidence in the Rongping Chemical Factory Pollution Case). Central Index (1/3680), 8 October 2003. http://www.clapv.org/about/news_save.asp?id=157

Zhongguo Jingji Shibao 中国经济时报. "*Hunan Cunzhuang Aizheng Bingli Pinfa Cunmin Chengshi Gongchan Wuran Suozhi* 湖南村庄癌症病例频发村民称是工厂污染所致" (Hunan Village Cancer Cases Repeatedly Occur: Villagers Say It Is Caused by Factory's Pollution). *Zhongguo Jingji Shibao* 中国经济时报 (China Economic Times), 31 January 2007. Accessed 5 August 2013. http://www.hero.ngo.cn/yntt/165.html#

Zhongguo Jingying Bao 中国经营报. "*Huanjing Gongyi Susong Poju Daqiye Ren Nanhan* 环境公益诉讼破局大企业仍难撼" (Environmental Public Interest Litigation Breakthrough: Large Enterprise Is Difficult to Shake). *Zhongguo Jingying Bao*中国经营报 (China Management Reporter), 22 January 2011. Accessed 23 May 2011. http://vnetcj.jrj.com.cn/2011/01/2216399054001-1.shtml

Zhonghua Quanguo Lyushi Xiehui 中华全国律师协会. "*Zhonghua Quanguo Lyushi Xiehui Guanyu Lvshi Banli Quntixing Anjian Zhidao Yijian* 中华全国律师协会关于律师办理群体性案件指导意见" (Guiding Opinion on Lawyers Handling Collective Cases). Issued 20 March 2006. Accessed 20 January 2010. http://www.chineselawyer.com.cn/pages/2006-5-15/s34852.html

Zhonghua Renmin Gongheguo Huanjing Yingxiang Pingjia Fa 中华人民共和国环境影响评价法 (Environmental Impact Assessment Law). Issued on 28 October 2002 by the Standing Committee of the State Council, put into effect 1 September 2003 by the president. http://zfs.mep.gov.cn/fl/200210/t20021028_84000.htm

Zhonghua Renmin Gongheguo Minzhengbu 中华人民共和国民政部. *Minzhengbu Guanyu Jinyibu Jiaqiang Shou Aizibing Yingxiang Ertong Fuli Baozhang Gongzuode Yijian* 民政部关于进一步加强受艾滋病影响儿童福利保障工作的意见 (The Ministry of Civil Affairs' Opinion on Strengthening the Welfare Protection of Children Affected by AIDS). Issued by the Ministry of Civil Affairs (No. 26), 17 March 2009. http://fss.mca.gov.cn/article/etfl/zcfg/200906/20090600031448.shtml

Zhonghua Renmin Gongheguo Weishengbu, Lianheguo Aizibing Guihuashu, Shijie Weisheng Zuzhi 中华人民共和国卫生部, 联合国艾滋病规划署, 世界卫生组织. *2009 Nian Zhongguo Aizibing Yiqing Guji Gongzuo Baogao* 2009 年中国艾滋病疫情估计工作报告(2009 Estimates for the HIV/AIDS Epidemic in China). Beijing, National Center for AIDS/STD Control and Prevention, China CDC, 2010.

Zhou, Bin and Luo Huiru 周斌 罗惠如. "*Shuxue Ganran Aizibing Qun Fa Anjian Lvshi Daili Tantao*" 输血感染艾滋病群发案件律师代理探讨 (An Analysis by Attorneys Representing a Group Who Contracted HIV/AIDS from Blood Donations). New York: Asia Catalyst (no date). Accessed 16 July 2014. www.asiacatalyst.org/Blood_transfusion_AIDS_cases.doc

Zhou, Weishe 周巍摄. "Aizibing Ganranzhe Lvzao Jiuyi Qishi Fan Qishi Fagui Weineng Luoshi 艾滋病感染者屡遭就医歧视反歧视法规未能落实" (AIDS Carriers Repeatedly Encounter Discrimination in Access to Health Care, Antidiscrimination Laws Are Unable to Have Effect). Yangcheng Wanbao 羊城晚报, 27 September 2011. Accessed 3 July 2013. http://www.chinavalue.net/Biz/Blog/2011-9-29/840212.aspx

Ziran Zhiyou et al.自然之友. "*Huanjing Gongyi Minshi Qisu Zhuang* 环境公益民事起诉状" (Environmental Public Interest Lawsuit Brief). Filed with Yunnansheng Qujingshi Zhongji Renmin Fayuan 云南省曲靖市中级人民法院, 28 November 2011.

Index

administrative responses to legal conflict, 11–12, 82–83, 221; AIDS carriers, 122–124, 135–137, 211–212, 213; pollution victims, 147, 156–157, 159–160, 168

AIDSCare China, 102–103, 106, 107

AIDS carriers:: estimates of number of, 6–7, 58, 65, 66, 70–71; fear of litigation, 125, 137, 138; infection rates, 6, 71–72; litigation by, 120–121, 123, 138; relations with China's state, 96–98, 135–137; stigmatization, 15, 65–66, 92. *See also* discrimination against AIDS carriers; discrimination cases, AIDS; protests

AIDS nongovernmental organizations (NGOs), 93–94, 95, 97, 98–99, 102–108; factions and rivalries, 106–107, 214. *See also* legal aid centers; international nongovernmental organizations (INGOs)

AIDS policies and regulations, China, 121–122, 125, 136; criminalization, 58, 59–61, 65–66, 96–97; harm reduction approach, 64–65, 72, 91, 93–94, 96–99

AIDS prevention teams (*gaogandui*), 98–99

AIDS, spread of, 65–72; by blood transmission and collection, 67–71; by heterosexual transmission, 58–59; by intravenous drug use, 58, 66–67, 71–72;
by MSM transmission, 58–59, 71–72; percentage of cases by type of transmission, 66. *See also* blood scandal

Aizhixing, 44, 101, 103–105, 107, 113, 133–134; exposure of blood scandal, 69

All-China Environmental Federation (ACEF), 112, 160, 198–199; environmental public interest litigation by, 185–186, 193–194, 198, 200–201; protection of state interests, 185, 194–197; state leadership in civil society, 179, 181, 186–187, 198, 200–201, 222. *See also* government-organized nongovernmental organizations (GONGOs)

All-China Lawyers Association (ACLA), 49–50, 154, 154–155, 222

alternative dispute resolution (ADR), 119–120, 137–138; AIDS carriers' legal claims, 119–120, 125–126, 128–129, 137–139; environmental legal claims, 190–191, 194–195, 199–200

antiretroviral drug treatment (ART). *See* Four Free, One Care policy

appeals process. *See* Civil Procedure Law

Arab Spring, Chinese reaction to, 3, 28–29

autonomy, civil society. *See* civil society

Blood Donation Law, 69

255

About the Author

Scott Wilson is the Alfred W. Negley Professor of Politics at The University of the South. His interest in China was piqued when he studied at Nanjing University in 1985. Since that time, he has lived in China for more than five years, conducting research on Chinese political economy and legal development. Wilson's research has been supported by grants from the Fulbright Commission, the Committee for Scholarly Communication with China, the U.S.-Japan Friendship Commission, and the Appalachian College Association. He is the author of a book on foreign investment in China, titled *Remade in China*, as well as several journal articles and book chapters.